The Experience of Revolution in Stuart Britain and Ireland

This volume ranges widely across the social, religious and political history of revolution in seventeenth-century Britain and Ireland, from contemporary responses to the outbreak of war to the critique of the post-regicidal regimes; from Royalist counsels to Lilburne's politics; and across the three Stuart kingdoms. However, all the essays engage with a central issue – the ways in which individuals experienced the crises of mid-seventeenth-century Britain and Ireland and what that tells us about the nature of the Revolution as a whole. Responding in particular to three influential lines of interpretation – local, religious and British – the contributors, all leading specialists in the field, demonstrate that to comprehend the causes, trajectory and consequences of the Revolution we must understand it as a human and dynamic experience, as a process. This volume reveals how an understanding of these personal experiences can provide the basis on which to build up larger frameworks of interpretation.

MICHAEL J. BRADDICK is Pro-Vice-Chancellor, Faculty of Arts and Humanities, University of Sheffield. His previous publications include *State Formation in Early Modern England* (Cambridge, 2000) and *God's Fury, England's Fire: A New History of the English Civil Wars* (2009).

DAVID L. SMITH is Fellow, Director of Studies in History, and Graduate Tutor, at Selwyn College, Cambridge. His previous publications include *Parliaments and Politics during the Cromwellian Protectorate* (as co-author, Cambridge, 2007), and *Royalists and Royalism during the Interregnum* (as co-editor, 2010).

This photograph of John Morrill is reproduced
by kind permission of Ariel Hessayon

The Experience of Revolution in Stuart Britain and Ireland

Essays for John Morrill

Edited by

Michael J. Braddick and David L. Smith

CAMBRIDGE
UNIVERSITY PRESS

CAMBRIDGE UNIVERSITY PRESS
Cambridge, New York, Melbourne, Madrid, Cape Town,
Singapore, São Paulo, Delhi, Tokyo, Mexico City

Cambridge University Press
The Edinburgh Building, Cambridge CB2 8RU, UK

Published in the United States of America by Cambridge University Press,
New York

www.cambridge.org
Information on this title: www.cambridge.org/9780521868969

© Cambridge University Press 2011

First published 2011

Printed in the United Kingdom at the University Press, Cambridge

A catalogue record for this publication is available from the British Library

Library of Congress Cataloguing in Publication data
The experience of revolution in Stuart Britain and Ireland / [edited by]
Michael J. Braddick and David L. Smith.
   p.   cm.
Includes bibliographical references and index.
ISBN 978-0-521-86896-9 (hardback)
1. Great Britain – History – Civil War, 1642–1649.   2. Great Britain –
History – Commonwealth and Protectorate, 1649–1660.   3. Great
Britain – History – Charles I, 1625–1649.   4. Great Britain – History,
Military – 1603–1714.   5. Religion and state – England – History –
17th century.   6. Scotland – History – 17th century.   7. Ireland – History –
17th century.   I. Braddick, M. J. (Michael J.), 1962–   II. Smith, David L.
(David Lawrence), 1963–
DA405.E97   2011
941.06 – dc22   2010052616

ISBN 978-0-521-86896-9 Hardback

Contents

Notes on contributors

IAN ATHERTON is Senior Lecturer in History at Keele University. He has written extensively on cathedrals, including the co-edited *Norwich Cathedral: Church, City and Diocese, 1096–1996* (1996), and work on Ely cathedral, and diocese, between the Reformation and Restoration. He also works on early Stuart politics and religion, and on the Civil War, and has co-edited an edition of Sir William Brereton's 1646 letter book for the Staffordshire Record Society (2007).

MICHAEL J. BRADDICK is Professor of History and Pro-Vice-Chancellor for the Faculty of Arts and Humanities at the University of Sheffield. He is the author of several books on early modern social and political history, including *State Formation in Early Modern England, c. 1550–1700* (Cambridge, 2000). He is also co-editor, with John Walter, of *Negotiating Power: Order, Hierarchy and Subordination in Early Modern England and Ireland* (Cambridge, 2001) and, with David Armitage, of *The British Atlantic World* (2nd edn, 2009). His most recent publications are *God's Fury, England's Fire: A New History of the English Civil Wars* (2008), and, as editor, *The Politics of Gesture: Historical Perspectives* (2009).

GLENN BURGESS is Professor of Early Modern History and Pro-Vice-Chancellor (Learning and Teaching) at the University of Hull. His major publications include *The Politics of the Ancient Constitution: An Introduction to English Political Thought 1603–1642* (1992); *Absolute Monarchy and the Stuart Constitution* (1996); *British Political Thought 1500–1660: The Politics of the Post-Reformation* (2009); and, as editor, *The New British History: Founding a Modern State 1603–1715* (1999); *English Radicalism, 1550–1850* (Cambridge, 2007); and *European Political Thought 1450–1700* (2007). He is a Fellow of the Royal Historical Society and served on the Society's council from 2005 to 2009.

DAGMAR FREIST is Professor of Early Modern History at the University of Oldenburg. She is the author of *Governed by Opinion: Politics, Religion and the Dynamics of Communication in London, c. 1637–1645* (1998). Her most recent book is *Absolutismus: Kontroversen um die Geschichte* (2008). She has co-edited a number of books, among them *Staatsbildung als kultureller Prozess: Strukturwandel und Legitimation von Herrschaft in der Frühen Neuzeit* (2005) and *Living with Religious Diversity in Early Modern Europe* (2009). Her research and publications focus on political culture and the public sphere in seventeenth- and eighteenth-century England and Germany, religious diversity in early modern England and Germany, and networks, economic and social interaction and cultural transfer in early modern northern Europe. She is co-founder of NESICT (www.nesict.eu).

MARY K. GEITER works for L-3 Communications Corporation, providing educational support services to US government agencies. Prior to joining L-3, she taught at the College of Ripon and York St John, University of Maryland, European Division, and Bloomsburg University and Immaculata University in Pennsylvania. Her publications include *William Penn* (2000) and, with W. A. Speck, *Colonial America from Jamestown to Yorktown* (2002) and *A Dictionary of British America 1584–1783* (2007). Currently she is working on a full biography of William Penn. She is also researching the Atlantic connections of the signers of the Declaration of Independence.

JAMES S. HART, JR, is Professor of History at the University of Oklahoma. He is the author of *The Rule of Law 1603–1660: Crown, Courts and Judges* (2003) and *Justice upon Petition: The House of Lords and the Reformation of Justice, 1621–1675* (1991), as well as a variety of articles. He recently contributed a chapter (with co-author Richard Ross) entitled 'The Ancient Constitution in the Old World and the New' to Francis J. Bremer and Lynn Botelho, eds., *The Worlds of John Winthrop: Essays on England and New England, 1588–1649* (2006).

ARIEL HESSAYON is a lecturer in the Department of History at Goldsmiths, University of London. He is the author of *'Gold Tried in the Fire': The Prophet Theaurau John Tany and the English Revolution* (2007), as well as the co-editor of collections of essays, *Scripture and Scholarship in Early Modern England* (2006) and *Reappraising Radicalism in Seventeenth- and Early Eighteenth-Century Britain, Ireland and Continental Europe* (2010). His current research is primarily focused on the reception of the writings of the German mystic Jacob Boehme,

Gerrard Winstanley and the Diggers, and Jews and crypto-Jews in early modern England.

JOONG-LAK KIM is an associate professor in the Department of History Education, Kyungpook National University, Daegu, South Korea. Most of his publications are in Korean, except for 'Firing in unison? The Scottish Canons of 1636 and the English Canons of 1640', *Records of the Scottish Church History Society* (1998).

MARK A. KISHLANSKY is the Frank B. Baird Professor of English and European History at Harvard University and the author of *A Monarchy Transformed*, volume 6 of the Penguin History of Britain. He has written extensively on the reign of Charles I and the English Revolution.

JOHN McCAFFERTY is Senior Lecturer in the School of History and Archives at University College Dublin. He is Director of the Mícheál Ó Cléirigh Institute for the study of Irish history and civilization, a partnership between UCD and the order of Friars Minor in Ireland. He is joint editor (with Edel Bhreathnach and Joseph MacMahon) of *The Irish Franciscans, 1534–1990* (2009) and (with James Kelly and Charles Ivar McGrath) of *People, Politics and Power: Essays in Irish History 1660–1850* (2009). He is author of *John Bramhall and the Reconstruction of the Church of Ireland 1633–1641* (Cambridge, 2007). He is a member of the Irish Manuscripts Commission.

ANTHONY MILTON is Professor of Early Modern History at the University of Sheffield. His publications include *Catholic and Reformed* (Cambridge, 1995), *The British Delegation and the Synod of Dort* (2005) and *Laudian and Royalist Polemic in Seventeenth-Century England: The Career and Writings of Peter Heylyn* (2007), as well as articles on religious politics, censorship, political thought and the public sphere in early Stuart England. He is currently working on a monograph provisionally entitled 'England's second reformation: the battle for the Church of England 1636–66', for which he was awarded a Leverhulme Trust Major Research Fellowship. *The Genesis of the Canons of Dort*, co-edited with Donald Sinnema, is also forthcoming.

D. ALAN ORR holds a continuing appointment in Intellectual History at the Maryland Institute College of Art (MICA) in Baltimore, Maryland. He is the author of *Treason and the State: Law, Politics, and Ideology in the English Civil War* (Cambridge, 2002). His work has also appeared in a number of journals including the *Journal of British Studies*, *History*, the *Canadian Journal of History*, *Albion* and *The Sixteenth-Century Journal*. His current research focuses on the contested constitutional relationship between England and Ireland in the first half of the seventeenth century, and the role of republican ideas in England and Ireland during the late sixteenth and early seventeenth centuries.

JONATHAN SCOTT is Professor of History at the University of Auckland. His books include *England's Troubles: Seventeenth-Century English Political Instability in European Context* (Cambridge, 2000) and *Commonwealth Principles: Republican Writing of the English Revolution* (Cambridge, 2004). He has a study of the relationship of geography to early modern British political identities forthcoming from Cambridge University Press.

DAVID L. SMITH is Fellow and Director of Studies in History at Selwyn College, Cambridge. His books include *Constitutional Royalism and the Search for Settlement, c. 1640–1649* (Cambridge, 1994), *A History of the Modern British Isles, 1603–1707: The Double Crown* (1998), *The Stuart Parliaments, 1603–1689* (1999), and, with Patrick Little, *Parliaments and Politics during the Cromwellian Protectorate* (Cambridge, 2007). He has also co-edited several collections of essays, including most recently, with Jason McElligott, *Royalists and Royalism during the English Civil Wars* (Cambridge, 2007) and *Royalists and Royalism during the Interregnum* (2010).

TOM WEBSTER is a lecturer in British History at the University of Edinburgh. His previous works have included a monograph entitled *Godly Clergy in Early Stuart England* (Cambridge, 1997), editing and introducing the *Diary of Samuel Rogers* (2004), and editing and contributing to *Puritans and Puritanism in England and America: A Comprehensive Encyclopedia* (2006). In addition he has produced a series of articles, both general and particular, on Puritan spirituality, demonic possession, religion in early Stuart Britain and the philosophy of history. He is currently completing a monograph on demonic possession and the spirituality of divine union, which ties in with his epistemological interests.

Preface

This book is a tribute to John Morrill by a number of his former students, published to coincide with John's sixty-fifth birthday, an appropriate moment to celebrate his extraordinary achievements as a teacher and scholar.

It is very difficult to capture the career and influence of such an eminent and influential figure, but a crucial feature of John's contribution is that it has been made not simply through his own writing but across a much broader front, particularly through his teaching and wider advocacy for both his field and his profession. This volume is edited by two of his former students, and all the contributions are written by his students engaging with central themes in his work; that is, we hope, a fitting way to mark this distinctive contribution.

John's teaching has always moved in step with his research interests. His advanced courses engaged successively with the study of English government, the British problem, the life and reputation of Oliver Cromwell and latterly with the Irish rebellion of 1641, while his outline courses followed a similar trajectory, also taking in his thesis about the religious roots of seventeenth-century political conflict. Always the concern with personalities came through, sometimes explicitly, as in a 1995 course on 'Stuart politics and personalities: eight case studies'. The overview of John's published work offered in the introduction therefore summarizes an oeuvre that has unfolded in symbiosis with the teaching that means so much to him.

Just as John has always sought to communicate the subject as widely as possible, not least in his tireless work for the Royal Historical Society, the Historical Association and the Cromwell Association, so much of his writing seeks to make the fruits of his research available to the general reader and the student. This is most apparent in his works of synthesis, such as his chapter for the *Oxford Illustrated History of Britain* (1984) – reprinted in 2000 as *Stuart Britain: A Very Short Introduction* – or *The Oxford Illustrated History of Tudor and Stuart Britain* (1996). John has often consciously written for a student readership, as in the book on Charles I which he co-authored with Christopher Daniels in 1988. Indeed, he was first attracted to the idea of writing *The Revolt of the Provinces*, a book which has exercised a huge influence on research in this field, because he 'wanted to write a book that would be read first and foremost by students, while being research-rooted'.

Just as importantly for our current purposes, John has exercised a significant influence on the field through his postgraduate teaching: he has in fact supervised well over one hundred graduate students. Those taught by him have all responded to his own passion for history, as well as his exacting and rigorous scholarly standards. In this case, however, his teaching has not directly mirrored his research agenda; indeed, the diversity of his graduate students, in terms of personality, interests or methodology, is possibly the greatest tribute to his success. John has never sought to impose his own interests on his students, much less form any kind of 'school', but rather to guide each student to develop their own understanding of the past, to make sense of it in their own particular way, and to find their own scholarly voice. It is in that sense that his postgraduate teaching has marched in close step with his approach to the past.

We could not, of course, include contributions from all of John's students. To narrow it down, we identified those who fulfilled each of the following criteria: that John had been the sole supervisor of their Cambridge Ph.D.; that after the Ph.D. they had published at least one monograph; and that they hold, or have held, a permanent position in a university history department. All those who met these requirements were invited to contribute, and this volume is the result. The resulting essays, like John's own work, range widely across the period, from Smith's examination of Sir Benjamin Rudyerd to Scott's reinterpretation of Harrington; across the political spectrum from Milton's sensitive reading of Royalist counsel to Orr's insights into the political thinking of John Lilburne; and across the three kingdoms, with Kim's analysis of the Scottish Prayer Book, McCafferty's study of the memorialization of dead Irish bishops and Braddick's analysis of the relationship between mobilization and political argument at the outbreak of war in England. But they all engage with a central theme – the way in which individuals experienced the momentous events of mid-seventeenth-century Britain – a theme which engages with John's own work and in particular with his preoccupation with reconstructing the lived experience of individual people.

John's concern for the people of the past is mirrored by his concern for those of the present. We have all benefited from John's friendship and loyalty as well as from his selfless devotion to the pursuit of history and the immense generosity with which he shares his learning and ideas.

We are therefore delighted to include a personal tribute from one of John's closest friends within the historical profession, Mark Kishlansky of Harvard University, which brings to life the manifold contributions to the profession of this deeply humane man. This book is dedicated to John, with gratitude, affection and admiration.

MICHAEL J. BRADDICK
DAVID L. SMITH

Abbreviations

A&O	C. H. Firth and R. S. Rait, eds., *Acts and Ordinances of the Interregnum, 1642–60*, 3 vols. (1911)
AHR	*American Historical Review*
BL	British Library
Bodl.	Bodleian Library, Oxford
CJ	*Journals of the House of Commons*
Clarendon	W. Dunn Macray, ed., *The History of the Rebellion and Civil Wars in England by Edward, Earl of Clarendon* (6 vols., Oxford, 1969 edn)
CSPD	*Calendar of State Papers, Domestic series*
EEBO	Early English Books Online (http://eebo.chadwyck.com/home)
EcHR	*Economic History Review*
EHR	*English Historical Review*
ESTC	English Short Title Catalogue (http://estc.bl.uk/)
Gardiner	S. R. Gardiner, *History of the Great Civil War* (4 vols., Moreton-in-Marsh, 1991 edn)
Gardiner, *CD*	S. R. Gardiner, ed., *The Constitutional Documents of the Puritan Revolution 1625–1660* (3rd edn, Oxford, 1906)
HEH	Henry E. Huntington Library, San Marino
HJ	*Historical Journal*
HMC	Historical Manuscripts Commission
HR	*Historical Research*
HLQ	*Huntington Library Quarterly*
JBS	*Journal of British Studies*
LJ	*Journals of the House of Lords*
ODNB	H. C. G. Matthews and B. Harrison, eds., *Oxford Dictionary of National Biography* (61 vols., Oxford, 2004) (available online at http://www.oxforddnb.com/)
PP	*Past and Present*

TNA	The National Archives
TRHS	*Transactions of the Royal Historical Society*
TT	Thomason Tracts

Throughout this book, place of publication of printed works is London unless otherwise stated.

JSM
A tribute to a friend

Mark A. Kishlansky

I

I first met John Morrill in February 1974. David Underdown had arranged lunch with Christopher Hill and we arrived on the Oxford train an hour before the appointed time. Underdown led me over Worcester bridge and on to Broad Street. But instead of turning into Balliol he took me through an almost unseen gate that led to the warren of buildings that comprised Trinity College. We entered one of them; he knocked at a door, and upon a muffled response opened it. Behind billows of pipe smoke sat John Morrill at work on a thick stack of papers. When he saw David his face lit up with a smile of almost preternatural warmth, his eyes revealing genuine pleasure at Underdown's unexpected arrival. I crossed the threshold hesitantly since I still had no idea as to the purpose of our detour. In his usual laconic way Underdown simply said, 'you two should know each other', and pronounced our names, Morrill's resonating immediately in my historiographical memory, mine as yet meaningless to him. John regretted, as he would habitually in future years, that he was pressed for time, but immediately made us welcome. After an exchange of pleasantries with Underdown he turned his attention to me and asked what I was working on. I delivered a hundred-word synopsis of my doctoral research (which, further pared, made its way into a footnote in *The Revolt of the Provinces* the next year). John asked a question or two, looked at his watch and put on his gown to go off to teach. But as he was ushering us out he said to me, 'You must come back and visit again. We have much to talk about.'

Such perfunctory invitations occur hundreds of times in one's life – 'come see me in Vienna'; 'if you are ever in Portland' – and almost never are they taken up. For some inexplicable reason I felt a sincerity in his casual remark and the next time I was in Oxford I found my way to his Trinity rooms where this time the electric smile and warm welcome were for me. As he predicted, we had much to talk about, though the pressure of John's impossibly overbooked schedule always hurried along these early conversations. But the intellectual engagement and conviviality were never feigned and I left each encounter eager for the next.

I returned to America to write my thesis while John braved a job market that had suddenly collapsed. He had not originally aspired to an academic career; indeed, his initial goal was to become a prison governor, an ambition wryly recalled by his daughters during what they described as their periods of incarceration. But an early encounter with R. N. Dore turned his talents and energies to history. A British historian entering the profession in the early 1970s had few opportunities and could not rely on talent alone. Many of John's contemporaries had either bolted for America or were attempting to. The British market was still regulated through the iron hand of patronage, and here John was disadvantaged. He had studied with J. P. Cooper, a man of immense learning but few students. At Oxford Christopher Hill and Hugh Trevor-Roper brokered power; at Cambridge Jack Plumb and Geoffrey Elton did it. All were masters of the game. They moved their students around the academic checkerboard, kinging the favourites and sacrificing the others.

John's anxiety, expressed in his first letters to me, was genuine and clear-eyed. He thought he was unlikely to survive this four-fronted war. But then he caught a break. Trevor-Roper had already placed both of his newly minted students when a job opened late in the hiring season at Stirling University in Scotland. Not content to have taken that year's two plum positions he sought someone to back for the third. This turned out to be John (Cooper had been Trevor-Roper's steadfast ally in the gentry controversy, in which Trevor-Roper's thesis of the declining 'mere' gentry was supported by Cooper's extensive research). Thus was launched the academic career of John Morrill, albeit at a fledgling university in a different university system. The following year fortune smiled again in the same manner. An opening occurred at Oxford and Trevor-Roper secured it for one of his protégés, who in turn vacated a teaching fellowship at Selwyn College, Cambridge. This post had its obvious attractions, but it came without tenure. In those days a college teaching fellowship was either associated with an anticipated vacancy for a university lectureship or ran for a fixed term. Not only was the Selwyn position unattached to any foreseeable opening, but also John would be second in seniority if any unexpectedly arose. So the decision to move his family from the security of Scotland to the uncertainty of Cambridge in 1975 was a spin of the roulette wheel. Sure enough, his number came up. The young scholar senior to him moved to America and shortly afterward an unexpected departure suddenly created a vacancy for a university lectureship. His nearly half-century at Cambridge had begun.

If the beginning of his career can be attributed in part to chance, its prospering was the product of ambition and a willingness to take risks. These qualities constantly marked his scholarship and his professional accomplishments. He may seem an example of Cromwell's dictum – 'no one rises so high as he who knows not whither he is going' – but like the Lord Protector, whom he so admires, he has an iron rod of determination that keeps him on course as the winds blow.

The story of John and the lobster may illustrate the point. John loves lobsters. Over the decades we have used lobster dinners to celebrate whatever triumphs have come our way and I frequently entice him to visit Boston with news of the year's bounteous catch and low prices. Lobsters in Britain were a rare indulgence and John could seemingly remember every occasion on which he had been served one. I learned that we shared this culinary passion when John told me a story about his days as a research fellow at Trinity College. It was this occasion that provided me with the parable for his career.

We were idly swapping anecdotes about awkward situations that we had experienced when suddenly the conversation turned deadly earnest. 'I remember the most traumatic social situation I have ever encountered', he began. 'To this day, I feel badly about what I did.' I suppose this is why seats have edges, and my piqued interest overcame his reluctance to tell the tale. 'I was the second most junior member of college, below the salt as we say. When dining we sat in strict order of seniority and I always sat but one from the end. This occasion was my first college gaudy, a celebration in which the senior members treat themselves to the fine wines in the cellars and the best meal the college cook can provide. Everyone appears in evening dress, there are all manner of formal and informal toasts, and the general conviviality of a fellowship is shared. I looked forward to it for weeks, especially after I discovered that my favourite food, lobster, was on the menu. Not only did I have to endure the good-natured grousing of my wife, excluded in those days from all college activities as a woman, but her more pointed observations on the fit and quality of my shabby dinner jacket. Still, nothing could dull the anticipated pleasure of feasting on lobster and it only grew as the scouts heaved laden silver platters along the high table inviting each member to select their own. But when it came to me the salver arrived with a dilemma. Only one lobster remained and beyond me sat the junior-most fellow. My choices were plain: either decline the offering on some weak excuse – I could hardly deny my love of shellfish for the scouts never forgot and I would be perpetually deprived of all subsequent shrimp, oysters, and crabs – or I could place the lonely lobster on the gleaming china and make it someone else's problem. I understood the options instantly, but

I couldn't choose. I sat there for what seemed like an eternity paralysed between my pleasure and his. Finally, I reached up and filled my plate.'[1]

For me the story illuminated both John's remarkable career and his even more remarkable personality. In his hesitation, his obvious empathy for the plight of the junior fellow, was displayed all the compassion that has made him such a trusted member of the profession and that draws students and colleagues to him for advice, solace, and encouragement. But in the end he had his lobster as well. The hesitancy and desire were in equal measure John Morrill. He has always attained his goals and achieved his ambitions, either through instinct or shrewd calculation. But they never again came at the expense of the junior fellow.

II

In the 1970s, British academic careers proceeded very much according to the old ways. It was still the case that hardly any lecturers ever rose above that rank and the monetary incentives to do so were meagre. Professors were administrators and few in number. Initial appointment brought tenure and entitled its holder equally to all available perquisites. At Oxford and Cambridge there was a venerable tradition of college teaching that commanded respect on its own terms, and the faculties were still a mix of older members without doctoral degrees and newer hires with them. Research and writing was an avocation rather than a requirement and it was undertaken as its own reward. John took to it immediately. His early study with Dore had introduced him to the joys of local history, particularly that of the county of Cheshire.

Local history had been a mainstay of British historical writing, but by the 1970s it was being undertaken with a great scholarly seriousness and purpose. The light and heat of the gentry controversy still illuminated the historiographical landscape, but its intellectual pyrotechnics were beginning to burn out. Historians turned away from large-scale generalizations concerning aristocrats in crisis and rising or declining gentry to local case studies where they could be tested. By the time John began his dissertation research the enterprise of county history was thriving and bringing with it a localist interpretive perspective, typified by the aphorism that when Englishmen said their 'country' they meant their county. John's work on Cheshire combined both perspectives. His major figures were

---

[1] If John were telling the story he would want to add two facts unknown to him at the moment of choice: that someone ahead of him had taken two and that the cook had held at least one back in the kitchen. The junior fellow was not ultimately deprived by John's choice.

gentry who aligned their interests in their quest for social and political power within their community. Blood relationships, geographical propinquity and competition for official favour: these were the gears that turned the larger political wheels. Though he was sensitive to questions of economic and social status within the cohorts that he studied, he was even more attuned to the non-quantifiable determinants of their behaviour, to religion and ideology. In homage to Dore, he wrote compelling military history; in homage to Cooper he studied rent rolls and land transactions. But his attention to ideas and beliefs was his own original contribution.

Cheshire 1630–1660 earned accolades for its painstaking research and mastery of complex social and political interactions, yet it was one of several similar studies each of which reluctantly concluded that it was particularity rather than commonalty that defined a given county's history. Aristocratic rivalry in Somerset, administrative organization in Sussex, partible inheritance in Kent, all were believed to be differently determinative. What was needed was a more synthetic study, one that would be true to both the particular and the common and would render the local experience of early modern England significant. This was the achievement of *Revolt of the Provinces*, John's most influential book. It became standard reading for generations of undergraduates, the definitive statement of the localist perspective. Shifting focus from Westminster to the counties uncovered critical elements of Civil War experience that had been all but ignored. Neutrals, who existed in such profusion in the counties and who wished for nothing so much as peace, now found their voice and *Revolt of the Provinces* provided impetus for subsequent studies of groups like the Clubmen. The war may have dominated life at the centre, but it came mostly as an unwelcome interruption to ordinary activities in the localities. The refusal of trained bands to cross county boundaries and the efforts of local gentlemen to create and enforce neutrality pacts were as much a feature of the Civil Wars from this perspective as were the creation of Parliamentarian and Royalist armies.

A similar interest in the recovery of traditionalism, consensus and survival in the religious sphere drew John to the study of Anglicanism. His work reconstructed the experiences of outlawed Anglicans, a history long buried beneath the mountain of works on revolutionary Puritanism. *Revolt of the Provinces* displayed John's unique combination of skills. It presented a bold interpretation – so bold that it became caricatured and necessitated a title change to *Revolt in the Provinces* – it displayed fresh evidence drawn from archival research, it revealed considerable synthetic power and, above all, it was at the very cutting edge of its subject. The bibliography included a long list of as yet unpublished doctoral research and the footnotes reported the results of conversations with young scholars, like myself, whose work was at an even earlier stage. Moreover, *Revolt of the Provinces* was written to be accessible to students. For all of the novelty of its argument and originality of its material it never sacrificed lucidity for detail. Its ostensible aim was to initiate undergraduates into a new area of Civil War studies, give them a thesis to test, and provide them with excerpts from sources to do so. But it was in fact much more than this. Though the book followed the format of its series, it achieved success on a far greater scale.

Because John never published another monograph comparable to his Cheshire book it is easy to overlook his life-long engagement with archival materials. For years family holidays were scheduled around whatever exotic locations were convenient to record offices he had not visited. The beauties of Somerset were reduced to a small radius around Taunton; a picnic at Delapré Abbey was the occasion for a working session with the Montague papers. Even trips into Wales, in partially reliable motor cars provided by his brother-in-law, had a multiple purpose. The results of these forays found their way into numerous articles on subjects as diverse as the northern gentry and the Church of England. His wife, Frances, and their growing brood of daughters patiently endured the quest for churchwarden accounts and vestry minute books. None of them ever caught the history bug but their support created a stable centre for John's life away from scholarship and the university. Frances ran the home like a Fortune 500 company, albeit one whose finances were always precarious. Activities were not so much planned as they were choreographed. I remember once watching the family's mesmerizing breakfast routine. Boxes, jars and containers appeared all at once from multiple cupboards without a word being spoken. Bowls and plates were dealt on to the table seemingly as they were being filled, while the eldest Morrill daughter dressed the youngest and the two middle girls prepared lunches all to the steady tick of Frances's internal stopwatch. Four young children were up, dressed, fed, inspected and out the door within the compass of twenty minutes. John's job (and mine as well on this occasion) was to keep absolutely out of the way for fear that one of us elephants would trample a ballerina. The girls presented their own joys and challenges, each one a personality so distinct as to cause wonder whether nature and nurture are the only possible categories of formative influence. They seemed to have no inkling of their father's growing fame and stature. Frances, in particular, knew how to keep an ego at a proper level of inflation. She once accompanied John to a public school history day where he and two other dons sang the praises of their subject. Frances's silence in the car on the way home prompted John to beg for a compliment. 'I came top, didn't I?' he ventured. 'You came second,' was the piquant reply. 'First prize wasn't given.' Living as a lone male within a household of five women was not the least of John's lifetime achievements.

The results of his archival vacations appeared in the comet spray of important articles that followed John's initial scholarly efforts. His Cheshire interests led to deeply researched studies of Sir William Davenport and Sir William Brereton and to forays into Chester diocesan history. In two seminal pieces he offered a rereading of church history during the Interregnum. In 'The Church in England 1642–9' he explored the survival of Anglicanism during the dark years of civil war and argued that conventional religion continued to exert a strong hold on the English populace. In 'The religious context of the English Civil War', perhaps his most influential piece, he provocatively construed the Civil Wars as 'England's wars of religion', and pushed back against the secularity that was still historiographically dominant. This was a profound interpretive redirection with lasting consequences. It placed English (and later British) experience clearly within the compass of European developments, inviting continental historians to explore the British dimension of the Thirty Years War and inviting British historians to contemplate comparative history. It enriched both fields. It also reframed the dispute between revisionists and post-revisionists over the role of ideology in the English Revolution. Religion itself was a form of ideology and exploring it as the underlying motive of participants uncovered a wider and more diverse set of causes for political events. Nor was John's war of religion limited to the Puritan avant-garde. He had already uncovered the durability of Anglican belief and practice and soon he began to contemplate varieties of Catholicism that were another part of Britain's theological composition.

The turn toward religion was another example of John's sensitivity to the direction in which his field was moving. While producing his own original scholarship he was already publishing surveys of the work of others. His *Seventeenth-Century Britain* was much more than an annotated bibliography, and it required him to keep abreast of the latest work in all aspects of the field. The guide to local sources that he co-edited with G. E. Aylmer also demanded intimate familiarity with scholarly trends. During these years he was frequently called upon to write review essays that allowed him to deploy his massive historiographical erudition while prodding the field in directions he wished it to go. There can be no better example of this knack for agenda setting than his multiple interventions in what came to be called the British problem. John did not invent this subject but no one did more to promote it. Alone among the so-called 'new British historians' he conducted serious research on the history of all three Stuart kingdoms. He was the first to explore the problems of

Ireland as separate from, but implicated in, those of Britain, and he formatively encouraged a generation of young Irish historians to explore their country's history in the context of its relations with England and Scotland.[2] He was now renaming the revolutionary period the 'wars of the three kingdoms' or 'the British civil wars' and arguing not only for a comparative perspective but also for an integrative one. He was instrumental in organizing three-kingdom conferences, symposia and essay collections (two of which, *The Scottish National Covenant in its British Context* and *The British Problem 1534–1707*, he edited). His contributions to the new British history were both substantive and definitional and while his enthusiasm for the subject was genuine he never went overboard in thinking that it would provide the silver bullet in explaining the mid-century crisis.

Indeed, as the presses poured forth new histories oriented around this British perspective, John was drawn back to a figure who was one of the touchstones of his lifelong passion for Civil War history. And while there was surely a British dimension to this subject – the consequences of his actions in Scotland and especially Ireland would reverberate down the centuries – there was also no more quintessentially English figure than Oliver Cromwell. Throughout his career, John has had a fascination with Cromwell. He published an early essay in *Cromwelliana* and one of his first edited collections was a landmark volume on *Oliver Cromwell and the English Revolution*. His contribution to the study of Cromwell came on many fronts. He published on the Army Revolt in 1647, the Putney Debates of that same year, and on Cromwell's unexpected conversion to supporting regicide in 1648–9. Most of all, he wrote sympathetically about Cromwell's religion and on how everything he did was controlled by his relation with the Almighty. The discoveries he made about the Lord Protector's early life and career, his activities as a government tax collector, his almost fulfilled intention to emigrate to America in the early1630s, his participation in prophesying circles added freshness to a subject that was once thought exhausted. His life in the *Oxford Dictionary of National Biography* is one of the gems of that collaborative venture and has been published as a stand-alone volume. He served as president of the Cromwell Association for a decade, and late in his career became general editor and participated in the project to re-edit Cromwell's letters and speeches according to modern standards.

---

[2] For his many services to Irish historical studies – including stints as external examiner to both undergraduate and graduate programs, membership on Irish University appointment panels, and as an advisor to the Irish Higher Education Authority – he was elected a member of the Royal Irish Academy in 2010.

John's versatility as an historian is apparent in any summary of his publications. He is equally at home in political and religious history and has made seminal contributions to both. His debunking of the myth of 'King Pym' by the seemingly simple device of comparing the many speeches published in his name to the many fewer that he is actually recorded as giving was inspired. His *ODNB* articles included lives of a Roman Catholic martyr and a Puritan iconoclast; of Charles I and Oliver Cromwell. His debate with David Underdown over the ecology of Civil War allegiance displayed his own mastery of local sources and his wariness about the limits of their explanatory power. His forays into Scotland and Ireland evinced a willingness to master new subjects and open new frontiers.

But an assessment of John's scholarly contributions cannot end with a description of his monographs, or of his surveys written for a popular and student audience (though the *Oxford Illustrated History of Tudor and Stuart Britain* has been a triumph), or even with his many seminal articles. Impressive as these achievements are, his greatest contribution to the vitality of his field lies in his editing and collaborating, where he was not only able to make his own contributions but also to stimulate others to write and publish on important, cutting-edge topics. He was the founding and guiding editor of the Cambridge Studies in Early Modern British History, which has produced more than eighty monographs over the past quarter century, including the first books of many of the most distinguished young historians in the field's recent generations. He has edited or co-edited thirteen collections of essays, including festschrifts, conference proceedings and volumes on new subfields of research. In all of these he has encouraged the work of young historians above all. None of his volumes were trophy collections for the wellknown and wellestablished. Additionally, he has himself contributed thirty-eight essays to collections edited by others, and there are no signs that he is slowing down. John has served continuously for thirty years as a member of the editorial board and for ten as editor of the *Historical Journal*, one of the leading venues for research on British and European history. While John Morrill's own scholarship places him in the first rank of his generation, as a facilitator of the work of others he stands alone.

III

Simon Schama once told me a story about an experience he had when researching in the private Rothschild archives. It seemed so apropos of John. After a preliminary exchange of letters, he arrived at the chateau and was greeted by the baron's personal archivist. He was shown into a richly furnished library, with glass-fronted cases filled from floor to ceiling with beautifully bound volumes. The heavy curtains were drawn, the air was still, and the room was silent. Schama would sit at one end of a long table meticulously studying the relevant documents while his chaperone sat silently at the opposite end, his gaze fixed on space. This routine was repeated day after day until Schama neared the conclusion of his research. Then one morning the heavy oak door that separated the library from the massive vestibule opened and an elderly man, immaculately turned out and with the kind of self-possession that could only have been bred over generations, entered. The archivist, as if he had been sentinel against this very occurrence, leapt to his feet. Schama, slower on the uptake, turned back to his document, but something almost magnetic brought his work to a halt and he too stood. Slowly, the man crossed the carpeted floor to Schama's end of the polished table. He introduced himself as the Baron de Rothschild, politely inquired into the nature of Schama's study, and made small talk for a few minutes. He then turned his mesmerizing gaze directly upon the historian and asked: 'Professor Schama, do you know the motto of this family?' Fortunately, this detail had escaped Simon's notice and he obliged his host with the mystification the moment so obviously required. 'No, I do not,' Schama admitted. 'Service,' Rothschild intoned deeply. Then, glancing down to the other end of the table, he added, 'and we get it!'

   If early modern British history received its service in the late twentieth century, it was in large part the result of the labours of John Morrill. Perhaps John really did have the soul of a prison governor, for there was no onerous task that he would not willingly take up for the sake of scholarship or collegiality. Beyond his own writing and editorial duties he came to be in charge of a host of collaborative projects that succeeded one another with uncanny regularity. Geoffrey Elton, a model of tireless commitment to advancing historical study, deftly offloaded on to John the responsibility for compiling the early modern section of the annual bibliography of British and Irish history. This Herculean project required tracking all current books produced by the many publishers that then existed; surveying the contents of all the serials that filled the periodicals room of the University Library; and, most valuably, cataloguing the contents of the annual output of the innumerable local record societies whose volumes were rarities in libraries outside the United Kingdom. In the days before computers, all this required manual labour of the most pitiless kind. Entries were handwritten, typed and printed all in separate stages with arduous proofreading at each phase. John went on to become the founding editor of the Royal Historical Society's bibliography. When personal computers became available, John instantly exploited them and when CD-ROM was developed he transferred the accumulated bibliographic records of generations onto an easily portable and fully searchable medium. He had a technical savvy atypical of his generation and was one of the few Cambridge historians who could give even a partially intelligible explanation of Boolean connectors. The bibliography of British and Irish History on CD-ROM was an invaluable research tool for years until it was supplanted by an online version.

If the *Annual Bibliography* required scholarly compilation on a massive scale, John's editorial role on the *Oxford Dictionary of National Biography* involved coaxing hundreds of other historians to write the lives of more than 6,000 seventeenth-century historical figures. John was the perfect choice to head up the early modern section of the *ODNB* and to serve on the editorial board of such a global collaborative effort. Again, his enthusiasm for the project was irresistible. Here was a once-in-a-century opportunity to honour those who had made significant contributions to Britain's past and it was John's task not only to co-ordinate the work of section editors and individual authors but also to decide which figures, neglected by the Victorian *Dictionary of National Biography*, should be introduced. The original *DNB* was to be updated but not discarded. The first requirement was a machine-readable version of the original volumes that would be consulted by authors but also linked to the digital version of the new *Dictionary*. Scanning was still error-prone when the project started. The editors needed a more reliable method. The solution they hit on was ingenious. Sets of the original volumes of the *DNB* were shipped to different regions of China where women unable to read English transcribed them onto computers. Then a software program compared the massive files. The likelihood that two typists would make the same errors was acceptably small to make the solution both effective and affordable.

How John found the time to concentrate on these decisions remains mysterious, for at the same time he was editing and writing at his usual frenetic pace and was assuming administrative roles both at Cambridge and nationally.

Loyalty is perhaps John's bedrock value: loyalty to family, to church, to friends, and to institutions. At Cambridge he held nearly every office of his college (except chaplain) and served as Vice-Master for a decade. His term as college librarian was typical, as he threw himself into book acquisition so fervently that he became expert in Asian history. He took great pride in his college, whose intellectual stature and financial stability improved steadily during his tenure there. For twenty years he has been a syndic of the Cambridge University Press and, for a number of those, a member of its all-important finance committee. In 2001 he began a term as Deputy Director of the Centre for Research in the Arts, Social Sciences and Humanities (CRASSH), responsible for developing university-wide programmes and raising and disbursing funds in support of research. He would have been a natural director of the Centre, but found that he could not generate enthusiasm for other disciplines that would match his love of history. He confessed to me that his mind wandered during presentations of even the most distinguished luminaries of other fields, something that never happened to him when attending the modest early modern history seminar that he had helped to found decades earlier. There the work of the greenest novice riveted his attention.

In the Cambridge History Faculty John rotated through a succession of offices, including secretary. He participated in curriculum reforms and chaired the Part I Examinations Board – an office of some peril (he once recalled a marking dispute that left an earlier chairman bloodied). He also sat on innumerable appointment committees. Appointments were his métier, and I cannot recall a conversation with him over thirty years that did not include discussions of the British and American job market. True, we both constantly have had students to place and swapped useful information about anticipated vacancies and people on the move. But John has grown into the kind of patron that had so fortuitously launched his own career. When a junior position opened at Brown, he submitted references for no fewer than seven contenders for the post. There were some years when his Ph.D.s were stacked like planes landing at Heathrow in a storm and, not unlike an air traffic controller, he inevitably brought each one in safely.

John relishes faculty meetings as if they were Premier League fixtures. He loves the subtleties of academic politics and he studies the preferences and interests of his colleagues as if he were betting on the pools. He once won a wager on the proposition that Elton would speak first on every item of the agenda, though he had to give odds. He has an almost super-stitious belief in veiled intentions, and delights in decoding the concealed meaning in seemingly innocent events. He once had to interview a senior member of the faculty with whom he had lukewarm relations. 'He asked me to come at two o'clock,' he complained to me. 'Do you know what that means?' I was completely mystified. Two o'clock: low biorhythms? A late nooner? What could two o'clock possibly mean? John explained, 'It is absolutely the only time of day that he wouldn't have to offer any kind of refreshment. He would see me, but I wasn't welcome.' He would never attend a committee meeting without a multi-pronged strategy. His after-battle reports were an education in itself. He was master of the game and played it with a subtlety unknown to me.

By the middle of his career, John was making his mark well beyond East Anglia. He became a presiding presence in those national institutions that keep both historical study and the pursuit of knowledge alive and thriving. In the Royal Historical Society he became a member of council and then vice-president. His chief interest was in the society's publication efforts. He strongly supported the subvention that kept the Studies in History monograph series alive, and used his connections among publishers to stabilize its finances. Studies in History primarily published the work of young historians, a service increasingly eschewed by university presses. John not only kept the series afloat but also ensured its quality by directing worthy scholarship its way. He persuaded the society to take control and financial responsibility for the bibliography on which he had laboured for so long. Once online it quickly became the essential site for bibliographical information on all areas of British and Irish history.

John has received many honours, but none pleased him as much as his eventual election to the British Academy. From the outside this may have looked like a foregone conclusion, but John never considered it as such and there were some bumps and bruises along the way. The politics of the early modern section of the Academy's history group delight him even more than do those of Cambridge, though to my voyeuristic disappointment he treats them as if they were the *arcana* of the papal curia. Now and then he asks my views on the accomplishments of one or another historian, to gauge 'international opinion' as he calls it. Otherwise he keeps secret deliberations secret, though I can tell he is occasionally bursting to rehearse some remarkable development. John quickly became devoted to the Academy and accepted time-consuming membership on various committees. During one rather hectic year he served on both the Academy's grants committee and the Arts and Humanities Council Research Board. Together he sorted through hundreds of grant proposals and developed an encyclopaedic knowledge of what was being done throughout the field. Eventually he was elected vice-president of the Academy. When I asked him about the duties of the vice-president he responded with only a touch of sarcasm that while the president waved the flag of British academia in Paris and Rome, the vice-president did the same in Aberystwyth and Hull. He had a reverence for the Academy and its members and is especially honoured when asked to write obituaries of its members. His piece on John Kenyon was a remarkable labour of love, though he hardly knew the man in life. He had to negotiate the sensibilities of a skittish widow and colleagues who developed sudden memory lapses. Not only did he reread Kenyon's considerable corpus, but also gained access to his correspondence. There John found a kindred spirit in dozens of mischievous letters of recommendation, each of which required careful decoding. The one that delighted him most was ambiguously profound: the recommended candidate would fit into the department 'like a weevil into a ship's biscuit'.

I have experienced John's loyalty on many occasions, when he stood godfather to my son or performed the funeral service for my wife. But the occasion when it was most tested was when I submitted an essay to the *Historical Journal* during his editorship. The essay bluntly challenged the veracity of the work of another writer in the field who happened to hold a junior position at Cambridge. Since that work had been published in the *Historical Journal* it was only appropriate that the exposé appear there as well. The situation was awkward all around but John was predictably scrupulous in handling my submission, sending the essay to senior scholars in the field for vetting (to this day I don't know who they were). Their responses were less than pleased. The reviewers didn't like me or the exercise I had undertaken, but they believed it merited publication. Each fastidiously inspected numerous claims that I had made and pronounced them valid. On this basis John then set out to test my essay as well. He accepted the article, but asked that I either fortify or delete a number of charges that he found unpersuasive. He also informed me that the amended essay would then be submitted to the original author for response.

Once that happened, all hell broke loose. John was pressured from every direction with a single message: kill Kishlansky's essay. Unfounded rumours circulated that I was acting as his cat's-paw, or that he had penned the piece himself, or, more damaging, that he had abused his editorial responsibility. Though my target held only a position as a College fellow, in these fantasies he became rival to John himself, initiating unpleasant speculation as to his motives in printing so critical a piece. In a closed society like Cambridge these accusations reverberated unbearably. Finally, a senior member of the field sent him a menacing missive. He claimed to have examined over thirty of the points in dispute and found that I was wrong on every one of them. He warned John that if he published the essay the reputation of the *Historical Journal* would be damaged beyond repair and that John's own career would be ruined. These were not idle threats and this was the moment that a weaker man might have backed away. John had nothing to gain and much to lose. If he asked that I withdraw the essay questions about his judgement would be stifled and speculation about his motives ended. If, instead, he went forward he risked permanent rupture with distinguished colleagues and a controversy which, one way or the other, would imperil the reputation of the journal. For the next two days John did nothing but check these thirty-odd points, spending long hours in the University Library weighing three accounts of a scattered set of sources. Reassured of his original judgement he sent a reply conciliatory in tone but scathing in analysis. The essay was published and years of bitterness ensued.

IV

For several years in the early 1990s John and I spent a week together at a National Endowment of the Humanities summer institute. The institute was designed to rejuvenate the research interests of participants who held positions in American teaching colleges. They were to be introduced to the latest historiographical trends and the newest historical methods, while being afforded time to work on their own scholarship. John led a week's worth of sessions on the Civil War and invited me, as a visiting fireman, to conduct one on the New Model Army. But our real purpose was to spend time together away from the pressure of families and of our increasingly busy professional lives. The institute was held in a small southern Californian town, the kind of which it is observed 'it gets late early there'. Seminar leaders and participants had the choice of two family-style restaurants and one bar and sooner or later we would find ourselves all together talking about our historical interests and professional experiences. Once each year in this company either John or I would innocently ask the other a question that we had discussed on many occasions: 'If for the rest of your life you had to choose between only teaching or only producing scholarship which would you choose?' Before either of us provided an answer we turned the question on the seminar participants, most of them young historians in the early years of their career and all of them facing a life of college teaching. Their answers were usually predictable. Those already estranged from their positions or ambitious for a place at a prestigious university chose research and writing. Those who seemed happiest and treated the institute more as a social than an intellectual occasion plumped for a life in the classroom. When our turns finally came we both made the same choice. We held positions that allowed us to balance research and teaching and we had access to the best resources and the brightest students. For us this was purely hypothetical. But we were sure that if only allowed one of the two activities we would both choose teaching.

Our shared teaching experiences never extended to undergraduate education. The English and American systems were just too different for any of the innovations in which we were each involved to be of use to the other. To this day I have only a partial understanding of what reading history at Cambridge entails and find talk of tripos (which in defiance of mathematical law appears to consist of Part I and Part II), special subjects and firsts unintelligible. The seriousness with which British marking and examining is undertaken is beyond my experience, as is the communal responsibility that is taken for every aspect of undergraduate education. On the other hand, my lectures at Harvard are not optional for the students in my classes and they are expected to be highly polished performances. The fact that American students are compelled to study across the disciplines means that they are analytically sophisticated, even if empirically naïve. They require a special kind of teaching that has no analogue in Britain.

Where John and I did connect as teachers, however, was in graduate training. From the beginning of our careers we were involved with training Ph.D. students in our common field. Here we had lots to share, even if the structure of our respective programmes was different. John was always looking for innovation in his teaching. Once, when I invited him to the University of Chicago, I asked him to come and talk to my seminar about his career. For the benefit of my students I interviewed him about how he had become an historian, led him through his years as a teacher and scholar, and then asked him to reveal those requirements of the profession that he found most difficult. My purpose was to personalize someone whom my students only knew through his writings. After our interview, I went around the table and had each student pose their own questions. The occasion contained a hilarious incident that John has always threatened to repeat when it came my turn to speak to his pupils. The only time I could assemble all of my students was at lunch, which they were instructed to bring with them. Most brought sandwiches or yoghurt and fruit. But seated right next to John, elbow to elbow, was a student of more exotic tastes. He arrived with a can of sardines, fastidiously rolled it open, and released into our confined space an aroma so pungent as to be almost palpable. Never before had I seen an actual stiff upper lip. John resisted all temptation to comment though he could not resist some arch sidelong glances as one pilchard after another was devoured and, with a final slurp, the packing oil was drained down. I repeated this exercise – without the sardines – each year with another historian (unhappily John's openness and honesty was not often imitated) and John soon initiated it at Cambridge. It was especially valuable for our female students to hear the professional stories of female historians and we would often share the identity of successful visitors.

John's role as a graduate supervisor was enhanced by constant practice. Unlike many of his Cambridge contemporaries he never cherry-picks his students. He has been open to all comers in the field and increasingly to those from outside England. He welcomes Scots, Irish, Canadians,

Americans, Antipodeans, Asians and Europeans with genuine pleasure
and has kept a thriving graduate community orbiting around him. On
some days he would book as many as eight supervisions and as he fell
further and further behind schedule – before e-mail no fifteen-minute
period could pass without his phone ringing – they would gather on
his staircase and hold impromptu discussions of their work. Though he
had no interest in forming a school, his graduate students naturally took
their cue from his current interests. His path from subject to subject can
be plotted in an archaeology of the dissertations he directed: politics,
religion, the British problem and Cromwell. But he also encouraged
many who went in their own direction. His enthusiasm for the work of
his students was always genuine and he was able to find a nugget of value
in each one. When I came to his Cambridge he would assemble throngs
of them and make sure that each had the chance to tell me about their
research. Some I already knew of, others I would meet again in later
years when they would recall the strawberry and champagne party or the
time they sat cross-legged on his floor when I was there. To date he has
directed over one hundred doctoral theses, a record, no doubt, if records
of such things were kept.

John has not only been adviser to his own students. Every one of my
doctoral candidates has been sent to meet him to discuss their work and
they always come away enlightened. Beyond his own immense knowledge
of the field, he inevitably knows exactly whom each student must meet,
and this has been an invaluable service to each of them. They became
integrated into the community of scholars at Cambridge or in London
through the entrée of John's recommendation, and this usually resulted
in learning about work or sources that were previously unknown to them.
For some of my students he acted as surrogate advisor, bringing them
to Cambridge to deliver papers at his seminar, reading their chapters,
and ultimately publishing their books. And what has been true for my
students is true for those of others. The parade of visitors up the tower
staircase at Selwyn is seemingly inexhaustible and one never knew who
would arrive to sit at the master's feet.

V

From a distance, ours seems an unlikely friendship: a Manchester lad
and a kid from New York. Two cultures separated by a not so common
language. Indeed there is much we do not share. He is devout, I am
profane (in the technical sense). For him it is classical music, for me it
is classic rock. He is cool-tempered, I am volatile; he catches his flies
with honey, I kill mine with vinegar. I am cynical. But there are points of

contact as well and they matter more. *Mutatis mutandis* we share the same passion for sport, he for Manchester United, I for the New York Yankees. He once told me that during a cup final involving Man U he had to enter a lay-by on the road because he was screaming so violently at his radio that other drivers were becoming alarmed. I conduct similar invective-laden conversations with my television set, in violation of my father's admonition to 'never argue with inanimate objects'. We both knew what Tolstoy meant about happy families and we both had uxorious marriages cut short within a year of each other by cancer. The dignity he maintained through his ordeal became the blueprint for my own. We had our common intellectual and professional interests, and as the years passed a stock of common experiences that could be recounted and savoured.

Above all we've enjoyed each other's company and there was never a meeting and hardly a phone call where one or both of us did not dissolve into laughter. We share the same sense of humour despite having grown up in entirely different comedic traditions. Jokes we save to tell each other are always uproariously funny and when John gets going his bellowing effusions can only be described as guffaws, completely unrestrained deep belly laughs. These once got me banned from meetings of the Liberty Fund when, learning that *A Fish Called Wanda* was showing on television, we decided to play hooky from the open bar that capped the day's sessions in preference for one of our favourite movies. The antics of Kevin Kline and John Cleese soon had us literally rolling on the floor and one of John's great paroxysms of hilarity alerted the rest of our group – sombrely drinking themselves into stupors – to our absence. The next morning I was officially reprimanded for 'corrupting' him. When John subsequently learned of this he laughed even harder and for the period of my banishment he would delight in informing me of his most recent Liberty Fund invitations. My revenge came cruelly. One night in his family room one of my wry remarks so set him off that he tipped an entire cup of coffee on to the not-so-stain-resistant sofa. Hurrying for a solvent and cloth, an exasperated Frances observed 'you two are just like schoolboys', echoing my own wife's assessment that we were just like teenagers.

John has always had the knack of making and keeping friends. They come from all parts of his life, representing his different eras and broad interests. In the small world of British academia it is only natural that he would have professional friends from as long ago as his schooldays, but he has maintained connection with many others who have no attachment to professional history. They parade to Cambridge unceasingly. Over the years many of his students have passed from one category to the other and he loves visiting them *in situ*. His Christmas card list must rival those of political leaders, except his are always handwritten and personally addressed. He takes pleasure in introducing his friends one to another and delights when one of these connections endures. Nothing makes him prouder than their accomplishments and he is always bathing in reflected glory. Indeed, unlike Gore Vidal, every time a friend succeeds, he grows a little. To those who know him best, John Morrill is a veritable giant.

Introduction: John Morrill and the experience of revolution

Michael J. Braddick and David L. Smith

I

When John Morrill began his research career the most influential writing about mid-seventeenth-century England was essentially concerned with modernization, and, even in non-Marxist explanations, contained a strong strain of materialism. This was a prominent feature of the sometimes vituperative exchanges of the gentry debate, and John's first piece of extended writing about seventeenth-century England was written in response to that controversy; it was a long essay, composed during a summer vacation, which examined the relationship between the fortunes of particular gentry families and their Civil War allegiance. His interest in local realities, however, quickly gave rise to dissatisfaction with the broad categories of analysis with which the gentry controversy was engaged. By the time that he published the monograph based on his Oxford D.Phil. thesis, in 1974, he concluded (among other things) that 'the particular situation in Cheshire diffracted the conflicts between King and Parliament into an individual and specific pattern. As a result all rigid, generalized explanations, particularly of the socio-economic kind, are unhelpful if not downright misleading.'[1] A desire to do better than these generalizations has driven his work ever since, and has thereby provided a huge stimulus to scholars of early modern England.

His doctoral study of Cheshire marked the beginning of the first of three overlapping but distinct phases in the development of his work, in each of which he has been a leading figure. All have been a point of reference for the work of numerous scholars engaged in a critical reappraisal of the Whig and Marxist traditions. In his first phase, as a local historian,

---

[1] J. S. Morrill, *Cheshire, 1630–1660: County Government and Society during the 'English Revolution'* (Oxford, 1974), p. 330. He later distanced himself a little from this position: see John Morrill, *Revolt in the Provinces: The People of England and the Tragedies of War, 1630–1648*, 2nd edn (Harlow, 1999), especially p. 17. This Introduction should be read alongside the chronological bibliography of John's major writings at pp. 291–8. This bibliography obviates the need for detailed footnotes here, except to provide references for specific quotations.

John followed the lead given by Alan Everitt, and helped to breathe new life into a nineteenth-century genre of county histories, while stimulating a veritable research industry in the production of county studies. His own summary of much of this work, *The Revolt of the Provinces*, was published in 1976 and proved a seminal work, synthesizing John's own research with the large number of local studies that had appeared over the previous decade. In doing so, it offered a new explanation of the political, as opposed to social, conflicts that emerged in the reign of Charles I. The essence of John's argument was that 'England at this period is more like a federated state than a unitary national state', and that 'national issues took on different resonances in each local context and became intricately bound up with purely local issues and groupings'.[2] The titles of John's publications between the early 1970s and the early 1980s reflected this preoccupation with the local dimension, and especially with the dilemmas of that 'silent majority'[3] who strove to keep the Civil War out of their locality.

This view of the nature of the political relationship between centre and locality has been much revised in the last thirty-five years.[4] John's work has been criticized for underestimating the importance of political engagement in local societies, and for taking the ideology out of the Civil War and the Revolution. At a greater distance in time, however, it seems more accurate to suggest that the significance of neutralism and attempts to disengage from armed conflict were a means both to emphasize the importance of local commitments and an attempt to bring into sharper focus those issues which overrode that essential commitment. In any case, by 1981 he had come to feel that he 'had said all [he] wanted to say about "neutralism" and "localism"'.[5] In fact, the important and influential

---

[2] J. S. Morrill, *Seventeenth-Century Britain, 1603–1714* (Folkestone, 1980), p. 125; A. M. Everitt, *The Community of Kent and the Great Rebellion, 1640–60* (Leicester, 1966); A. M. Everitt, *The Local Community and the Great Rebellion*, Historical Association, General Series 70 (1969), repr. in R. C. Richardson, ed., *The English Civil Wars: Local Aspects* (Stroud, 1997), pp. 14–36.

[3] J. S. Morrill, 'William Davenport and the "silent majority" of early Stuart England', *Journal of the Chester and North Wales Archaeological Society*, 58 (1975), 115–29.

[4] Clive Holmes, 'The county community in Stuart historiography', *Journal of British Studies*, 19 (1980), 54–73; Ann Hughes, 'Local history and the origins of the Civil War', in Richard Cust and Ann Hughes, eds., *Conflict in Early Stuart England* (Harlow, 1989), pp. 224–53; Clive Holmes, 'Centre and locality in civil-war England', in John Adamson, ed., *The English Civil War* (Basingstoke, 2009), pp. 153–74.

[5] John Morrill, *The Nature of the English Revolution* (Harlow, 1993), p. 34. So effective was the stimulus to this kind of work that in 1984 his advice to Braddick was 'Whatever you do, don't do a county study'. John has subsequently acknowledged the limitations of the localist approach, while also restating and refining his argument: Morrill, *Nature*, pp. 179–90; Morrill, *Revolt in the Provinces*, pp. 1–23, 177–208.

body of work associated with his 'localist' phase already contained the seeds of John's second major historiographical contribution. In *The Revolt of the Provinces*, published in 1976, he wrote: 'while the great majority of men dithered or wrote petitions and talked of raising a third force for peace, it was the men who felt most strongly about religion who began the war'.[6] His emphasis on localism threw into sharp relief the difficulty of the choices people made at the outbreak of the war, as they tried to reconcile apparently contradictory impulses and commitments in order to make the 'agonizing' choices which events were forcing upon them.

From this position John famously presented in a lecture to the Royal Historical Society in December 1983 the thesis that 'The English Civil War was not the first European revolution: it was the last of the Wars of Religion'.[7] The importance of religion in shaping seventeenth-century British history has been a central theme in much of John's subsequent work. He has acknowledged the problems of the term 'war of religion',[8] but the significance of religious issues both in the lives of individual historical figures (such as Oliver Cromwell or William Dowsing) and in driving the course of events has remained central to his writings ever since. As he put it in an essay published in 2008, 'these were wars of religion as much as any wars in early modern Europe were wars of religion – that is to say, they were about many things other than religion, but confessional poles were those around which all kinds of other issues clustered'.[9]

The stimulus of this second creative departure in his understanding of the Civil War is still very much with us, and many of the essays in this collection engage with these questions. In particular, those by Glenn Burgess (Ph.D. 1988), David Smith (Ph.D. 1990), Ian Atherton (Ph.D. 1993) and Anthony Milton (Ph.D. 1989) all reflect in one way or another on the utility of interpreting these events as a war, or wars, of religion. Glenn Burgess's essay pursues the question of historical change, and the place of the Revolution in a longer history, through an examination of the thought of four individuals. For Stephen Marshall, Henry Ireton, Jasper Mayne and John Locke a key question posed by the experience

---

[6] J. S. Morrill, *The Revolt of the Provinces: Conservatives and Radicals in the English Civil War, 1630–1650* (1976), p. 50.

[7] Morrill, *Nature*, p. 68. This lecture, entitled 'The religious context of the English civil war', was first published in *Transactions of the Royal Historical Society*, 5th ser., 34 (1984), 155–78, and later reprinted in Morrill, *Nature*, pp. 45–68.

[8] See especially Morrill, *Nature*, pp. 33–44.

[9] John Morrill, 'The rule of saints and soldiers: the wars of religion in Britain and Ireland, 1638–1660', in Jenny Wormald, ed., *The Short Oxford History of the British Isles: The Seventeenth Century* (Oxford, 2008), pp. 83–115, at p. 84.

of revolution was 'could civil society survive the religious enthusiasm of its subjects (and its rulers)?'. All of them were forced to reflect on the relationship between the commitments of religious conscience and other social goods – in particular the role of law and the importance of civil peace. They, and others, 'were compelled to ask how civil society could survive among a diversity of religious beliefs' even if 'they were not compelled to agree on the answers'. In exploring the interaction between the political and religious dimensions of social life, these authors sometimes made secularizing moves – shifting the boundary in some respect so as to better secure civil peace – but none of them had a properly secularizing intent. All remained convinced of the public and political importance of religion; the difficulty they addressed was how to secure that without jeopardizing the stability of civil society.

These complexities are often best understood through the study of particular individuals. It is in this way that we get a sense of what was flexible and what was immoveable. David Smith examines the development of Sir Benjamin Rudyerd's political positions in the course of his long parliamentary career. There are strong consistencies in Rudyerd's commitment to godly reformation and to a strong relationship between crown and parliament based on trust (which implied adequate financial supply for the crown). His silver-tongued advocacy of these principles was remarkably consistent from the 1620s to the end of his career, and they supported a clear Parliamentarian allegiance in the Civil War, but they were difficult to sustain in the light of events. As further reformation threatened disorder in the early 1640s, for example, he became a defender of episcopacy, but not a Royalist; and throughout the war he supported attempts to make peace. At the core of this analysis lie two concerns which are also characteristic of Morrill's work: the place of specifically religious sentiments in shaping Rudyerd's attitudes and actions, and a desire to understand what was consistent and what was malleable about his politics – what constituted his essential psychology and what proved more flexible in the face of events.

The role of religious issues and motives is likewise examined in Anthony Milton's essay, which explores the content of the religious advice addressed to Charles, how it reacted to the immediate needs of particular moments, and how it seems to have been reflected in Charles's negotiating positions. Here was a group of highly principled and conscientious people seeking to respond to circumstances, maintaining what had to be maintained and giving away as little as possible of what was disposable. It reveals how this was a war of religion not just for the radical Puritans, but also for those with a higher view of the Church of England and its future.

Ian Atherton's essay explores the place of the cathedral in these arguments about the present and future of the English, Scottish and Irish churches. The practical complexity of reforming the church – the potentially competing pressures of local sentiment, legal right and reforming zeal, for example – are central to an explanation for the survival of the cathedrals, and their rapid re-establishment in 1660. What they came to represent for Parliamentarians and Royalists in the meantime also casts considerable light on some of the central issues of the Revolution, and on the differences between the wars of religion as they were experienced in the three kingdoms.

This focus on the three kingdoms brings us to the third major historiographical contribution that John has made, namely to encourage awareness of the importance of the 'British problem'. John's interest in what had prevented settlement, what in the politics of the crisis could not easily be negotiated, also informed his commitment to understanding the crisis in a British context. From about 1990 onwards, the titles of many of John's publications indicate a growing interest in the histories of Scotland and (especially) Ireland, and the ways in which those kingdoms interacted with England within the Stuart monarchies. This growing preoccupation is reflected in the fact that when John was elected to a Readership in the Cambridge History Faculty in 1992 he chose the title 'Reader in Early Modern History', but when six years later he was promoted to a personal chair he took the title 'Professor of British and Irish History'. John's key claim here is that 'some of the most stubborn and insoluble problems in the history of each kingdom require a British dimension in order to be fully understood'. He has therefore sought to reconstruct 'the story of three kingdoms in search of a defined relationship one to another, of four or more peoples in the process of refashioning themselves in the light of much heightened contact and friction'.[10] He wrote that in 1996, and many of his publications since then have explored the challenges and problems of constructing British history. As he put it in 2006, 'British history is . . . a story of not what is, or even what was, but what was in the process of becoming.'[11] Here he was influenced by the work of John Elliott and Conrad Russell, which understood seventeenth-century political instability in structural terms, but as distinctively early modern phenomena, namely those associated with the problems of

---

[10] John Morrill, 'The British problem, *c.* 1534–1707', in Brendan Bradshaw and John Morrill, eds., *The British Problem, c. 1534–1707: State Formation in the Atlantic Archipelago* (1996), pp. 1–38, at pp. 1–2.

[11] John Morrill, 'Thinking about the New British History', in David Armitage, ed., *British Political Thought in History, Literature and Theory, 1500–1800* (Cambridge, 2006), pp. 23–46, at p. 42.

multiple kingdoms and composite monarchies or (John's term for the Stuart kingdoms) 'dynastic agglomerates'.[12]

This body of work has also had a galvanizing effect on the field, a stimulus which is again reflected in the essays collected here. Joong-Lak Kim's (Ph.D. 1997) view of the Scottish Prayer Book depends on this extra-national perspective. Reconstructing both who was involved at each stage and what changes were introduced, he is able to build an argument about the direction and motives of reform. It was natural and plausible for Scots to see the Book as an effort at Anglicization, but by taking a cross-border view it is possible to see the Book as part of a programme for uniformity that would have required change in all three Churches. Here the influence of Laud and, behind him, Charles seems to have been crucial. For the framers of the Book, no less than those offended by it, the changes to the Scottish liturgy had to be understood in a British or three kingdoms perspective.

John McCafferty's (Ph.D. 1996) study of the life-writings about dead bishops reveals that the bishops appeared differently to readers in each of the three kingdoms. This attempt to understand the meaning of the Revolution through personal experience enjoyed a strong contemporary appeal: as Sharpe and Zwicker have argued, 'civil war and revolution not only and inevitably wrote and rewrote lives as texts of party and cause, they fashioned a desire, an appetite and market for lives, old and new, a market which printers and publishers rushed to satisfy'.[13] In these writings, the life of each bishop 'also functions as an argument for episcopacy', but the argument, and hence the significance to be lent to the life, depended on context. Six lives of three bishops (William Bedell, John Bramhall and James Ussher), written between 1656 and 1686, illustrate the shifting terrain of arguments about episcopacy (and

---

[12] Conrad Russell, 'The British problem and the English Civil War', *History*, 72 (1986), 395–415; Russell, 'The British background to the Irish Rebellion of 1641', *Historical Research*, 61:145 (1988), 166–82 (both reprinted in Russell, *Unrevolutionary England, 1603–1642* (1990), chs. 13 and 15); Russell, *The Causes of the English Civil War: The Ford Lectures delivered in the University of Oxford, 1987–1988* (Oxford, 1990), especially ch. 2; Russell, *The Fall of the British Monarchies, 1637–1642* (Oxford, 1991); Russell, 'Composite monarchies in early modern Europe: the British and Irish example', in Alexander Grant and Keith Stringer, eds., *Uniting the Kingdom? The Making of British History* (1995), pp. 133–46; J. H. Elliott, 'A Europe of composite monarchies', *Past and Present*, 137 (November 1992), 48–71. For John's use of the term 'dynastic agglomerates', see especially John Morrill, *"Uneasy Lies the Head that Wears a Crown": Dynastic Crises in Tudor and Stewart Britain, 1504–1746*, Stenton Lecture for 2003 (Reading, 2005).

[13] Kevin Sharpe and Steven Zwicker, eds., *Writing Lives: Biography and Textuality, Identity and Representation in Early Modern England* (Oxford, 2008), p. 19, quoted by McCafferty below, p. 259.

Ireland). These varying readings result perhaps in a paradoxical effect on the reader: 'Their very insistence on depicting their chosen bishops as exemplars of unity, piety, moderation and primitive episcopacy whose lives were played out in a discernible moral framework actually serves to highlight the traumatic uncertainties of the revolutionary years in the three kingdoms.'[14]

A number of the other essays, following the lead offered by interpretations of the British problem or the crisis of three kingdoms, also offer new insight on the basis of a shift of geographical focus. Dagmar Freist (Ph.D. 1992) brings to an understanding of the responses to the royal marriage an awareness of the wider European debate about mixed marriage, and its dangers. That awareness puts the issues in a different light, just as it did for many contemporaries. Crucial here is the attempt to understand the practical context of political action – not just the categories of understanding that contemporaries appeared to find helpful, but the precise political context in which they were thinking and acting on that understanding, and how that transformed (or failed to) those initial categories. Freist explores how standard views of the dangers of Catholicism became attached particularly to the person of Henrietta Maria. This was an important element of the dangerous fusing of anti-popery (hostility to remaining corruption in the church) with fear of a Roman conspiracy against the English Church, and suspicion of actual Catholics. As a result, pressure was placed on the practical toleration of the Catholic minority which had characterized English life, despite the presence of virulent anti-popery in discussions of the English Church and polity. The question she addresses is how experience – news and rumour about Henrietta Maria and her political influence – served to put pressure on these everyday practices; how 'specific (subjective) experiences' led to a re-evaluation of pre-existing structures and values. Of central importance to this was awareness of the terms of the royal marriage contract, which reflected wider European expectations about the confessional rights and duties of those in religiously mixed marriages. Once they became public, these rights and obligations, formally extended to Henrietta Maria, fed into fears about the place of Catholicism in the English state and church. Mary Geiter (Ph.D. 1993) likewise demonstrates how ideas forged in one geographical context were subtly transformed by the transplantation to another. She charts the development of William Penn's thought from its grounding in a naval and republican context to its colonial expression in America. Again we see core commitments – to religious toleration, mercantile and imperial expansion – and an interest in constitutional

---

[14] McCafferty, below, p. 269.

solutions to political problems tested, shaped and reframed by the experience of revolution and, in this case, transplantation. Penn's vision was European and Atlantic in both inspiration and expression.

II

All three of these lines of interpretation – the localist, the religious and the British – remain central to John's work, and they were prominent themes in his 2006 Ford Lectures in Oxford. They are united into a coherent whole not only by the formation of John's particular interests but also by certain broader characteristics of his historical approach. Of these, perhaps the most pervasive and profoundly important is a preoccupation with individual personalities, motives and experiences. This impulse marked his earliest research in the field, informing his work on Cheshire. He has written of this retrospectively as deriving from his 'dissatisfaction with and revulsion against modelling of civil war allegiance on the basis of putting individuals into one of three boxes labelled *royalist*, *parliamentarian* and *other*, and then tipping out the contents of each box and looking for statistical variants between them'.[15]

This reaction against aspects of social scientific history was not uncommon during the 1970s and 1980s, even if it took a particular form among Stuart political historians. One recent account of the origins of 'the new cultural history', for example, identifies similar discontents:

In describing the behavioral tendencies of social groups and emphasizing normative behavior, often in the abstractions of numbers and charts, social historians had moved beyond an elite-dominated political paradigm, but had ignored both the uniqueness of individual experience and the ways in which social life is created through politics and culture.[16]

This is perhaps the core of John's critique of the field as he found it, for the historiography of the English Revolution had of course been profoundly influenced by some of the most distinguished practitioners of that kind of social scientific history. We have already noted John's early engagement with the gentry controversy and he himself has commented on how Lawrence Stone's *Causes of the English Revolution* (1972), a masterpiece of social scientific history writing, was important in crystallizing the dissatisfactions with the whole approach.[17] While some of Stone's 'revisionist' critics subsequently engaged very explicitly with this cultural

---

[15] Morrill, *Nature*, p. 180.
[16] Paula S. Fass, 'Cultural history/social history: some reflections on a continuing dialogue', *Journal of Social History*, 37: 1 (2003), 39–46, at 39, 40.
[17] Morrill, *Revolt in the Provinces*, pp. 5–8, 17.

history – most notably, of course, Kevin Sharpe – John seems instead to have continued to stick with the original question – to strive to explain and characterize the Revolution as a general phenomenon – but to do so in ways that do not do violence to, or ignore, the importance of immediate human experiences.

Certainly John has written with great sympathy about the practical difficulties and dilemmas of life during civil war and revolution, the ambiguous personal experiences and the choices made by active politicians and those facing the practical consequences of social and political conflict. The result is a picture of fluid and dynamic politics, rather than a clash between fixed blocks of ideas or interests, out of which come surprising alliances and commitments. His interest is not so much in the history of political thought, but the history of political thinking: he seeks to understand how personal and ideological commitments are given life in the difficult choices made by individuals understood in close context.

Much of John's most powerful and moving writing is in this mode, engaging with the beliefs and dilemmas of particular historical figures and the relationship between their public and private behaviour. Pride of place in this cast of characters must surely go to Oliver Cromwell, who emerges frequently and explicitly in John's bibliography from 1981 onwards. It was natural that John should write the life of Cromwell for the *Oxford Dictionary of National Biography* in 2004, subsequently reprinted in the 'Very Interesting People' series (2007). Few historians have written more hauntingly or eloquently than John about Cromwell's complex character and ambivalent achievement, in passages such as this:

What makes Oliver Cromwell endlessly appealing and endlessly alarming is that he was true to his own vision. He never doubted his call to service or to salvation... If God called upon him to be the human instrument of his wrath, he would not flinch. His sense of himself as the unworthy and suffering servant of a stern Lord protected him from the tragic megalomanias of others who rose to absolute power on the backs of revolutions. Cromwell's achievements as a soldier are great but unfashionable; as a religious libertarian great but easily mis-stated; as a statesman inevitably stunted. No one who rises from a working farmer to head of state in twenty years is other than great... He was to himself and to his God most true, if at great cost to himself and others.[18]

John likewise co-authored with Mark Kishlansky the *ODNB* life of Charles I, and that he should write equally compellingly about these two arch-enemies speaks volumes about the range of John's historical empathy. His ability to enter into the hearts and minds of historical figures is equally apparent with less prominent characters, ranging from

---

[18] John Morrill, *Oliver Cromwell* (Oxford, 2007), pp. 121–2.

the moderate William Davenport to the chillingly fanatical William Dowsing. This achievement expresses not only the power of John's historical imagination but also his capacity to engage empathetically even with those personalities most different from his own. John must surely, for example, be the first Roman Catholic deacon to have served as president of the Cromwell Association. A passionate interest in, and concern for, other people characterizes John's attitude towards both past and present. In terms of historical method, this comes through in his interest in historical biography: he not only contributed twelve lives to the *ODNB* but also served as consultant editor for the over 6,000 seventeenth-century lives in that project.

Alan Orr's (Ph.D. 1997) study of John Lilburne's thought complements this approach by seeking to understand how his beliefs were shaped and formed by events, to recapture the 'complex, factionalized and ideologically messy' politics of the 1640s, and the ideas to which that could give rise. On this reading, Lilburne's view of liberty arose not from an engagement with other thinkers addressing that question, nor from a formal education in the law, but from an 'ongoing, and sometimes subjectively reactive process'. In that process the conditions of his imprisonment exercised a crucial influence, as he drew creatively (although not necessarily with a full understanding) on the traditions of common law to develop a negative theory of liberty – liberty as the absence of active constraint, freedom *from*, rather than freedom *to*. Seen from this perspective Lilburne's political views appear as the product of a 'haphazard, goal-directed process undertaken with the practical aim of securing his release'. Orr presents this as a methodological corrective to historians of political thought, often more concerned with traditions, formal learning and intellectual context; here political thought is understood in dialogue with the very immediate and subjective experience of incarceration.

Perhaps the most dramatic personal experience of revolution was the kind of intense spirituality explored by Tom Webster (Ph.D. 1993). For John Gilpin, a Quaker, revolutionary religion was an immediate and physical experience, and the understanding of that experience was mediated by long-standing debates about the presence of the divine and diabolic in both the world and the body. Such experiences were highly contested, and stood close to the core of religious controversy, and it is difficult to understand the nature of this experience without close attention to the longer history of debates about possession and diabolism. As was so often the case, the authenticity of religious experience was contested in relation not to formal theology, or scriptural authority, but to a more pragmatic religious knowledge which was grounded in the everyday and the physical. Reports of these very direct and personal religious

experiences were commonly the basis on which to redraw the boundaries of acceptable Christian practice or belief, and, Webster suggests, as
that argument progressed in the accelerated conditions of revolutionary
England, the terrain of those arguments shifted. The displacement of
the possessed individual, and the details of the experience of possession,
helped to inform the later denunciation of 'enthusiasm' or 'frenzy'. Here
we can see, perhaps, an exemplary case for understanding the nature and
consequences of the Revolution in terms of experience and its mediation.

It is hard to imagine a career more resistant to modern sociologi-
cal categorization than that of Thomas Violet, described here by Ariel
Hessayon (Ph.D. 1996). An English national of perhaps mixed ethnicity,
marginal in some ways to the structures of respectable society, Violet
nonetheless built up a considerable fortune and some impressive political connections. On the basis of these connections he sought to extort
money from the semi-clandestine Jewish community in London. It is a
deeply unappealing career, and in it the main political story of war and
revolution appears as something of a backdrop, or a series of opportunities to be grasped, rather than a structuring feature of Violet's life and
concerns. Instead, the sensitive reconstruction of his life reveals in fascinating detail dimensions of London's religious and commercial life that
have previously been hidden. It prompts us to rethink the outlines of
Anglo-Jewish history, our picture of London life, of international trade
and its alliances, and the variety of experiences of revolution in mid-
seventeenth-century London.

Michael Braddick's (Ph.D. 1988) essay explores these issues from the
other end, by examining the difficulties of making particular languages
work to describe new policies and changing conditions, and the problems
that posed for securing and maintaining allegiance. He shows how the
pressures of the Parliamentarian mobilization for the first year of the
real war in 1643 revealed the limitations of arguments as they were first
promoted in opposition to royal policies during the 1630s, and how this
prompted some individuals to re-examine their allegiance and to clarify
their original commitments. But this instability in political language was
also an opportunity to redefine standard forms of political argument
in creative ways: the tension between a commitment both to standard
political languages and to the innovations necessary to achieve political
victory was an important context for intellectual creativity, one way of
addressing the origins of revolutionary politics.

This view of ideas in motion, and the relationship between concepts
and languages, also characterizes James Hart's (Ph.D. 1985) essay which
explores the fate of two notions of Parliament as a Great Council as
the political crisis unfolded. There were medieval precedents both for

a notion of a baronial council of the king and also for the view that Parliament as a collective body was the Great Council: a Great Council in Parliament and a Great Council of Parliament, as it were. There were some tensions between these notions and, in any case, neither justified the executive role that Parliament had begun to claim by the time of the Ten Propositions in June 1641. The baronial notion was rendered obsolete under the pressure of events, and the notion of Parliament as the king's Great Council transformed almost beyond recognition. By October 1643, when the Commons secured the Lords' acquiescence to the issue of a Great Seal under its own authority, neither the baronial nor the monarchical element seemed crucial to the notion of the Great Council. This new claim about the constitutional and political role of Parliament apparently justified its position as an executive authority.

Jonathan Scott (Ph.D. 1986) returns to Harrington's *Oceana* in a similar spirit, placing it in the context of the search for settlement in 1656. Clearly articulated from within the traditions of humanism, or classical republicanism, *Oceana* was, nonetheless, a response to immediate conditions. The difficulty faced by successive attempts at settlement was not to do with their betrayal of principles or the cause so much as their failure to identify the necessary basis for political stability. The same was true of Hobbes's *Leviathan*, another work of theory with an immediate political purpose. Here the experience of conflict and constitutional stability sharpened Harrington's theoretical understanding of both the classical tradition that he inherited and the structures of the society he inhabited. Once again, ideas are most richly understood through a reconstruction of the specific personalities and circumstances of their exponents.

Many of the other essays here pursue the meanings of the Revolution through an understanding of individual experiences – notably those by Burgess, Smith, Freist, Geiter and McCafferty. For John, these attempts to understand individual experiences of the Revolution are central to the attempt to characterize its nature. In his treatment of individuals, John has sought to understand not just what was pliable but also what was not – what persisted or proved fundamental. This is crucial to his underlying view of historical change. So, for example, in one essay he drew an analogy that had become familiar to many of his students, that of the 1862 Solera Madeira kept in the cellar of his Oxford college. Every year a part of the vat is drawn off and another cask of wine is added, so that the wine drawn off each year is 'always developing and changing as the older vintage matures and the younger wine adds its own distinctive flavor'.[19] And,

---

[19] 'John Morrill', in Juliet Gardiner, ed., *The History Debate* (1990), pp. 90–5, quotations at pp. 90, 91–2.

we might add, although the identity of the whole is consistent, its actual composition is in continuous evolution. Historians, then, are dealing with 'the process of becoming', and that is best understood through the experiences of individuals wrestling with the dilemmas of an engaged political life. This is the real core of his response to the limitations of the impersonal categorizations that drove the social scientific history of the 1950s and 1960s. Putting 'individuals into . . . boxes' with simple labels not only fails to do justice to the complexities of their lives, but in so doing it limits our understanding of the nature of the Revolution.[20]

III

Throughout his academic career, John has been pre-eminently concerned with the lives and experiences of human beings, with their hearts and minds, their aspirations and sufferings: with the experience of revolution as a key to understanding its nature. This is the underlying concern which unites the essays in this volume, all of them written by John's students: the presumption that to understand the causes, trajectory and consequences of the Revolution we must understand it as a human and dynamic experience, as a process. Of course, as McCafferty points out, 'Individual experience, no matter how well contextualized nor how brilliantly articulated, can do no more than offer partial, if often vivid, insight'.[21] But an understanding of these personal experiences is certainly an important part of any attempt to define the nature of the Revolution, and can provide the basis on which to build up larger frameworks of interpretation. This has been John Morrill's project and while many of these authors disagree with him on the detail and pertinence of the larger frameworks he has proposed, they are all, in this more fundamental respect, following in his footsteps. They are profoundly conscious of the debt that they owe to his inspiration and example.

---

[20] The quality of imaginative empathy also characterizes John's sensitive, generous and candid appreciations of other historians in his field. This gift first became apparent in 1983, when he co-edited a collection of papers by his former tutor at Trinity College, Oxford, J. P. Cooper; this volume included John's essay on 'J. P. Cooper as a teacher'. Since then, John has written at length, often for the British Academy or the *ODNB*, about scholars as diverse as Christopher Hill, J. P. Kenyon, Austin Woolrych and Conrad Russell. These memoirs all display a compelling evocation of personality and a generous but not uncritical assessment of the subject's achievements as a historian. It is typical of John that his concern with the political and religious psychology of seventeenth-century people is combined with a similar desire to enter into the mindset of those scholars who have studied them.

[21] McCafferty, below, p. 269.

1   The Scottish–English–Romish Book: the character of the Scottish Prayer Book of 1637

Joong-Lak Kim

I

The riot against the Scottish Prayer Book of 1637 at St Giles in Edinburgh on Sunday, 23 July 1637, was the starting point of the British troubles in the mid-seventeenth century. The National Covenant, the two Bishops' Wars, the Long Parliament, and the English Civil War were inevitable chain reactions of the riot against the Prayer Book. It had been used as a piece of evidence for the Popish Plot by the Puritans on both sides of the border during the English Civil War. The Scottish Covenanters found the book 'popish' and accused William Laud of being a main composer of it. The archbishop was tried and executed amid the Scottish rage against the Prayer Book in January 1645.

But was it? Was it entirely popish? Could it be called an anglicization of Scottish worship? Was Laud alone responsible for that? What were the roles played by the king and the Scottish bishops? The Scottish Prayer Book of 1637 is the best key to the understanding of the nature of Charles's ecclesiastical policies of the 1630s in their British context. This is not simply because the composition and the imposition of this book occupied the whole of the 1630s, but also because from the first step to the last in this policy, its relation to the English liturgy dominated the British ecclesiastical policy of the 1630s. However, few historians have fully recognized the potential of a study of the Scottish Prayer Book in understanding Charles I's ecclesiastical policies more generally during the 1630s. Although the narrative work of Peter Donald illustrated the king's response to the troubles in a British context, it concerned the political style of Charles rather than the Prayer Book policy, and did not discuss the king's policies before 1637.[1] Gordon Donaldson's magisterial work, *The Making of the Scottish Prayer Book of 1637* (1954) lacks a British perspective on the king's ecclesiastical policies, and is in need of

---

[1] P. Donald, *An Uncounselled King: Charles I and the Scottish Troubles, 1637–1641* (Cambridge, 1990).

14

some correction. In order to discover the nature and changes of Charles I's liturgical policy, a slightly different narrative approach needs to be employed. Through a thick description of the making of the Scottish Prayer Book of 1637, and an analysis of the ritual formulae, we may find the true nature of the book.

In the *Large Declaration* written by the hand of Walter Balcanquhal, Charles had offered a historical background for the propriety of his liturgical policy, arguing that it was in line with his father's.[2] In the brief history of the liturgical policy of James in the *Large Declaration*, the story of the General Assembly of Aberdeen in 1616 was strongly emphasized. The Assembly had passed 'an Act, whereby they authorized some of the present Bishops, and divers others, to compile and frame a public form of Liturgie, or Booke of Common Prayer'.[3] 'While these things were in doing', the story continues, 'and before they could receive their much wished and desired period and consummation', King James died.[4]

We must ask why Charles told this story in the *Large Declaration*. It seems that Charles was answering the Covenanters, who accused him of imposing the new liturgy in an unlawful manner. In a pamphlet produced by the Covenanters in the previous year, it was argued that 'if a new one ought to be imposed, then it ought to come in by a lawfull manner: by a general assemblie, and men chosen to make it that are known to have the gift of prayer themselves'.[5] Although there had been no General Assembly since that of Perth in 1618, the king was claiming that he had carried out the same task which the Aberdeen Assembly had commissioned, through the same bishop who was alive then.

Another point made by Charles in the *Large Declaration* was that James found a lack of decency and uniformity in the worship of Scotland, indicating his agreement with his father.

Our Father of blessed memorie immediately after his coming into England, comparing the *decencie and uniformitie* of Gods worship here, especially in the Liturgie of the Church, with that diversitie, nay deformitie which was used in Scotland, where *no set or publike forme of prayer* was used, but Preachers or Readers and ignorant Schoolmasters prayed in the Church, sometimes so seditiously that their prayers were plain Libels, girding at soveraigntie and authorie; or Lyes,

---

[2] [Charles I], *A Large Declaration concerning the Late Tumults in Scotland* (1639), pp. 15–18.

[3] *A Large Declaration*, p. 16. The compilation of this liturgy had been led by William Cowper, bishop of Galloway. For the details of the making of this draft see G. Donaldson, *The Making of the Scottish Prayer Book of 1637* (Edinburgh, 1954), pp. 31–9.

[4] *A Large Declaration*, p. 17.

[5] [G. Gillespie], *Reasons for Which the Service Booke, Urged upon Scotland Ought to Bee Refused* (1638), p. C.

being stuffed with all the false reports in the kingdome: He did immediately, as became a Religious Prince, bethink himself seriously how His first reformation in that Kingdome might begin at the Publike worship of God.[6]

If Charles was suggesting here that the Scots had no set form of liturgy he was under an illusion. In its repudiation of the *Large Declaration*, the General Assembly of 1639 denied this accusation.[7] From the Reformation to the beginning of the Scottish troubles, the Book of Common Order was, as Donaldson argued, 'the official Scottish service-book'.[8] Alexander Henderson stated that the Book of Common Order was the Scottish liturgy 'to which the ministers are to conform themselves'.[9] It was apparent that the book was more than a mere directory, 'for an Order', as McMillan has pointed out, 'cannot be called *common* when every one pleases himself whether he uses it or not'.[10]

However, there is a certain truth in Charles's comment that 'no set or publike forme of prayer was used' in James's reign, if he simply meant that the public prayers contained in the Book of Common Order were not strictly enforced. It seems that a good deal of variation in public prayers was practised in the 1610s. This was confirmed by John Spottiswood, archbishop of Glasgow, in 1615: 'Thair is lacking in our Churche ane form of Divine service; and quiles every Minister is left to the framing of publick prayer by himself, bothe the people ar neglectit and thair prayeris prove often impertinent.'[11] This practice was something to do with the preaching-centred worship of Scotland and the reluctance to read prayers. The radical Presbyterian minister John Row was opposed to a 'prescript and stinted form of the words and prayers and exhortation'.[12] For these men, to read the prayers was to diminish the preaching ministry.

James also seems to have found a lack of 'decencie and uniformitie' in Scottish worship, as Charles observed.[13] He seems to have been pursuing the improvement of decent worship in Scotland by the introduction of

---

[6] *A Large Declaration*, pp. 15–16 (emphasis added).

[7] *Records of the Kirk of Scotland, Containing the Acts and Proceedings of the General Assemblies, 1638–51*, ed. A. Peterkin (Edinburgh, 1838), p. 266.

[8] Donaldson, *Making of the Scottish Prayer Book*, p. 13. The question of whether the Book of Common Prayer was a directory or not is best discussed in W. McMillan, *The Worship of the Scottish Reformed Church, 1550–1638* (1931), pp. 63–73.

[9] R. Baillie, *Letters and Journals*, ed. D. Laing, 3 vols. (Edinburgh, 1841–2), II, p. 2.

[10] McMillan, *Worship*, p. 65.

[11] *Original Letters Relating to the Ecclesiastical Affairs of Scotland, Chiefly Written by, or Addressed to His Majesty King James The Six*, ed. B. Botfield (2 vols., Edinburgh, 1851), II, pp. 445–6; G. W. Sprott, *Scottish Liturgies of the Reign of James VI* (Edinburgh, 1901), p. xvi.

[12] J. Row, *History of the Kirk of Scotland, from the Year 1558 to 1638* (Edinburgh, 1842), pp. 404–6.

[13] *A Large Declaration*, pp. 15–16.

the Five Articles. Just before the General Assembly of Perth in 1618, he clearly expressed his intention of introducing the Five Articles: 'God knows my intention is, and ever was to have his true worship maintained, and a decent and comely order established in the Church.'[14] However, the introduction of the Five Articles brought more confusion in Scottish worship, particularly in the communion service. The diversity of worship and sacraments in the late 1620s was greater than that of any previous period. No doubt this made Charles regard the situation of the Scottish Church as one of 'deformity'.[15] It was the succession to James's 'pietie and religious care of the Publique Service of God' that Charles considered 'a greater honour' than the 'crownes'.[16]

Another aim of the king was to establish a British uniformity in worship. In the preface to the Scottish liturgy, the king declared that one of his main aims with the Prayer Book was to achieve uniformity in the three kingdoms.

It were to be wished that the whole church of Christ were one, as well in form of public worship as in doctrine, and that as it hath but one Lord and one faith, so it had but one heart and one mouth. This would prevent many schisms and divisions, and serve much to the preserving of unity. But since that cannot be hoped for in the whole Catholic Christian church, yet at least in the churches that are under the protection of one sovereign prince the same ought to be endeavoured.[17]

Clarendon also observed that 'the king . . . inherited that zeal for religion, and proposed nothing more to himself than to unite his three kingdoms in one form of God's worship and in a uniformity in their public devotions'.[18]

However, there is no evidence at all that this Caroline policy of uniformity was aiming at anglicization in either canons or liturgy. Conrad Russell has argued that the Caroline programme of uniformity involved 'in its fully developed form, a common acceptance throughout the King's dominions of the Thirty-Nine Articles, a common liturgy, Episcopacy, a Court of High Commission, a body of canons for ecclesiastical discipline, and a common Royal Supremacy'.[19] If he means by this that

---

[14] J. Spottiswood, *The History of the Church of Scotland* (1655), p. 533.
[15] *A Large Declaration*, p. 16.   [16] Ibid., p. 17.
[17] *The Booke of Common Prayer and Administration of the Sacraments And other Parts of divine Service for the use of the Church of Scotland* (Edinburgh, 1637), sig. a3. This book is reprinted in Donaldson, *Making of the Scottish Prayer Book*, pp. 97–247.
[18] Clarendon, I, p. 111.
[19] Conrad Russell, *The Fall of the British Monarchies, 1637–1642* (Oxford, 1991), pp. 38–9.

Charles wanted anglicization or conformity with English practice, he is mistaken as to the nature of this British uniformity.

Although the Thirty-Nine Articles were introduced in Ireland in 1634, it was not without a compromise.[20] If Charles had wanted to introduce the articles into Scotland later, there should have been a hint in the Scottish Canons of 1636. Although there were mentions of the Book of Common Prayer, which was introduced later, the Thirty-Nine Articles were never mentioned. If Russell meant by 'a body of canons' a common or a similar set of canons in the three kingdoms, this also was wrong. It is true that the Irish Canons were largely copied from the English Canons of 1604, although not without some changes. However, the Scottish Canons were too different from either the English Canons of 1604 or the Irish Canons to be defined as a part of a programme of anglicization.[21]

II

In August 1629, John Maxwell, then a minister of Edinburgh and later bishop of Ross, was sent to the king by 'a meeting of the bishops and some ministers in Edinburgh'. Maxwell's official mission was to ascertain 'the king's will toward the papists'.[22] However, his more important mission, if not an official one, was to bring another copy of the manuscript of the draft liturgy to the court.[23] This does not mean that the king had decided at this stage to introduce a new liturgy based on the draft made by his father's command. The king had another option, which was to introduce the English Prayer Book, with or without any variation. In a meeting with William Laud, Maxwell argued that 'their countrymen would be much better satisfied if a Liturgy were framed by their own clergy, than to have the English liturgy put upon them'.[24] It seems that Maxwell represented

---

[20] John D. McCafferty, 'John Bramhall and the reconstruction of the Church of Ireland', Ph.D. dissertation, University of Cambridge, 1996, pp. 97–8.

[21] For the three sets of canons see Joong-Lak Kim, 'Firing in unison? The Scottish canons of 1636 and the English canons of 1640', *Records of the Scottish Church History Society*, 28 (1998), pp. 35–77.

[22] In July 1629, many complaints were made against the activities of the papists. In particular, many Scots were offended by the king's protection of the marquis of Huntly at the court. A meeting of the bishops and some ministers in Edinburgh commissioned John Maxwell to discover the King's will towards them. Row, *History*, pp. 348–9.

[23] Stirling understood that the person who presented another copy was Patrick Lindsay, then bishop of Ross, later archbishop of Glasgow. But Laud's account of his experiment in 1629 tells that Dr John Maxwell, later bishop of Ross, was in London for the project of the new liturgy. Baillie, *Letters and Journals*, I, p. 444; W. Laud, *The Works of the Most Reverend Father in God, William Laud, D.D.*, ed. W. Scott and J. Bliss, 7 vols. (Oxford, 1847–60), III, p. 427.

[24] Donaldson, *Making of the Scottish Prayer Book*, p. 41.

a majority of the Scottish bishops, who knew that the draft liturgy would be less offensive than the English liturgy.

However, it seems to have been Laud who advised the king to impose the English Book of Common Prayer without any alteration. In August or September 1629, while discussing the liturgical programme with Maxwell, Laud expressed his clear opinion that the best way would be 'to take the English Liturgy without any variation to be established there'.[25] Maxwell returned to Scotland in November 1629 with a letter from the king. The king instructed him 'to intimate that it was his Majesty's pleasure that the whole of the order of the English Kirk should be received here'.[26] This early decision to introduce the English liturgy without variation seems to have been a victory for Laud. As far as the early 1630s were concerned, it is apparent that Laud devoted himself to this project; as he said, 'in this condition, I held that business for two or three years at least':

if his Majesty would have a Liturgy settled there, it were best to take the English Liturgy without any variation, that so the same Service Book might be established in all his Majesty's dominions; which I did then, and do still think, would have been a great happiness to this State, and a great honour and safety to religion.[27]

However, this plan met serious opposition among the Scottish bishops. Heylyn's account alludes to the existence of the opposition and Laud's response before 1633: 'on these terms it stood till this present year [1633], Laud standing hard for admitting the English Liturgy without alteration; the Scottish Bishops pleading on the other side'.[28] The king witnessed this opposition in person when he visited Scotland to be crowned in 1633.[29] Laud accompanied him. In a conference with the Scottish bishops and some ministers, Laud was brought face to face with the opposition from the old bishops to any liturgical change, apart from

---

[25] Laud, *Works*, III, p. 427.   [26] Sprott, *Scottish Liturgies*, p. xlii.

[27] Laud, *Works*, III, p. 427; Peter Heylyn, *Cyprianus Anglicus, or the History of the Life and Death of... Lord Archbishop of Canterbury* (1688), p. 236.

[28] Heylyn, *Cyprianus Anglicus*, pp. 236–7.

[29] Sir James Balfour described the ceremony as 'the most glorious and magnifique coronatione that ever was seine in this kingdome': J. Balfour, *Historical Works of Sir James Balfour*, ed. J. Haig, 4 vols. (Edinburgh, 1824–5), II, p. 199. There were two groups in the ceremony distinguished by their clerical dress, one group in 'white rockets and white sleeves and loops of gold, having blue silk to their foot', the other in black gowns. Cited in J. Morrill, 'The National Covenant in its British context', in J. S. Morrill, ed., *The Scottish National Covenant in its British Context* (Edinburgh, 1990), p. 3. Patrick Lindsay, the archbishop of Glasgow, did not attend the English-style service, as the Scottish bishops were expected 'to bow thair knie and bek': J. Spalding, *Memorialls of the Troubles in Scotland and in England, 1625–1645*, ed. J. Stuart (Edinburgh, 1850), pp. 36–7.

the issue of having the English liturgy without alteration. The old bish- ops feared that it might cause a 'very sad' consequence, reminding Laud how the project had been stopped in James's reign.[30] They were afraid that the English liturgy would inflame Scottish national sentiment against England.[31]

Laud recalled the situation later. In a letter to the earl of Traquaire on 11 September 1637, he wrote,

why did they not then admit the Liturgy of England without more adoe? But by their refusall of that, and the dislike of this, 'tis more then manifest they would have neither, perhaps none at all, were they left to themselves.[32]

The fact seems to be that the Scottish bishops did not want any liturgical change, and that if it was inevitable, they wanted the new liturgy to be different from that of England. In the latter case, it was necessary for the bishops to draw it up by themselves. This opposition may explain well why a simple task like preparing the English Prayer Book for Scotland took a long time.[33]

Although the debate about the Scottish liturgy was pursued afresh after his return from Scotland, Charles seems to have been inclining to the opinion of the Scottish bishops and against that of Laud. It was, however, not until 13 May 1634 that the king, persuaded by the Scottish bishops, at last resolved that they 'should draw up a Liturgy, as near that of England as might be'.[34] Given the fact that Laud did his best in this debate,[35] and given the king's confidence in his archbishop, this decision against Laud suggests that the Caroline ecclesiastical policy was dominated by the king himself. Although there is a basic similarity between the English liturgy and the Scottish Prayer Book of 1637, this decision indicates that the Caroline ecclesiastical policy was far from aiming at a narrow uniformity in the three kingdoms.

Clarendon offers us another reason why Charles was not interested in anglicization in liturgical policy:

---

[30] H. Guthry, *Memoirs of Henry Guthry*, ed. G. Crawfurd (1702), p. 18.

[31] Clarendon, I, p. 113.

[32] W. Prynne, *Hidden Workes of Darkenes Brought to Publike Light, or A Necessary Introduction to the History of the Archbishop of Canterburie's Triall* (1645), p. 169; Laud, *Works*, VI, p. 506.

[33] The first Scottish edition of the Book of Common Prayer was published in 1633 and two more editions followed in 1634: Donaldson, *Making of the Scottish Prayer Book*, p. 43.

[34] W. Alexander, Earl of Stirling, *The Earl of Stirling's Register of Royal Letters Relative to the Affairs of Scotland and Nova Scotia from 1615 to 1635*, ed. C. Rogers, 2 vols. (Edinburgh, 1885), II, pp. 752–3; Laud, *Works*, III, pp. 278, 428.

[35] Laud, *Works*, III, p. 428.

He was in his nature too much inclined to the Scots nation, having been born amongst them, and as jealous as any one of them could be that their liberties and priviledges might not be invaded by the English, who, he knew, had no reverence for them: and therefore the objection that it would look like an imposition from England, if a form settled in Parliament at Westminster should without any alteration be tendered (though by himself) to be submitted to and observed in Scotland, made a deep impression in his majesty.[36]

The king seems to have understood Scottish national sentiment, as he later confirmed that 'they might have taken some offense, if we should have tendered them the English service book *totidem verbis*, and that some factious spirits would have endeavoured to have misconstructed it as a badge of dependence of that Church upon this England'.[37] The fact that Charles had sympathy towards Scotland was also confirmed by Laud. Laud recorded,

I wrote to the late Reverend Archbishop of St Andrews, Sept. 30th 1633, concerning Liturgy, that whether that of England or another was resolved on, yet they should proceed circumspectly, because his Majesty had no intendment to do anything but that which was *according to honor and justice, and the laws of that kingdom.*[38]

Thereafter, the history of the composition of the new book can be divided into two periods: the first takes us up to the partial printing of the Scottish bishops' preparation at the end of 1635, and the second is from Wedderburn's intervention to the publication of the Scottish Book of Common Prayer.

III

Within three months of the king's order, the Scottish bishops seem to have made some progress in the business of the new liturgy. A draft was sent to the court, through Maxwell, in August 1634. In a letter Maxwell carried there was 'an account anent the Liturgy'.[39] We have no detail about what progress the bishops had made and about what the 'account' in the letter was. The king was satisfied with what they had done: 'Right Reverend – We are well pleased, and count it acceptable service that you are so careful, according to our command, to have a Book of Common Prayer.'[40]

[36] Clarendon, I, p. 114.   [37] *A Large Declaration*, p. 18.

[38] Laud, *Works*, III, p. 278.

[39] This letter, 'written and subscribed by the Archbishop of St Andrews, 8 August 1633', later fell into the hands of Covenanters: Baillie, *Letters and Journals*, I, pp. 427–8.

[40] *Register of Royal Letters*, II, pp. 796–7.

The king's involvement in the composition of the new liturgy was most active at this stage. As well as giving a compliment to Spottiswood in the same letter, the king ordered him to 'cause frame it [the Scottish Book of Common Prayer] with all convenient diligence and that as near as can be to this of England'. It is apparent that the king sent with this letter a copy of the English Prayer Book, on which he made some alterations and instructions.[41]

Bishop Maxwell was again in London in April 1635. Maxwell's mission at this time was to inform Laud 'what they did in that Service Book', to give 'some account of their diligence and care in that behalf' by the king's command, and to get the royal warrant for the publication of the revised draft of the Book of Canons.[42] However, from the end of the debate on the general shape of the new liturgy in the previous May to this time, Laud's involvement in the composition of the Scottish Prayer Book has to be considered as less deep than before. Dissatisfied with the decision against his opinion, Laud seems to have been very reluctant to be involved. As he confessed,

Then his Majesty commanded me to give the bishops of Scotland my best assistance in this way and work. I delayed as much as I could with my obedience, and when nothing would serve, but it must go on, I confess I was then very serious, and gave them the best help I could.[43]

In the letter to Laud which Maxwell conveyed in April 1635, some Scottish bishops apologized that although they wished for 'a full conformity in the Churches', 'this must be the work of time'.[44] We have no evidence that Laud had any correspondence with the Scottish bishops in reference to the composition of the liturgy before this.[45] We have also no evidence that Laud made any comment on the work of the Scottish bishops or any alteration to it. The confession that he gave 'the best help he could', says no more than that he had obeyed the king's commands as his clerk, by 'acquainting' the king with the procedure of the composition of the liturgy about which he had been informed by the Scottish bishops,

---

[41] A reference to this book was made in the warrant from the king to Laud in 1636, as follows: 'signed by himself at Hampton Court, Sept. 28, 1634'. See Sprott, *Scottish Liturgies*, p. l.

[42] Laud, *Works*, III, p. 337.   [43] Ibid., p. 428.

[44] The Scottish bishops who signed the letter were the archbishops of St Andrews and Glasgow and the bishops of Moray, Dunblane and Brechin. Prynne, *Hidden Workes*, p. 150.

[45] But Laud kept writing to Bellenden, the bishop of Dunblane, on the keeping of the English service in the Royal Chapel and his promotion. For the letters, see Baillie, *Letters and Journals*, I, pp. 430–6.

and by sending the king's order to Scotland at the king's command.[46] Nonetheless, Laud's relative detachment in this period was due to his deep obsession with the English Prayer Book rather than to any reluctance to be involved in Scottish affairs.[47]

Seeing the draft of the liturgy Maxwell brought, the king seems to have considered that the draft was acceptable without further revision. Thus the king approved this draft with some corrections and instructions he had made. The king's response to this draft of the liturgy seems to imply that he would not allow any more variation from the English liturgy. Alternatively, his action might show that he was ready to accept the considerable variations already made. The content of the variations is unknown. The only known change was substitution of 'priest' by 'presbyter'.[48] This might well represent a victory for Scottish sentiment. The king permitted the printing of the draft and 'much of it' was printed in Edinburgh before Christmas 1635.[49] It would soon prove premature, however, for further significant changes were to come.

The tide turned against the Scottish bishops in February 1636, when the Chapel Royal and the bishopric of Dunblane went to James Wedderburn, who had an English background.[50] Sometime after his consecration Wedderburn sent 'certain notes' to the king on a further revision of the Prayer Book in print.[51] The king referred them to Laud, Wren and Juxon for their consideration. Without Juxon, who was busy with other business, Laud and Wren submitted their conclusion that most of Wedderburn's suggestions were acceptable. Laud was then asked to make alterations on a copy of the English Prayer Book, and

---

[46] Laud's only letter to the Scottish bishops about the liturgy in this period, dated 19 September 1635, was about the preparation of the printing of the draft, at the king's command. There was no mention of the content. Laud, *Works*, VI, p. 434; Baillie, *Letters and Journals*, I, pp. 317–21.

[47] Laud, with Bishop Juxon, was taking part in the alteration of the final draft of the Book of Canons between May 1635 and its publication in January 1636. Laud, *Works*, III, pp. 317–21.

[48] In the letter to the bishops in which the king approved the draft, he used the term 'Presbyter'. See *Register of Royal Letters*, II, p. 856; Sprott, *Scottish Liturgies*, p. liii. In the printed book in 1635, 'Presbyter' was used: Donaldson, *Making of the Scottish Prayer Book*, p. 49.

[49] Baillie, *Letters and Journals*, I, p. 4; Donaldson, *Making of the Scottish Prayer Book*, p. 48. Laud often referred to this draft as 'Ross's book': Laud, *Works*, VI, pp. 456, 457.

[50] Wedderburn, educated at St Andrews University, was appointed Professor of Divinity at St Andrews. He went to England in 1626, and held benefices in the dioceses of Ely and of Bath and Wells before his appointment as the dean of the Royal Chapel in 1635 and bishop of Dunblane in 1636. He was the only Caroline bishop with an Anglican background.

[51] In a letter to Wedderburn on 20 April 1636, Laud made a reference to Wedderburn's consecration which indicated that Wedderburn had given information in his earlier letter to Laud about suggested alterations.

it was sent to Scotland with the king's warrant on 20 April. As Baillie wrote, this led to the destruction of the edition which was already partly printed.[52] However, the draft on which Maxwell had worked does not seem to have been completely abandoned. In a letter to Wedderburn, Laud instructed him that the printing should 'follow the book which my Lord Ross brought, and additions which are made to the book I now send'. However, priority was given to the book Laud sent, in case there was any difference between them.[53]

When Laud was charged with making these alterations and additions by the Scottish Commissioners in London in 1641, he defended himself by arguing that some of the Scottish bishops 'were very earnest to have some alterations and some additions'. Although Laud referred to 'some', it is unlikely that the 'some' was more than Bishop Wedderburn alone. There was a distinct difference between the attitude of those who argued that 'a full conformity must be the work of time' in April 1635, and that of those who argued that 'if they did not then make that book as perfect as they could, they should never be able to get it perfected after'.[54] More or less all the Scottish bishops may have been frustrated by Wedderburn.

However, it seems that Laud was the mastermind at this period. The phrase in the king's warrant for the changes, 'I gave the Archbp. of Canterbury command to make the alterations expressed in this book, and to fit a liturgy for the Church of Scotland', is ample evidence that Wedderburn's suggestions were decided under Laud's influence. Given Laud's close relationship with Wedderburn, we cannot rule out the possibility that Wedderburn's suggestion might have been guided by Laud. It was also Laud himself who marked the alterations on a copy of the English Book of Common Prayer which was sent to Scotland. This copy seems to have been returned to Laud later with some further alteration by a Scottish hand. When this copy was found in Laud's library in May 1643, William Prynne, Laud's greatest enemy, noticed that the copy had 'all the additions and alterations wherein it varies from the English, written, made and inserted by archbishop's own hand, as it was afterwards printed and published in Scotland, Anno 1637'.[55] As he admitted in his letter to Wedderburn, Laud changed the rubrics of the Holy Communion of his own will, inserting rubrics before every prayer and action.[56]

---

[52] Baillie, *Letters and Journals*, I, pp. 31–2.   [53] Laud, *Works*, VI, p. 456.

[54] Ibid., III, pp. 342–3. For the charge made by the Scottish Commissioners against Laud, see *The Charge of the Scottish Commissioners against Canterburie and the Lieutenant of Ireland* (1641), pp. 1–22.

[55] Prynne, *Hidden Workes*, p. 156. This copy is now in the library of Christ Church, Oxford. Donaldson, *Making of the Scottish Prayer Book*, p. 89.

[56] Laud, *Works*, VI, p. 458.

The king, in his warrant, gave the Scottish bishops the liberty – if they saw apparent reason to the contrary – to reject these alterations. It was Laud who gave a different interpretation of this liberty in his letter to Wedderburn, ordering him to inform the other bishops that 'his Majesty having viewed all these additions, hopes there will be no need of change of any thing, and will be best pleased with little or rather no alteration'.[57] Donaldson's assertion that Laud had been acting merely as clerk even in 1636 seems to be far wrong.[58]

Nonetheless, it is wrong to say that Laud alone was responsible for the new liturgy. It is true that the role of the king at this stage seems not to have been as great as before. Given the fact that most of Wedderburn's suggestions were too complicated and too doctrinal for a king whom Donaldson calls 'a somewhat small-minded and sacerdotally inclined layman' to understand, it may be right to say that the role played by the king at this stage was quite limited.[59] However, the king was still an active part of the project. Referring to the alterations, Laud said in his letter to Wedderburn that 'so many of them as his majesty approved, I have written into a service book of ours'.[60] Laud also denied the Covenanters' accusation that he 'surreptitiously' inserted the additions 'without the king's knowledge': 'I inserted nothing without his Majesty's knowledge nor anything against his purpose.'[61] Some further changes which were not desired in Scotland were to come from the king. In the final instructions dated 18 October 1636, the king, ordering 'the Preface to the Book of Common Prayer signed by our hand, and the Proclamation authorising the same, to be printed and inserted in' it, ordered the insertion of some chapters of the Book of Wisdom and of Ecclesiasticus in the lessons and to add 'the peculiar Saints of that our Kingdom' to the 'Catholic Saints as are in the English'. The instructions give no hint that Laud was involved in these final alterations. A comparison of these alterations with the previous ones shows the distinctive difference in the interests of the two compilers. A part of the final alterations are certainly the king's work.

Donaldson blamed the Scottish bishops for the new changes, releasing the king and Laud from responsibility for them. He argued that since the last alterations in addition to those of Laud were done in Scotland, the Scottish bishops alone were responsible.[62] However, as Donaldson himself noted, most of the last alterations, such as the English offertory sentence, which were done in Scotland were done at Laud's request.

---

[57] Ibid., pp. 458–9.   [58] Donaldson, *Making of the Scottish Prayer Book*, p. 80.
[59] Ibid., p. 47.   [60] Laud, *Works*, VI, p. 456.
[61] *Charge of the Scottish Commissioners*, p. 11; Laud, *Works*, III, p. 342.
[62] Donaldson, *Making of the Scottish Prayer Book*, p. 55.

The only alteration modified in Scotland was one of the rubrics of Holy Communion which might savour of the Mass.[63] Besides this, Donaldson seems to have deliberately ignored the fact that Wedderburn was the only Scottish compiler of the new liturgy at this stage.

IV

On 20 December 1636 the Scottish Privy Council, on the king's instruction, issued a proclamation commanding the use of the new liturgy. However, it was not until May 1637 that the book came out.[64] It was basically similar to that of England, as Charles had intended it to be. However, it had also enough of its own features to be called the 'Scottish liturgy' or 'Laud's liturgy'. The complex character of the book was a result of continuous changes of royal policy during its composition. In fact, the history of the composition of the new liturgy divided into two periods which were dominated by different compilers, and were guided by the king's two different presuppositions.

At the core of Charles's liturgical policy in the first period of composition lay a tension between the king's two presuppositions: that the liturgy should be as close as possible to the English Prayer Book, and that it should also be altered a little to fit with Scottish sensibilities. The king tried to hold these two together, but accommodation proved to be impossible. The Scottish bishops who dominated the first period of the composition hoped to relax the demand that the new book was to be as near as possible to that of England. They found that the king's two presuppositions could not be reconciled. Their demand for further variation to satisfy their countrymen was denied by the king. In the second period of composition, some considerable variations were made as the king dropped his presuppositions. Thus the changes went in the opposite direction to the king's presuppositions, with more variation from the English book, but going against Scottish national and religious sentiment. The dropping of the king's principles gave Laud an opportunity to make a liturgy containing Laudian features.

The two presuppositions on which the composition of the Scottish Prayer Book of 1637 was based caused the book to contain two elements, a Scottish element and an English element. However, a Roman element was also introduced into the book when the king revised his attitude. If the Scottish–English–Romish character of the book is open to criticism, the king must take responsibility, for it was an inevitable result of his confusion. However, if we have to judge the book by the variations

---

[63] Ibid., p. 56.   [64] Baillie, *Letters and Journals*, I, pp. 4, 16.

from the English book and by its difference from the traditional Scottish practice, we need to examine the changes and the differences before we blame any compiler.

These alterations and the differences were discussed at length by Donaldson. However, he distorted some facts and many of his arguments need to be corrected. Donaldson was right when he said that 'if the compilers are to be judged, they are to be judged not on the general resemblance of their book to the book of England – for in that they had no choice; but on the changes which they made, and on the further changes which they proposed'.[65] However, most of his observations on the changes were misleading, as he had a strong bias towards the view that the Scottish bishops were mainly responsible for the changes, and that many of the major changes were concessions to Scottish or Puritan opinion.

It is true that some changes made by the Scottish bishops followed Scottish demands and usage. However, few of these have great importance. Many changes Donaldson regarded as being in a Scottish or Puritan direction were not unambiguously so. For him, even the inclusion of an apology for the new festivals and rites, and the omission of the word 'ceremonies' on the title-page, were concessions to the Scottish or Puritan view.[66]

Donaldson also argued that even some crucial changes which were undoubtedly against Scottish wishes were in a Puritan direction. He suggested that 'the insertion of the feasts of the Conversion of St Paul and St Barnabas in the list of holy days and their elevation to red letter rank in the Kalendar' met a Puritan demand.[67] This is hardly true. Although Easter and Christmas were enjoined by the Five Articles, for most Scots only the sabbaths were true holy days. John Row's criticism of this inclusion contradicts Donaldson: 'twenty-nine holie dayes equalised in holiness to the fifty-two Sabbaths, or Lord's dayes'.[68]

Donaldson's argument that some changes in the communion had been made to meet Presbyterian demands is most seriously misleading. A crucial change in the Scottish book was the omission of the second phrase of the administration of elements at the Eucharist, which said, 'do this in remembrance of Him'. Donaldson asserted that this omission would have fitted with the high Scottish doctrine of Communion. He has argued that there was no second phrase in Alexander Henderson's

---

[65] Donaldson, *Making of the Scottish Prayer Book*, p. 60.   [66] Ibid., p. 65.   [67] Ibid.

[68] Row, *History*, p. 400. John Row's attack on the Scottish book seems to have copied that of *Reasons for Which the Service Booke*, but the comparison in the number of holy days must have been his work, as he had found that the Scottish book had twenty-nine 'holie festivities (England's booke has but twenty-seven)'.

administration words, suggesting that the Scots had never used it.[69] This assertion is entirely untrue. The Scottish doctrine of Communion was low, and Henderson used the second phrase, 'do this in remembrance of Him'.[70] The fact is that the Scottish reformers and their successors carefully reproduced the formula found in the accounts of the Lord's Supper in the New Testament, adding nothing to 'the Word of Christ'.[71] In the paragraph entitled 'To the Reader' in the order in the Book of Common Order, they wrote that they rehearsed the 'words of the Lord's Supper'. The Scottish Covenanters later attacked the omission of the second phrase,[72] John Row, a radical Covenanter minister, condemning it as taking away 'the spirituall eating and drinking by faith mentioned in the Inglish Liturgie'.[73] The purpose of this omission, as Laud himself confessed, was to get rid of 'the Zuinglian tenet, that the Sacrament is a bare sign taken in remembrance of Christ's passion'. Although this change had been seen by Laud as 'no hurt', it seemed to the Scots to have reeked of the Catholic tenet of transubstantiation.[74]

Donaldson argues that a rubric on the 'taking' of the elements at the Holy Communion was inserted in the new book to meet Scottish practice.[75] No doubt, the four actions in the Scottish Communion – taking, thanksgiving, breaking and delivering – had been used. However, Donaldson seems to have failed to notice the difference between the rubric of *taking* in the new Scottish Prayer Book and that in the Book of Common Order. In the Book of Common Order, the action of *taking* was to be done *before* the prayer of thanksgiving.[76] But in the new Scottish liturgy the actions, 'took bread' and 'took the cup', were enjoined to be performed *during* the prayer.

As we can see from the rubric that 'he is to take the chalice . . . as *he intends to consecrate*', the Prayer of Consecration in the new liturgy could have meant elevation of the elements rather than thanksgiving. Row referred to it as 'the verie popish consecration'.[77] Moreover, given the fact that the other three actions of the Scottish Holy Communion were hardly emphasized in the new prayer book, there is no reason why the insertion of the action of *taking* only should be interpreted as a concession to the Puritan view.

---

[69] Donaldson, *Making of the Scottish Prayer Book*, p. 69.
[70] For Henderson's formula of the Communion service, see A. Henderson, *The Government and Order of the Church of Scotland* (1641), p. 23.
[71] McMillan, *Worship*, p. 172.   [72] Laud, *Works*, III, p. 355.
[73] Row, *History*, p. 400.   [74] Laud, *Works*, III, pp. 355–7.
[75] Donaldson, *Making of the Scottish Prayer Book*, p. 69.
[76] G. W. Sprott, *The Worship and Offices of the Church of Scotland* (Edinburgh, 1882), pp. 115–6.
[77] Row, *History*, p. 399.

The Prayer of Consecration in the Scottish book has more phrases than that of England. The additions were regarded by the Scots as a popish consecration which supported the doctrine of transubstantiation or the corporeal presence of Christ.[78] The shift of the Oblation Prayer from after the distribution to before it, following the Consecration Prayer, was attacked by the Covenanters because 'the memorial and sacrifice of praise in it may be understood according to popish meaning'.[79]

As we have seen before, not only had the king played a key role throughout both stages, but Laud had also been involved seriously in the entire process of composition.[80] Although Laud distanced himself from one moment of the first stage, his deep interest in the project of the Scottish liturgy and canons was long-standing. Even before 1621, Laud had drawn up canons and a liturgy for Scotland by himself, without the king's order.[81]

What then, were Laud's motivation and aim? It is difficult to answer this question unless we understand that what Laud cared for was the whole Catholic Church.[82] For Laud, 'the Catholic church of Christ' was neither Rome nor the Church of England.[83] However, he seems to have believed that, as John Morrill argues, 'the Church of England came closest to that ideal, but it too had some way to go; the Churches of Scotland and Ireland had to abandon much false practice even before they began to join the English church in the final strivings after perfection'.[84] Furthermore, in order to establish his ideal of the pure Catholic Church, Laud did not mind adopting and then adapting the practice of the Church of Rome.[85]

The Scottish commissioners told Laud in December 1640 that the Scottish service book contained many changes and supplements which were taken from the Mass-Book, and rituals in it which varied from those of the English book. While denying his 'popish spirit', Laud admitted

---

[78] *Charge of the Scottish Commissioners*, pp. 11–12; Laud, *Works*, III, pp. 353–5; *Reasons for Which the Service Booke*, p. 2; Row, *History*, pp. 400–1.

[79] Laud, *Works*, III, pp. 343–5.

[80] K. Brown, *Kingdom or Province? Scotland and the Regal Union, 1603–1715* (1993), p. 109.

[81] J. Hacket, *Scrinia Reserata, A Memorial Offered to . . . John Williams* (1693), p. 64.

[82] In a collect in the Communion service of the Scottish book, 'the whole congregation' was replaced by 'the holy Catholic Church', which was followed by the addition of a phrase, 'and in this particular Church in which we live'. For the text, see Donaldson, *Making of the Scottish Prayer Book*, p. 185.

[83] Laud, *Works*, II, p. xvii.

[84] J. Morrill, 'A British patriarchy? Ecclesiastical imperialism under the early Stuarts', in A. Fletcher and P. Roberts, eds., *Religion, Culture and Society in Early Modern Britain* (Cambridge, 1994), pp. 225–6.

[85] For the Laudian understanding of the Church of Rome see A. Milton, *Catholic and Reformed: The Roman and Protestant Churches in English Protestant Thought, 1600–1640* (Cambridge, 1995).

that these variations were taken from 'the First Book of Edward VI and some ancient liturgies', probably including the 'Mass-Book'. Laud gave the reason: 'for every line in the Mass-Book or other popish rituals, are not all evil and corruption. There are many good prayers in them; nor is anything evil in them'.[86] The fact that there were some words of the Mass-Book in the Scottish liturgy, but not in both the Edwardian book and the English book, reflects Laud's view.[87] In fact, the Scottish liturgy inclined more towards Catholic practice than did the English liturgy. The most visible difference, one which has never been noticed by historians, is that the Scottish book had many more pictures and decorated letters than the English Prayer Book, which to the Scottish and English Puritans looked idolatrous. If the Covenanters accused Laud of being a main composer of the new Scottish liturgy, they do not seem to have missed their target.

However, the role played by the king, particularly in providing the principles of composition for the whole project, was no smaller than that of any other individual. If there was a person who was responsible for the general outlook of the new Scottish liturgy, it was the king. As we have seen before, although he abandoned the introduction of the English book without any change at the first stage, he still wanted the Scottish book to be as close as possible to the English one. It was the king who stopped the Scottish bishops deviating further from the English book in May 1635.[88] Then he dropped this principle when Wedderburn's suggestion of a further change was forwarded.

Was conformity to the English liturgy the king's main aim at the first stage of composition when he established the principle that the Scottish book should be as close as possible to the English book? The answer seems to be negative. The fact that many variations from the English book were made at this stage suggests that the king was not interested in mere conformity with England's liturgy. What the king was most concerned about seems to have been a national uniformity of decent worship in Scotland, as he thought that the existing Scottish worship had neither decency nor uniformity. Ironically, as we have seen, the most distinguishable alterations from the English Prayer Book were made in the second period, when the king and Laud were most deeply involved.

As we have seen before, the king clearly explained in the preface to the Scottish Prayer Book that he intended it to lead to British uniformity. If this British uniformity was not anglicization, we can conclude that the king had a plan of British uniformity which envisaged Scotland and England being brought into conformity with his own ideal. We cannot

---

[86] Laud, *Works*, III, pp. 340–1.   [87] Ibid., pp. 353–4.
[88] Donaldson, *Making of the Scottish Prayer Book*, p. 60.

rule out the possibility that the king would have imposed the new prayer book on England, if it had not been rejected by the Scots. In particular, Laud's comparison between the English liturgy and the Scottish one strengthens this possibility: 'though I shall not find fault with the orders of prayers, as they stand in the Communion-book of England (for, God be thanked, 'tis well); yet, if a comparison be made, I do think the order of the prayers, as they stand in the Scottish liturgy, to be better, and more agreeable to use in the primitive Church'.[89] He was also 'sorry' that the English Book of Common Prayer lacked 'the oblation of the element' which was prescribed in the Scottish Prayer Book.[90]

Ironically, it was the Scottish Covenanters who rightly understood the nature of Caroline ecclesiastical policies. It was a constant claim of the Scottish Covenanters that if the innovations were successfully introduced into Scotland, they would be imposed in England. The Scottish Commissioners to the Peace Treaty in 1640 criticized these innovations as being in conformity to Rome: 'By this their doing, they [the bishops] did not aim to make us conform to England, but to make Scotland first . . . and therefore England, conform to Rome, even in those matters wherein England have separated from Rome, even since the time of Reformation.'[91]

We have no hard evidence that the Caroline ecclesiastical policies in the two nations were aimed at bringing the two churches into line with the Church of Rome. The Covenanters confused Laud's 'Catholic church' with the Church of Rome itself.[92] However, the confusion was inevitable for the opponents of the king and the archbishop, as many of the Caroline ecclesiastical policies looked similar to those of the pre-Reformation church. Besides this, the Covenanters seem to have intended to exploit anti-Catholic sentiment by this attack. Nevertheless, we cannot deny that the policy aimed at British uniformity in religion by congruity.

It may be exaggerating somewhat to argue that the king and Laud used the Kirk as a guinea pig for their ecclesiastical experiment. However, given the fact that England in the late 1630s was troubled by many other innovations, and had already become a religious battlefield, it is understandable that they tried to achieve their aims by pushing for change in

---

[89] Laud, *Works*, III, p. 335.   [90] Ibid., p. 359.

[91] *Charge of the Scottish Commissioners*, p. 20; Laud, *Works*, III, pp. 381–2. The Covenanters seem to have believed that Laud 'did negotiate with Rome about the frame of our service book and Canons, that with his own hand he altered, and interlyned diverse passages thereof, tending to conformity with Rome: A plot so perilous, that had not the Lord disappointed it, First, *Scotland* and then *England* by him, and such as cooperate with him, had become, in their Religion, Romish.' *The Remonstrance of the Nobility, Barrones, Ministers, and Commons within the Kingdome of Scotland* (1639), pp. 17–18.

[92] Laud strongly denied this accusation: Laud, *Works*, III, p. 381.

the smaller and supposedly more manageable country first. They thought that Scotland was, in Hugh Watt's words, 'a possible strategic base for ending the deadlock in England'.[93] However, this was a miscalculation which proved fatal for both of them.

[93] H. Watt, 'William Laud and Scotland', *Records of the Scottish Church History Society*, 7 (1941), 188.

2 Popery in perfection? The experience of Catholicism: Henrietta Maria between private practice and public discourse*

Dagmar Freist

I

An important strand of recent work on the history of Catholicism has been an attempt to move beyond studies of martyrdom and survival, or of a deep-rooted collective anti-Catholicism, by concentrating instead on the possibilities of coexistence and practical toleration.[1] Studies of the perception of religious difference and various forms of interaction across confessional boundaries in everyday life have demonstrated that religious coexistence was generally peaceful and characterized by pragmatism or even curiosity. This trend has been accompanied by a greater awareness of the fluidity of religious identities, even among the highly educated.[2] This emphasis contrasts with an awareness of the successful revival and instrumentalization of anti-Catholic sentiments on the eve of the English Civil War,[3] despite the evidence that anti-Catholicism does not seem to have been a powerful collective phenomenon during the 1630s.

Based on new research on the experiences and perceptions of religious differences in early modern Europe, this chapter will shed new light on

---

* This article is based on my inaugural lecture at the Carl von Ossietzky University of Oldenburg on 29 June 2005, which was entitled 'Private Practice and Public Discourse: Königin Henrietta und der englische Anti-Katholizismus'.

[1] Alexandra Walsham, *Church Papists: Catholicism, Conformity and Confessional Polemic in Early Modern England* (Woodbridge, 1993); Alexandra Walsham, *Charitable Hatred: Tolerance and Intolerance in England, 1500–1700* (Manchester, 2006); for a European perspective see Benjamin J. Kaplan, *Divided by Faith: Religious Conflict and the Practice of Toleration in Early Modern Europe* (2007); Andreas Höfele, Enno Ruge and Gabriela Schmidt, eds., *Representing Religious Pluralization in Early Modern Europe* (Münster, 2007); and Scott Dixon, Dagmar Freist and Mark Greengrass, eds., *Living with Religious Diversity in Early Modern Europe* (Aldershot, 2009).

[2] See, e.g., David L. Smith, 'Catholic, Anglican or Puritan? Edward Sackville, fourth earl of Dorset and the ambiguities of religion in early Stuart England', *TRHS*, 6th ser. II (1992), 105–24.

[3] For the instrumentalization of anti-popery in the face of political events on the eve of the civil war see John Walter, *Understanding Popular Violence in the English Revolution: The Colchester Plunderers* (Cambridge, 1999).

the complex interdependencies of religious politics, the experience of religious differences in everyday life and anti-Catholic discourses in mid-seventeenth-century England. At its heart lies the question of why Queen Henrietta Maria came to stand for the threat of popery with such force that the traditions of practical coexistence were threatened. Essential for understanding this phenomenon are the terms of the marriage contract, whose impact has never been analysed. It will be argued that the precise detail of the treaty transformed the experience of Catholicism, not least by suggesting that international Catholicism had acquired a voice in the inner councils of government. Vital for its impact on a larger segment of society, especially in London, was the very public Catholic presence in the capital. In print and on the streets of the capital, Catholicism was visualized in various forms, and among them the personification of Catholicism in Henrietta Maria in her role as missionary was of critical importance.

On the eve of the English Civil War the apparent contradiction between the traditional anti-Catholic discourse on the one hand and peaceful religious coexistence on the other was suspended, at least in some localities and among some groups. For Puritans and many moderate Anglicans alike the 'popishness' of religious politics under Charles I and Archbishop William Laud was associated with an actual Catholic influence at court.[4] Fears about the Catholic threat were no longer nourished simply by theories of foreign conspirators who joined forces with a few surviving English Catholics to overturn the kingdom; instead, it was experienced as immanent, as being at the heart of the kingdom.[5] As William Prynne warned in 1643,

there is and hath bin in his Majesties Reigne till this instant, a most strong... desperate confederacie prosecuted (*wherin the Queen Majestie hath bin cheife*) to set up Popery in perfection, unlesse Gods owne Almighty Power, and our unanimous, vigilant strenuous opposition, prevent its small accomplishment.[6]

Prynne's view was mirrored in numerous pamphlets of the time, as well as in seditious talk. The universal message of this line of argument was that Henrietta Maria secretly – and successfully – plotted the recatholicization of England, and these fears were not completely

---

[4] For the distinction between anti-popery and anti-Catholicism see Michael Braddick, *God's Fury, England's Fire: A New History of the English Civil Wars* (2008), pp. 47–8.

[5] For the basis in reality of anti-Catholic sentiments see Caroline Hibbard, *Charles I and the Popish Plot* (Chapel Hill, 1983), pp. 41–60, 177–80; and Kevin Sharpe, *The Personal Rule of Charles I* (New Haven, 1992), pp. 168–208.

[6] William Prynne, *The Popish Royal Favourite: or, A Full Discovery of His Majesties Extraordinary Favours to, and Protections of notorious Papists [. . .]* (1643), p. 35.

groundless.[7] Previous work has assessed the nature and significance of Henrietta Maria's political influence and the importance of the European context, but, to date, little attention has been paid to the importance of the marriage treaty. However, this treaty, it will be argued, is crucial to an understanding of the pamphlets which 'demonized the Queen'[8] and which can be understood as a product of the precise political context, rather than simply part of a wider Puritan attack on popery on the eve of the Civil War.

I shall argue that a central feature of the conflation of anti-popery with anti-Catholicism since the 1630s has been overlooked: that the union between Charles and Henrietta Maria was a formally agreed mixed marriage. Its validity rested on a papal dispensation, which Urban VIII would only grant in return for far-reaching rights for Catholics in England and sufficient securities that the queen would not be forced to convert.[9] Moreover, from a Catholic perspective, Henrietta Maria would have been expected to achieve the conversion of her husband. Although these conditions for a papal dispensation were not unusual by European standards,[10] the specific conditions in early Stuart England, and the fact that Henrietta Maria took her role as the saviour of English Catholics very seriously, gave the marriage contract unusual political weight. During the 1630s we can observe both the implementation of the marriage contract and an increasingly public presentation of Catholicism, especially in London, which was not confined to the court.

Rather than judge the queen's actions by their actual political impact, I shall concentrate instead on how her role as a Catholic queen who openly engaged in politics was appropriated and experienced by different groups of society.[11] In order to do so I shall seek to historicize abstract anti-Catholic discourse in relation to the different levels of perception

---

[7] Gordon Albion, *Charles I and the Court of Rome: A Study in 17th-Century Diplomacy, with a Foreword by David Mathew* (Louvain, 1935); Hibbard, *Charles I*; Sharpe, *Personal Rule*.

[8] Caroline Hibbard, 'Henrietta Maria', *ODNB*.   [9] See below, pp. 38–40.

[10] For a survey see Friedrich Kunstmann, *Die Gemischten Ehen unter den Christlichen Konfessionen Teutschlands, Geschichtlich Dargestellt* (Regensburg, 1839).

[11] For a study of the impact her involvement in politics had on the English people, with particular emphasis on 'popular perceptions of the queen, her court and her machinations', see Michelle Ann White, *Henrietta Maria and the English Civil Wars* (Aldershot, 2006) (quotation at p. 6). Her approach is similar to that in my inaugural lecture 'Private Practice and Public Discourse', which forms the basis of my argument. For the perception of religious and political controversies on the eve of the English Civil War through the eyes of the wider public, see Dagmar Freist, *Governed by Opinion: Politics, Religion and the Dynamics of Communication in Stuart London 1637–1645* (1997).

and experience, and thereby shed new light on the public impact of Catholicism on the eve of the English Civil War.

II

The concept of experience as a historical category is of vital importance here. As an analytical category it focuses on how people's perceptions, judgements and actions are guided by their experiences and how this helps us to explain historical phenomena and change. It has proved difficult to develop a general method for conceptualizing these relationships, however, and I should therefore like to offer one possible approach by drawing on cultural studies, anthropology and phenomenology.[12] One characteristic of 'experience' is that it is first-hand, subjective and unmediated. At the same time, however, experiences are pre-structured by numerous influences and are always shaped, reshaped, challenged and confirmed in communication and social interaction. The key issue is the relationship between subjective experience and objective structures, between appropriation and meaning, which becomes evident in everyday practice.[13] Everyday practice is shaped by the interdependence of structures and value systems and specific (subjective) experiences that serve as orientation and create a sense of familiarity and normality. Thus peaceful coexistence between Catholics and Protestants in seventeenth-century England created a sense of familiarity and normality without extinguishing religious differences or the problematic status of Catholics in England. Consciously or subconsciously, lines were drawn between what was experienced as normal and what was experienced as abnormal, a process which could turn religious differences into a challenge if the framework changed.[14] Catholicism in England offered spiritual power and might create a sense of belonging and of achievement of social status and symbolic capital,[15] not just at court but elsewhere in English society.

---

[12] For a general discussion see Paul Münch, ed., *'Erfahrung' als Kategorie der Frühneuzeitgeschichte* (Munich, 2001). For the difficulties see ibid., 'Einleitung', pp. 11–27.

[13] Heiko Haumann and Martin Schaffner, 'Überlegungen zur Arbeit mit dem Kulturbegriff in den Geschichtswissenschaften', *Uni Nova: Mitteilungen aus der Universität Basel*, 70 (1994), 18–21. By 'everyday practice' I mean the 'sum of concrete and lived experiences that characterize the actions of those' who, 'through mutual orientation . . . seek their bearings and define their own position within the historical and biographical conditions of a society that is always already given': Richard Grathoff, *Milieu und Lebenswelt: Einführung in die Phänomenologische Soziologie und die Sozialphänomenologische Forschung* (Frankfurt am Main, 1995), p. 93 (author's translation).

[14] Grathoff, *Milieu und Lebenswelt*, pp. 338–53.

[15] Pierre Bourdieu, *Sozialer Sinn: Kritik der Theoretischen Vernunft* (Frankfurt am Main, 1987), pp. 205–21.

It could become threatening, however, if it was perceived to endanger the values, norms and belief systems of non-Catholics or the power relations between different religious groups. Divergent religious beliefs could be familiar, because they were part of everyday experience, without necessarily being considered normal or welcome. Even if religious difference was part of people's experience and thus something familiar, it could turn into something abnormal and threatening. Through the perception of something as unfamiliar or abnormal, individuals and groups became more conscious of their own identity, practices and values.

In order to explain the place of (the image of) Henrietta Maria in the rhetoric of anti-Catholicism, and based on these theoretical and methodological considerations, I shall focus on popular perceptions of Henrietta Maria based on the interplay of subjective experiences and social norms, values and the (re)assignment of meanings which are communicated in word, images, symbols and prints. I shall look, first, at political considerations, and in particular the royal mixed marriage that might have helped to create anti-Catholic sentiments and distrust that focused on the queen. I shall then consider the visualization of Catholicism at court and in London. Third, I shall explore the extent to which these developments were being discussed in print and by word of mouth. Finally, I shall consider the queen's secret political networking in and outside England on the eve of and during the English Civil War.

III

A crucial element of this conjuncture was the royal mixed marriage. According to canon law, mixed religion was a matrimonial impediment and a dispensation requested the conversion of the heretic partner.[16] In practice, however, there was 'a clear understanding of canonical tolerance as the peculiar legal expedient taken by the Church, when an enforcement of her law would result only in greater evil and harm'.[17] Especially in cases of *matrimonia illustra*,[18] exceptions were made for political reasons[19]

---

[16] Alfred J. Connick, 'The canonical impediment of mixed religion from the Council of Trent to the pontificate of Benedict XIV', Ph.D. dissertation, Catholic University of Louvain, 1961. One chapter is published as 'Canonical doctrine concerning mixed marriages – before Trent and during the seventeenth and early eighteenth centuries', *Jurist*, 20 (1960), 295–326, 398–418.

[17] Connick, 'Canonical impediment', p. 295.

[18] Michael Stolleis, 'Staatsheirat', in Adalbert Erler and Ekkehard Kaufmann, eds., *Handwörterbuch zur Deutschen Rechtsgeschichte*, IV (Berlin, 1990), pp. 1822–4.

[19] Most recently on this issue Michael Stolleis, 'Die Prinzessin als Braut', in Joachim Bohnert, ed., *Verfassung – Philosophie – Kirche: Festschrift for Alexander Hollerbach for his 70th Birthday* (Berlin, 2001), pp. 45–57.

and the conversion of the heretic partner was waived under condition that on oath he or she would not be hindered to exercise the Catholic faith freely and that the children would be brought up as Catholics. The specific arrangements were usually fixed in a marriage contract.[20] Despite the carefully worded contracts, it was commonly believed that mixed marriages were bound to lead to conflict, and this was widely debated by contemporaries.[21] Reservations among Protestants are evident not only in numerous theological treatises but also in official *concilia* of the leading theological faculties of early modern Germany, which refer extensively to the relevant literature.[22] Debate was stimulated whenever marriage negotiations for *matrimonia illustra* involving mixed religion became publicly known. Apart from matters of conscience and marital discord, one of the main evils was the fact that a mixed marriage was used by church authorities as a welcome instrument for conversion politics. In particular, the Catholic Church, which had installed the *Sacra Congregatio de Propaganda Fide* in 1622 under Pope Gregory XV with the explicit aim of winning back Protestant Europe, put pressure on the heretic partner in a mixed marriage to convert. In 1638 it was decided that

In terris haereticorum, ubi haereses impune grassantur, maxime si ibi catholicae fidei liber cultus non permittur, matrimonia cum ipsis haereticis per exhortationes potius quam per censuras prohibenda.[23]

In cases of *matrimonia illustra* of mixed religion Rome tried to negotiate the best conditions possible for the Catholic marriage partner and their fellow believers before granting a dispensation. As we have seen, the pope was only willing to grant the marriage dispensation to Charles and Henrietta Maria in return for far-reaching rights for Catholics in England

---

[20] August Knecht, *Handbuch des Katholischen Eherechts* (Freiburg/Br., 1928), p. 286; Connick, 'Canonical doctrine', p. 319.

[21] For a very full example see Friedrich Benedict Carpzov, *Dissertatio Altera Ex jure ecclesiastico: De eo, quod consultum est, in nuptis personarum diversae religionis* (Wittenberg, 1735).

[22] This material has not been systematically studied nor indexed. For printed material see, e.g., Georg Dedeken, *Thesauri consiliorum et decisionum*, 3 vols., 2nd enlarged edn by Johann Ernst Gebhard (Hamburg, 1671).

[23] 'In heretical countries, where heresies spread unpunished especially if the Catholic faith is not permitted to be practised there freely, mixed marriages are to be prevented better by exhortations than by law' (author's translation). Quoted in Knecht, *Handbuch des katholischen Eherechts*, p. 287, n. 4; see also Hermann Tüchle, *Acta S.C. Propaganda Fide Germaniam spectantia: Die Protokolle der Propagandakongregation zu deutschen Angelegenheiten, 1622–1649* (Paderborn, 1962).

and sufficient securities that the queen would not be forced to convert,[24] a danger that was being widely discussed in Europe.[25]

Other conditions of the treaty included the repeal of penal laws against Catholics, the abolition of the oath of allegiance, and the Catholic baptism and upbringing of the children of the marriage up to the age of thirteen (the age at which, it was commonly assumed, children reached the age of reason and could decide independently to which faith they wanted to belong).[26] Henrietta Maria had to confirm in a letter to Pope Urban VIII that she would do all she could to support the English Catholic minority and to bring up her children as good Catholics.[27] At the same time, the French crown used the marriage negotiations to seek protections for English Catholics.[28] Louis XIII and his negotiators insisted that Henrietta Maria should be allowed to practise her religion publicly without hindrance and that she could be accompanied by a Catholic priest and court ladies. Concerned that the English parliament might not approve the marriage in the aftermath of the Spanish match, the English marriage negotiators argued for an unwritten agreement on these issues, despite insistence from the papacy and the French that they be part of the formal contract.[29] The final outcome of intense diplomatic activity between Rome, France and England was a secret addendum to the official marriage contract, the basis for far-reaching concessions to

[24] I was unable while writing this essay to gain access to the Vatican library in Rome, which holds most of the relevant correspondence, because it was closed for rebuilding works. The best and most detailed account of the negotiations is Albion, *Charles I*, pp. 49–77, but see also S. R. Gardiner, *History of England from the Accession of James I to the Outbreak of the Civil War, 1603–1642*, 10 vols. (1883–4), V. In older studies of the mixed marriage problem in German estates the English case has regularly been referred to. See, e.g., Friedrich Kunstmann, *Gemischten Ehen*, pp. 143–62.

[25] For the safeguards for Henrietta Maria's religion see especially paragraph IX: *A True Relation of the Treaty and Ratification of the Marriage concluded[...]* (1642). For the broader discussion see Dagmar Freist, 'Toleranz und Konfessionspolitik: Konfessionell gemischter Ehen in Deutschland 1555 bis ca. 1806', unpublished habilitation, Osnabrück, 2003.

[26] Dagmar Freist, 'Kinderkonversionen in der Frühen Neuzeit', in Ute Lotz-Heumann, Jan-Friedrich Missfelder and Matthias Pohlig, eds., *Konversion und Konfession in der Frühen Neuzeit* (Gütersloh, 2007), pp. 393–429; Dagmar Freist, 'Lebensalter und Konfession. Zum Problem der Mündigkeit in Religionsfragen', in Arndt Brendecke, Ralf-Peter Fuchs and Edith Koller, eds., *Die Autorität der Zeit in der Frühen Neuzeit* (Münster, 2007), pp. 47–70.

[27] This she did: 'Henrietta Maria to Pope Urban VIII', Paris, 6 April 1625, in Mary Anne Everett (Wood) Green, ed., *Letters of Queen Henrietta Maria* (1857), pp. 9–10.

[28] Albion, *Charles I*, pp. 55–62.

[29] In a petition to the King just after the marriage plans had become public the English parliament requested that there should be no concessions to Catholics in the kingdom: ibid., p. 52.

Catholics in England wrested from the English crown by the Catholic powers.[30]

From a French Catholic perspective, Henrietta Maria had left France in order to marry a heretic king. Consequently, she was expected to use all her power to convert the king to the true Catholic faith and to improve the life of Catholics in England, and there is no doubt that her marriage was seen by some as a mission. Pope Urban VIII admonished the fifteen-year-old to take on the role of guardian angel of the English Catholics, to be 'the Esther of her oppressed people, the Clotilda who subdued to Christ her victorious husband, the Alderbirga whose nuptials brought religion into Britain; for that the eyes of the whole world, and of the spiritual world too, are turned upon her'.[31] On 26 March 1625 the pope wrote that 'her mission in England was not so much to reign as to procure the reign of popery'.[32] For her part, Henrietta Maria made it clear in numerous letters that she was aware of her duties. She thanked her brother, King Louis XIII of France, that 'in contracting the marriage between the Prince of Wales and me, there is none which more sensibly touches my heart, and the memory of which I cherish more cordially, than the particular care you have taken about the things that concern the surety of my conscience', adding, 'as I desire religiously to keep and observe your majesty's sincere intentions, as well in what concerns me and mine, as in what may be useful and advantageous to the religion and to the Catholics of Great Britain, I give your majesty my faith and word of conscience'.[33]

These expectations found an echo in contemporary literature.[34] During the 1630s a number of books and poems were published about heroines who achieved the conversion of their heretic husbands to the true faith through piety, sexuality and, finally, seduction. In 1626 Nicolas Caussin's work *La Cour sainte* appeared in English under the title 'The Holy Court'. Caussin was one of the leading French Jesuits at the court of Henrietta Maria's brother, Louis XIII. The English translation of his work was dedicated to Edward Sackville, earl of Dorset and lord chamberlain to Henrietta Maria. Dorset was explicitly chosen for his proximity to the queen and the work was obviously meant to evoke parallels to the English court, taking Clotilda, who laboured to convert her husband to the true faith, as a role model for the queen – Clotilda, so the story went,

---

[30] Kunstmann, *Gemischten Ehen*, p. 155; Albion, *Charles I*, pp. 60–4.
[31] Green, *Letters*, p. 7; see also Erica Veevers, *Images of Love and Religion: Queen Henrietta Maria and Court Entertainments* (Cambridge, 1989), p. 76.
[32] Green, *Letters*, p. 7.
[33] Henrietta Maria to Louis XIII, 29 Dec. 1624, in Green, *Letters*, p. 8.
[34] Veevers, *Images of Love*.

succeeded in the conversion of her heretic husband to Christianity with the help of her piety and her beauty.[35] Caussin devoted chapter 4 of his book to *The Lady* and focused on her vital role in the 'advancement of Christianity'.[36] Under the heading 'the Prudence, which the Queene used in the Conuersion of her Husband', Caussin described in detail conversion tactics of Clotilda so 'that she found the King dayly disposed the better and better towards her religion'.[37] These writings must be seen in the wider context of theological treatises on mixed marriages which regularly touched on the interplay of piety, sexuality and seduction while they were quite ambivalent about mixed marriages; they posed both the danger of seduction to heresy and the chance of seduction to the true faith.[38]

For Catholics, Henrietta Maria's mixed marriage thus implied the natural task of converting a heretic king to the true Catholic faith, and it was expected that she would employ her powers of seduction. For the same reasons Protestants dreaded the mixed marriage of their king. William Prynne argued that 'wee have great cause to fear (if Adams, Solomons, or Abrahams seducements by their wives be duly pondered) that his Majesty . . . may ere long be seduced to their Religion [Catholic], as well as to their Party'.[39]

The first years of marriage, however, gave little cause for fear.[40] The marriage was characterized by misunderstandings and confessional disagreements, which provide a rare insight into the everyday life of mixed-marriage couples.[41] While the queen refused to submit to Anglican church rituals, she was accused of turning her chambers into Jesuit headquarters.[42] Charles and the duke of Buckingham repudiated the secret articles of the marriage treaty in order to appease Parliament, and stepped up enforcement of the laws against recusancy.[43] These measures provoked fierce protests in Catholic Europe and diplomatic

---

[35] Nicolas Caussin, *The Holy Court* (1626), p. 516.   [36] Ibid., p. 467.
[37] Ibid., p. 520; see also Veevers, *Images of Love*, p. 83.   [38] Freist, 'Toleranz'.
[39] William Prynne, *The Popish Royall Favourite: A Full Discovery of his Majesties Extraordinary Favours to, and Protections of Notorious Papists [. . .]* (1643).
[40] Albion, *Charles I*, pp. 80 ff.
[41] Caroline Hibbard, 'Translating royalty: Henrietta Maria and the transition from princess to queen', *Court Historian*, 5 (2000), 15–29.
[42] Caroline Hibbard, 'The role of a queen consort: the household and court of Henrietta Maria, 1625–1642', in Ronald G. Asch and Adolf M. Birke, eds., *Princes, Patronage, and the Nobility: The Court at the Beginning of the Modern Age c.1450–1650* (Oxford, 1991), pp. 393–414.
[43] Malcolm Smuts, 'Religion, European politics and Henrietta Maria's circle, 1625–41', in Erin Griffey, ed., *Henrietta Maria: Piety, Politics and Patronage* (Aldershot, 2008), pp. 13–38, at p. 16.

strategies were developed to set Henrietta Maria and her household against Buckingham.[44]

Life became easier for Henrietta Maria after Buckingham's assassination in August 1628. She replaced him as the confidante of the king, and the royal couple seem to have developed a strong emotional relationship characterized by mutual affection and respect. The queen's position at court grew stronger and, as Malcolm Smuts has shown, she was willing to promote the interests of Puritans and Catholics, drawn together by their hostility to the Spanish and support for the French alliance.[45] In return she sought political protection for English Catholics. This atmosphere of hope for English Catholics encouraged the presentation of a petition to the king pleading for toleration during his coronation visit to Scotland in 1633, which invoked the example of his father-in-law, Henry IV of France.[46] Catholicism, then, established an increasingly public presence at the court and in London during the 1630s, and as a result began to enter people's experiences.

IV

After the expulsion of her Catholic household in 1626, the queen had practised her Catholic faith in private, undisturbed and little noticed. Yet she assured the pope in a letter of the same year that she continued to work for the peace and comfort of English Catholics, hoping despite the current disappointments that her perseverance would eventually receive divine assistance.[47]

The arrival of twelve Capuchin friars in London in 1630, however, turned Henrietta Maria's faith into a public affair. After initial disagreements about their status – disagreements which reflected French factionalism and rivalry at the English court – the friars were settled at Somerset House. They were permitted to wear the religious habit which visualized their Catholic faith in public, and the execution of the penal laws against recusants was suspended.[48] The fraternity of the Capuchins was one of the most successful missions worldwide, and the friars started their missionary work in London immediately, securing a notable list of conversions.[49] The most obvious public manifestation of the queen's Catholic faith, however, was her chapel, designed by Inigo Jones and finished in 1635, a late fulfilment of her marriage contract. With Charles's

---

[44] Ibid., p. 18.
[45] R. Malcolm Smuts, 'The Puritan followers of Henrietta Maria in the 1630s', *EHR*, 93 (1978), 26–45.
[46] Henrietta Haynes, *Henrietta Maria* (1912), p. 105.   [47] Quoted in ibid., p. 98.
[48] Ibid., pp. 104–6.   [49] Albion, *Charles I*, pp. 196–202.

approval not only were priests permitted to reside in London but English Catholics were allowed to attend the chapels of the queen and the ambassadors and to participate in regular religious instructions. The centre of Catholic revival in the city was the chapel of the papal agent, George Conn, which he had set up in his lodgings in Long Acre. As in the Roman churches, Conn had erected the Barberini arms and mass was held in the 'pope's chapel' up to eight times daily, even during the plague, attracting large crowds.[50] All the houses in the neighbourhood were soon taken by prominent Catholics.[51] In a way, Catholicism had almost become fashionable, not only at court but in London. It certainly had become a public sight and thus started to enter the horizon of ordinary men and women of either religion. These sites became the focus for anti-Catholic riots during the 1640s.[52]

The growing prominence of Catholics at court and the political impact and impression that this had in and outside London again changed dramatically with the establishment of the Roman agency in England. Gregorio Panzani was sent to London in 1634, and was succeeded by the Scot George Conn in 1636. At the same time negotiations were under way over establishing an English agent in Rome.[53] Among the political objectives was the promotion of a church union and a change in the administration of the oath of allegiance.[54] Conn was well liked by both Protestants and Catholics. The intense theological discussions he had with leading courtiers and with the king, and his proselytization, are well known. Under his influence Henrietta Maria began to play a more aggressive role in promoting her faith, and together with her Catholic court ladies started to campaign for her religion.[55] In a letter to Cardinal Barberini in 1637, the queen repeated her 'strongest passion, the advancement of the Catholic religion in this country'.[56] The conversion of several prominent women courtiers in 1637–8 was interpreted by Puritans as a sign of the missionary activities of the queen and her papal agent;[57] as one contemporary put it, 'Our great women fall away every

---

[50] Ibid., p. 162.   [51] Ibid., p. 203; Hibbard, *Charles I*, p. 160.

[52] Albion, *Charles I*, pp. 338–9; Freist, *Governed*, p. 236; David Cressy, *England on Edge: Crisis and Revolution 1640–1642* (Oxford, 2006), p. 120.

[53] Albion, *Charles I*, pp. 152 ff.

[54] *The Memoirs of Gregorio Panzani: Giving An Account of His Agency in England in the Years 1634, 1635, 1636*, translated from the Italian Original and introduced by Joseph Berington (first published 1793), pp. 160 ff.; Albion, *Charles I*, p. 153; Hibbard, *Charles I*, ch. 3.

[55] Hibbard, 'Henrietta Maria'.   [56] Quoted in Haynes, *Henrietta Maria*, p. 123.

[57] Albion, *Charles I*, pp. 203–15; Elisabeth Hamilton, *Henrietta Maria* (1976), p. 145; Sarah Poynting, '"In the Name of all the Sisters": Henrietta Maria's notorious whores', in Clare McManus, ed., *Women and Court Culture at the Courts of the Stuart Queens* (2003), pp. 163–85, at p. 179.

day.'[58] A royal edict was eventually issued forbidding proselytism under severe penalties of the law.[59]

Anti-Catholic sentiment commonly resulted in a negative attitude to these conversions, and this has influenced the judgements of historians. However, under the influence of Queen Henrietta Maria, her visible and sincere devotion, her court entertainments and the fashions, dresses and luxuries which she regularly received from France, it became fashionable to be Catholic as it was in some other European courts. Papal agents showered courtiers, especially court ladies, with Catholic emblems of all sorts and fed the king's fascination with the fine arts by importing paintings, sculptures and exotica from Italy.[60] This cultural transfer from France may have had an important role in signifying the exclusiveness and status of noble society, although that question has yet to be addressed in detail.[61] Certainly, though, the trend was a powerful one: there were further conversions among court women between 1638 and 1641, when the queen's mother, Maria de' Medici, and the duchess of Chevreuse, Marie de Rohan-Montbazon, and their households joined the English court.

Henrietta Maria had successfully shaped court life according to her personal fondness for the fine arts, festivals, piety and ideals of platonic love, and this contributed to the visualization of Catholicism in London.[62] These ideals found expression in a close interrelationship of festivities and piety, theological discussions and intense forms of religious practice such as the cult of the holy virgin, which the queen cultivated at court.[63] French theologians of the seventeenth-century Counter-Reformation drew a connection between neo-Platonic ideals of beauty and love and the cult of the holy virgin. This proved popular among Capuchin friars of the queen's household. Among the most well-known authors were Zacharie de Lysieux, a former chaplain of Henrietta Maria, and his close friend, Yves de Paris. Central to their arguments was the idea that love which opened the immediate way to God exceeded reason.[64] The ideal of Platonic love strove to unite souls of true Catholic believers, not bodies. In court masques these ideals were put on stage and re-enacted in court life: it is tempting to draw parallels between these

---

[58] Hibbard, 'Henrietta Maria'.
[59] *A Proclamation restraining the withdrawing His Majesties subjects from the Church of England, and giving scandal in resorting to Masses.* See Albion, *Charles I*, p. 215.
[60] Haynes, *Henrietta Maria*, p. 111.
[61] For a study of these issues see Gesa Stedman, 'Early modern cultural exchange: England and France in the seventeenth century', unpublished habilitation, Berlin, 2005.
[62] Veevers, *Images of Love*, pp. 1–8.   [63] Ibid., pp. 92–3, 103–09.
[64] Ibid., pp. 92–3.

ideals and the image of Clotilda and others who had been recommended to Henrietta Maria as role models. In this context the fact that George Conn had 'evidently contemplated subjecting the whole realm through women' appears in a new light.[65] Such allusions were quickly discerned by Puritans, who accused the queen of publicly promoting a lascivious life at an increasingly corrupt court with the explicit aim of seducing courtiers to the Catholic religion. In *Histriomastix*, his well known onslaught on the immorality of the theatre, William Prynne not only compared actresses to whores but also attacked the seduction to the Catholic faith.[66] Lord Dorset, the lord chamberlain of Henrietta Maria and hence responsible for her theatrical court entertainments, made a 'robust defence of the queen's "vertues" [which] was matched only by his intense desire to see Prynne punished'.[67]

This image of an utterly immoral court culture was widespread in print and seems to have been a central ingredient of anti-popery on the eve of the English Civil War. Sexual slander was commonly used to discredit political opponents in seventeenth-century England.[68] In this context, however, there was a specific cultural resonance in concern about the dangers of courtship and seduction to Catholicism.

As a result of the marriage contract and changes in court culture, the potential for an anti-Catholic reaction was building. But these might seem concerns for the political elite, and the question remains how this potential for conflict and hostility actually gave rise to a revival of anti-popery, despite the record of peaceful religious coexistence, and the attractions of Catholicism for some English people. In order to address this question it is important to examine what the public knew of these things and how they were interpreted.

V

Since the 1620s newsbooks and broadsides had communicated political and religious news to a wide audience. The imperative of the *arcanum politicae*, which defined politics as the exclusive realm of the king and his first ministers, as well as censorship, were increasingly undermined. It is no surprise, therefore, that details of the marriage negotiations between Charles and Henrietta Maria were already circulating in manuscript in

---

[65] Albion, *Charles I*, p. 162.
[66] William Prynne, *Histriomastix: The Players Scorge or Actors Tragedy* (1633).
[67] Smith, 'Catholic', p. 112.
[68] The literature on this point is large. For an overview and further references see Alasdair Bellany, 'Raylinge Rymes revisited: libels, scandals and early Stuart politics', *History Compass*, 5 (2007), 1136–79.

Europe during the 1620s,[69] and that numerous pamphlets discussed this unnatural alliance in the tradition of theological treatises on mixed marriages.[70] At the height of hostilities against the French queen in 1642, the marriage contract was published in London under the title *A True Relation of the Treaty and Ratification of the Marriage [. . .]*, thus confirming to a wider public the basis of court Catholicism and politics.[71] The most direct references to the regulations of the marriage contract can be found in the Great Remonstrance. At the heart of the Remonstrance lies the conviction that the Kingdom was ruled by a 'malignant party' of Catholics and popish agents who influenced the king and contrived the overturn of the kingdom, and the concessions consequent on the marriage contract provided evidence of this threat.[72] Catholics, so the argument went on, formed a state within the state and laboured against the freedom and privileges of the English people.[73] In 1642 Parliament issued a *Declaration of Causes and Remedies* which focused on Henrietta Maria, her Catholic court and her role as adviser.[74] This laid the foundation for the subsequent Nineteen Propositions which parliament presented to Charles in June 1642.[75] The propositions requested the king's assent to a bill requiring that children born by Catholics should be brought up by Protestant parents and educated in the Protestant religion. Likewise the king was requested to execute penal laws against recusants.[76] These provisions were, in effect, directed against the conditions of the marriage treaty.

These declarations publicized details about the role of Catholics in the royal household as well as detailed information about the concessions made to Catholics in the marriage treaty. As a result, a wider audience was drawn into the political and religious conflicts. The names of Catholics and crypto-Catholics who should not be pardoned were published in proclamations, and the king was asked to free himself from malignant and evil councillors.[77] Religious and political requests merged, while Puritans were in no doubt that the causes of the crisis lay in the immediate Catholic surroundings of the king and his wife. In a petition to the king, several of the peerage complained in 1640 of 'the great increase in popery and the employing of popish recusants . . . in places of power'.[78] The joint effort of John Pym and the City of London, which warned of the 'concourse of

[69] Smuts, 'Religion', p. 15.   [70] Albion, *Charles I*, p. 54.
[71] *A True Relation of the Treaty*.
[72] See, e.g., paragraph 88, or the hostility to the residence of the papal nuncio: Gardiner, *CD*, pp. 202–32, at p. 219.
[73] Ibid.   [74] *Declaration of Causes and Remedies[. . .]* (1642).
[75] Gardiner, *CD*, pp. 262–7.   [76] Ibid., p. 264.
[77] Mary D. R. Leys, *Catholics in England, 1559–1829: A Social History* (1961), p. 85.
[78] *CSPD, 1640*, pp. 639–40.

papists' in November 1640, led to the formation of a committee which was ordered to investigate papists and to disarm them.[79] These fears were echoed in cheap print, ballads and woodcuts, which flooded the London market in the 1640s.[80]

It is, of course, difficult to know how ordinary men and women appropriated politics and how they related to Catholicism, but a systematic analysis of court records on seditious talk and slander which touched on politics and religion in the kingdom has shown that ordinary people were intensely involved in these debates and that they took sides depending on their personal outlook, experiences and convictions.[81] Opinions diverged on how to judge the complex political and religious conflicts of the 1640s, and this was also true for the public assessment of the queen's religious and political influence on Charles.[82] In June 1640, the Catholic widow Elizabeth Thorowgood and the Anabaptist Alexander West regularly met in the house of a certain Mr and Mrs Parkman in the parish of St James. Incited by 'certeine Popish tenenth', they had several arguments about the 'popish and the protestant religion'.[83] While West criticized the 'Papists many treacheryes against this Nation', Thorowgood insisted that 'now the kinge loveth the Papist better than the Puritans and hee would sooner trust them [meaninge the papists] then hee would the Puritans . . . will the kinge say My wife is a Papist shall I not love them'.[84] The Catholic Mary Cole, on the other hand, was not so positive about the queen's influence on Charles, and remarked in 1638, 'if shee wear as the Queene shee would quickly make away with the king for dealing so hardly with that Religion.'[85] Joan Worrall of St Martin-in-the-Fields was seemingly convinced that Charles shared the religious practices of his wife when she reported, 'She hoped ere long there would be crucifixes in all houses and that the king's majesty had a crucifix in his chamber and did bow to it.'[86] People also noted that Charles accompanied the queen at the inauguration of her chapel in 1635 and that he had gone to Mass. Statements such as the following were representative of the general atmosphere: 'And now the King goes to Mass with the Queen',[87]

---

[79] Hibbard, *Charles I*, pp. 171–2.

[80] Freist, *Governed*; David Zaret, *Origins of Democratic Culture: Printing, Petitions, and the Public Sphere in Early-Modern England* (Princeton, NJ, 2000).

[81] Freist, *Governed*; more recently, Cressy, *England*, esp. pp. 321–9.

[82] For a full discussion of public political opinions see Freist, *Governed*, and Cressy, *England*.

[83] State Papers (SP) 16/457.3i–4i, 1640.   [84] Ibid., and Freist, *Governed*, pp. 272–6.

[85] SP 16/392.61 and SP 16/393.24i, 1638, and Freist, *Governed*, pp. 29–30.

[86] John C. Jeaffreson, ed., *Middlesex County Records (Old Series)*, III: 1625–1667 (1974), p. 74 (24 November 1640).

[87] SP 16/454.42, 1640.

or 'now the kinge commonly went to Masse, and was turned to bee a Papist'.[88] From then on many believed that the king was about to convert to the Catholic faith. Catholics expressed their hopes for an advancement of their cause with increasing self-confidence and regularly referred to the influence of Queen Henrietta Maria as well as the queen mother. Elizabeth Shipley of the Strand was accused of steering 'the people to rebellion and insurrection and the praise of the Roman religion'.[89] While Catholics were ambivalent about what to expect of the queen's political influence, Protestants, too, were divided in their judgements about the queen's potential danger. It is important here to note that awareness of the issue, and debate about its implications, reached out on to London's streets.

News of the Scottish war in 1639 and the Irish rising in 1641 had an even greater impact on perceptions of the role of Catholics at court. Rumours of popish plots are well known and have been dealt with by historians as part of Puritan propaganda.[90] Although Puritans clearly did promote these rumours, they do not seem to have invented them.[91] Many of these rumours, too, were accompanied by detailed descriptions of the role Henrietta Maria played in these conspiracies. In fact, she was widely believed to be at the centre of it; it was these pamphlets that were summarized by Caroline Hibbard as a 'campaign that demonized the queen'.[92]

Henrietta Maria's commitment to raise money from Catholic subjects throughout England to finance the king's army in 1639 gave rise to one such rumour.[93] Her efforts were supported by George Conn as well as by the Catholic courtiers Kenelm Digby, Walter Montagu and her secretary John Walter. In letters to leading Catholic families throughout the kingdom she assured them of her personal protection and asked for money in acknowledgement of the support they had received from the royal couple. The network she created to support this effort was uncovered and reported anonymously in a pamphlet published 'at London in the yeare of the discovery of the Plots' under the title *A Copy of the letter sent by the Queenes Majestie concerning the collection of the Recusant Mony for the Scottish Warre, Apr. 17, 1639.* Parliament, too, sought to uncover these conspiracies, searching houses for weapons, among them the residences of George Conn and Count Carlo Rosetti, the papal agent in London.[94]

---

[88] SP 16/457.3i–4i, 1640.

[89] Jeaffreson, ed., *Middlesex County Records, III*, pp. 73–4 (6 November 1640).

[90] Anthony Fletcher, *The Outbreak of the English Civil War* (1981); Hibbard, *Charles I*, chs. 8–9.

[91] Cressy, *England*, pp. 43–50.   [92] Hibbard, 'Henrietta Maria'.

[93] Albion, *Charles I*, pp. 334–6; Leys, *Catholics*, p. 84; Hibbard, *Charles I*, pp. 121–2. Hibbard does not mention the involvement of Henrietta Maria.

[94] Hibbard, *Charles I*, p. 166 and n. 184.

Parallel to the domestic mobilization of loyal Catholics, the queen was involved in negotiations with France, Spain and Rome to supply men and money to the royal army.[95] The aim behind these activities was to empower the king to conduct the war against Scotland without summoning Parliament.[96] Tension heightened when it became public that the king's army was supported by Catholics from Ireland, Scotland and Wales. Here, too, Queen Henrietta Maria played a vital role when she supported plans of Randal MacDonnell, second earl of Antrim, to recruit Irish Catholics for the king's army.

Concern about the Catholic networks centred on the queen formed a staple element of parliamentary propaganda thereafter. The attack on the five members, for example, was quickly linked to theories of a popish plot[97] and the queen was publicly identified as the prime mover of events. The anonymous author of a letter, in which he had warned the House of Commons of the impending danger, wrote that

> though I am of opinion the king's majesty be a good Protestant in his heart, yet I am persuaded that by the persuasions of the queens majesty, and the advice of the Catholic lords and other gentlemen, the wished design may take full effect.[98]

Shortly afterwards, the royal couple left London, and in February 1642 the queen escaped to the Continent, fearing an imminent impeachment by the English parliament. Earlier attempts by her to leave the country had been discovered and defeated because it was rightly assumed that she would be more successful in drumming up foreign support for Charles. The reasons 'to stay the Queens going into Holland' were printed immediately.[99] The queen negotiated her desire for departure with the Parliament, and her speech, too, was printed.[100]

After her departure the queen's correspondence was frequently intercepted and her letters were printed as proof of the continuing threat she posed to the kingdom. Almost all of her movements and intentions on the Continent could be closely followed in print.[101] The publication of the

---

[95] Hibbard, 'Henrietta Maria'.   [96] Hibbard, *Charles I*, p. 166.

[97] See, e.g., Anon[?], *The Papists' Design Against the Parliament and the City of London Discovered* (1642).

[98] Hibbard, *Charles I*, p. 222.

[99] John Pym, *Reasons of the House of Commons to Stay the Queens Going into Holland: Delivered to the Lords at a Conference the 14 of July 1641* (1641).

[100] *The Queenes Speech as it was Delivered to the House of Commons by Sir Thomas Jermyn Comptroller* (1641).

[101] *The Queens Majesties Declaration and Desires to the States of Holland June 18, 1642 [...] With Her Majesties Message and Proposition to the States of Holland, Concerning the Kings Levying of Forces [...]* (1642). Many of these pamphlets listed her political activities on the title page: *Strange and Terrible News from the Queene in Holland Shewing plainly the Intelligence of the Kinge of his Intention to raise Armes. And the Queene of Englands*

king's letters following their capture at Naseby fuelled this propaganda effort, although its impact was not straightforward. Thomas Sampson of Spitalfields, a turner, argued 'that the letters that were taken in the King's cabinet were not of the Kinges owne handwriting, but that the State did counterfeit his hand', thus implying a political plot on Parliament's side.[102] Both Caroline Hibbard and Michelle Anne White have stressed in recent studies the impact of the meticulous record of the queen's political activities on the wider public in England.[103] There can be little doubt that 'the political reverberations of the queen's efforts were at least as important as any contribution to the royalist military effort that they made'.[104]

VI

Public interest in the private religious practices of the queen as they had been guaranteed by the marriage contract grew with increasing proof of her support for Catholics in England. Not only were members of the royal household and courtiers attracted to the Catholic faith, so the public noted, but the queen used all her influence to enhance the rights of her Catholic subjects. Her attempts to mobilize Catholics in England and abroad in the unfolding crisis following the Scottish Prayer Book rebellion fanned the fear of a Catholic revival and plot to take over the kingdom. Her letters were published as an unquestionable proof of her political designs and also demonstrated that she continued to be one of the king's most influential advisers. Yet not all the people were impressed by the anti-Catholic rhetoric and not all deduced danger from the presence of Catholics at the court and in London and the country at large. In fact, for many contemporaries, the growing sectarianism and egalitarianism posed a greater threat to the social status quo. Consequently, apart from searches of Catholic houses for weapons authorized by act of Parliament and almost ritualized attacks on Catholic lodgings on feast days or as the result of rumours, there were no major attacks on Catholics in general. To the same degree that Henrietta Maria posed a threat to some segments of society as 'popery in perfection', for others she became a symbol of hope and an icon of Catholicism, piety and devotion. Her court life, her behaviour and her fashions were a magnet for a younger generation of nobles of either religion.

---

providing many Barrels of gunpowder, diverse Pistols, and to be sent suddainely over to the King [. . .] (1642).

[102] Jeaffreson, ed., *Middlesex County Records, III*, p. 99 (24 March 1647).

[103] Hibbard, 'Henrietta Maria'; White, *Henrietta Maria*.

[104] White, *Henrietta Maria*, ch. 4, and quote from Hibbard, 'Henrietta Maria'.

In 1643 Henrietta Maria returned to England and marched at the head of a 'popish army'. This not only earned her the name of 'Catholic crusader' but also led to her impeachment by the House of Commons. At the same time Parliament launched a renewed campaign of iconoclasm which included the demolition of the queen's chapel in Somerset House. The malign influence attributed to Queen Henrietta Maria is summed up in a *Declaration of both Houses of Parliament* in 1643, which demanded

That your Majesty would be pleased not to entertaine any advice or mediation from the Queene in matters of Religion, or concerning the Government of any of your Majesties Dominions, &c.

That for the further securing of the Kingdom in this behalf (being a matter of such greate importance for the preservation of Religion, and the safety of the Kingdom) the Queen would be pleased to take a solemn oath in the presence of both houses of Parliament, that she will not hereafter give any Counsell, or use any meditation to your Majesty concerning the displacing of any offices or places, or at all intermeddle in any affairs of State and government of the Kingdome.[105]

Under the impact of these developments, the familiar experience of religious differences and pragmatic forms of religious coexistence which characterized life in London and the countryside in the 1630s turned for some groups in society into conflict and segregation: the mere fact that people were familiar with different religious beliefs and practices within a given social setting did not prevent them from perceiving a fundamental threat in that familiar phenomenon. However, this campaign was mirrored by positive images of Henrietta Maria, especially her piety and devotion. The visualization of Catholicism in London served as an argument for the presence of danger, yet it also aroused curiosity and even fostered attraction. It seems that the experience of religious coexistence was characterized by everyday pragmatism on the one hand, and a tension between fascination and repulsion on the other.

---

[105] *The Declaration of both Houses of Parliament to the Kings Most Excellent Majestie. Concerning the Queene with the evill Councell about them* (1643).

3   Sir Benjamin Rudyerd and England's 'wars of religion'*

David L. Smith

I

This essay examines the public career of Sir Benjamin Rudyerd (1572–1658), especially during the period 1640–5. After first considering Rudyerd's activities during the 1620s and 1630s by way of context, the essay will then focus on his career during the two years before the outbreak of the English Civil War, and the first three years or so of the war itself (after which he became less and less active in political affairs). In particular, the essay will explore the development of Rudyerd's political and religious ideas, and their impact on his actions. A reconstruction of how Rudyerd's position evolved in the years leading up to war and during the early part of the conflict allows us to assess the significance of ideology, especially religion, as against other motives, in shaping his moderate Parliamentarian allegiance. The essay thus engages with John Morrill's work at two levels: first, by reconsidering the importance of religion in causing the Civil War and influencing the choice of sides; and, second, by offering a case study of the 'political psychology' of one prominent and well-documented, but hitherto little studied, individual. The essay will explore the intertwining of religious and political attitudes in this period. It will also grapple with the challenge of reconstructing the relationship between beliefs and actions, and hence of explaining the nature of political motivation. It thus offers a case study of moderate Parliamentarian allegiance that can be situated within the wider context of some of the

* I first became interested in Sir Benjamin Rudyerd back in 1984–5, when I wrote a Cambridge B.A. dissertation on his career, supervised by John Morrill. It therefore seems appropriate for this volume, over a quarter of a century later, to revisit a subject that I first explored under John's expert guidance. An early version of this article was presented at the seminar on the religious history of Britain, 1500–1800, at the Institute of Historical Research in May 2007, and I am grateful for their helpful comments to all those who were present, especially Ken Fincham, Tom Freeman and Nicholas Tyacke. I also wish to thank Mike Braddick for his valuable advice on the first draft of this piece, and the History of Parliament Trust for permitting me to see prior to publication Simon Healy's article on Rudyerd's career up to 1629.

central concerns and approaches of 'revisionism' in general and of John Morrill's work in particular.

II

Rudyerd's parliamentary career began relatively late in his life; born in December 1572, he was aged nearly fifty when he first entered the Commons in 1621. He sat in every parliament from then until 1648, and he was one of the thirteen oldest members of the Commons by the time the Long Parliament assembled in November 1640.[1] Educated at Winchester College and St John's College, Oxford, he was later admitted to the Middle Temple in April 1590, and called to the Bar in October 1600. At an unknown date he married Mary Harrington, and in 1610 he obtained a licence to travel abroad for three years. After his return he was knighted, in March 1618, and the following month was appointed Surveyor of the Court of Wards for life. He held that lucrative office until the court's abolition in February 1646, whereupon the Long Parliament voted him £6,000 as compensation. In 1619 he was also granted an annuity of £200 that was apparently still being paid in the 1640s.[2] Rudyerd was noted for his eloquence, and Sir Edward Dering referred to him in the Long Parliament as 'that silver trumpet'.[3] Sir John Eliot was less impressed, and once wrote that Rudyerd 'did speak never but premeditated, which had more show of memory than affection and made his words less powerful than observed',[4] but what Rudyerd's speeches may have lacked in spontaneity they made up for in rhetorical prowess and colour of language. His attitudes can be reconstructed principally from these parliamentary speeches, and his concerns ranged broadly across the public issues of the period, from foreign policy to the crown's finances and the future of the Church of England.

The key influence on Rudyerd's political career appears to have been his friendship with William Herbert, third earl of Pembroke, and with his younger brother Philip Herbert, earl of Montgomery and fourth earl of Pembroke. Rudyerd's connection with the Herberts apparently grew out of his early association with Robert Sidney, Lord L'Isle, whose elder

[1] Mary Frear Keeler, *The Long Parliament, 1640–1641: A Biographical Study of its Members*, Memoirs of the American Philosophical Society 36 (Philadelphia, 1954), p. 19, table 4.

[2] For biographical accounts of Rudyerd see J. A. Manning, ed., *Memoirs of Sir Benjamin Rudyerd, Knt* (1841); C. H. Firth's life of Rudyerd in the old *DNB*; and my life of Rudyerd in the *ODNB*.

[3] *The speeches of Sr. Edward Deering in the Commons House of Parliament* (1641), p. 4 (Wing, D 1116).

[4] Maija Jansson and W. B. Bidwell, eds., *Proceedings in Parliament, 1625* (New Haven and London, 1987), p. 507.

son he tutored on a grand tour. The third earl of Pembroke, to whom
Rudyerd owed his appointment as Surveyor of the Wards, was L'Isle's
nephew. Rudyerd sometimes answered letters for both the third and the
fourth earls of Pembroke, and he also acted as a surety for some of
their legal transactions, such as indentures conveying land. Similarly, his
return to Parliament for Portsmouth (1621, 1624, 1625), and then for
the Wiltshire constituencies of Old Sarum (1626), Downton (1628–9)
and Wilton (1640–8) was directly due to the earls of Pembroke, whose
seat was at Wilton House. During this period the earls of Pembroke
nominated both members for Wilton and at least one for each of the
three other constituencies that Rudyerd represented.

Throughout his parliamentary career Rudyerd co-operated closely with
his patrons. Conrad Russell described him as 'the chief House of Commons spokesman for Pembroke'.[5] Both the third and fourth earls were
strongly committed to godly Protestantism, an outlook with which Rudyerd appears to have been instinctively in sympathy. Vehemently anti-
Catholic, Rudyerd, like the Herberts, advocated a pan-Protestant, pro-
Dutch, anti-Spanish foreign policy, and was prepared to contemplate a
French alliance if that helped to isolate Spain. Rudyerd's view of diplomacy was guided primarily by his horror that 'our religion [was] battered
abroad and mouldered away at home'.[6] More specifically, this outlook
translated into a deep concern about scandalous livings as well as scandalous ministers, and a wish to alleviate the poverty of the Church.

This theme occurred repeatedly in Rudyerd's parliamentary speeches
during the 1620s, and was clearly among his highest priorities for the
reform of the Church. Thus, on 15 May 1621, in his maiden speech
in the Commons, he advocated an oath to prevent patrons selling clerical livings: 'Here in this place have many good laws been made against
papists; but the best that I know would be to employ the best ministers, for matter of belief is not to be compelled, but persuaded.'[7] His
concern with ecclesiastical matters was evident again on 25 June 1625,
when he spoke against inserting a proviso into the petition on religion
that aimed to allow silenced ministers to preach on agreed points of doctrine and discipline, on the grounds that 'moderate bishops would do it
of themselves'.[8] During the later 1620s he became ever more preoccu-
pied with the problems of scandalous livings and the under-endowment
of the Church of England. Thus, on 10 February 1626, he urged the

---

[5] Conrad Russell, *Parliaments and English Politics, 1621–1629* (Oxford, 1979), p. 13.
[6] Wallace Notestein, F. H. Relf and H. Simpson, eds., *Commons Debates, 1621*, 7 vols.
(New Haven, 1935), II, p. 445.
[7] Ibid., IV, p. 344.   [8] *Proceedings in Parliament, 1625*, p. 248.

Commons 'to enlarge ministers' livings, and lamented the case of two Lancashire ministers whose livings yielded 'but £6 per annum', and who had been 'found to be unlicensed alehousekeepers'. There was, he complained, 'scarce such blindness or ignorance in Christendom as in some parts of this kingdom'.[9] He called for a bill to improve the endowment of scandalous livings, and subsequently suggested that this be paired with another bill concerning scandalous ministers.[10] A subcommittee was appointed to draw up such a bill, but it does not appear to have reported before the parliament was dissolved.[11]

Two years later Rudyerd explored these problems much more fully in a major speech, probably delivered on 21 April 1628, and later published as a separate, entitled *Sir Beniamin Ruddierd's speech in behalfe of the Cleargy*.[12] He maintained that 'there were some places in England, which were scarce in Christendom, where God was little better known than amongst the Indians'. These places included 'the utmost skirts of the north, where the prayers of the common people are more like spells and charms than devotions', and Rudyerd detected 'the same blindness and ignorance . . . in divers parts of Wales'. He insisted that 'to plant good ministers in good livings was the strongest and surest means to establish true religion', and that 'it would prevail more against papistry than the making of new laws or executing of old'. He believed this was 'absolutely within our power'. Rudyerd was tough on scandalous ministers – 'there is no man shall be more forward to have them severely punished than I will be' – but also tough on the causes of scandalous ministers: 'let us provide them convenient livings, and then punish them, in God's name; but till then, scandalous livings cannot but have scandalous ministers'. The 'glorious and religious work of King James' offered an inspiring example: 'within the space of one year he caused to be planted churches through all Scotland, the Highlands, and the Borders, with £30 a year apiece, with a house and some glebe land belonging to them; which £30 a year, considering the cheapness of the country, and the modest fashion of ministers living there, is worth double as much as anywhere within an 100 miles of London'. He asserted that 'though Christianity and religion be established generally throughout this kingdom, yet until it be planted more particularly, I shall scarce think this a Christian commonwealth'.

[9] Maija Jansson and W. B. Bidwell, eds., *Proceedings in Parliament, 1626*, 4 vols. (New Haven and London, 1991–6), II, pp. 12, 15, 17.

[10] Ibid., II, p. 128; III, p. 101.   [11] Ibid., II, pp. 26–9.

[12] For the problems of dating this speech, and a convincing case for regarding 21 April 1628 as the most probable date, see M. F. Keeler, M. J. Cole and W. B. Bidwell, eds., *Proceedings in Parliament, 1628*, 6 vols. (New Haven, 1977–83), III, p. 17n. *Sir Beniamin Ruddierd's speech in behalfe of the Cleargy* (London, 1628) is ESTC, S2865, 21435.7.

This matter would, Rudyerd declared, 'lie heavy upon Parliaments until it be effected', and he concluded, 'I will never give over soliciting this cause as long as Parliaments and I live together'. Rudyerd believed that until Parliament took radical steps, the Church's economic problems would remain unresolved. When, on 16 May 1628, the scandalous ministers bill received a third reading, he again urged that it might go 'hand in hand' with the scandalous livings bill, although the latter was never reported to the House.[13]

By the later 1620s, Rudyerd had another growing concern about the state of the Church of England, namely the increasing influence of Arminianism. His anxieties became evident in April 1626, when he informed Sir Francis Nethersole that Pembroke 'does not think fit his Majesty should stand neutral towards the Arminians lest he should give them too much countenance'.[14] A few days later, he supported Pym's investigation of Richard Montagu and urged that the charges against him should be related to the Lords.[15] In the 1628 Parliament, Rudyerd was named to the committees that drew up charges against two other divines, Roger Maynwaring and Richard Burgess.[16] Parliamentary fears of creeping Arminianism came to a head in the 1629 session, and on 29 January Rudyerd made a remarkable speech in the committee of religion that offers an important insight into his conception of the Church of England and the dangers that it faced. According to Sir Edward Nicholas, Rudyerd argued that

His Majesty hath already publicly declared to keep the unity of love in the bond of peace; popery is ancient amongst us and in that we complain only of the want of execution of laws against recusants. Arminianism lately crept in and crept up into high places. Moves that we should consider of the articles of our faith long since agreed, 1552, and published again lately; the ancient catechism appointed and published in our book of common prayer, and to consider also of those also at Lambeth: from all which he would have us to take our proceedings, to express what those were, and to advance against all that shall vary from those, without disputing for or against particulars nor upstart opinions.[17]

By highlighting the 1552 Articles and the Lambeth Articles of 1595, Rudyerd was espousing a strongly Protestant – indeed, Calvinist – vision of the Church of England. Small wonder, then, that he was deeply opposed to any signs of growing Arminian influence, and about two weeks later, on 10 February, he urged the Commons to write to the

---

[13] *Proceedings in Parliament, 1628*, III, pp. 431, 438, 440.
[14] *Proceedings in Parliament, 1626*, IV, p. 309.   [15] Ibid., III, p. 101.
[16] *Proceedings in Parliament, 1628*, IV, pp. 36, 60.
[17] Wallace Notestein and F. H. Relf, eds., *Commons Debates for 1629* (Minneapolis, 1921), p. 116.

universities of Oxford and Cambridge requesting details of the 'public censures and recantations...made on such as have held tenets of Arminianism and popery'.[18] The House duly resolved that the Speaker should do this.[19]

Rudyerd's religious outlook was consistent not only with Pembroke's, but also with that of other members of the Commons with whom he regularly collaborated politically, not least in seeking an overhaul of crown revenues, most notably Sir Nathaniel Rich, Sir Dudley Digges and John Pym. These members aimed both to enlarge the monarch's income and to safeguard the future of parliaments. Politically, Rudyerd was probably the least radical of them, and throughout the 1620s he mainly confined himself to advocating the grant of a generous number of subsidies. For example, on 26 November 1621 he moved that 'we would not suffer the instrument to be strained too high to the ruin but proceed to bounty speedily'.[20] Rudyerd consistently urged the Commons to back up its advice on foreign policy, and especially its calls for war, with generous grants of supply. Thus on 22 June 1625 he hoped that members would 'carry [them]selves in this first session' of Charles I's reign 'with sweetness, with duty, with confidence in and towards his Majesty', who had been 'bred in Parliaments'.[21] Eight days later he reminded members that 'the King's domestical charges [were] exceeding great; for funeral, entertainment of ambassadors, and coronation. The charge of the navy like to be 3 hundred thousand pounds', and he wanted the House to 'give...in some proportion to this great charge'.[22] In a similar vein, Rudyerd declared on 22 March 1628 that 'the way to show that we are the wise counsellors or that we should be so is...by giving a large and ample supply, proportionable to the greatness and importance of the work in hand, for counsel without money is but a speculation'.[23] He recognized that Parliament's 'power of the purse', if pushed too far, could force the king to resort to non-parliamentary means of raising money, and this fear lay behind his celebrated warning to the Commons, earlier in that same speech, that 'this is the crisis of Parliaments: we shall know by this if Parliaments live or die'.[24]

Rudyerd's repeated calls for generous supply closely resembled Pembroke's own views, and their attitudes towards the duke of Buckingham were similarly aligned. Throughout, they remained at heart suspicious of the duke, but they were prepared to co-operate with him for tactical reasons, especially after 1623–4, when Buckingham became committed

---

[18] Ibid., pp. 57, 137.   [19] *CJ*, I, pp. 928, 930.   [20] *Commons Debates, 1621*, II, p. 445.
[21] *Proceedings in Parliament, 1625*, p. 219.   [22] Ibid., p. 274.
[23] *Proceedings in Parliament, 1628*, II, p. 59.   [24] Ibid., II, p. 58.

to an anti-Spanish foreign policy. This reconciliation was, however, only skin-deep; it was a member of the Pembroke 'interest', Dr Turner, who launched the attack on Buckingham in the 1626 parliament, and Rudyerd was among the sixteen members of the Commons appointed to assist the managers of the duke's impeachment.[25] A further attempt at reconciliation, in the form of a marriage agreement concluded in early August 1626 between Buckingham's daughter and Pembroke's nephew, appears to have had some effect,[26] and probably explains why both Rudyerd and Pembroke took a moderate line in the debates over the Petition of Right in 1628, and in particular opposed naming the duke in the Petition.

Rudyerd indicated his view of the Petition on 28 April 1628, when he told the Commons that 'if justice and wisdom may be stretched to desolation, let us thereby learn that moderation is the virtue of virtues and wisdom of wisdoms. Let it be our masterpiece so to carry the business that we may keep parliaments on foot; for as long as they be frequent there will be no irregular power, which though it cannot broken at once, yet in short time it will be made and moldered away.' Rudyerd was pleased to see 'that old decrepit law Magna Carta, which has been so long kept and lain bedridden . . . walk abroad again with new vigour and lustre'. Equally, he insisted that 'the King is a good man who is greater than any king who is not so', and he reminded members that 'the King has intimated that he would have the abuses of power reformed: a happiness to us.'[27] Pembroke's stance in the Lords, while supportive of the Petition in principle, was likewise conciliatory. On 9 May, he reportedly 'occurs [*sic*] with the petition. Moved to sweeten the manner, not to lay down the particulars so at large . . . As many of the particulars to stand as may stand. None to be omitted, but such as will distaste the King.'[28] Rudyerd spoke in very similar terms on 11 June in the Commons: 'We have daily experience of his Majesty's grace. I desire that we be so provident that we gratify his Majesty with a good turn so as we may have the benefit. The work we are about must have a future operation if his Majesty consider how dangerous the counsel is that has been offered him. If we name the person we may give a distaste to his Majesty.' According to another version of this speech, Rudyerd warned that 'if we give the King distaste, our counsel will not go down with him'.[29] Rudyerd's attitude towards the Petition – and even his specific language about the need to avoid causing Charles I 'distaste' – was thus strikingly close to that of his patron.

---

[25] *Proceedings in Parliament, 1626*, II, pp. 261–2, 268–9; III, pp. 140, 147.

[26] Roger Lockyer, *Buckingham: The Life and Political Career of George Villiers, First Duke of Buckingham, 1592–1628* (Harlow, 1981), p. 333.

[27] *Proceedings in Parliament, 1628*, III, pp. 128–9, 138.   [28] Ibid., V, p. 401.

[29] Ibid., IV, pp. 247, 260.

These political and religious associations remained very much in evidence during Charles's Personal Rule. The third earl of Pembroke died on 10 April 1630 and was succeeded by his younger brother Philip Herbert, earl of Montgomery. Rudyerd shared his new patron's interest in colonial enterprises, and on 4 December 1630 he became one of the original incorporators of the Providence Island Company. Here again we find him working regularly with Pym and Rich. Although this company was not the hotbed of Puritan opposition that has sometimes been claimed, many of its members shared Rudyerd's commitment to godly Protestantism.[30] One particular letter, written in 1633 on behalf of his brother to the governor of Providence Island, Philip Bell, is very useful in throwing further light on Rudyerd's religious attitudes. Rudyerd wrote,

[P]icking here a Verse, and there a Verse to be sung after the Sermon, wherein two Reverend Preachers were cited for Examples: this is a Course I never heard, or heard of, and I am sure that in London congregations it is not used, neither can it be conveniently performed, where the Clerk doth publicly direct what Psalm, or what part, or what parcel by itself, is to be sung; and although it be no ill nor unlawful thing, to sing the scattered collected pieces of a Psalm, yet certainly it is no discretion to be unnecessarily singular.[31]

This letter suggests that Rudyerd wanted a clear liturgical framework, and his defence of the established order of worship is consistent with his comments in January 1629 about the Book of Common Prayer.

Rudyerd's religious concerns again came to the fore when Parliament was recalled in 1640. In a major speech on 16 April,[32] he reportedly lamented that 'in so long a vacation between Parliaments many disorders must needs grow in upon us as deviation in religion, violation of laws, invasion upon liberties'. He argued that 'the best religion makes the best subjects' and declared,

Let us set up more and better lights to lighten their darkness, burning, shining lights, not lukewarm glow-worm lights; that the people in all places of the kingdom may be diligently taught, carefully instructed, in soundness of doctrine by God's example in their pastors . . . The best way to suppress all other religion is to uphold our own to the height.

---

[30] See especially Karen Ordahl Kupperman, *Providence Island, 1630–1641: The Other Puritan Colony* (Cambridge, 1993).

[31] Ibid., p. 232.

[32] The fullest surviving accounts of this speech are found in Esther S. Cope, ed., *Proceedings of the Short Parliament of 1640*, Camden Society, 4th series, 19 (1977), pp. 138–40, 248–51. The following quotations are taken from these texts unless otherwise stated. There is another, rather more abbreviated, version in Thomas Aston, *The Short Parliament (1640) Diary of Sir Thomas Aston*, ed. Judith D. Maltby, Camden Society, 4th series, 35 (1988), pp. 3–4.

This emphasis on improving the quality of the ministry was entirely consistent with Rudyerd's recorded words in the parliaments of the 1620s. His commitment to conciliation between crown and parliament, and to the granting of generous supply, remained equally striking. He reportedly warned the Commons that 'it is wisdom in us to preserve temper and moderation' lest 'we may turn the medicine into a worse disease and so undo all, even root out the race of parliaments for ever'. Parliament was 'the bed of reconciliation between a King and his people', and Rudyerd continued to regard the speedy and generous granting of supply as essential to achieving this: 'Before the ending of this Parliament, the untimely breaking whereof would be the breaking of us, I doubt not but His Majesty's revenues may be so settled, that he may live plentifully at home and abroad.' However, his warning to the Commons not to 'fall with too much vehemence on our own grievances, before we look on the king's occasions'[33] went largely unheeded, and Charles I, faced with a majority of members who refused to grant supply until their grievances were fully aired, dissolved the parliament after only three weeks.

III

When the Long Parliament met the following November, Rudyerd's rhetoric became rather more forceful, yet his two central concerns – religion and supply – remained the same. In a lengthy speech on 7 November 1640, he stressed the primacy of religious issues: 'let religion be our *primum quaerite*, for all things else are but *etcaeteras* to it'.[34] He bitterly denounced Laudian innovations and complained that they 'would evaporate and dispirit the power and vigour of religion, by drawing it out into some solemn, specious formalities – into obsolete, antiquate ceremonies, new furbished up.'[35] He felt that

they have so brought it to pass that under the name of Puritans, all our religion is branded . . . Whosoever squares his actions by any rule, either divine or human, he is a Puritan. Whoever would be governed by the King's laws, he is a Puritan. He that would not do whatsoever other men would have him do, he is a Puritan. Their great work, their masterpiece, now is, to make all those of the religion to be the suspected party of the kingdom.[36]

Rudyerd lamented the 'disturbance [that] hath been brought upon the Church for vain, petty trifles. How the whole Church, the whole kingdom,

---

[33] Aston, *Diary*, p. 4.
[34] *Five Speeches in the High and Honourable Court of Parliament, by Sir Beniamin Rudyerd* (1641), p. 8 (Wing, R 2184).
[35] Ibid., p. 9.   [36] Ibid., p. 10.

hath been troubled where to place "a metaphor" – an altar. We have seen ministers, their wives, children, and families undone, against all law – against conscience – against all bowels of compassion – about not dancing upon Sundays... These inventions are but sieves made on purpose to winnow the best men, and that's the devil's occupation.'[37] Rudyerd insisted that these religious issues should be the parliament's highest priority, and argued that

> if we secure our religion, we shall cut off and defeat many plots that are now on foot by them and others. Believe it, our religion hath been for a long time, and still is, the great design upon this kingdom. It is a known and practised principle, that they who would introduce another principle into the Church must first trouble and disorder the government of the state, that so they may work their ends in a confusion which now lies at the door.[38]

He was, he declared, 'zealous of a thorough reformation in a time that exacts, that extorts it'.[39]

Equally, Rudyerd remained sympathetic to the crown's financial problems. In this same speech he went on to call for the removal of what he termed the 'subverting, destructive counsels', who rang 'a doleful, deadly knell over the whole kingdom', and who had 'not suffered his Majesty to appear unto his people in his own native goodness' and had 'eclipsed him by their own interposition'.[40] Once these counsels had been removed, he argued, the king would be able to shine 'in his own splendour',[41] and Rudyerd hoped that the Houses would then grant generous supply. He continued to affirm the innate symbiosis between the monarch and his subjects: 'the King must always, according to his occasions, have use of his people's power, hearts, hands, purses. The people will always have need of the King's clemency, justice, protection; and this reciprocation is the strongest, the sweetest union.'[42] He hoped that 'as we shall be free in our advices, so shall we be the more free of our purses, that his Majesty may experimentally find the real difference of better counsels'.[43] Here again, we can see a direct continuity with Rudyerd's earlier speeches during the 1620s in his promotion of good relations between crown and parliament, his attack on evil advisers, and his advocacy of a generous grant of supply.

Rudyerd returned to this last point on 23 December 1640, when he asserted that 'the principal part of this business is money; and now we are about it, I shall be glad we may give so much as will not only serve the turn for the present, but likewise to provide that it comes not quick upon

---

[37] Ibid., pp. 8–9.   [38] Ibid., p. 11.   [39] Ibid., pp. 15–16.   [40] Ibid., pp. 12, 14.
[41] Ibid., p. 14.   [42] Ibid., pp. 14–15.   [43] Ibid., p. 15.

us again.' He declared that 'this is the business of all the businesses of the House – of all the businesses of the kingdom; if we stand hacking for a little money we may very shortly lose all we have'. Convinced that 'four subsidies will do the work, if they be given presently', he urged members to 'do this whilst we may'.[44] Rudyerd's speech appears to have had the desired effect, for the Commons resolved to grant two further subsidies in addition to the two on which they had already agreed.[45]

Rudyerd's religious and financial concerns, and the close connection between them, were further illustrated in a speech that he made the following month, probably on 21 January 1641.[46] He regarded the Scottish commissioners' demand for £514,000 as 'a portentous apparition which shows itself in a very dry time, when the King's revenue is totally exhausted, his debts excessively multiplied, the kingdom generally impoverished by grievous burdens and disordered courses'. He felt that it would lead to 'the utter draining of the people, unless England be *puteus inexhaustus* [an inexhaustible well], as the Popes were wont to call it'. Nevertheless, he would 'most willingly and heartily afford the Scots whatsoever is just, equitable, and honourable, even to a convenient, considerable, round sum of money towards their losses and expenses'. He regarded the Scots as 'being truly touched with religion, according to their profession', and hoped that such a settlement would 'contract a closer, firmer union between the two nations than any mere human policy could ever have effected, with inestimable benefits to both in advancing the truths of religion; in exalting the greatness of the King; in securing the peace of his kingdoms against all malicious, envious, ambitious opposites to religion, to the King, [and] to his kingdoms'. Rudyerd's sympathy for the Scots as a nation 'truly touched with religion' was thus consistent with his more general commitment to godly Protestantism.

That Rudyerd did not, however, want the Church of England to be reformed along Scottish lines became increasingly clear as Parliament found itself faced with demands for radical reform, such as the London 'root and branch' petition. When the Commons debated whether or not to commit this petition on 8 February 1641, Rudyerd argued that 'it now behoves us to restrain the bishops to the duties of their functions, as they may never more hanker after heterogeneous, extravagant employments', and he stressed the need 'to regulate them according to the usage of ancient churches in the best times, that, by a well-tempered government,

---

[44] Manning, *Memoirs of Sir Benjamin Rudyerd*, pp. 166–7.   [45] *CJ*, II, p. 57.
[46] Maija Jansson, ed., *Proceedings in the Opening Session of the Long Parliament*, 7 vols. (Rochester and Suffolk, 2000–7), II, pp. 239–40.

they may not have power hereafter to corrupt the Church, to undo the kingdom'.[47] He was not, however, in favour of the outright abolition of episcopacy, and declared that 'this superintendency of eminent men, bishops, over divers churches, is the most primitive, the most spreading, the most lasting government of the Church'. He warned the Commons, 'Whilst we are earnest to take away innovations, let us beware we bring not in the greatest innovation that ever was in England. I do very well know what very many do very fervently desire. But let us well bethink ourselves, whether a popular, democratical government of the Church (though fit for other places) will be either suitable or acceptable to a regal, monarchical government of the State.'[48] Rudyerd concluded by moving that

we may punish the present offenders, reduce and preserve the calling for better men hereafter. Let us remember, with fresh thankfulness to God, those glorious martyr-bishops, who were burnt for our religion in the times of popery, who by their learning, zeal, and constancy, upheld and conveyed it down to us. We have some good bishops still, who do preach every Lord's day, and are therefore worthy of double honour. They have suffered enough already in the disease; I shall be sorry we should make them suffer more in the remedy.[49]

Rudyerd's godly Protestantism and hatred of Laudianism were typical of many who became Parliamentarians in the Civil Wars; where he was somewhat less usual was in his continuing attachment to the institution of episcopacy and his mistrust of 'root and branch' reform.

Rudyerd returned to these issues in a major speech on 11 June 1641, when the Commons debated at length a bill for the abolition of episcopacy. This speech contained perhaps the fullest and most eloquent statement of Rudyerd's view of the church and the nature of church government. He began by stating that 'one thing doth exceedingly trouble me, it turns me quite round, it makes my whole reason vertiginous, which is, that so many do believe, against the wisdom of all ages, that now there can be no reformation without destruction, as if every sick body must be presently knocked on the head as past hope of cure'.[50] Conrad Russell wrote perceptively that this statement revealed 'the frustration which increasingly afflicted those who had been happy with Archbishop Abbot'.[51] This is a very telling point, because the debate over church government was rapidly moving into uncharted waters in which Rudyerd felt increasingly out of his depth. He was not, he affirmed, 'of their

---

[47] *Five Speeches*, p. 21. Cf. *Proceedings in the Opening Session of the Long Parliament*, II, p. 390.
[48] *Five Speeches*, p. 22.   [49] Ibid., p. 23.   [50] Ibid., pp. 24–5.
[51] Conrad Russell, *The Fall of the British Monarchies, 1637–1642* (Oxford, 1991), p. 345.

opinion who believe that there is an innate ill quality in episcopacy, like a specifical property, which is a refuge, not a reason'. He hoped that 'there is no original sin in episcopacy, and though there were, yet may the calling be as well reformed as the person regenerated'.[52] Rudyerd remained committed to episcopacy, albeit of a reduced kind: 'Let them be reduced according to the usage of ancient churches in the best times, so restrained that they may not be able hereafter to shame the calling.'[53] He warned that 'if we pull down bishoprics, and pull down cathedral churches, in a short time we must be forced to pull down colleges too'. This was, he felt, 'the next way to bring in barbarism, to make the clergy an unlearned, contemptible vocation, not to be desired but by the basest of the people; and then, where shall we find men able to convince an adversary?'[54] This brought Rudyerd back to his long-standing concern with the under-endowment of the clergy. 'It will', he declared, 'be a shameful reproach to so flourishing a kingdom as this, to have a poor, beggarly clergy. For my part, I think nothing too much, nothing too good for a good minister, a good clergyman . . . Burning and shining lights do well deserve to be set in good candlesticks.'[55] Rudyerd concluded by summing up his position thus: 'I am as much for reformation, for purging and maintaining religion, as any man whatsoever: but I profess, I am not for innovation, demolition, nor abolition.'[56]

What is perhaps most interesting about this speech is that from late summer 1641 such an attachment to a moderate, primitive episcopacy inclined some members of the Long Parliament to rally to the king.[57] Yet Rudyerd remained at Westminster, and his deep commitment to godly Protestantism and 'reformation' probably contributed strongly to this decision. Conrad Russell included Rudyerd straightforwardly on his list of 'members of the Commons in favour of further reformation'.[58] Rudyerd broadly shared this religious outlook with his patron the fourth earl of Pembroke, and the close political alignment between them continued to be apparent throughout 1641–2. Pembroke became progressively more estranged from the court during summer 1641, and on 3 May he promised the crowds at Westminster that he would 'move his Majesty that justice might be executed' against Strafford 'according to their requests'.[59] Charles I never forgave Pembroke for these words to the crowd and dismissed him as Lord Chamberlain of the King's Household

[52] *Five Speeches*, p. 25.   [53] Ibid., p. 25 [*recte* = p. 26].   [54] Ibid., pp. 28–9.
[55] Ibid., p. 29.   [56] Ibid., p. 29.
[57] Cf. John Morrill, *Revolt in the Provinces* (Harlow, 1999), p. 70.
[58] Conrad Russell, *The Causes of the English Civil War* (Oxford, 1990), p. 224.
[59] *A Perfect Journal of the Daily Proceedings and Transactions in that memorable Parliament, begun at Westminster, 3 November 1640* (1641), p. 90.

the following July.[60] During Strafford's trial, Rudyerd's main concern appears to have been that the Commons should act in close consultation with the Lords and follow the lead of the upper House as much as possible. Thus on 12 April 1641 he 'showed the great treason of the Earl of Strafford and yet said that one full third part of the evidence was not heard and that divers of the Lords who were present at the opening thereof were not satisfied that it was treason'.[61] Rudyerd went on to decline 'the reading of the bill to that effect', and moved 'for a conference with the Lords'.[62] Four days later Rudyerd warned the Commons, 'invert not the saying "slow to speak and swift to hear". Judges must first fully hear and then justly determine.'[63] In addition to his looking to the upper House for a political lead, these contributions to the debates over Strafford's fate also show a judiciousness that was highly characteristic of Rudyerd.

This quality was evident again the following November in the ambivalent view that Rudyerd took of the Grand Remonstrance. He accepted that it was 'requisite we should publish a declaration, because there are so many depravers of this Parliament',[64] such as 'papists, delinquents, and libertines [who] accuse us falsely'.[65] It was, he felt, important to make it clear that 'we have done great things in this Parliament. Things of the first magnitude.' These included 'something of religion', which he 'reckoned last because least done!'[66] Regarding the Grand Remonstrance, his vote went 'along in general with the narrative historical part of it; but for the prophetical part, to foresee the whole work of this Parliament to come, and to bind it up by anticipation and engagement of votes beforehand, for ought I know, Sir, we have no such custom'.[67] He could agree to 'the narrative part . . . , but not the prophetical part, lest we fail of our performance'.[68] He was thus 'for the narrative [but] against the prophetical part [because] to engage by way of anticipation this Parliament is new and wherein he cannot satisfy himself'.[69] Rudyerd was willing to endorse the Long Parliament's previous measures but not the

---

[60] TNA, SP 16/482/95 (Thomas Wiseman to Sir John Pennington, 29 July 1641).

[61] *Proceedings in the Opening Session of the Long Parliament*, III, pp. 512–13.

[62] Ibid., p. 517.

[63] H. Verney, ed., *Notes of Proceedings in the Long Parliament . . . by Sir Ralph Verney*, Camden Society, 1st series, 31 (1845), p. 49.

[64] Manning, *Memoirs of Sir Benjamin Rudyerd*, pp. 221–3.

[65] Verney, *Notes of Proceedings in the Long Parliament*, p. 122.

[66] Simonds D'Ewes, *The Journal of Sir Simonds D'Ewes from the First Recess of the Long Parliament to the Withdrawal of King Charles from London*, ed. Willson H. Coates (New Haven, 1942), p. 184.

[67] Manning, *Memoirs of Sir Benjamin Rudyerd*, pp. 221–3.

[68] Verney, *Notes of Proceedings in the Long Parliament*, p. 122.

[69] D'Ewes, *Journal*, p. 184.

demands for future reforms, and this important distinction may well have reflected a desire to avoid further inflaming relations between the king and Parliament. Certainly a wish to secure an accommodation between Charles and the Houses was entirely characteristic of Rudyerd, as was a feeling that religious reform had not yet been given as high a priority as it deserved. Both these attitudes continued to be evident in Rudyerd's speeches as England moved closer towards civil war.

The outbreak of rebellion in Ireland strengthened Rudyerd's instinctive anti-Catholicism, and when the Commons debated Irish affairs on 29 December 1641, he warned of 'the great danger this kingdom is in through the practices of priests and Jesuits, and all of the popish religion'. There were hazards, he argued, in 'not removing . . . those popish officers in this state that have places of great trust and strength committed to their fidelity', and he hoped 'that they may by degrees remove such dangerous officers, and place good Protestants in their room'. He also wished to see 'the bishops and such lords as favour[ed]' the retention of their votes in the upper House 'speedily brought to trial and by the sword of justice taken out of the way', so that they 'may be removed from the presence of his Majesty, by whom he is mis-counselled and his mind somewhat averted from complying so willingly with the Parliament as otherwise it is conceived he would be'. Rudyerd thought it 'of absolute necessity to remove such as are not inclined towards the Protestant religion', and he reminded the House of 'the treacherous stratagems that have been attempted against not only the persons of the princes of this kingdom that have been Protestants, by papists and the favourers of that part, but also against the whole state, to bring it to confusion and place themselves and their religion herein'.[70] In Rudyerd's mind, these defensive measures against Catholicism were closely associated with a continuing desire for further reform of the church, and on 26 March 1642 he moved 'to appoint a speedy day to consider of the matter of religion, to settle the distractions of the church for the present, and to provide for the future'.[71]

Following the king's withdrawal from London in January 1642, Rudyerd repeatedly tried to encourage reconciliation between Charles and Parliament. On 7 February he 'desired that we might move his Majesty to return and to give thanks'.[72] Interestingly, when, on 10 June, Rudyerd advanced £100 for Parliament's military preparations, he did so 'freely without interest for defence of king, kingdom, and parliament

---

[70] *Sir Beniamin Rudyerd his Learned Speech in Parliament on Wednesday, being the twenty ninth day of December 1641* (1641), pp. 2–4 (Wing, R 2186).

[71] Willson H. Coates, Anne Steele Young and Vernon F. Snow, eds., *The Private Journals of the Long Parliament*, 3 vols. (New Haven and London, 1982–92), II, p. 89.

[72] *Private Journals of the Long Parliament*, I, p. 297.

conjunctively'.[73] Such a form of words seems consistent with someone who, like Pembroke, tried vigorously to promote an accommodation between the crown and the two Houses. On 9 July 1642, for example, they can be found presenting the same message; that morning, Pembroke made a speech 'laying open the means for that happy union',[74] while later that day Rudyerd begged the Houses 'to compose and settle these threatening ruining distractions' and 'make a fair way for the King's return hither'. He praised the reforms of 1640–1 as a 'dream of happiness' and cited in particular the abolition of High Commission, Star Chamber and forest fines, the provision for triennial parliaments, and the fact that 'the bishops' votes' had been 'taken away'. He urged Parliament not to 'contend for such a hazardous, unsafe security as may endanger the loss of what we have already' and, in a memorable phrase, warned that the Houses 'cannot make a mathematical security'. He concluded by stating that 'we are at the very brink of confusion and combustion', and that 'every man here is bound in conscience to employ his uttermost endeavours to prevent the effusion of blood'.[75] Similarly, two weeks later, on 23 July, when the Commons was considering how to react to Charles I's *Answer to the XIX Propositions*, Rudyerd moved that they should 'embrace an accommodation of peace'.[76]

IV

Rudyerd's support for peace negotiations continued during the Civil War. For instance, on 17 February 1643, as the Commons debated Charles I's responses to the Oxford Propositions, Rudyerd warned the House that 'we have already tasted the bitter bloody fruits of war, [and] we are grown exceedingly behind-hand with our selves since we began it'. He implored members to consider

who shall be answerable for all the innocent blood which shall be spilt hereafter, if we do not endeavour a peace, by a speedy treaty? Certainly, God is as much to be trusted in a treaty as in a war: it is he that gives wisdom to treat as well as courage to fight, and success to both, as it pleases him. Blood is a crying sin, it pollutes a land: why should we defile this land any longer? . . . Let us stint blood as soon as we can. Let us agree with our adversaries in the way, by a present, short, wary treaty.[77]

---

[73] Ibid., III, p. 467.
[74] *A Perfect Diurnall of the Passages in Parliament, from 4 to 11 July 1642* (1642), p. 6.
[75] *A Worthy Speech spoken in the Honourable House of Commons, by Sir Benjamin Rudyerd, this present July, 1642* (1642), pp. 2–4 (Wing, R 2207).
[76] *Private Journals of the Long Parliament*, III, p. 120.
[77] *Sir Benjamin Rudyerd His Speech in the High Court of Parliament the 17 of February [1643], for a speedy Treaty of Peace with His Majestie* (1643), pp. 4–5 (Wing, R 2196).

Like other moderate Parliamentarians such as Sir Simonds D'Ewes, Bulstrode Whitelocke and John Selden, Rudyerd advocated peace talks with the Royalists at every possible opportunity.

Rudyerd likewise remained strongly committed to godly reformation, and on 12 June 1643 he and Pembroke were among those who were appointed lay members of the Westminster Assembly.[78] Rudyerd does not appear to have spoken often in the Assembly and such contributions as he did make suggest that his ecclesiastical position was complex and difficult to categorize in simple terms as either Presbyterian or Independent. He seems to have been nervous about the activities of the more radical Independents and on 14 November 1643, when some members of the Assembly expressed concern about 'the Independents gathering churches in the city and elsewhere', he 'promised to present [the matter] to the Houses' of Parliament.[79] This would seem consistent with the reservations he had expressed in connection with Providence Island in 1633. Rudyerd's first priority appears to have been reformation within an orderly framework, and this may have made him suspicious of the assertions of *ius divinum* that Presbyterians and Independents alike asserted against those who favoured a more Erastian approach.

This concern came through in Rudyerd's speech in the Assembly on 30 April 1646, when a delegation from the Commons presented a series of nine queries to the Assembly on the subject of church government. Rudyerd asserted that

> The matter you are now about, the *jus divinum*, is of a formidable and tremendous nature. It will be expected you should answer by clear, practical and express Scriptures, not by far-fetched arguments which are commonly told before you come to the matter . . . I have heard much spoken of the pattern in the mount so express . . . I could never find in the New Testament . . . The first rule is let all things be done decently and in order to edification. Decency and order are variable and therefore cannot be *iure divino*. Discipline is but the hedge.

Rudyerd continued by hoping that the Assembly would make its 'answer in plain terms'. He had

> heard it often very well said, the present Assembly are pious and learned men, but a Parliament is to make laws for all sorts of men. It hath been often objected, this power is so strongly opposed bec[ause] it makes a strict discipline . . . I believe we have done nothing against the word of God, neither do all the churches agree throughout. The civil magistrate is a church officer in every Christian

---

[78] *A&O*, I, p. 181.
[79] Cambridge University Library, MS Dd.XIV.21 (Journal of John Lightfoot), fo. 36r.

commonwealth. In Scotland, nobility and gentry live commonly in the country and so the clergy are moderated as by a scattered Parliament.[80]

These words seem to reflect sympathy with an Erastian approach to church government, and this possibility is reinforced by the fact that Pembroke, to whom Rudyerd continued to be close, apparently had leanings in the same direction. From 1643 Pembroke also served as a member of the Westminster Assembly and, as the 1640s progressed, his most consistent priority was an Erastian hostility to the more radical demands of both the high Presbyterians and the Independents. In early November 1644 he and the earl of Warwick went to the Westminster Assembly and 'chide[d] the Independents for retarding the work of reformation'.[81] He supported Laud's attainder in January 1645, but in March 1646 he voted to reject the high Presbyterian petition submitted by the City of London. Interestingly, Pembroke, like Rudyerd, remained sympathetic to the preservation of episcopacy, and evidence of the earl's moderate episcopalianism may be found in his choice of the future bishop of Winchester, George Morley, as his domestic chaplain, as well as in the nature of his ecclesiastical patronage within the parish of St Martin-in-the-Fields, of which he was a resident.[82]

The continuing friendship between Rudyerd and Pembroke was evident in other ways. Both were appointed commissioners for the plantations in the West Indies on 2 November 1643.[83] On 14 June 1645, in the Committee of Both Kingdoms, 'two letters were brought in by Sir Benjamin Rudyerd, one directed to himself and the other to the Earl of Pembroke'.[84] In his will, dated 1 May 1649, Pembroke stipulated that Rudyerd was to continue to occupy the premises in Kent that the earl had assigned to him by an indenture of 21 February 1639. At his death in January 1650, Pembroke owed Rudyerd a debt of £260, which was discharged shortly afterwards by the earl's executors.[85]

During the second half of the 1640s Rudyerd became less and less active in political affairs. He made fewer speeches in the Commons and

---

[80] Chad B. Van Dixhoorn, 'Reforming the Reformation: theological debate at the Westminster Assembly, 1643–1652', Ph.D. dissertation, University of Cambridge, 2005, VII, p. 546.

[81] Thomas Juxon, *The Journal of Thomas Juxon, 1644–1647*, ed. Keith Lindley and David Scott, Camden Society, 5th series, 13 (1999), p. 62. See also Van Dixhoorn, 'Reforming the Reformation', V, pp. 449–50.

[82] For a fuller discussion see my life of Pembroke in the *ODNB*.   [83] *A&O*, I, pp. 331–3.

[84] TNA, SP 21/8 (Committee of Both Kingdoms, fair day book), pp. 335–6.

[85] Sheffield Archives, Elmhirst MS (Pye deposit), EM 1358/1, EM 1358/2, EM 1360; Hatfield House, Accounts, 168/2, pp. 22, 28.

was appointed less regularly to committees. Early in 1646 he adopted a characteristically judicious position on the fate of the Court of Wards, of which he had been Surveyor since April 1618. He urged that 'if in any part of it there be any thing unfit, or exorbitant, it may be reduced and rectified by a better law; but if there be found corruption, extortion, or bribery in any of the officers, let them be prosecuted and punished to the utmost'. Rudyerd claimed that 'I have always endeavoured to perform my best service to the King, yet my tenderness hath been to the subject, because we do meet with many estates sore bruised and broken with debts and children.'[86] As usual he struck a balance between the interests of the crown and those of the subject, and was an inveterate foe of corruption and injustice. When the Court of Wards was abolished, the Commons granted him a sum of £6,000, together with the continuation of his existing annuity of £200, in compensation for his office.[87] Rudyerd's reduced activity during the later 1640s may partly have been a consequence of old age – he turned seventy-five in December 1647 – but it may also have owed something to growing disillusionment with the course of events and with the conduct of Parliament and the New Model Army. In his last recorded speech, on 5 August 1648, Rudyerd lamented that 'we have sat thus long, and are come to a fine pass; for the whole kingdom is now become Parliament all over. The army hath taught us a good while what to do; the city, country, and reformadoes, teach us what we should do; and all is, because we ourselves know not what to do. Some men are so violent and strong in their own conceits that they think all others dishonest who are not of their opinion.'[88] These words reflected Rudyerd's deep unhappiness at the turn that events had taken and his yearning for a settlement between crown and Parliament.

The following month, Pembroke was one of the Parliamentarian commissioners appointed to negotiate with the king at Newport, while back in London, on 5 December, Rudyerd voted that the talks should continue. The next day, he was among those arrested, and briefly imprisoned, by Colonel Pride.[89] However, Rudyerd was released later the same day, and David Underdown has commented that 'Rudyerd was too old and decrepit to be dangerous, and had powerful friends like his patron Pembroke.'[90] Immediately after his release Rudyerd, who was then just short of his seventy-sixth birthday, retired to his seat at West Woodhay in Berkshire. He lived out his remaining years there very quietly until his death on 31 May 1658, and he was buried in the chancel of the church at

[86] Manning, *Memoirs of Sir Benjamin Rudyerd*, pp. 241–2.   [87] *CJ*, V, p. 46.
[88] Manning, *Memoirs of Sir Benjamin Rudyerd*, p. 244.
[89] *Mercurius Elencticus*, no. 55 (5–12 December 1648), 527.
[90] David Underdown, *Pride's Purge* (1971), pp. 147–8.

West Woodhay. Rudyerd's will, which he composed earlier that month, survives, but reveals little that was individual about Rudyerd's religious beliefs. The opening form of words reads,

I do freely bequeath my soul unto Almighty God my creator and to his beloved son my Saviour Jesus Christ, by and through whose only death and passion I doe already trust to have remission of my sins and to enjoy everlasting life. My body I do commit to the earth from whence it came.[91]

It may be, however, that the absence of a dogmatic religious position in Rudyerd's will is in itself revealing of someone who apparently felt most at home within the broad church of Elizabeth and James. That church could accommodate Rudyerd's commitment to a well-endowed preaching ministry within an episcopalian framework that preserved order and decency while allowing freedom from antiquated formality.

A similar conclusion may perhaps be drawn from a hymn that Rudyerd composed in his later years:

> O God! My God! What shall I give
> To thee in thanks? I am and live
> In thee; and thou dost safe preserve
> My health, my fame, my goods, my rent:
> Thou makest me eat, while others starve,
> And sing, whilst others do lament.
> Such unto me thy blessings are
> As though I were thine only care.
> But, Oh! My God, thou art more kind.
> When I look inward on my mind,
> Thou fill'st my heart with humble joy,
> With patience meek, and fervent love
> (Which doth all other loves destroy),
> With faith which nothing can remove,
> And hope assured of Heaven's bliss:
> This is my state, my grace is this.[92]

It is possible that the closing reference to 'hope assured of Heaven's bliss' would tend to place Rudyerd at the more clearly Calvinist end of the Jacobean spectrum, and this would be entirely consistent with the picture of him that emerges from his parliamentary speeches.

V

Rudyerd's religious and political views, as they evolved during the course of his life, thus provide a fascinating case study of how a strongly

---

[91] TNA, PROB 11/284.   [92] Manning, *Memoirs of Sir Benjamin Rudyerd*, pp. 255–6.

Protestant layman reacted to the changing circumstances of early and mid-seventeenth-century England. Having been happy with the church led by Archbishop Abbot, and having advocated improving reforms within this Jacobean framework, Rudyerd felt much less at ease in the more polarized atmosphere of Charles I and the Laudians. He felt equally unhappy with the more radical Parliamentarian responses to Laudianism, and as both official policies and reactions to them moved further apart, Rudyerd, who disliked confrontations and always preferred persuasion to coercion, proved less able to cope and became a progressively more marginal figure. In that sense, he was, perhaps, a 'Jacobethan' whose long life meant that he saw events turn in directions that he regretted.

He believed in the English Reformation and praised the 'martyr-bishops' of the 1550s. He was deeply committed to further reformation of the church, and especially to improving the endowment of the clergy, but he did not want destruction or liberty to turn to licence. He sought orderly reformation, and believed that this could best be achieved by more generous funding of the Church of Elizabeth and James. Rudyerd abhorred the hijacking of that church by Laud and his allies; but he was equally suspicious of the more radical measures that Parliament adopted in response during the 1640s. He deprecated both the Laudians' actions and the Long Parliament's reactions. Instead, his heart really lay in the Church of Elizabeth and James, in which he had grown up and which he had sought to reform.

Politically, Rudyerd consistently sought harmony between crown and Parliament. He believed in the innate constitutional symbiosis of the two, and throughout his public career he strove to overcome differences between them. In practical terms this often led him to advocate reform of the royal finances accompanied by generous grants of supply as evidence of Parliament's trust in the monarch. The more that that trust became eroded, the more Rudyerd sought to restore it and to promote an accommodation between crown and Parliament. If his religious attitudes helped to make him a Parliamentarian, his political attitudes ensured that he always remained a moderate. This was a pattern that he shared with his patron, the earl of Pembroke, who appears to have been a further influence behind Rudyerd's Parliamentarian allegiance. Rudyerd's behaviour was thus the product of a complex blend of motives in which political, religious and personal considerations were fascinatingly intertwined.

These points bring us back, in conclusion, to the two problems with which this essay began, namely the role of religion as an influence on the choice of sides in the Civil War, and the nature of 'political psychology' in motivating behaviour. Like many of those who were committed to godly Protestantism and further reformation of the Church, Rudyerd became a Parliamentarian. His allegiance was thus consistent with, and directly reflected, his religious attitudes. These were not, however, his only motive, for other aspects of his behaviour owed much to his political and constitutional beliefs. In particular, his long-standing desire to preserve harmony between crown and Parliament was crucial in ensuring that he remained a moderate and tried constantly to achieve an accommodation between Charles and the Houses in the years immediately before and during the Civil Wars. Furthermore, his characteristic religious and political beliefs placed him in close accord with his patron, Pembroke. This brings us to the second problem, for it shows that 'political psychology' often involved a complex blend of motives which merged to form an integrated whole within which they were distinguishable but not separable. Rudyerd's religious, political and personal motives were analytically distinct but they cannot be fully understood in isolation from each other. This in turn suggests the fundamental – and psychologically plausible – conclusion that an individual with several reasons for doing something is even more likely to do it than someone with only one reason. In a case like Rudyerd's, to assert the primacy of any one consideration would be to risk distorting the complexity of the multiple motives that guided his behaviour. He saw the world in terms of an integrated vision that unified both political and religious elements, and the integrated quality of his ideas comes through strongly in the accounts in his own words quoted throughout this essay.

Rudyerd's tragedy was to live in a period when the harmonies that he wished to preserve – between crown and Parliament, and between the established Church and Protestant reform – steadily became incompatible with each other, and in the end events forced him to make choices between them. His search for gradual, orderly religious reform, within a framework of political and constitutional harmony, took place against a background where opinion was becoming ever more polarized and the nation ever more deeply divided, and as a result his quest ultimately turned out to be in vain. He nevertheless pursued it with a singular eloquence and integrity that make it still worthwhile to reconstruct the sounds of the 'silver trumpet' of the early seventeenth-century House of Commons. In the voice of that trumpet, we can hear the authentic anguish of a prominent 'Jacobethan' who, in his advancing years, had to experience the trauma of England's 'wars of religion'.

4   Rhetoric and reality: images of Parliament as Great Council

James S. Hart, Jr

I

The Long Parliament which convened in November 1640 has always been seen as being of central importance to the broader narrative of English history. Its notoriety derives, in the first instance, from the critical role it played in the onset – and subsequent conduct – of the English Civil War and Revolution. But it is also seen to be critically important to the history of the institution itself and to Parliament's evolving sense of its own role and responsibilities. The collapse of the king's government in 1640, the resulting (and immediate) need to fill the administrative vacuum and the eventual demands of governing in wartime all worked inevitably to bring about a fundamental transformation during the ensuing decade. Traditionally (and certainly through the parliaments of the 1620s) Parliament had been called primarily to do 'the king's business' and it did so in three clearly defined ways: by offering advice and counsel to the king's government on contemporary problems; by joining the king in passing legislation to correct those problems and any others which they or the king's ministers might have identified; and (rather less conspicuously) by enforcing the king's laws through the judicial process of impeachment or through appellate review in the House of Lords. Parliament's functions were advisory, legislative and judicial. They were not, and until 1640 were not presumed to be, either administrative or executive in nature. The crises engulfing all three kingdoms in 1640 and Charles I's seeming inability to navigate through them, rendered those traditional expectations effectively immaterial, and in part through default and in part by deliberate design, Parliament took responsibility for determining the direction of the king's government.[1] At least initially, they did so with wholly conservative intentions and through entirely conventional means. But political intransigence and the pressure of events

---

[1] For the most recent detailed narrative account of this process see John Adamson, *The Noble Revolt: The Overthrow of Charles I* (2007).

conspired against tradition, and ultimately required bolder initiatives and more radical arguments to support them.

The assumption of executive authority by the Long Parliament has obviously attracted considerable attention from historians over the years. We know that it was a crucial (if not necessarily decisive) issue for many members of parliament in choosing sides in the Civil War. But what did it actually mean for those who stayed? Despite the speed with which events took shape and the sometimes irrational fears which came into play, those responsible were clearly aware that they were 'crossing the line', that they were abandoning traditional restraints and breaking new constitutional ground. That was not something that came easily or that could be taken lightly. It required a serious rethinking about the purpose and identity of the institution itself and, more particularly, about the role and responsibilities of MPs. That process has not, I think, been taken as seriously as it deserves to be. Historians have tended to concentrate on the evolving Parliamentarian arguments which justified taking up arms against the king: the arguments from necessity, the doctrine of the king's two bodies, contract theory and the like. But those arguments were themselves predicated on a prior assumption about parliament's institutional status and about its right and obligation to assume sole responsibility for the welfare of the nation. It is really that which I think warrants more attention. On what was that assumption based and what impact did it have on the long-term course of events?

In the eyes of most MPs, the crisis in 1640 was, first and foremost, a by-product of Charles I's near-pathological reliance on private counsel. As it was later expressed in parliamentary declarations, the 'causes of our misery and danger' had been 'the managing and transacting of the great Affaires of the Realme in private and Cabinet Councels, by men unknown, not trusted by the Wisdome of the Law, nor well affected to the publique good of the Kingdome'.[2] They were determined, as a consequence, and conversely, to resurrect the primacy of public counsel and to reassert the historic responsibilities of the estates as guardians of the public welfare.[3] In order to do so, however, that claim had to be couched in the language and imagery of tradition; it had to speak to precedent and carry the weight and authority of history. Otherwise, it could too

---

[2] *The Declaration of Both Houses of Parliament to the King's Most Excellent Majestie, concerning the Queene, with the Evil Councell about them both; and the Vindication of the Fidelity of Both Houses to King and State* (1643).

[3] For an important and illuminating discussion of these ideas in a sixteenth-century context, see John Guy, 'The King's Council and political participation', in Alistair Fox and John Guy, eds., *Reassessing the Henrician Age: Humanism, Politics and Reform, 1500–1550* (1986), pp. 121–47.

easily be denounced as innovation and, fatally, condemned as rebellion. Consequently, reformist MPs in the Long Parliament carefully – and rather self-consciously – recast their proceedings and refashioned their rhetoric to recreate the new/old image of Parliament as the 'Great Council of the Realm'.

Michael Mendle has argued, in his important study of parliamentary ordinances, that Parliament's willingness effectively to legislate without the king in 1641 and 1642, up to and including the Militia Ordinance, was based almost entirely on that perception; on a belief that, as the Great Council, Parliament had a fundamental duty to remedy, by executive action, any defects of policy which the welfare and safety of the realm required.[4] It was this perception which allowed MPs to argue from a posture of self-defence, to claim a higher responsibility to save the nation from the machinations of evil advisers and, finally, to protect the office of the king from the person of Charles I. But, as Professor Mendle also suggests, there was little universal agreement about what the term 'Great Council' actually meant. The term was certainly not new in 1640. It had deep historical antecedents and, like so much English history in this period, it resonated in many directions, leaving it open to contest and reinterpretation.

That is what I want to explore here – the notion of Parliament as a Great Council. I want to see what the concept really meant to MPs in the 1640s and how seriously it was argued by those who took up the parliamentary cause. I want to see as well the extent to which the concept may have influenced parliamentary policy both prior to the war and during the protracted negotiations for peace which followed. I am going to attempt to approach the problem, as it were, from the inside out. That is, rather than depend on the opinion of contemporary political theorists in published tracts, I want to limit myself primarily to a study of Parliament's own rhetoric: the language of official declarations, position papers, proclamations and orders. I do not want to suggest for a moment that this is the only way to assess contemporary political opinion or constitutional theory. Clearly it is not; and admittedly there are important caveats which have to be entered with regard to these sources. The most important of these is the fact that many of them were the product of an intense and critically important propaganda war being waged between the respective camps. The published declarations may not always reflect the private thoughts of some members. The best that can be said is that they represent the consensus (or in some cases simply the majority) view

---

[4] Michael Mendle, 'The Great Council of Parliament and the first ordinances: the constitutional theory of the Civil War', *Journal of British Studies*, 31 (1992), 133–62.

of Parliamentarians at any given point. But that is, I think, an appropriate and useful guide to the political ethos at Westminster during this critical period.

II

There were at least two distinct (albeit overlapping) notions of the 'King's Great Council' at work in 1640. The first was essentially baronial in nature and paid tribute to the long and important history of aristocratic counsel. In its medieval context, the term itself initially referred to the series of special, non-parliamentary, non-legislative meetings of royal advisers, called by the crown at fairly regular intervals and for a variety of purposes during the Middle Ages.[5] In some cases, these meetings had been purely ceremonial, in others, the occasion for serious discussion of current political issues, approval of financial exactions or consideration of pending legal cases. But what distinguished these meetings (with rare exceptions) was the composition of the assembly itself. The attendees were almost exclusively great magnates of the realm, all of whom had, by birth, title and property, inherited the duty to advise the crown on matters of public policy and welfare. This was not yet an institution. It was instead 'a contrivance of government',[6] but the consistent resort to such meetings (eventually in, as well as out of, Parliament) over two centuries conferred on the participants permanent status as *Consiliarii nati*. That authority had in turn persuaded the baronage to assume direct responsibility for the government of the realm in moments of national crisis, as they had done famously in 1215, 1258 and 1311, in efforts to restrain the excesses of arbitrary government.

If meetings of such Great Councils had declined noticeably in the latter half of the sixteenth century – largely as a consequence of the growing institutional power of Parliament and, subsequently, the Privy Council – the appreciation of the aristocracy's historic responsibilities certainly had not.[7] Indeed, John Adamson has recently argued that consciousness of that tradition became the centrepiece of the baronial conspiracy which ultimately brought down the government of Charles I. The baronial effort to strong-arm the king into summoning Parliament in summer 1640 – the famous Petition of Twelve Peers – drew heavily on medieval

---

[5] For a concise discussion of the medieval Great Council and its relation to Parliament, see G. O. Sayles, *The King's Parliament of England* (1974), pp. 21–47. See also John Guy, *Tudor England* (1990), pp. 309–30, and P. J. Holmes, 'The Great Council in the reign of Henry VII', *English Historical Review*, 101 (1986), 840–62.

[6] Sayles, *King's Parliament*, p. 32.

[7] P. J. Holmes, 'The last Tudor Great Councils', *HJ*, 33 (1990), 1–22.

precedent and directly from the powers claimed and exercised by the Council of Barons in the Provisions of Oxford of 1258. Research on the matter appears to have been commissioned from Oliver St John and the results of his studies on the applicable legal authority to summon a parliament had been disseminated among leading dissident peers by the earls of Bedford and Warwick – and became the focus of their planning – in late summer 1640.[8] In fact, the historical parallels were all too obvious: the barons in 1258 had confronted a government in shambles: isolated, secretive and committed to misguided war policies abroad which had left it bankrupted by a king who was by turns uncommunicative, uncooperative and untrustworthy. But these noble conspirators could have (and may have) just as easily looked for precedent to the famous 'security clause' of Magna Carta (1215), which had empowered a baronial committee of twenty-five to authorize the use of force to compel the king to honour his commitment to good government.[9] Or they could have drawn from the example of the Lords Ordainers of 1310–11, who seized control of the government of Edward II in order to preserve and protect the institution of parliament and the concept of counsel.[10] Such baronial coercion in the face of royal misgovernment had become almost commonplace in the thirteenth and fourteenth centuries, and the men who laid claim to the status of Great Councillors in summer 1640 seem to have understood that history and followed the leads it provided.

Of course, Charles I understood the concept of Great Councils as well. At the suggestion of the earl of Manchester, his Privy Council had considered calling one into session during a discussion on war finance on 2 September, some days before the king had been confronted with the threats of the so-called Twelve Peers. Manchester's resort to historical example – although markedly different – was equally astute: he cited the role of 'Great Councils of Lords' who had assisted Edward III in raising money.[11] That recommendation was the one the king chose to follow, calling a Great Council into session in September 1640. However, his purpose was less to draw on the collective wisdom of the assembled peerage in order to extricate himself from crisis, and more to blunt the power

---

[8] Adamson, *Noble Revolt*, pp. 47–48, 56. For a discussion of the political context and the evolution of the Provisions of Oxford, see Sayles, *King's Parliament*, pp. 48–69.

[9] Carl Stephenson and F. G. Marcham, eds., *Sources of English Constitutional History*, vol. 1 (1972), p. 125 (clause 61).

[10] Ibid., pp. 193–8, the Ordinances of 1311. The influence of the Ordinances of 1311 on the subsequent Nineteen Propositions of 1642 is discussed by John Morrill, 'Charles I and Tyranny', in Morrill, *The Nature of the English Revolution* (Harlow, 1993), p. 299, and by John Adamson in 'The baronial context of the English Civil War', *Transactions of the Royal Historical Society*, 5th series 40 (1990), 93–120, at 97.

[11] S. R. Gardiner, *History of England, 1603–42*, 10 vols. (1883–4), IX, p. 200.

and influence of the rebel minority with what he assumed (mistakenly) was the greater weight of a loyalist majority.[12] His miscalculation and the failure of the Great Council to follow his lead (or provide him with political cover) necessitated the calling of the Long Parliament.

The meeting of the Long Parliament in November 1640 brought forward the second operative notion of the king's Great Council. This one drew its weight from medieval example as well, but, unlike the first, which emphasized the exclusively baronial nature of ancient councils – and the primacy of political leadership they seemed to confer on the aristocracy – the second made the term synonymous with Parliament itself, and with the combined authority of both Houses. This was the tradition which had, in a sense, evolved from the *Modus Tenendi Parliamentum*, the famous handbook on parliamentary procedure dating from the crisis years of Edward II (probably 1322).[13] The *Modus* had plainly been written as a legal treatise, not as a political manifesto, but, intentionally or otherwise, at least two of its clauses had significant, long-term, political implications.[14] In the first, clause XXIII ('Concerning Aids to the King'), the author had argued that the presence of the Commons, the 'community of the realm' – here specifically distinguished from bishops, earls and barons – was essential to the legitimacy of any parliament:

[If] the communities, clerical and lay are summoned to parliament, as by right they should, and for certain reasons are not willing to come, if, for example, they argue that the king does not govern them as he should, and mention particular matters in which he has not ruled correctly, then there would be no parliament at all . . .[15]

In the second, clause XVII ('Concerning Difficult Cases and Decisions'), he had insisted that the representatives of the Commons had a mandated role in the resolution of national conflicts, as 'when a dispute, doubt or difficult case arises of peace or of war, within or without the Kingdom'. When such conflicts 'between the King and some magnates or perhaps between the magnates themselves' could not be resolved by reference to 'a full parliament', a committee of twenty-five was to be appointed to recommend resolution, a committee on which the commonality – 'five knights of the shire, five citizens, and five burgesses' – had a majority.[16] What these provisions clearly suggest is that by 1322 the 'Great

---

[12] Adamson, *Noble Revolt*, pp. 76–82.

[13] For a thorough and comprehensive analysis of this text, see Nicholas Pronay and John Taylor, *Parliamentary Texts of the Middle Ages* (Oxford, 1980).

[14] Ibid., pp. 28–30. I am indebted here to the arguments made by John Guy, 'King's Council', pp. 123–4.

[15] Ibid., p. 90.   [16] Ibid., p. 87.

Council', at least in its public, institutional guise, had been transformed. The increasingly frequent invitations extended to the 'lower orders' to participate in Parliament over the preceding two reigns had ultimately turned a 'high court of the baronage' into a broader-based representative assembly and conferred on it ever wider responsibilities.

The influence of the *Modus* is well known. As the oldest, and, indeed, the only parliamentary handbook in existence, it achieved a wide circulation within and outside the legal profession and established over the subsequent centuries a foundation of parliamentary procedure which would be used (in a variety of ways) by clerks and commentators from Hooker to Lambarde, to Hakewill and to Elsyng.[17] But the work clearly had a polemical influence as well. 'The representative ideal' evolving from the *Modus* gradually established itself as the dominant political paradigm, at least in so far as it argued in favour of relying on counsel drawn from the widest possible range of voices.[18] The collective influence of the aristocracy, of those 'natural born' councillors, waned in the fifteenth and sixteenth centuries, in part because they gradually came to be seen (not without some reason) as too self-interested and self-serving to protect the broader interests of the commonwealth, and in part because the increasing Tudor reliance on legislation institutionalized consultation with the lower orders. The subsequent use (or misuse) of the *Modus Tenendi Parliamentum* in the seventeenth century to establish the pre-Norman 'antiquity' of Parliament (and the controversy that followed from it) should not obscure the enduring importance of the representational model it described.[19] Eventually, early modern England inherited a clear sense of ascending political power (just as surely as a notion of descending authority) and that inevitably gave shape to a broader, more inclusive definition of the king's Great Council.[20]

III

I do not want to suggest for a moment that these two notions either were hostile or were antithetical to one another. After all, those 'Great Councillors' who met in the summer of 1640 were determined to use their power for one particular end: the calling of a new parliament. They fully

---

[17] Ibid., pp. 51–5. Pronay and Taylor provide a detailed assessment of the influence of the *Modus* on subsequent generations.

[18] Guy, 'King's Council', p. 124. Professor Guy traces the evolution of this idea through the writings of Sir John Fortescue, Christopher St German and Thomas Starkey.

[19] For a discussion of the controversy see J. G. A. Pocock, *The Ancient Constitution and the Feudal Law*, 2nd edn (Cambridge, 1987).

[20] Guy, 'King's Council', p. 124.

appreciated that lasting reform could only be secured through legislation. But there remained an inherent tension between the two nonetheless, an unspoken tension, perhaps, between a Great Council *in* Parliament and the Great Council *of* Parliament; between those who had by tradition acted for the crown and who were, in the first instance, accountable to the king; and those who saw themselves (at least in 1640) as equally accountable to their constituents and who increasingly felt the need to act in the broader interests of the commonwealth.

During the first few months of the Long Parliament, it seems clear that the former concept prevailed, that is, the running remained with a largely aristocratic 'Great Council', with the lead taken by Bedford, Warwick, Saye and Essex, those so-called 'Junto lords' who had engineered the calling of the parliament in the first place. And it seems clear that they were willing initially to pursue a moderate, traditional path, one which (at least in theory) held the king blameless and placed the responsibility for misgovernment on his advisers. They therefore engineered the removal of errant officials – Strafford, Laud, Finch, Windebanke and an assortment of judges and bishops – through impeachment or the threat of same – and urged the king to replace them with the so-called bridge appointees. Charles appointed Bristol, Bedford, Essex, Hertford, Saye, Mandeville and Savile to the Privy Council in mid-February (and Oliver St John a fortnight earlier) but he did so with the greatest reluctance and without a genuine commitment to reform. The appointments were made, cynically, to win votes in the House of Lords for the earl of Strafford – whose trial for treason loomed ominously – and to hold out the 'expectation of future favour'.[21] Charles used the tactic carefully over the following months as well. Key appointments were made to crown offices, but rarely with the view towards the acquisition of wise counsel and almost always towards achieving short-term political advantage. The appointment of Essex to the office of Lord Chamberlain, for example, was designed in large part to engender jealousy and discord among the aristocratic critics of Charles's government.[22] That seems to have been true as well of Saye's appointment as Master of Wards (and as Treasury Commissioner) and may well have been of the earl of Leicester's as Lord Lieutenant of Ireland. Charles understood that taking a place at the king's table carried certain inherent risks for the appointee, not the least of which was the suspicion of disloyalty to the cause and the appearance (if not more) of self-serving careerism. The tension was inherent in the situation in any case and was certainly well understood by the likes of Essex and Saye, although perhaps with differing degrees of moral angst. Saye certainly developed a

---

[21] Gardiner, *History of England*, IX, pp. 292–3.   [22] Ibid., p. 409.

reputation for being susceptible to the lure of the 'sweet Refreshments of Court favours', and seems progressively to have undermined the trust of his fellow-travellers as a consequence.[23] In the case of the earl of Hertford, political favour engendered a wholesale political transformation. One of the original Twelve Peers, Hertford was made a privy councillor in February 1641 and subsequently appointed Governor to the Prince of Wales in August, and eventually abandoned his allies and transferred his loyalty to the king.[24] His story was exceptional, however. He was the only one of the original twelve signatories to change his political stripes. Indeed, the king's tactic of divide and conquer could only have worked if the Great Councillors were actually pursuing separate agendas. As long as they remained unified in their commitment to 'saving' Charles's government, such potential risks could be overcome – or at least finessed.

Even so, it became clear over spring and summer 1641 that Charles was not on board with their notions of constructive reform and, despite some appearances to the contrary, never had been. He shared neither the Great Council's perception of his misgovernment nor the resulting case for correction, and he had no intention of taking direction from people he imagined were his political 'enemies'.

The revelations of the Army Plot, in May 1641, exposed the ruse. Charles's betrayal indicated his true intentions and made a mockery of the traditionalist expectations that good government and constructive reform could be achieved through the careful guidance of reformist peers alone. More drastic measures were needed. If Charles I could not be trusted, his powers and authority would have to be forcibly restrained or directly assumed by others. Inevitably, as that realization sank in, a fissure opened up within the ranks of the Great Councillors: between traditionalists still willing to work with the king (either for reasons of personal advancement or genuine ideological commitment) and radicals determined instead to usurp his authority (presumably for the short term, during his alleged 'indisposition'). The division drove a wedge between former allies, leaving moderates such as the earls of Bristol, Hertford, Savile and Digby increasingly at odds with radicals such as Essex and Warwick and newfound allies such as Hamilton, Holland, Pembroke and Northumberland.[25]

Those committed to seizing the reins of government in late spring 1641 had necessarily to re-imagine and then recast their own role. It

[23] Arthur Wilson, *The History of Great Britain being the Life and Reign of King James the First* (1653), p. 162.

[24] David L. Smith, 'Seymour, William, first Marquess of Hertford and second Duke of Somerset (1587–1660)', *ODNB*.

[25] For a detailed and illuminating discussion of this process see Adamson, *Noble Revolt*, pp. 309–12.

was not enough simply to exercise executive authority; they had to be seen to be doing so legitimately and that meant broadening both the meaning and the composition of the king's Great Council. In practical terms it meant relying ever more heavily on their like-minded clients in the lower House. Defining and enforcing public policy was a process not dissimilar to making law, and if Parliament was to assume executive authority, realistically it could only do so – as it did all things legislative – as a co-operative, bicameral exercise. In essence, the king's Council *in* Parliament had to give way to the king's Council *of* Parliament.

The first sign of the new paradigm was probably the appearance of the famous Ten Propositions in June 1641. The proposals are too well known to be rehearsed here, but at their core were three key issues over which Parliament now sought to exert greater influence: the protection of the Protestant religion; the management of national defence and security; and the appointment of crown officers and counsellors. On the face of it, the propositions remained within the bounds of propriety, appearing only to request greater and more consistent parliamentary input in decision-making. But there were striking intrusions all the same, and the language made it clear where accountability now lay. The king's advisers were to be such as 'the parliament may have just cause to confide in'; Parliament was to be informed about the current personnel in charge of the kingdom's forts and ports – 'that those persons may be altered upon reason' – and about the current state of his majesty's navy; and even the queen's court was to be reconstituted with new and trusted noble advisers, at the king's urging and 'by advice of his parliament'.[26] That the authors imagined this as a more or less permanent state of affairs – at least during this king's reign – was clear; the 'Tenth Head' requested the appointment of 'A select committee of Lords to join with a proportionable Number of the House of Commons, from Time to Time, to confer about these particular Courses as shall be most effectual for the reducing of these Propositions to Effect for the Public Good'.[27]

It seems clear that their passage was the result of a fair degree of co-ordination between like-minded members of both Houses. Given the truly radical nature of the proposals, the ease with which they sailed through the House of Lords – with little debate and few amendments – is remarkable. Equally so was the speed with which their joint oversight committee was appointed. The Ten Propositions were presented to the Lords by Pym on 24 June and were approved only two days later. The

[26] *LJ*, IV, pp. 285–7.   [27] Ibid., p. 287.

requested committee had been appointed by the end of business that same day.[28]

For his part, Charles remained adamantly opposed to any such notions of shared responsibility over the appointment of his officers and advisers, and rejected outright any pretence that he had ever or would ever entertain 'ill counsellors'. In a rather pointed riposte, the king suggested to the Lords' messengers that his counsellors should be afforded as great a measure of free speech when advising him as were members of parliament.[29]

If nothing else, the Ten Propositions sharpened the battle lines. The king's impending departure for Scotland did as well, by throwing Parliament's own role into high relief. In late July, MPs proposed the appointment of a *Custos Regni*, an officer akin to the medieval Justiciar, whom they imagined would assume command of the military and exercise the king's legislative responsibilities in his absence. With their own candidate in mind (likely Northumberland)[30] MPs rather overstated his presumptive powers and consequently torpedoed the idea. It would, in any case, have been untenable to the king, and eventually proved to be so even to the moderate majority in the Lords. But having failed, some MPs moved instead to assert custodial authority for Parliament itself. One member, Harbottle Grimston the younger, actually claimed that 'the power of *Custos Regni* is in the Parliament'.[31] That assertion could only have come from a growing understanding of Parliament's collective responsibilities as the king's Great Council. William Strode's similar (and contemporaneous) assertion, that Parliament had the power to make ordinances 'as binding as an Act of Parliament', should be seen in the same light.[32] So, too, should the efforts made a day earlier, on 9 August, by Strode and fellow MPs in the Commons – Haselrig, Holles and Hotham – to nominate candidates to two of the most powerful offices of state: the earl of Salisbury as Lord Treasurer and the earl of Pembroke as Lord Steward.[33] Precisely how efforts were co-ordinated between the two Houses is not entirely clear, but there can be little doubt that co-ordination took place and that it reflected a sense of shared purpose. The men involved were consciously and deliberately infringing – or indeed, attempting to usurp altogether – powers and prerogatives which had always belonged to the

---

[28] Ibid., p. 290. The provisions regarding the queen's court were tabled, pending a review of their marriage contract. The committee of two dozen members included a large number of reforming lords, including Warwick, Essex, Saye, Paget and Brooke.

[29] *LJ*, IV, pp. 310–11.   [30] Adamson, *Noble Revolt*, pp. 339–40.

[31] BL, Harl. MS 5047, fo. 62. Cited in Conrad Russell, *The Fall of the British Monarchies, 1637–1642* (Oxford, 1991), p. 366.

[32] Ibid.

[33] Adamson, *Noble Revolt*, pp. 339–40. See also Russell, *Fall of the British Monarchies*, pp. 365–6, for another view of this episode.

crown. At this point, in all likelihood, the majority imagined that they were doing so on a temporary basis, in a custodial capacity, and with a clear view to the authority provided by historical precedent. But the claims themselves were striking all the same.

So long as the two Houses continued to work – and were seen to work – in harness, such pretensions could be convincing. Unfortunately, that could not always be guaranteed. Both houses could and did act independently. Indeed, the Lords had already done so in striking fashion in early May, when it moved unilaterally to seize military control of the critically important Tower of London.[34] The Commons then repaid the favour in September by attempting to force the Lords into sweeping religious reform with its famous ordinance against superstition and idolatry – its attempt to dismantle the Laudian innovations. Both episodes were highly contentious and in that latter case, deeply divisive. The appearance of unity was seriously compromised and was arguably preserved only by the September–October recess and by the overwhelming importance of subsequent events.

The news of the Irish Rebellion brought things back into focus. The dangers it posed allowed, or indeed required, the Great Council to assume the mantle of national leadership and declare its intent in the so-called Additional Instruction, addressed to the king in Scotland (via Parliament's Scottish commissioners) in early November. The Irish crisis had only highlighted for MPs the imminent dangers posed by 'evil counsel', and the Commons now insisted that responsibility for appointing those given 'places of Counsel and Authority' should now shift to Parliament, 'who are his [Majesty's] greatest and most faithful Council'. The challenge to the royal prerogative was striking (although clearly presaged by the Ten Propositions) and was therefore cushioned by a pledge of MPs that they would 'always continue with reverence and faithfulness to [the King's] person and his Crown, to perform those duties of service and obedience to which, by the laws of God and this Kingdom we are obliged'. Nonetheless, the king's failure to co-operate on this issue would, they claimed, 'force' them to take their own measures for the defence of Ireland 'in discharge of the trust which we owe to the State, and to those whom we represent'.[35] MPs were already deeply involved in planning an Irish campaign, so the implied usurpation of the king's prerogative on national defence was perhaps less notable than it seems. What was

[34] Adamson, *Noble Revolt*, pp. 286–7. Dr Adamson has rightly emphasized the significance of this episode because, as he suggests, it marks the first time the Lords had deployed military forces without reference to either the king or the lower house, and because the men involved were acting without the authority of public office.

[35] *LJ*, IV, p. 431.

remarkable, however, was the phraseology. The use of the word 'State' –
as opposed to 'Kingdom' – may have been inadvertent, but in this context
it seems unlikely. The authors – Pym and his Junto allies – seem to have
been making a deliberate point here (if perhaps only a semantic one) by
divorcing the king's person and the crown from the entity of the state,
and by contrasting the duty and obedience owed to the former with the
ostensibly greater obligations owed to the latter. In this passage at least,
the two are clearly not seen as one and the same. In addition, the notion
of accountability expressed here abandons any pretence that this Great
Council was acting as an advisory body to the king. The trust these MPs
were exercising was unequivocally that of their constituents.[36]

To a considerable extent, the Grand Remonstrance, drawn up later the
same month, reflects similar thinking, at least in so far as the document,
with its litany of self-serving complaints against the king, his government
and a 'malignant party' in the Lords, was unashamedly designed for
public consumption and, indeed, to win public support. Beyond that, it
is hard to claim that the Remonstrance reflects one consistent political
ideology. This was, after all, a long and complex presentation, composed under pressure of time and by a number of different hands, and
it should not be surprising that there is little uniformity in either tone or
terminology. All the same, in those sections which propose reform – and
particularly those which deal with the much-sought-after religious reformation – there are some rather striking assertions being made. Indeed,
early on, the king seems almost absent from the process of reformation
itself. 'What hope have we', the authors ask, 'but in God, when as the
only means of our subsistence and power of reformation is under him in
the parliament.'[37] The authors do acknowledge the king to be 'entrusted
with the ecclesiastical law as well as with the temporal, to regulate all the
members of the church of England', but they insist that he does so 'by
such rules of order and discipline as are established by Parliament which
is his *great council* in all affairs both in Church and State'.[38] Certainly
it is possible to read this as a perfectly conventional assertion that the
king is bound to govern his church according to the laws enacted by
Parliament. But in this particular context, the authors seem to be saying
something more. Certainly Charles would have argued strenuously with

---

[36] This is the position articulated much more fully by Henry Parker in 1642 in his essays
Some Few Observations and *Observations Upon Some of His Majesties Late Answers and
Expresses*. See Mendle, 'First ordinances', 159–60. See also Adamson, *Noble Revolt*,
p. 427.

[37] J. Rushworth, *Historical Collections*, 6 vols. (1703–8), IV, pp. 437–51, cited in J. P.
Kenyon, *The Stuart Constitution: Documents and Commentary*, 2nd edn (Cambridge,
1986), p. 216.

[38] Ibid., p. 215 (emphasis added).

the notion that Parliament was responsible for establishing the 'order and discipline' of the Church of England; that was the duty of the king and his bishops in convocation. However, as the Remonstrance had already made clear by this point, that had been the central problem and it was that that was now going to change. Moreover, the king's Great Council as presented here is emphatically not an advisory body. This is a council which makes policy (ostensibly through legislation) and which does so not so much with the king as for him. Certainly the language in the subsequent clauses of the Remonstrance suggests that the direction of policy with regard to religion would henceforth be the responsibility of the Commons. The clauses speak of 'our intentions', 'our purposes', 'our desires', and it was certainly no accident that the General Synod of the Church demanded by the Remonstrance was ultimately 'to represent the results of their consultations unto the Parliament, to be there allowed of and confirmed, and receive the stamp of authority, thereby to find passage and obedience throughout the Kingdom'. However much the king himself was symbolically encompassed within each parliament, his direct influence, legislative or otherwise, over matters ecclesiastical had disappeared from this equation altogether.

Of course, it needs to be kept in mind that neither the Additional Instruction nor the Grand Remonstrance had sufficient support to pass in the upper House and, indeed, only passed the Commons itself by the narrowest of margins. But it was those majorities that mattered and it was those members who would establish Parliament's corporate identity during the 1640s. Admittedly, one also has to be careful not to make too much of what are in fact isolated passages in only two parliamentary documents. But these are, undeniably, important declarations, and at the very least they suggest that the more radical members of both Houses had begun to fashion a new concept of parliamentary authority – as a Great Council – which would make it relatively easy and logical to assume responsibility for the nation's welfare without the king's legislative concurrence. The pivotal moment in this rather awkward transition was undoubtedly the Militia Ordinance of March 1642. In fact the decision to legislate without the king in the Militia Ordinance may have been less dramatic (or traumatic) for MPs than we have usually assumed, not (or not simply) because of the fact that Parliament had employed ordinances before, but because the underlying conceptual framework had already begun to take shape.[39] Certainly, the king's departure from London had heightened anxiety and raised genuine fears about his immediate intentions, and his recalcitrance in the face of Parliament's pleas accounted for some of the hardened attitude evinced by the leadership.

[39] Mendle, 'First ordinances', 156–8.

But Parliament's claims here were all of a piece with the positions already articulated. As they later explained, they had acted to secure the militia – had usurped the king's powers to appoint military personnel – because 'the advice of Evil and wicked counsels [was] receiving still more credit with [the king] than that of his great Councell of Parliament'. Given the very real threats from abroad, this represented a national emergency, and Parliament had been compelled to intervene because 'the Lords and Commons were intrusted with the Safety of the Kingdom'.[40]

Again, what seems striking here is the language. The deliberate attempt to draw a distinction between the king's private and public councils is notable. But so, too, is the seeming exclusion of the king from the responsibilities of national defence. Parliament – presumably encompassing the king – was not responsible, the Lords and Commons were.[41] Given the nature of political developments in May 1642 and the need to enlist public support, such distinctions were understandable, but they were dramatic all the same. In Parliament's declaration of 19 May, the argument is made explicitly:

> Let all the world judge whether we have not reason to insist upon it, that the strength of the Kingdom [the Militia] should rather be ordered according to the direction and advice of the Great Council of the land, equally entrusted by the king and the Kingdom, than that the safety of the King, Parliament, and Kingdom should be left to the devotion of a few unknown counsellors, many of them not entrusted at all by the King in a public way, not at all confided in by the Kingdom.[42]

While this declaration acknowledged that the responsibility for national defence was in 'his Majesty and in his Parliament together', it stressed that the prince was only one person and 'subject to accidents of nature and chance.' Therefore,

> The wisdom of this State hath entrusted the Houses of Parliament with a power to supply what shall be wanting on the part of the prince, as is evident by the constant custom and practice thereof in cases of nonage, natural disability and captivity. And the like reason doth and must hold for the exercise of the same power in such cases where the royal trust cannot be or is not discharged and the Kingdom runs an evident and immanent danger thereby.[43]

---

[40] Edward Husbands, *An Exact Collection* . . . (1643), p. 172.

[41] This appears to have been intentional. Similar wording was proposed when Parliament responded to the king's rejection of the Militia Ordinance in mid-March. Defending their right to define the law by ordinance, the Commons defined the 'Supreme Court of Judicature in the Kingdom' as 'the Lords and Commons in Parliament', thereby appearing to remove the king's presence in the assembly. The effort was challenged and the words 'Lords and Commons in' were removed. *LJ*, IV, p. 650.

[42] Husbands, *Exact Collection*, p. 206.   [43] Ibid., p. 208.

In a sense, this declaration represents an amalgamation of the two previous conceptions of a great council. It makes clear reference to medieval tradition and the baronial assumption (or usurpation) of royal authority in times of crisis and, at the same time, acknowledges that those responsibilities need to be shared with the representatives of the wider public. For at least one key leader, those public statements reflected private feelings. In an exchange of letters with Chief Justice Bankes on 19 May, the earl of Northumberland made clear what he thought was the central problem standing in the way of peace. 'We believe that those persons who are most powerful with the King do endeavor to bring Parlaments to such a condition that they should only be made instruments to execute the commands of the King, who were established for his greatest and most supreme council.'[44]

The themes are replayed time and again in the critical months before the outbreak of civil war. By the time of the Nineteen Propositions of 1 June, they had become almost axiomatic, perhaps not surprisingly, given Northumberland's central role in the ongoing negotiations. It was he who led the committee of the Lords appointed to draft the proposals, in co-operation with a committee of the Commons, in late May.[45] Accordingly, the subject took pride of place in just the second proposition. Parliament requested that the king refrain from transacting and concluding the 'great affairs of the Kingdom' with the advice of private men and of unknown or unsworn counsellors. Instead, all matters which 'concern the public and are proper for the High Court of Parliament, which is your Majesty's great and supreme council, may be debated, resolved, and transacted only in Parliament and not elsewhere'.[46] The use of the word 'supreme' here is clearly not accidental and was used to draw a not so subtle distinction between what were now seen as the respective authorities of Privy Council and Parliament. The former had now become the king's advisory body, the latter his executive one.

Less than a week later, on 6 June, the Houses issued another public defence. Among its many startling claims is a key passage relating to the institutional nature of Parliament itself. It is worth quoting here at length:

The High Court of Parliament is not only a court of judicature enabled by the laws to adjudge and determine the rights and liberties of the Kingdom . . . but it is likewise a council to provide for the necessities, prevent the imminent dangers, and preserve the public peace and safety of the Kingdom, and to declare the King's pleasure in those things that are requisite thereunto; and what they do therein hath the stamp of Royal authority, although his majesty, seduced by

---

[44] Russell, *Fall of the British Monarchies*, p. 514.   [45] *LJ*, V, pp. 85, 88, 90.
[46] Ibid., p. 98.

evil counsel, do in his own person oppose or interrupt the same; For the King's supreme and royal pleasure is exercised and declared in this high court of law and council, after a more eminent and obligatory manner than it can be by personal act or resolution of his own.[47]

In actual fact this was a response to the king's own proclamation on the Militia Ordinance (and therefore part of a crucially important propaganda campaign) and its tone is necessarily more aggressive and confrontational. Even so, the claims being made here are dramatic. Parliament – or, as they proceed to call themselves in this declaration, 'His Majesty's High and Great Council' – has now been entirely transformed into the governing body of the kingdom, directly responsible for providing the 'necessities' of public peace and safety, even as they are being opposed by the king himself. Their claim was justified on the by now standard grounds that the king had been 'seduced' by evil counsel, and as a consequence, royal authority now resided in his parliament, where the king's commands were, in any event, always more powerful and persuasive than when issued on their own.

Even allowing for the contextual caveats that need to be made here, these arguments suggest very clearly that Parliament was, by this stage, developing a revolutionary ideology of its own, or at least a sense of corporate identity which would allow the members remaining in London comfortably to assume the mantle of government and to justify doing so to the public.

It must be said, however, that the new ideology emerged with some difficulty and could only be maintained by continually overcoming the inescapable tensions it created between the two Houses. By June 1642, of course, those who had found part or all of Parliament's reform measures untenable had already parted company with their colleagues and abandoned Westminster: attendance rates in the House of Lords rarely rose much above a dozen members after May. But even those lords who remained were not always (or altogether) willing to embrace bold claims to executive authority for Parliament without qualification. After all, the Militia Ordinance itself had had to be forced through the upper House under enormous pressure – seventeen members registered their dissent[48] – and even then the membership had initially insisted that the king should at least be asked to give his assent.[49] The wording of the aforementioned defence of the Militia Ordinance – with its rather tortured attempts to lay claim to the expression of the royal will and to the exercise of royal authority – was in all probability a concession, not just to

---

[47] Ibid., pp. 112–13.   [48] *LJ*, IV, p. 627.
[49] For an illuminating discussion of this process, see Mendle, 'First ordinances', 153–4.

the demands of propaganda, but to the demands of the House of Lords. At this stage, it was a concession willingly made. It was absolutely crucial that unity (or the appearance of unity) between the Houses be strictly maintained. No concept of a Great Council could seriously be advanced without it. But an underlying tension existed all the same.

Where problems arose they usually did so when members of the upper House sensed that the Commons were moving outside what they saw as the Council's more limited mandate. Most of the Lords held to the principle that all (or certainly most) of the Council's executive responsibilities were temporary. The powers they assumed and the changes they engineered (those to the church apart) were not intended to be permanent. They were simply the expedients of war and would no longer be necessary once the king had come to his senses. The prevailing leadership in the Commons, however, did not always share that assumption. Indeed, the practical demands of war inevitably forced the lower House to adopt expedients which seemed directly to challenge royal authority itself, and which seemed, to some lords at least, to represent the prospect of permanent constitutional change. That led to difficulties. One could cite a number of examples, but an important episode here was the dispute between the Houses over the commissioning of a new Great Seal.[50] From late May 1642 the Great Seal of England had been in the king's possession and had been used (*inter alia*) to issue commissions of array and proclamations seizing the estates of Parliament's supporters. The Commons were anxious to counteract those proceedings, but were also determined to create their own icon. The Great Seal was the most powerful symbol of executive authority in the realm, and the Commons argued that it ought to 'attend the Commands of Parliament', presumably in order continually to remind the public where executive authority now lay.[51] Throughout spring and summer 1643 they pressed the Lords to join them in an ordinance authorizing the creation of a new seal. The Lords resisted. They twice rejected the Commons' proposal outright and recommended instead that the Houses proceed by conventional means: 'the Parliament, having in all of their resolutions and actions, gone upon the power of their Ordinances, their Lordships conceive that it will be proper to continue on that ground'.[52] This was not, for the Lords, a simple matter of propaganda and symbols. Creating a new seal (and declaring null and void all process under the king's seal) represented too decisive a break with the king and too unequivocally an attempt

---

[50] For a detailed discussion of this episode see J. S. Hart, *Justice upon Petition: The House of Lords and the Reformation of Justice 1621–1675* (1991), pp. 186–90.
[51] *LJ*, VI, p. 55.   [52] Ibid., p. 96.

to erect an alternative sovereign authority. This was not co-ordination, it was usurpation, and it clearly betrayed the fiction on which (in the eyes of most of the Lords) all of their actions had rested heretofore: the premise that they were acting as the *king's* Great Council, in exceptional, emergency circumstances, while the king was 'indisposed'.

The Lords held to that position until October 1643. Ominously, the Commons proceeded without them, ordering on their own authority that a seal be made in July, but they continued to press for their concurrence – the seal would presumably have carried little of its intended weight without the sanction of the upper House – and the Lords finally capitulated in November. They did so in part because the composition of their house had changed in the meantime, with the desertion of a number of key moderates, and in part because the collapse of the Oxford peace negotiations made the Commons demands for the seal more compelling. On the day they finally considered the Commons' demand, 1 November, there were only thirteen members in attendance, and that number was only increased by three when the final vote was taken on the 10th.[53]

But their capitulation marked an important turning point all the same. At least symbolically, the ties to the original notion of a *king's* Great Council were now largely broken. The medieval, baronial model had already disappeared, subsumed within the larger parliamentary Great Council, and now that body had taken on a corporate identity – and laid claim to a measure of executive authority – that was unrecognizable and without precedent. The king's fear that his enemies sought 'an alteration of government' seemed now to be justified, and their earlier claim to be 'saving' his government through conscientious reform could no longer be seriously sustained.[54] The seal's supporters had instead embraced an ideology which seemingly transferred the locus of political sovereignty.

Nor was this simply an expedient of war. It was evident as well in the programme for peace which followed, and most particularly in the Newcastle Propositions of 1646. The Propositions make it clear that the governing 'Great Council' was unwilling to relinquish much of the executive authority it had accumulated over the previous four years. Quite apart from the well-known demands made for the reformation of the church to parliamentary specifications, and for the control of English and Irish military forces for a twenty-year period, Parliament made two signal demands which suggest just how accustomed it had become to

---

[53] Ibid., pp. 87, 300–1. The committee appointed to consider the ordinance consisted of Northumberland, Salisbury, Lincoln, Denbigh, Stamford, Bolingbroke, Saye and Wharton.

[54] Russell, *Fall of the British Monarchies*, p. 514.

wielding final authority in the realm. First, and most importantly, it continued to insist on its ability to legislate without the king. The point is made not once but twice. The wording is the same in both cases and reads as follows:

And if that the Royal assent to such Bill or Bills shall not be given in the House of Peers within such time after the passing thereof by both Houses of Parliament as the said Houses shall judge fit and convenient, that then such Bill or Bills so passed . . . shall nevertheless after declaration of the said Lords and Commons made in that behalf, have the force and strength of an Act or Acts of Parliament, and shall be as valid to all intents and purposes as if the royal assent had been given thereunto.[55]

It is perhaps important to note that this passage referred to prospective bills needed by the Houses to raise taxes and pay for military forces *after* the expiration of the twenty-year limitation on the king's authority.

The other demand made by the Propositions involved the Great Seal. Parliament continued to insist that its seal, rather than the king's, was to remain the legitimate emblem of executive authority, and demanded as well that all acts, grants, commissions, writs and assorted proceedings authenticated by their seal be confirmed by Act of Parliament – with the king's assent – as legitimate and of full force and effect. Acts which had, alternatively, been confirmed by any other seal – that is, the king's – were to be declared null and void. Although the wording is not altogether clear, the Propositions seem to suggest in addition that the seal would remain for the foreseeable future in the hands of the parliamentary commissioners. Quite apart from anything else, these two provisions suggest that Lords and Commons had clearly decided that parliamentary sovereignty was to be as much a condition of the peace as of the war.

The king's summary rejection of the Newcastle Propositions as unworkable and 'destructive to his just regal power' was therefore understandable and entirely predictable. Their failure led to a collapse of parliamentary unity, and any sense of a shared corporate identity quickly gave way to the forces of party and faction.[56] Conflict within and between the two Houses seemed to make a mockery of claims that Parliament could serve either as an effective administrative body or, indeed, as an advisory one. The ensuing disarray, however, did little to diminish enthusiasm for the underlying premises which had given birth to the resurgent Great Council in the first place. The Heads of Proposals, offered to the king

---

[55] Ibid., pp. 295–6.

[56] For a detailed discussion of this process, see Mark Kishlansky, 'The emergence of adversary politics in the Long Parliament', *Journal of Modern History*, 49 (1977), 617–40.

the following July, while far more respectful of constitutional tradition and the royal prerogative, still contained striking claims to an intrusive administrative authority. Control of military forces was vested in Parliament for a shorter period (ten years), but the deployment of those forces remained thereafter dependent on the consent of both Houses. Likewise, Parliament relinquished the right to appoint to the great offices of state after ten years, but not the right to select the only potential nominees. The Heads would also have established permanent parliamentary committees to oversee these responsibilities during intervals between parliaments. Fittingly as well, perhaps, the king's Privy Council was to be replaced with a 'Council of State', appointed by the present participants, and given responsibility over both the militia and foreign relations.

Of course, the Heads were no more successful in 1647 in eliciting genuine co-operation from Charles I than were the more draconian Newcastle Propositions of 1646, and subsequent events in spring and summer 1648 irrevocably altered the terms of debate and the possibilities for negotiation. The second civil war had doomed to failure Parliament's attempts to preserve the traditions of the ancient constitution. Real power now lay with the army, and its suggested settlement, the Remonstrance of 1648, vested sovereignty instead in the freely elected representatives to 'a common and supreme Council or Parliament'. Tripartite government itself was under siege and when it disappeared in the Revolution of 1649, notions of accountability, of advice and consent, and of counsel, went with it. They would return only with the re-establishment of a supreme magistrate and with the end of the 'state of emergency' which had driven parliament to assume executive authority in the first place. By 1657 that had been accomplished, when Parliament willingly resumed its place as junior partner, and when the *Humble Petition and Advice* could inform the Lord Protector that Parliament was once again 'your great Council in whose affection and advice yourself and this people will be most safe and happy'.

IV

The relative ease and speed with which the second Protectorate Parliament abandoned any claim to executive authority and restored Parliament to its traditional role should not mislead us into believing that earlier claims during the crisis years were simply exercises in casuistry or rhetorical grandstanding. Most (if not quite all) of the presumptive members of the king's Great Council would have accepted that the powers they were exercising were temporary expedients, necessary only to preserve the fabric of the English church and state from the machinations of a dangerous and irresponsible monarch. But that did not diminish their underlying authority. Indeed, the alacrity with which these claims were made, in the first instance, and the consistency with which they were then applied to the changing circumstances of the 1640s are telling. The concept had a powerful resonance. Key members of the Long Parliament clearly believed that history had conferred on the king's Great Council (however variously imagined) the responsibility to assume sovereign authority, in emergencies, in the best interests of the king's subjects and in the broader interests of the state. Whether, in the event, the Council had actually or always exercised its authority convincingly, to best effect, or with equanimity and fairness was a matter of debate (indeed, it could hardly be otherwise, given the circumstances of civil war and revolution). But what mattered was that they had acted with proper intent – to preserve and protect a sacred public trust. That was critically important because it was a responsibility – inalienable and unavoidable – that they would be called on to exercise again another day.

5   Cathedrals and the British Revolution

Ian Atherton

I

The British Revolution began and ended in a cathedral. The first act of violence of the three kingdoms' civil wars was the famous riot in St Giles's cathedral, the High Kirk of Edinburgh, on 23 July 1637, in protest at the first reading of the Scottish Prayer Book.[1] The symbolic end of the Revolution came on Sunday 27 May 1660, the first church service that Charles II attended after his return to any of his kingdoms: in Canterbury cathedral (albeit 'very much dilapidated and out of repair') and using the Book of Common Prayer, episcopalian church and crown symbolically reunited.[2] For many others in the three kingdoms, the Revolution did not end so neatly; nonetheless, across all three kingdoms, from Winchester to Dublin to Aberdeen, the restoration of monarchy and church was marked and celebrated in cathedrals or their sister institutions, collegiate churches, or by the remnants of cathedral choirs. The resumption of choral services and episcopal ceremony in a cathedral was an important marker of the restoration of monarchy.[3]

Cathedrals framed the British Revolution because there had been considerable unease as to their purpose, even their existence, since the Reformations of the mid-sixteenth century. Cathedral and collegiate churches, with their choirs of priests, laymen and boys, had been established for the ceaseless round of Catholic devotion; what role could they have in a Protestant church where the Word of God was supreme? There were long-standing English Puritan condemnations of cathedrals as dens of

---

[1] Many contemporaries began their accounts with the 1637 broyle, including *All the Memorable & Wonder-Strikinge, Parlamentary Mercies* (1642) and R. Baillie, *Letters and Journals*, ed. D. Laing, 3 vols. (Edinburgh, 1842), I, p. 295. The research and writing of this chapter were assisted by grants from the Arts and Humanities Research Council and the British Academy.

[2] Clarendon, VI, p. 233.

[3] *Mercurius Publicus*, no. 21, 17–24 May 1660, and no. 28, 5 July 1660; Bodl., MS Ashmole 1521B(iv), p. 161, MSS Carte 45, ff. 55–6, 61–2, Carte 221, f. 156r; D. Loftus, *The Proceedings Observed* (1661); *CSPD, 1661–2*, p. 171.

non-preaching, pluralist, fat canons who thought only of their own bellies and nothing for spreading the gospel, as well as alarm that cathedrals were the natural home of superstition and crypto-Catholic ceremonialism.[4] Protestant Ireland saw less debate about its cathedrals, but during Elizabeth's reign there were three separate campaigns to convert St Patrick's, one of Dublin's two cathedrals, into a 'more useful' institution, a university for Ireland,[5] while doubts about the role of cathedrals probably lay behind the foot-dragging over the rebuilding of Derry cathedral in the early seventeenth century.[6] In Scotland, the fate of cathedrals had been close to the heart of the problems from which the Civil Wars arose. The two Presbyterian Books of Discipline (1560 and 1578) had demanded the abolition of cathedrals, but the restoration of bishops in Scotland by James VI and I had brought first a return of cathedrals and chapters and then, in 1633, a new cathedral to Scotland in the form of the elevation of St Giles in Edinburgh to cathedral status. That creation had raised fears of creeping English and popish influence.[7] Scottish cathedrals did not survive the revolution of 1637–8: bishops were abolished and the Glasgow Assembly endorsed the view of the 1596 Edinburgh Assembly that 'all titles of dignitie, savouring more of Poperie than of Christian libertie, as chapters . . . deans . . . chanters, sub-chanters, and others having the like title, flowing from the Pope and Canon law only . . . bee also banished out of this Reformed Kirk, and not to bee usurped or used hereafter under ecclesiasticall censure'.[8]

As the case of Scotland shows, the fate of cathedrals was closely (but not, as we shall see, altogether inseparably) linked to that of episcopacy in the Revolution. It has been a key part of John Morrill's work to show how religious divisions, over the form of the church and the nature of its government, deepened the crisis of 1640–1 in England and made the

---

[4] C. Cross, '"Dens of Loitering Lubbers": Protestant protest against cathedral foundations, 1540–1640', in D. Baker, ed., *Schism, Heresy and Religious Protest*, Ecclesiastical History Society, Studies in Church History, 9 (1972), pp. 232–7.

[5] J. Murray, 'St Patrick's cathedral and the university question in Ireland *c.* 1547–1585', in H. Robinson-Hammerstein, ed., *European Universities in the Age of Reformation and Counter-Reformation* (Dublin, 1998), pp. 1–33.

[6] D. A. Chart, ed., *Londonderry and the London Companies* (Belfast, 1928), pp. 54, 75, 109.

[7] *The First and Second Booke of Discipline* ([Amsterdam], 1621), pp. 26, 85; Robert Keith, *An Historical Catalogue of the Scottish Bishops, Down to the Year 1688* (Edinburgh, 1824), pp. 44–60; National Library of Scotland, Wodrow MSS Quarto IX, ff. 408r, 346r and Quarto CVI, ff. 111v–12r; J. Row, *The History of the Kirk in Scotland*, ed. D. Laing (Wodrow Society, Edinburgh, 1842), pp. 369–70; *The Charge of the Scottish Commissioners against Canterburie* (Wing S1001AD, 1641), p. 3.

[8] T. Pitcairn, ed., *Acts of the General Assembly of the Church of Scotland 1638–1842* (Edinburgh, 1843), pp. 1–35.

outbreak of war possible.[9] That, and work by others, has concentrated on divisions over episcopacy,[10] leaving debates about the role and continuance of cathedrals relatively unexplored;[11] and yet an examination of the cathedral question can help to expand and refine issues relating to the religious context of the Civil Wars. It can also help to re-evaluate arguments about the creation of Anglicanism in the 1640s and 1650s.

II

While Scottish cathedrals were summarily dismissed in 1638, those in England and Ireland suffered a much more lingering death, enduring a half-life through most of the 1640s. Censorship during the Personal Rule had ensured that public criticism of English cathedrals had been restricted to the circles of aspiring martyrs, such as the Puritans William Prynne and Henry Burton, who had both committed to print trenchant attacks on cathedrals, or the prophetess Lady Eleanor Davies, who had in 1636 defaced with tar the hangings and the bishop's seat in Lichfield cathedral.[12] With the opening of the Long Parliament, however, not only Scottish example and encouragement, but also a century of reformed doubts capped by the recent experience of Laudianism, meant that cathedrals seemed to many to be an easy and necessary target. The flood of petitions in the opening weeks of the Parliament included attacks on individual cathedrals and chapter members for Laudianism;[13] after the London Root and Branch petition of December 1640 called for the abolition of 'archbishops and lord bishops, deans and archdeacons, etc.', individual cases were swept up into a growing sense that cathedrals were part of a popish conspiracy.[14] While the issue of deans and chapters was

[9] Particularly 'The religious context of the English Civil War' and 'The attack on the Church of England in the Long Parliament, 1640–1642', reprinted in J. Morrill, *The Nature of the English Revolution* (Harlow, 1993), pp. 45–90.

[10] A. Fletcher, *The Outbreak of the English Civil War* (1981), and W. M. Abbott, 'The issue of episcopacy in the Long Parliament, 1640–1648: the reasons for abolition', D.Phil. dissertation, Oxford University, 1982.

[11] S. Lehmberg, *Cathedrals under Siege: Cathedrals in English Society, 1600–1700* (Exeter, 1996), for example, does not consider those debates.

[12] W. Prynne, *A Quench-Coale* ([Amsterdam], 1637), pp. 161, 196–9; H. Burton, *For God, and the King* ([Amsterdam], 1636), pp. 160–3; R. F. Williams, ed., *The Court and Times of Charles the First*, 2 vols. (1848), II, p. 259; E. Davies, *Bethlehem Signifying the House of Bread* (London?, 1652), pp. 2–5.

[13] M. Jansson, ed., *Proceedings in the Opening Session of the Long Parliament*, 7 vols. (Rochester, NY, and Woodbridge, 2000–7), I, pp. 79–80, 224, 226–7, 232–4, 236–7, 351, 359, 371; II, pp. 182, 184, 245–8, 623, 628–9, 645, 649–50, 707–8.

[14] Jansson, *Proceedings*, I, pp. 157, 261, 289–90, 571–5; II, pp. 122, 124–5, 188–9, 415, 506. For the argument that Parliamentary managers such as Pym sought to link individual complaints into a grand conspiracy, see Morrill, *Nature*, pp. 80–1.

often thereafter subsumed into the wider question of church government, discussion of cathedrals did form an important and often distinct strand of that debate for a number of reasons.

First, the wealth of cathedrals attracted calls for their abolition. Their riches had been a tempting target since the later Middle Ages,[15] and between the 1530s and 1620s every English foreign war had brought forth calls for their despoliation.[16] Against a background of calls for ecclesiastical reform in the 1640s, cathedrals seemed ripe for plucking, especially in the midst of the financial crisis caused by the need to pay the Scots (in the first half of 1641) or the New Model Army (in the later 1640s).[17] By spring 1641 the downfall of deans and chapters was confidently predicted: 'Adiue good Organ pipe' noted one newswriter.[18]

The idea that the crown should asset strip the cathedrals, however, faced three significant problems, two of them almost insuperable. The least of the hurdles was the hostility of capitular tenants, since the scheme envisaged increased rents and entry fines.[19] A second and more serious problem was Charles's own opposition to the idea: he had told his Privy Council on 24 January 1640/1 that he 'would rather starve than have any of the church lands or livings', and he repeated the promise to Oxford University in April.[20] Third, and most problematic of all, even many opponents of cathedrals shared Charles's sense that it was sacrilege to employ any of their revenues for anything but spiritual ends. As one surprised MP put it during a Commons debate about cathedrals, 'both sides agree that it is sacrilege to take those lands away'.[21]

---

[15] M. Day and R. Steeloe, eds., *Mum and the Sothsegger*, Early English Text Society, os, 199 (1936 for 1934), ll. 553–59, pp. 43–4; W. Tyndale, *The Obedie[n]ce of a Christen Man* ([Antwerp], 1528), f. lxxvi^r; A. Peel, ed., *The Seconde Parte of a Register*, 2 vols. (Cambridge, 1915), I, p. 178; II, pp. 12, 44, 211; Burton, *For God*, p. 160.

[16] L. Stone, 'The political programme of Thomas Cromwell', *Bulletin of the Institute of Historical Research*, 24 (1951), 1–18, at 7, 9–10; BL, Cotton MS Galba B xix, f. 19r, Add. MS 48066, ff. 10v, 14; Lambeth Palace Library, MS 2016, ff. 25–34; J. Hacket, *Scrinia Reserata* (1693), pp. 203–6.

[17] For the connection between abolition and revenue pressures see Jansson, *Proceedings*, II, pp. 674–5; C. Russell, *The Fall of the British Monarchies 1637–1642* (Oxford, 1991), pp. 236–43; Woburn Abbey, Bedford Estate Archives, 'Notes on a scheme to obtain £420,000 for the Crown out of the lands of the clergy' (I am grateful to the archivist, Mrs Ann Mitchell, for assistance in locating this document). See Jansson, *Proceedings*, IV, pp. 320, 326, for a very similar scheme discussed in the Commons on 11 May 1641.

[18] G. L. Owens, ed., 'Two unpublished letters of Thomas Knyvett of Ashwellthorpe, 1641–1642', *Norfolk Archaeology*, 35 (1973), 428–32, at 429. See also Baillie, *Letters and Journals*, I, pp. 298–9.

[19] Russell, *Fall*, pp. 254–5; TNA, SP16/470/112, SP16/482/96; Jansson, *Proceedings*, IV, p. 334.

[20] Russell, *Fall*, p. 245; A. Wood, *The History and Antiquities of the University of Oxford*, 2 vols. (Oxford, 1792–6), II, pp. 431–2.

[21] Jansson, *Proceedings*, IV, pp. 339, 341–2, 345, 349.

There were also tactical reasons why the future of cathedrals remained on the political and religious agenda in 1640–1. As the abolition of episcopacy met considerable opposition in 1641, the abolition of cathedrals looked like an easy first step for root and branchers, a means of kicking off church reform, as well as a way to mollify the Scots, who watched English delays over abolition impatiently.[22]

Conversely, some defenders of episcopacy may have hoped that deans and chapters might be a sufficient sacrifice to buy off enough Puritan antipathy to bishops to save the established church. Support for the Church of England did not have to mean defending every last jot and tittle of episcopacy.[23] Alongside such an approach was the willingness of some city corporations in 1640–1 to exploit the climate of antipathy and opposition to cathedrals not to abolish them, but to tame and humble deans and chapters both as revenge for judgments in the 1630s which had seen chapters lord it over boroughs, and as a means of ensuring that cathedrals danced more to the city's tune.[24] The final explanation for the position of cathedrals at the forefront of debate in 1641 was their role in plans for reduced or primitive episcopacy. One answer to a common diagnosis of the problems of the 1630s church – the sole authority of bishops – was to revive the role of deans and chapters as the bishop's council to make them, as Sir Benjamin Rudyerd put it, 'assessors with the Bishops . . . in actions of moment, in causes of importance'. That, argued Prebendary John Hacket, was 'the native, the proper, the sure way' to reduce episcopacy to its common form. A number of ideas circulated in 1641 for primitive cathedrals, made both centres of preaching and 'Colledges of Bishops', as a part of wider schemes for primitive episcopacy.[25]

Several commentators have placed great emphasis on the schemes for reducing episcopacy, and on Bishop John Williams's subcommittee of the House of Lords' committee for religion, established in March 1640/1, which was a key forum for devising such plans. Thomas Fuller thought

---

[22] It was widely assumed that cathedrals had few friends and the case for abolition required no argument: Jansson, *Proceedings*, II, pp. 677–8.

[23] *CSPD, 1640–41*, pp. 484–5; A. Milton, 'Anglicanism and Royalism in the 1640s', in J. Adamson, ed., *The English Civil War: Conflict and Contexts, 1640–49* (Basingstoke, 2009), p. 73.

[24] See the dispute in Worcester: Jansson, *Proceedings*, II, p. 459; Worcester Cathedral Library, D312, D143, and A75, ff. 148–50; S. Bond, ed., *The Chamber Order Book of Worcester 1602–1650*, Worcestershire Historical Society, ns, 8 (1974), pp. 342–4, 349.

[25] B. Rudyerd, *Sir Beniamin Rudyerds Speech; Concerning Bishops Deans and Chapters* (1641), sig. A3r; *To the Right Honorable the Lords and Commons assembled in Parlament. The Humble Petition of divers of the Clergie* (1641), pp. 4–5; J. Hacket, *A Century of Sermons*, ed. T. Plume (1675), p. xxi; BL, Stowe MS 184, f. 29r.

that the subcommittee was the last chance to build a consensus that might have prevented war in England.[26] John Adamson has suggested that modified episcopacy (rather than root and branch reform) represented the true wishes of the leading lords and MPs who sought to strip the king of effective power; while Conrad Russell suggested that the deliberations of Williams's subcommittee mark both the collapse of the Bedford–Pym projected settlement and the 'centrepiece' of the king's new policy to raise his own party based around defence of the episcopal Church of England.[27] The reason for the collapse of such schemes in summer 1641 thus becomes a key question, but one which historians have struggled to answer: Samuel Gardiner, for example, was mystified by their failure.[28]

Most explanations blame external causes for the failure of reduced episcopacy to carry the day, seeing them as the moderate middle ground eroded by a polarized debate or, like Alan Ford, condemning the king's 'stubbournness [sic] and political ineptitude' in refusing to occupy the middle ground.[29] What historians have failed to recognize are the internal divisions over the nature of any modified episcopalian system, divisions that focused on what role, if any, deans and chapters should play. Much of the deliberations of Williams's subcommittee in fact concerned cathedrals, in an attempt to build a consensus over deans and chapters before moving to the more divisive question of bishops. The two tracts associated with that subcommittee both made proposals for the reform of cathedrals, calling for changes in music and singing, for cathedrals to be made preaching centres and for reorganization to strengthen links between cathedral and diocese, and between bishop and chapter, as a way of meeting criticisms of the sole authority of bishops.[30] Cathedrals, then, were at the heart of the debate.

Some plans saw a dean and chapter as the bishop's council, and put cathedrals at the heart of preaching and teaching,[31] but a number of plans for primitive episcopacy had no place for cathedrals,[32] drawing

---

[26] T. Fuller, *The Church-History of Britain* (1655), book 11, p. 175.

[27] Russell, *Fall*, pp. 268–71; J. Adamson, *The Noble Revolt: The Overthrow of Charles I* (2009), pp. 168, 174–5, 322.

[28] S. R. Gardiner, *The History of England from the Accession of James I to the Outbreak of the Civil War, 1603–1642*, 10 vols. (1884), IX, p. 387.

[29] A. Ford, *James Ussher: Theology, History and Politics in Early-Modern Ireland and England* (Oxford, 2007), pp. 235–56; Fletcher, *Outbreak*, p. 122; Russell, *Fall*, p. 250; Adamson, *Noble Revolt*, pp. 328–9; Milton, 'Anglicanism and Royalism', pp. 73–4.

[30] *A Copy of the Proceedings of Some Worthy and Learned Divines* (1641); *Humble Petition of Divers of the Clergie*. For evidence linking the tracts to Williams's subcommittee, see TNA, SP16/472/72; Jansson, *Proceedings*, IV, p. 336; Russell, *Fall*, pp. 251, 271.

[31] E.g. H. Thorndike, *Of the Government of the Churches* ([Cambridge], 1641), pp. 205–8.

[32] E.g. H. Grimston, *Master Grimstons Argvment concerning Bishops* (1641).

instead on a tradition of plans to modify episcopal government through the increased role of parochial clergy that stretched back to the middle of the sixteenth century.[33] The most famous of all these schemes, that of Archbishop James Ussher, made no mention of deans and chapters, envisaging an episcopal church where a diocesan synod functioned as the co-adjutor of the bishop.[34] By contrast, Williams's own scheme, set out in a bill in July 1641, put cathedrals at the centre of a reformed church: deans and chapters were envisaged as the bishop's council, while cathedrals would be made both preaching centres and a means of augmenting poor livings.[35] Adamson's assumption that there were 'Ussher–Williams proposals for "primitive episcopacy"' and that an 'impressively broad consensus' for a reformed episcopate emerged out of Williams's subcommittee ignores these crippling differences over cathedrals.[36] Moreover, it seems likely that the reason why Ussher's scheme, widely discussed in 1641, was not published until after his death, a fact which has often puzzled historians, lies not in the primate's fear of religious radicalism (as William Abbott has argued) but because the failure to find agreement over so simple a matter as cathedrals ensured that the plan was stillborn.[37]

The divisions over cathedrals even within Williams's subcommittee were made public when the Commons debated deans and chapters on 12 May 1641. That day MPs heard what was in effect a public meeting of Williams's subcommittee before falling to their own debate, listening to divines from the subcommittee speak for and against cathedrals.[38] John Hacket made the most detailed defence of cathedrals articulated in the early modern period, stressing their role as a crucial prop to learning,[39]

---

[33] P. Collinson, *Godly People: Essays on English Protestantism and Puritanism* (1983), pp. 155–90.

[34] J. Ussher, *The Reduction of Episcopacie* (1656). Ussher was drawing on his experience in the early 1620s as bishop of Meath, a diocese without cathedral or chapter, where the archdeacon and beneficed clergy met twice a year 'to supply the place of a dean and chapter'. *Calendar of State Papers, Ireland, 1608–10*, p. 415.

[35] Gardiner, *CD*, pp. 167–79.   [36] Adamson, *Noble Revolt*, pp. 186, 209–10, 322.

[37] W. M. Abbott, 'James Ussher and "Ussherian" episcopacy, 1640–1656: the primate and his *Reduction* manuscript', *Albion*, 22 (1990), 237–59. Compare Ford, *Ussher*, pp. 247–55.

[38] Jansson, *Proceedings*, III, pp. 334–49. For the subcommittee membership see Fuller, *Church-History*, book 11, p. 174; O. Foulis, *Cabala* (1664), p. 44; BL, Harleian MS 6424, ff. 49v, 54r.

[39] Jansson, *Proceedings*, IV, pp. 338–9, 344–7; J. Maltby, 'Petitions for episcopacy and the Book of Common Prayer on the eve of the Civil War 1641–42', in S. Taylor, ed., *From Cranmer to Davidson: A Church of England Miscellany*, Church of England Record Society, 7 (1999), pp. 118–21. His speech was posthumously published in Hacket, *Century of Sermons*, pp. xviii–xxv.

and his case was seconded by petitions from the universities.[40] Cornelius Burges put the contrary case: he attacked cathedral singing and solemnity as undermining their role as houses of prayer; he denied that cathedrals contributed much to learning or preaching; he asserted that cathedrals were a post-Conquest novelty and their wealth could and should be put to better uses within the church for the benefit of the Commonwealth.[41]

That debate proved inconclusive. When deans and chapters were next disputed in the Commons, on 15 June, their opponents made a major concession, abandoning hopes to enrich the crown at cathedrals' expense. On the condition that capitular lands would be used 'to the advancement of learning and piety', and that pensions would be paid to dispossessed cathedral clergy and officers, MPs voted by a significant margin, 211 to 42, 'that all deans, deans and chapters, archdeacons, prebendaries, canons, chanters, and petty canons, and their officers shall be utterly abolished and taken away forth of the Church'. Sir John Culpepper mourned that 'now we are come to the funeral of the dean and chapters', but rumours of their demise proved premature.[42]

No further legislative progress on the dissolution of cathedrals was made for eight years after July 1641, although Parliament occasionally returned to the subject.[43] When bishops were finally abolished in October 1646, deans and chapters remained.[44] What had looked so easy a target, a mere first step to the abolition of episcopacy, had proved more difficult than ever imagined. Legislation stalled for three reasons. Since there was no agreement that capitular estates could be sold for secular ends, it proved more immediately profitable to sequester the estates of deans and chapters as delinquents.[45] Second, the most objectionable aspects of cathedrals – their ceremonies, choirs and music – were removed, abolished or simply withered away as each cathedral came under Parliamentarian control.[46] Most cathedrals became instead preaching houses often under the control of city corporations, with some of their revenues used to maintain one or more preachers at the cathedral and to support parish ministers, or itinerant preachers in Wales, thereby removing much local

---

[40] Jansson, *Proceedings*, IV, pp. 334, 339, 345–8.   [41] Ibid., pp. 341, 345, 349–50.

[42] Jansson, *Proceedings*, V, pp. 162–8, 175–6.

[43] *CJ*, II, pp. 747–8, 858, 906–7, 938; IV, p. 678; *LJ*, V, p. 569.

[44] *A&O*, I, pp. 879–83.

[45] *LJ*, V, p. 402; *CJ*, II, pp. 814, 852, 856, 965–6, 986; III, p. 458; IV, p. 275.

[46] I. Atherton et al., eds., *Norwich Cathedral: Church, City and Diocese 1096–1996* (1996), pp. 552–4; I. Atherton, 'The dean and chapter, Reformation to Restoration: 1541–1660', in P. Meadows and N. Ramsay, eds., *A History of Ely Cathedral* (Woodbridge, 2003), p. 190; J. Spraggon, *Puritan Iconoclasm during the English Civil War* (Woodbridge, 2003), p. 195.

pressure for their abolition.[47] Third, pressure for immediate abolition was lessened for as long as the fate of cathedrals was one of the negotiating points between king and Parliament.[48] The long legislative road to dissolution began again in May 1648; an ordinance slowly crawled through the Commons, an act finally being passed on 30 April 1649.[49] The lands of deans and chapters were then surveyed and sold to pay the army's arrears.[50] The abolition of Irish cathedrals was more piecemeal. The lands of St Patrick's cathedral were confiscated for Trinity College Dublin in March 1649/50, and the English ordinances for 'the abolishing of the hierarchy' were applied to Ireland in December 1650.[51] The history of cathedrals in the British Isles, stretching back more than a thousand years, had apparently come to a full stop.

III

Throughout the 1640s, cathedrals and cathedral clergy were to English Parliamentarians symbols and agents of the popish Antichrist ranged against them. An engraved, broadside copy of the Solemn League and Covenant printed in Edinburgh 1643 illustrates the clause about the extirpation of prelacy not with a bishop, but with a cathedral choir cast out of church.[52] The link between Royalism and cathedrals seemed obvious to many. Throughout 1642, English cathedral clergy appeared in the forefront of preaching opposition to Parliament, feeding Parliamentarian suspicions that cathedrals and collegiate churches were nests of malignancy.[53] Cathedral clergy and officers were depicted as the shock troops of the Royalists.[54] The legendary wealth of cathedrals now seemed part of the king's arsenal, making the search for hidden treasure at a number of cathedrals a legitimate activity for Parliamentarian soldiers.[55] Even

---

[47] *CJ*, III, pp. 421, 577, 597, 620, 655; IV, pp. 43, 97, 106, 113, 242, 334, 395, 493, 622, 635, 719.

[48] J. Rushworth, *Historical Collections*, 6 vols. (1703–8), V, pp. 47–8, 454; VI, pp. 35, 277, 283, 514, 528.

[49] *CJ*, V, pp. 552–3, 602; VI, pp. 197–8; *A&O*, II, pp. 81–104.

[50] Lehmberg, *Cathedrals under Siege*, pp. 41–3.   [51] *A&O*, II, pp. 355–7, 494–5.

[52] *A Solemne League and Covenant* (Edinburgh, 1643), Wing C4264.

[53] J. Eales, 'Provincial preaching and allegiance in the first English civil war, 1640–6', in T. Cogswell, R. Cust and P. Lake, eds., *Politics, Religion and Popularity in Early Stuart Britain* (Cambridge, 2002), pp. 194–5, 199–200, 203–4; I. Atherton, ed., 'An account of Herefordshire in the first civil war', *Midland History*, 21 (1996), 136–55, at 144, 149.

[54] BL, Add. MS 70003, f. 99r; *The Spie*, no. 2, 30 January–5 February 1643/4, 11; *Some Speciall and Considerable Passages*, no. 2, 16 August 1642; *Speciall Passages*, no. 4, 30 August–6 September 1642, 29.

[55] Spraggon, *Puritan Iconoclasm*, pp. 213–14; *Speciall Passages and Certain Informations*, no. 22, 3 January 1643, 185.

the very buildings themselves were dangerous: cathedrals were personified as demonic monsters with 'bloody Anthems' and 'murdering Organ pipes'.[56]

Interconnecting associations were drawn between idolatry, spiritual fornication, carnal lust, gluttony and idleness, between Laudian ceremonies and bodily delight, between Rome, the Whore of Babylon, Italy and sexual immorality, between medieval monasteries and cathedrals as the new abbeys, between monks and prebendaries.[57] Such connections meant that it was easy to portray cathedral clergy as immoral, eliding religious transgression and sexual immorality.[58] The reformation of cathedrals was, thus, driven on by a number of imperatives: combating opposition to the Parliament and winning the war, the godly reformation of manners, the putting down of popery and the religious purification of the land. With their downfall so often predicted in the 1640s, frustration at the failure to abolish deans and chapters doubtless increased iconoclastic violence against cathedrals during the first civil war, while copes and other 'popish relics' purged from cathedrals were sent to the Commons like so many trophies of war or standards of battle.[59]

Once defeated and cleansed, the question of what to do with the foundations and buildings arose. Parallels drawn between cathedrals and abbeys suggested the precedent of the dissolution of the monasteries.[60] Unlike so many monastic churches, English and Welsh cathedrals avoided wholesale demolition, but it was not for want of trying. There was repeated, often local pressure to demolish individual cathedrals including Winchester, Norwich, Rochester and Ely, with proposals to reuse the materials for other building works, or sell them for charitable purposes.[61] In April 1651 the Rump voted to dispose of Lichfield cathedral and use the profits for the poor of the former diocese. At the end of that year the lead from the roofs, and the bells, were offered for sale; much of the proceeds, however, were apparently embezzled.[62] There were also

---

[56] N. Smith, *Literature and Revolution in England 1640–1660* (New Haven and London, 1994), p. 64; *Mercurius Britanicus*, no. 17, 14–21 December 1643, 133.

[57] E.g. R. Culmer, *Cathedrall Newes from Canterbury* (1644); Corpus Christi College, Oxford, MS 206, f. 10r.

[58] E.g. *Mercurius Britanicus*, no. 19, 28 December–4 January 1643[4], 146.

[59] *Weekly Account*, no. 62, 31 October–6 November 1644; *CJ*, III, p. 583.

[60] R. Culmer, *Dean and Chapter Newes from Canterbvry*, ed. R. Culmer the younger (1649), sig. A2r.

[61] *CJ*, V, p. 478; Spraggon, *Puritan Iconoclasm*, pp. 189, 198–9; HMC, *Ninth Report*, 2 vols. (1883–4), I, p. 320; *CSPD, 1657–8*, pp. 121–2, 362, 398.

[62] *CJ*, VI, p. 556; Bodl., MS Ashmole 826, f. 125r; *Severall Proceedings in Parliament*, no. 118, 24 December 1651–1 January 1651/2, 1836; *Victoria County History*, *Staffordshire*, III, p. 174.

plans, and rumours of plans, at various times during the Commonwealth to pull down several or even all cathedrals,[63] but no cathedral church was demolished, and many continued to be used for worship in the 1650s.

The failure of the Interregnum regimes to demolish cathedrals requires some explanation.[64] The survival of the buildings in part reflects the long-standing disagreement over whether to use the proceeds for temporal or spiritual ends. It was these latter pressures that led to the creation of a short-lived university out of the church and prebendal houses of Durham cathedral in 1657.[65] The survival of cathedral churches also reflects local struggles for control of the cathedral church, and attempts by civic authorities to assert their control. It is perhaps significant that the first proposal to demolish a cathedral in its entirety, in March 1647/8, concerned Ely, not only a city firmly under the control of radical elements in the army, but a town without a corporation to act as a rival power base.[66] Many cathedrals were effectively municipalized in the 1640s and 1650s. In the mid-1640s a number of corporations secured the appointment of preachers at the cathedral,[67] but some Zions went much further in realizing the Protestant dream of a church as a true nursing mother of the city, providing preaching, charity and education. The corporation might take over the cathedral church, absorb the precincts into the city, use some of the buildings for civic purposes, oversee the preaching of regular sermons, control the cathedral school, appoint the almsmen, establish a library and make the cathedral the corporation's church (as at Gloucester),[68] or divide it up between competing congregations (as at Edinburgh, Exeter and Worcester).[69] York minster was so effectively taken over by the city corporation that Claire Cross has argued that 'for

---

[63] T. Carte, ed., *A Collection of Original Letters and Papers*, 2 vols. (Dublin, 1759), I, p. 276; *CJ*, VII, pp. 152, 245; T. Birch, ed., *A Collection of the State Papers of John Thurloe*, 7 vols. (1742), I, p. 387.

[64] Lehmberg's suggestion (*Cathedrals under Siege*, p. 43) that the Commonwealth regime had no intention of demolishing cathedrals seems mistaken.

[65] T. Burton, *Diary of Thomas Burton*, ed. J. T. Rutt, 4 vols. (1828), II, pp. 531–42.

[66] *CJ*, V, p. 478.

[67] *CJ*, III, pp. 343, 597; Parliamentary Archives, HL/PO/JO/10/1/179; *LJ*, VII, p. 489; *A&O*, I, pp. 840–1; W. A. Shaw, *A History of the English Church during the Civil Wars and under the Commonwealth 1640–1660*, 2 vols. (1900), II, p. 329; Lehmberg, *Cathedrals under Siege*, p. 48.

[68] S. Eward, *No Fine but a Glass of Wine: Cathedral Life at Gloucester in Stuart Times* (Salisbury, 1985), pp. 79–117; Gloucester Record Office, GBR/B/3/2, pp. 330, 381, 496, 503, GBR/B/3/3, p. 103, GBR/H/2/3, pp. 138–41.

[69] A. I. Dunlop, *The Kirks of Edinburgh*, Scottish Record Society, 15–16 (1989), pp. 17–18, 24, 28; W. Cotton and H. Woollcombe, *Gleanings from the Municipal and Cathedral Records relative to the History of the City of Exeter* (Exeter, 1877), pp. 122, 131–2, 156, 169, 171–9; Lehmberg, *Cathedrals under Siege*, pp. 48–9.

the first time the Minster seems to have been fully integrated in the life of the city'.[70] That civic desire to control cathedrals frustrated the hopes of others to see them all pulled down is suggested by the discussion in the 1654 Parliament that 'All cathedral and collegiate churches to be bestowed upon the cities and counties where they stand, to be kept up and maintained'.[71]

Ireland offers both the most dramatic examples of competition between congregations for cathedrals and the most extensive damage to cathedral fabric. Irish cathedrals suffered considerably during the wars of the 1640s and 1650s (as they had done during Tudor wars and would do so again during the Williamite wars): at least seven were attacked and badly damaged by one side or another, including Armagh, Kilkenny and Ross.[72] Control of a cathedral see-sawed from one side to another according to the ebb and flow of the war. Catholic control would mean reconsecration, repair, the installation of the paraphernalia of Catholic worship and even, as at Kildare and Kilkenny, the ritual purging of the church by the removal of bodies from Protestant graves. Catholic deans were appointed not only for at least eleven cathedrals under Catholic control, but also for at least four more still in Protestant hands in anticipation of a Catholic takeover. Protestant rule, meanwhile, might mean contests between rival congregations for control of what could still be recognized as a 'High Place', particularly in the case of Christ Church, Dublin, where its role as the church of the Dublin administration and symbolic heart of the Protestant church in Ireland ensured that it reflected the twists and turns of official religious policy as a model for the rest of the island.[73] Throughout the British Revolution, and even despite their abolition, cathedrals

---

[70] C. Cross, 'From the Reformation to the Restoration', in G. Aylmer and R. Cant, eds., *A History of York Minster* (Oxford, 1977), pp. 214–15; A. Raine, ed., 'Proceedings of the Commonwealth Committee for York and the Ainsty', in C. E. Whiting, ed., *Miscellanea vol. VI*, Yorkshire Archaeological Society Record Series, 118 (1953), pp. 1–30.

[71] Burton, *Diary*, I, p. cxxi.

[72] C. Diamond, 'The cathedral system of Ireland in the Stuart Period, 1603–91', Ph.D. thesis, Trinity College Dublin, 2007, pp. 113–14, 121–3; Armagh Public Library, Walter Harris, 'Some Account of ye Cathedral Church of Armagh'. For earlier and later damage to Irish cathedrals see also National Library of Ireland, MS 2669, part 1, p. 1, MS 8013, part ix; Trinity College Dublin, MS 1188, f. 18r.

[73] St. J. D. Seymour, 'The storming of the Rock of Cashel by Lord Inchiquin in 1647', *EHR*, 32 (1917), 373–81, at 374, 381; Diamond, 'Cathedral system', pp. 123, 143, 304–8; A. Fuller and T. Holms, *A Compendious View of some Extraordinary Sufferings of the People call'd Quakers* (Dublin, 1731), pp. 106–7; K. Milne, ed., *Christ Church Cathedral Dublin: A History* (Dublin, 2000), pp. 205–16. During the Williamite wars, possession of Irish cathedrals was again contested between Catholics and Protestants. Armagh Public Library, Dopping State Papers connected with Meath, I, nos. 87, 89, 92, 98, 116, 121, 125, 127, 130, II, nos. 142, 151; Public Record Office of Northern Ireland, DIO/4/19/2/5.

retained a symbolic, even cultic status, as focal points for an often contested religious identity.

Such a role, together with local and civic pride in cathedrals, also lay behind various attempts to protect them from iconoclasm and ensure their repair. York minster was protected from the iconoclastic attention of Parliamentarian soldiers in 1644 by the intervention of Sir Thomas Fairfax, a Yorkshireman, who then sought to make the cathedral a centre for godly learning and a university in the north. In 1649 the mayor of York and two other leading citizens described the minster as an 'ornament' to the city, even though two of them had been involved in enforcing official iconoclasm in the city's churches.[74] While Julie Spraggon has suggested that the 'Puritan approach' to cathedrals once they had been reformed and purged was 'pragmatic',[75] preservation of a cathedral depended on more than the practicalities of needing a building capacious enough to hold a large assembly for preaching or assizes. Cathedrals were not uncommonly praised for their 'stately', 'goodly' or 'beautiful' fabric.[76] Such statements nonetheless stand alongside the removal of lead, stone and other materials from nearly all English and Welsh cathedrals that became something of a national pastime in the 1640s and 1650s.[77] But a number of cathedrals did see campaigns of repair and restoration in the 1650s, either with official sponsorship (as at Carlisle, Gloucester and York) or through individual initiative (as at Norwich, Salisbury and Winchester).[78]

Just as some former Parliamentarians could see purged cathedrals as great ornaments and goodly fabrics, so for others defaced and ruinous cathedrals could be significant landmarks, carrying further meanings. Richard Franck, a Nottinghamshire Cromwellian officer, noted all the cathedrals he passed on his journey from England to the north-east of

---

[74] A. Hopper, *'Black Tom': Sir Thomas Fairfax and the English Revolution* (Manchester, 2007), pp. 153, 168, 219; J. Raines, ed., *The Fabric Rolls of York Minster*, Surtees Society, 35 (1859), pp. 332–3; Rushworth, *Historical Collections*, VI, pp. 283–4; Spraggon, *Puritan Iconoclasm*, p. 193.

[75] Spraggon, *Puritan Iconoclasm*, p. 200.

[76] As in Gloucester and Worcester: J. Dorney, *Certain Speeches* (1653), p. 82; J. Dorney, *A Briefe and Exact Relation* (1643); W. R. W. Stephens and F. T. Madge, eds., *Documents relating to the History of the Cathedral Church of Winchester in the Seventeenth Century*, Hampshire Record Society (1897), p. 97.

[77] Lehmberg, *Cathedrals under Siege*, pp. 41–50; W. B. Jones and E. A. Freeman, *The History and Antiquities of Saint David's* (1856), pp. 171–2.

[78] D. Weston, *Carlisle Cathedral History* (Carlisle, 2000), p. 19; Lehmberg, *Cathedrals under Siege*, pp. 47–9; Gloucester Record Office, GBR/B/3/3, pp. 30, 94, 97; Raine, 'Commonwealth Committee for York', pp. 23–4, 28–9; Atherton et al., *Norwich Cathedral*, p. 560; D. H. Robertson, *Sarum Close: A History of the Life and Education of the Cathedral Choristers for 700 Years* (1938), p. 196; Stephens and Madge, *Documents*, pp. 98–9.

Scotland and back in the mid-1650s. For him, the ruins of such 'imbelish'd Fabricks', now 'blotted and blurr'd by the Dates of Time', provoked contemplation on 'the Unconstancy of Men and Times': Aberdeen, for example, was 'an old weather-beaten Cathedral, that looks like the Times, somewhat irregular'.[79] Others may have viewed the ruins more as monuments of the victory over popery, as Spraggon has suggested.[80] D'Ewes, for example, had argued in 1641 that certain relics of popery should be retained as a 'monument of the miserable ignorance of those times'.[81] Between the abolition of deans and chapters in 1649, and their restoration in 1660, cathedral churches stood in limbo, neither up nor down, typically but not universally still described as cathedrals despite their loss of cathedral status,[82] some decaying, others repaired. Where in 1640–1 cathedrals had been seen by Puritans only as monuments of superstition, from the mid-1640s no single Parliamentarian view prevailed.

IV

In Royalist views, by contrast, there is a simpler shift, from embarrassed silence to glorification. Cathedrals rarely featured in early defences of episcopacy. Only one county petition in 1641–2 in defence of the established church made any explicit mention of cathedrals.[83] While the presses and street corners rang to the tune of anti-cathedral tracts and satires,[84] little was published in defence of cathedrals in the early 1640s; such apologies as there were tended to be brief asides in tracts devoted to bishops.[85] The status of cathedrals within a Protestant church was too questionable to make deans and chapters a good rallying call in the early

---

[79] R. Franck, *Northern Memoirs* (1694, but written 1658), pp. 59, 185–6, 193, 223, 225; C. H. Firth, 'Franck's *Northern Memoirs*', *Scottish Historical Review*, 25 (1927–8), 230–3.

[80] Spraggon, *Puritan Iconoclasm*, p. 200.

[81] Simonds D'Ewes, *The Journal of Sir Simonds D'Ewes: From the First Recess of the Long Parliament to the Withdrawal of King Charles from London*, ed. W. H. Coates (New Haven, 1942), p. 6. I am grateful to Paul Jones for reminding me of D'Ewes's speech.

[82] The godly London fishmonger John Harper always referred to 'the Cathedriall Church of St Paul' when recording sermons there in the 1650s. William Andrews Clark Memorial Library, Los Angeles, MS B8535 M3, 1625–65, 21 August 1657 (a reference I owe to the kindness of Ann Hughes).

[83] Maltby, 'Petitions for episcopacy', 116–67.

[84] Examples include *An Answer to the Petition sent from the Vniversitie of Oxford* (1641); *The Organs Eccho* (1641); *Saint Pauls Potion prescribed by Doctor Commons* (1641); T. Pury, *A Reply made by Mr. Thomas Pury* (1641); J. White, *A Speech of Mr. Iohn White* (1641); W. Thomas, *Master William Thomas Esquire his Speech* (1641); *The Organs Fvnerall* (1642); D. Cressy, *England on Edge: Crisis and Revolution 1640–1642* (Oxford, 2006), p. 337.

[85] T. Aston, *A Collection of Sundry Petitions* (1642), pp. 4–8; Thorndike, *Government of the Churches*, pp. 205–8; but see *To the High and Honourable Court of Parliament, the Humble Petition of the University of Oxford, in Behalfe of Episcopacy and Cathedrals* (Oxford, 1641).

1640s. However, attacks by soldiers against cathedrals which began as soon as the war in England commenced (by April 1643 at least eight cathedrals had been purged by Parliament's soldiers)[86] led to a focus in Royalist propaganda on cathedrals as victims of the anarchy unleashed by rebellion and an increasing identification between Royalism and the fate of cathedrals. The process is revealed in Bruno Ryves's newsbook chronicling the 'plunderings' and 'outrages' committed by the rebels, *Mercurius Rusticus*. The first seventeen issues, from May to December 1643, concentrated on violence against individuals, especially gentlemen and country ministers, or against objects associated with them, such as tombs, monuments and church furnishings, completely ignoring cathedrals. From issue 18 (16 December 1643) onwards, however, the newsbook concentrated almost exclusively on cathedrals, signalling the change in a new subtitle, so that the final few issues became a 'Catalogue of Plundered Cathedrals'.[87]

Mercurius Rusticus ceased in spring 1644, but it was republished as a single volume at least twice in the 1640s, each new edition increasing the prominence and importance of cathedrals as victims. The 1646 edition emphasized the importance of the cathedral section: it was given a separate title page, and it concluded with a new address to the reader drawing further attention to the glories of England's twenty-eight cathedrals, with a catalogue of those and three collegiate churches.[88] A further edition in 1647, retitled *Angliae Ruina, or, Englands Ruine*, reinforced the message of the sacrilege suffered by cathedrals. A new engraved title page depicted some of the events recounted within: at the head stood 'Canterbury Minster' assailed by soldiers. And the cathedral section was extended, with a new fifth chapter describing the despoliation of Peterborough at the hands of Oliver Cromwell.[89]

Ryves's change in focus suggests a different way of looking at cathedrals. In the first seventeen issues, churches are little more than mausoleums, their contents to be smashed by Parliamentarian soldiers;

---

[86] Spraggon, *Puritan Iconoclasm*, pp. 204–6.

[87] *Mercurius Rusticus*, 21 issues, Oxford, 1643–4. A complete facsimile set is available: P. Thomas, ed., *Newsbooks 1 Oxford Royalist Volume 4, The English Revolution III* (1971), pp. 117–302. Numbers 1–17 were subtitled 'The Countries Complaint of the Murthers, Robberies, Plunderings, and other Outrages committed by the Rebells on his MAJESTIES *faithfull Subjects*'; from number 18 that became 'The Countries Complaint of the Sacriledges, prophanations and Plunderings, Committed by the REBELLS ON THE CATHEDRALL CHURCHES of this KINGDOME'. The change may have been prompted by Ralph Culmer's iconoclasm at Canterbury, which started on 13 December 1643. Culmer, *Cathedrall Newes*, p. 20.

[88] *Mercurius Rusticus* ([Oxford], 1646).

[89] *Angliae Ruina, or, Englands Ruine* (n.p., 1647).

such a view echoes pre-war accounts of cathedrals that focus almost entirely on monuments, epitaphs and heraldry.[90] Descriptions of the sack of cathedrals, however, suggest a view of ecclesiastical fabric where the stones of the building are sacred and where the magnificence of the building itself can inspire devotion. Ryves's account of each despoiled cathedral begins with a short account of its history, emphasizing the antiquity of the building (without any mention of their Roman past) and stressing any royal connections, noting the kings and queens associated with or buried in the cathedral. Ryves's point is to connect cathedrals with monarchy and suggest that behind the attack on individual cathedrals lay an anti-monarchical spirit. Hence the soldiers assailing Chichester attack a picture of Edward VI; those at Winchester smash parts of a statue of Charles I; and those at Exeter a statue of Edward the Confessor.

Ryves's account also hints at connections in Royalist thinking between cathedrals and their founders and patron saints. When Lord Brooke was killed by a shot from the tower of the cathedral church of St Chad in Lichfield while besieging the close on St Chad's day, 2 March, the coincidence of patron saint, day and victim, well known for his antipathy to cathedrals, was noted by many.[91] Ryves pointed out the 'accursed rage, and madness' of the iconoclastic soldiers at Winchester cathedral, dedicated to the Holy Trinity, as if the attack was aimed at God. A further connection made by accounts of sacrilege at cathedrals was to link those churches with Christ himself. Chichester was attacked on Holy Innocents' day (28 December) and the cathedral plundered on the following day, as if the soldiers were Herod's agents and the cathedral itself were one of the innocent babes slaughtered in place of the infant Christ.[92]

By 1648, then, cathedrals were linked to the king and to Christ, making available the essential ingredients for a further jump in Royalist thought. Just as the martyred king was compared to the crucified Christ,[93] so cathedrals as a type of Christ could also be an emblem of the regicide. In *The Terrible, Horrible, Monster of the West*, Parliament is imagined as a monstrous beast devouring the land: on coming to London it swallowed

[90] E.g. W. Camden, *Reges, reginae, nobiles, & alij in ecclesia collegiata B. Petri Westmonasterij sepulti* (1600); H. Holland, *Monumenta sepulchraria Sancti Pauli* ([1614]); BL, Add. MS 71474.

[91] W. Sanderson, *A Compleat History of the Life and Raigne of King Charles* (1658), p. 613; Hyde, *History*, II, p. 474; N. Ellis and I. Atherton, 'Griffith Higgs's account of the sieges of and iconoclasm at Lichfield Cathedral in 1643', *Midland History*, 34 (2009), 233–45, at 240; *Mercurius Aulicus*, 10th week, 5–11 March 1643.

[92] See also J. Gauden, *A Sermon preached in the Temple-Chappel* (1660), pp. 157–8.

[93] A. Lacey, *The Cult of King Charles the Martyr* (Woodbridge, 2003), especially pp. 29–32, 117, 140–5.

St Paul's cathedral but, its hunger undiminished, it then killed the king and 'banqueted in his bloud', before consuming most of the rest of the Commonwealth.[94] It became a Royalist commonplace that the fate of cathedrals was a precursor to the regicide, and that thereafter they shared in the royal martyrdom.[95] The connection between cathedrals and monarchy was reinforced by the coincidence between the regicide and the abolition of deans and chapters in the first months of 1649, meaning that thereafter cathedrals were seen as one of the first and most iconic victims of the English republic.[96] Royalists collected stories of the grizzly ends of cathedral iconoclasts as further evidence of God's displeasure at rebels and sectaries.[97] The sight of Lichfield's ruins led John Taylor to muse on the Hebrew slaves weeping by the rivers of Babylon (Psalm 137), as if Royalists, too, were now held captive in a strange land.[98]

Taylor's comparison, however, held out hope to Royalists, for if they were enduring a Babylonian captivity under the Rump, there remained the promise that Babylon would be destroyed, the church restored and their exile ended. Others, in prophecy, made the connection more explicit: as king and cathedrals fell, so, like Christ, they would rise again and return.[99] Such hopes were manifest in the careers of the Royalist prophets Jacob Freeman in Norwich and Walter Gostelow and his dream in Lismore cathedral.[100]

The Interregnum witnessed not only a focus on the meaning of ruined cathedrals, but a renewed interest in their pre-war state. Both Fuller's *Church-History* and the first volume of Dugdale and Dodsworth's *Monasticon Anglicanum* (both 1655) carried plates showing cathedrals in their pre-war, undefaced state, with none of the scars of the Revolution showing.[101] That there was a significant commercial market for views of pristine cathedrals in Interregnum England is suggested by the

[94] *The Terrible, Horrible, Monster of the West* (1650) – copy in Worcester College, Oxford, AA 2.4 (88).

[95] Cambridge University Library, MS 151, f. 3r; Bodl., MS Ashmole 826, f. 125r; J. Nalson, *An Impartial Collection of the Great Affairs of State*, 2 vols. (1682–3), I, frontispiece.

[96] W. Dugdale, *A Short View of the Late Troubles in England* (Oxford, 1681), p. 560.

[97] Norfolk Record Office, DCN 107/3; *Mercurius Rusticus*, 18th week, 16 December 1643, 144–51; Lehmberg, *Cathedrals under Siege*, p. 35; Bodl., MS Ashmole 826, f. 125r; S. Gunton, *The History of the Church of Peterburgh* (1686), p. 92.

[98] J. Taylor, *A Short Relation of a Long Iourney* [London, 1653], p. 8.

[99] An engraving of Lichfield cathedral (Fuller, *Church-History*, frontispiece) bore the motto 'Resvrgam' (I shall rise again).

[100] Norfolk Record Office, DCN 107/3; M. Stevenson, *Norfolk Drollery* (1673), pp. 85–7; W. Gostelo, *Charls Stuart and Oliver Cromvvel United* (1655), pp. 1–40. See also Bodl., MS Top. Staffs. c. 1, no. 47.

[101] Fuller, *Church-History*, frontispiece; R. Dodsworth and W. Dugdale, *Monasticon Anglicanum* (1655).

publications of Daniel King.[102] The idea of representing cathedrals in an idealized, perfect state was taken furthest in Dugdale's *History of St. Pauls Cathedral* of 1658, which included a drawing of the cathedral as it would have looked in 1640 if the medieval spire (which had collapsed in 1561) had been replaced under Elizabeth.[103]

The image of cathedrals played a much greater role in the survival and rebirth of Anglicanism as a significant force after 1642 in England than the bishops (who failed to provide significant leadership between 1641 and 1660),[104] and perhaps as great a role as the ordinary clergy. The focus of concern was on cathedrals first as buildings and then as institutions; there was little public discussion of the fate of ejected cathedral clergy or other cathedral officers. And yet cathedrals have been overlooked by studies of Anglicanism during the Revolution, which have stressed instead attachment to the Prayer Book and its festivals, especially Christmas, and on individuals, lay such as the diarist John Evelyn or clerical such as the Warwickshire parson Christopher Harvey.[105] Studies of Anglican survivalism and the creation of an Anglican identity during the British Revolution have concentrated on the ways in which individuals and worshipping communities hung on to that which the Puritan regimes of the 1640s and 1650s had sought to remove, so that prayer-book Protestants became Anglicans through what survived (often illegally) of the pre-war church. The extent to which an Anglican identity was formed by what had been lost, however, should not be overlooked. The absence of a functioning cathedral, the losses to cathedral fabric and the contrast between the engravings of cathedral churches published in the 1650s and the present state of them, were central to the ways in which many people thought about the Church of England. The more damaged and broken a cathedral, the more it could stand as an emblem of the church; Taylor, for example, commented more fully on the more ruinous cathedrals he encountered in his travels than those, like Gloucester, where the fabric was in better repair.[106] The circulation of ideas and

---

[102] D. King, *The Cathedrall and Conventuall Churches of England and Wales* (1656), Wing K484, K485, K485A; E. Benlowes, *On St. Paul's Cathedral represented by Mr. Dan. King* (1658).

[103] D. Keene et al., eds., *St Paul's: The Cathedral Church of London, 604–2004* (New Haven and London, 2004), pp. 131, 173, 182–3, 317–18.

[104] P. King, 'The episcopate during the civil wars 1642–1649', *EHR*, 73 (1968), 523–37; Morrill, *Nature*, pp. 159–60.

[105] J. Morrill, 'The Church in England 1642–1649', in Morrill, *Nature*, pp. 148–75; J. Maltby, 'Suffering and surviving: the civil wars, the Commonwealth and the formation of "Anglicanism", 1642–60', in C. Durston and J. Maltby, eds., *Religion in Revolutionary England* (Manchester, 2006), pp. 158–80.

[106] John Taylor, *John Taylors Wandering, to see the wonders of the west* (1649), pp. 19, 21; Taylor, *Short Relation*, pp. 9, 26.

drawings in print meant that the case of cathedrals was not restricted to the inhabitants of cathedral cities, but was effectively nationalized. And although evidence about the ways in which cathedrals were viewed in Ireland and Scotland is largely lacking, Gostelow and Franck show that the English could be as interested in and influenced by Irish and Scottish cathedrals as they were by those in England and Wales.

V

There is no space here to consider in detail the re-establishment of the cathedrals in 1660–1, but it is clear that it happened rapidly in England and Ireland, and often in advance of the restoration of episcopacy. No doubt it was in part a self-interested move, but, more importantly, it reflected a desire to obliterate the wounds of Puritan rule and, at the same time, to preserve a memory of the providential survival of church, crown and individual Royalists. Opposition to deans and chapters had not disappeared, but their defence had found a new voice; no longer were they the Anglican institution that dare not speak its name. Cathedrals and cathedral worship were rapidly re-established in England and Ireland as a considered act of Anglican identity, and as the reflection of a high earthly ideal of harmony and order.

As John Morrill has so significantly demonstrated, the British Revolution was in many ways a series of interlocking religious crises, with disputes about the nature of the church lying at the heart of the conflict, although in different ways in each of the three kingdoms. In Scotland and England, and between the two, those disputes are typically considered in terms of the debate over episcopacy, and yet questions about the existence and nature of cathedral churches could prove as significant and divisive, if not more so. While episcopacy was rarely publicly questioned in England or Ireland before the end of the 1630s, there had been a century of puzzlement over cathedrals and their place in the reformed English and Irish church, with various proposals to strip some or all of their wealth, to convert some to alternative uses, or to dissolve them all. Any defence of cathedrals was muted, and generally along limited, practical lines. Throughout the debates over the church in Scotland 1637–8 and England 1640–2, cathedrals were treated as secondary to bishops. In Scotland there was only limited debate about cathedrals; there, opposition to the Laudian church focused on the new service book and bishops as instruments of popery.[107] Scottish cathedrals disappeared without

---

[107] E.g. National Library of Scotland, Wodrow MSS Quarto XXVI and CVI, and Advocates MS 33.2.32.

ceremony as part of the abolition of bishops. In England, proponents of root and branch reform decided early in 1641 to attack cathedrals first as a potentially softer target than bishops, and as a first step towards the abolition of episcopacy. That step failed unexpectedly, not because of any trenchant defence of or public support for cathedrals as they then existed, but because opponents were divided over whether the spoils could be applied to secular uses and, second, because of divisions over whether to abolish cathedrals entirely or reform them into preaching colleges. The tactical decision to treat cathedrals before bishops separated their fates, so that when bishops were abolished in 1646, cathedrals did not follow for a further three years. Ireland then dutifully followed England. The lack of public concern for cathedrals in 1641–2 is in marked contrast with the concentration from the end of 1643 on cathedrals as victims of radical iconoclasts and then as an analogue of the royal martyrdom. They became a far more visible and public sign of religious change than the cowed, largely inactive bishops. At the Restoration, cathedrals returned in summer and autumn 1660 not as the junior partners of bishops but in many cases in advance of the return of bishops to their palaces and the re-establishment of episcopal administration. From the Restoration cathedrals could symbolize both the suffering of the church *and* its resurgence.

The British Revolution had transformed the fate of the cathedrals of the three kingdoms. Scottish cathedrals never fully recovered from their abolition in 1638. Returning in 1661, they were pale shadows of what their supporters had intended before the Revolution: in neither worship nor ornament could English or Scots episcopalians distinguish the Scottish episcopalian church from its Presbyterian cousin, and they were to be abolished once again in 1689 alongside episcopacy.[108] By contrast, English and Irish cathedrals emerged from the Revolution strengthened and with a renewed purpose at the heart of the church.[109] Their suffering ensured that throughout the long eighteenth century they were insulated against the need for change or reform – so much so that, when the Victorian Ecclesiastical Commission refocused attention on cathedrals and a vigorous pamphlet dispute was conducted over their utility, the terms

[108] G. Mackenzie, *A Vindication of the Government in Scotland* (1691), p. 9; T. Morer, *A Short Account of Scotland* (1702), pp. 47–50, 88; C. Jackson, *Restoration Scotland, 1660–1690* (Woodbridge, 2003), pp. 109–110, 122–3; D. Stevenson, *St Machar's Cathedral and the Reformation: 1560–1690*, Friends of St Machar's Cathedral Occasional Papers, 7 (Aberdeen, 1981), pp. 14–17.

[109] I disagree here with Carl Estabrook's argument that cathedrals emerged at the Restoration humbled and trimmed: 'In the mist of ceremony: cathedral and community in seventeenth-century Wells', in S. D. Amussen and M. A. Kishlansky, eds., *Political Culture and Cultural Politics in Early Modern England* (Manchester, 1995), pp. 133–61.

of that debate had changed little: early modern arguments were plundered wholesale, and Hacket's 1641 speech was even republished in its entirety.[110] Through their trials and tribulations in the mid-seventeenth century, English and Irish cathedrals had discovered an essential truth of the Christian religion: in seeking to save their life they had lost it, but in losing their life they had saved themselves eternally.

[110] W. Selwyn, *Are Cathedral Institutions Useless?* (1838), p. 11; W. Selwyn, *An Attempt to Investigate the True Principles of Cathedral Reform, Part II* (Cambridge and London, 1840); J. Hacket, *Apology for Cathedral Establishments* (1838 and 1861); J. Hacket, *Ecclesiastical Duties and Revenues Bill. A Speech in Behalf of Deans and Chapters, Made before the Long Parliament in 1641* (1840); P. J. Welch, 'Contemporary views on the proposals for the alienation of capitular property in England (1832–1840)', *Journal of Ecclesiastical History*, 5 (1954), 184–95.

6   History, liberty, reformation and the cause: Parliamentarian military and ideological escalation in 1643

Michael J. Braddick

I

As civil war broke out in 1642, both sides claimed to be acting defensively: the war was defined in terms of what it was intended to prevent, rather than what it was hoped it would achieve. Partisans sought military strength in order to secure a safe peace, with the result that there was a contrapuntal relationship between fighting and talking. But there was an inherent difficulty in this: the increasing demands of the military mobilizations put pressure on the initially defensive claims. In summer 1642 there had been tussles for control over local military resources and in the autumn one significant pitched battle, which proved inconclusive. Early in 1643, these military considerations looked rather different and rather more challenging. As peace negotiations were about to start in Oxford, Parliament was also preparing for a sustained campaign on several fronts. Innovative financial and military demands forced Parliament to claim powers that were difficult to justify in legal and constitutional terms acceptable before the war. This pressure for administrative innovation, built into the effort to secure a peace by fighting a war, generated new claims to political legitimacy – either in the sense of novel uses of pre-existing forms of argument, or entirely new political and religious claims. As the practical costs of military mobilization escalated, in other words, so, too, did the ideological claims of the cause, with the consequence that the campaign might come to seem quite different from the one being championed in January or even September 1642. As a result there was an inherent instability in the ways in which military and political action were justified, which gave rise to both anxiety and creativity. One implication of this, the one that I want to draw out here, is that the radical, revolutionary, potential in the parliamentary cause was present in the first year of the war. Creativity and anxiety were born out of the experience of war, or of mobilizing for war; but the roots of that radical potential lay in the difficulty of fixing a definition of the parliamentary cause that had been present at the very inception of the war.

II

One common response to this difficulty was to historicize it, to offer a narrative of recent events that placed the current situation on a trajectory towards a predictable future. This was a common reflex throughout the 1640s – from the Grand Remonstrance to the Engagement or the army Declaration justifying the Vote of No Addresses in February 1648, for example.[1] To the extent that this future was desirable or undesirable, such narratives invited either renewed commitment to the cause or a revision of that commitment. History offered fixity, therefore, but also the terrain over which the legitimacy of the cause was fought.

A case in point was a short pamphlet published in early January 1643, *A Complaint to the House of Commons*. It opened with an account of the threats posed to liberties and religion during the 1630s, but quickly turned to the even greater threat now posed by the Parliamentary war effort: 'we have lived to see many changes in Church and State, as make our hearts ake, because for the most part they are still for the worst, and when we could not believe a degree beyond our miseries, and thereupon built hopes of amendment, our sense of suffering taught us new degrees of comparison'.[2] It concentrated in particular on the use of ordinances and the undermining of the clerical estate, and seems to have made quite a splash: at least two versions survive, as well as a number of rebuttals.[3] The pamphlet clearly touched a raw nerve in Parliament, too. Preparations for the Oxford treaty were broken off while the Commons took measures to track down the author, and it was ordered to be burnt.[4]

The anxious reaction to *A Complaint*, in the context of preparations for the treaty, points up the close relationship between, on the one hand, the need to mobilize for war, in part by maintaining a purposeful unity, and, on the other hand, the often simultaneous attempt to make peace.

---

[1] Gardiner, *CD*, pp. 202–32, 348–9, TT E. 427[9]. For a full discussion of related themes see Gary Rivett, '"Make use both of things present and past": Thomas May's histories of parliament, printed public discourse and the politics of the recent past, 1640–1650', unpublished Ph.D. dissertation, University of Sheffield, 2010.

[2] Anon., *A Complaint to the House of Commons* (Oxford, 164[3]), sig. A2r.

[3] Peter Bland, *An Answer to the late scandalous and libellous pamphlet entituled A Complaint* (1643), Thomason date 4 January 1643; Anon., *A Complaint to the House of Commons* (Oxford, 1643), Thomason date 12 January 1643. The title page of the spoof is a good imitation and publication details ostensibly identical. The original is Wing, 2nd edn/C5621; the York edition is Wing, 2nd edn/C5623B; the spoof is TT E.245[5] (another copy: TT E.244[31]). See also Anon., *A ivst complaint or the loud crie of all the vvell-affected Protestants in England* ([1643]).

[4] *CJ*, II, pp. 910–11.

And this was made more difficult because mobilizing for war presented an increasingly difficult task of reconciling the ideological and material claims of the cause with a reasonable understanding of what the war had originally been about.

Crucial to the legitimacy of Parliament's escalating financial and military mobilization was the claim to be in defensive arms, that Parliament's actions were driven by necessity in the face of the manifest threat posed by armed popery. This case had been made in 1642 and was implicit in what was probably the largest publishing venture of the early months of 1643 – Edward Husbands's *Exact Collection*. It opened with a supposed breach of privilege by Charles, when he commented on a measure in Parliament that was still under discussion, and ended with the assessment ordinance – in one view a profound challenge to property rights, but justified by the need to maintain defensive arms against a threat to parliamentary privilege. This may have been an officially sanctioned selection; Husbands had been publishing for Parliament for some time, and seeking payment for it, and it is possible that he had been commissioned to take on this risky venture which tied up a large amount of stock for a customer with an evidently imperfect record of payment.[5] This chronological collation, free of editorial comment, silently narrated a central justification of the Parliamentary cause, in legitimation of measures that could have been said to have posed a greater threat to the constitution than the innovations of the 1630s.

Reformation, another fundamental point of reference in the Parliamentary cause, was also, of course, an historicized concept. Anti-popery had a narrative to hand in the history of successive encroachments of papal corruption and the progressive liberation from bondage. However, within the Parliamentary cause such narratives had different end points. Some saw the Reformation as an achieved settlement, an event or events in the past whose legacy was now being defended, although it was of course possible to identify differently the moment at which the Reformation had been achieved. Others thought reformation was an experience in the present that was still unfolding. This open-ended and enabling view of the past and its implications for the future[6] was a potentially unsettling one, and it induced much anxiety. For those anxious about this view of reformation, both Parliamentarians and Royalists, there was another

---

[5] Michael Braddick, *God's Fury, England's Fire: A New History of the English Civil Wars* (2008), pp. 272–3.

[6] Cheney Culpeper's letters are particularly revealing of this sense of the Reformation as an unfolding process and its creative potential, because they also reveal his sense of the direction of reformation as it developed in the light of events: Michael J. Braddick and Mark Greengrass, eds., 'The letters of Sir Cheney Culpeper, 1641–1657', in *Camden Miscellany xxxiii: Seventeenth-Century Political and Financial Papers*, Camden 5th series, 7, Royal Historical Society (Cambridge, 1996), 105–402.

well-established narrative to hand: anti-Puritanism, the polemical counterpart to anti-popery, which was now largely rendered as hostility to sectarian excess. Catalogues of spiritual errors and heresies placed the post-Laudian religious scene in the longer context of zealous error – a history that reinforced the need for learned divinity.[7] Here, some of the most vituperative writing against Parliamentarian excess came from within the Parliamentary alliance – from those who used history to fix points of reference, rather than to open the way to a different future.

Debates about the meaning and direction of current events were shaped by histories of the Reformation, the threats posed to and by it, and by histories of English liberties. The fluidity with which these terms were deployed and redeployed made it a pressing but apparently impossible task to fix an authoritative or durable version of the cause; the resulting tension contained considerable radical potential.

III

A Complaint spoke to these tensions at a crucial moment in Parliamentary mobilization both for war and for peacemaking. They were resolved in the Parliamentary coalition largely by a mixture of agreement and selective silence – in spring 1643, for example, agreement around the attack on idolatry and superstition and a continuing diplomatic silence on the issue of church government. It was in these months that the Harley Committee began its official iconoclasm in London, that Cheapside Cross was pulled down and that the *Book of Sports* was burned on the site of the Cross in maypole season. But even here the dangers were clear. The increasingly direct attacks on the court Catholicism centred on Henrietta Maria led into very difficult territory, raising diplomatic issues and tending perhaps towards a direct attack on the king. On the other hand, it clearly had some resonance – Anne Smith, accused at quarter sessions of scandalizing the queen in 1648, argued that 'it is dubious . . . whether any suit can justly be commenced against [her] in the name of the Queen, so long as she is declared traitor by both Houses of Parliament'.[8]

The attempt to fix meanings was continually challenged by the implications of practical measures taken to shore up the negotiating position. As a result the practical meaning of these terms was continually debated – reformation, popery, legality, rights, liberties were key words in the

---

[7] Michael J. Braddick, 'Prayer Book and Protestation: anti-popery, anti-puritanism and the outbreak of the English Civil War', in Glenn Burgess and Charles Prior, eds., *Britain's Wars of Religion* (Farnham, forthcoming).

[8] Braddick, *God's Fury*, esp. pp. 273–5, 312–15; TNA, SP24/76 petition of Anne Smith.

political vocabulary of Stuart England, but their meanings were increasingly slippery once exposed to close interrogation. Indeed, another of the very damaging features of *A Complaint* was that it drew attention to this. It opposed Parliament's actions not by juxtaposing an alternative vocabulary – of loyalty or regality, for example – but by contesting the validity of Parliament's claims to its own preferred language of legitimation.

There was in fact a wider public battle being fought for control of particular political languages and terms, a battle sharply satirized in *The Interpreter*.[9] In this case it took the form of brief queries as to the meanings of key terms, starting with the leading institutions of government:

> *Quest. What is the King?*
> *A.* Charles Stuart
> *Q. What is C. R.?*
> *A.* King of Great Brittaine as much as of France, or Ireland
> *Q. What is the Queene?*
> *A.* A Subject, an Incendiarie, An over active Lady
> *Q. The Prince?*
> *A.* A Heire apparent, for the time being
> *Q. The Lords and Commons?*
> *A.* A Parliament
> *Q. A Parliament?*
> *A.* A Perpetuall Senate, an Omnipotent Counsell, Oracle, an Ephod

And so it goes on, covering crucial terms such as 'The Protestant religion by law established', 'The Common Prayer Book' and 'Votes and Ordinances'. Bruno Ryves's *Mercurius Rusticus* also took up this line of attack with some gusto in May 1643, retailing stories of the depredations of Parliamentary soldiers and supporters in order to contest the public claim to be acting for security of religion and property.[10] On this view the language was being stretched so far as to have lost its meaning – the claims had become almost comically incredible.

---

[9] This can, I think, be dated to January 1643: it satirizes the Nineteen Propositions, not the Oxford Propositions, its religious satire refers to the sectarian scare that ran from late 1641 to the start of the war, but not to the iconoclasm sponsored by Parliament from spring 1643, and makes no mention of the Solemn League and Covenant (September 1643). A manuscript copy in the Huntington Library (HEH, EL 7801) is numbered alongside a satire which is clearly from January 1643: 'The humble petition of diverse Matrons and Virgins in Petticoat Lane Smock alley and Conny Court and diverse other well affected places in and about the Cities of London and Westminster', HEH, EL 7802. The line is similar to that of *A Complaint*. This satire, in its turn, might be a response of some kind to a printed petition: Anon., *The Mid-wives just petition* (1643). It claimed to be a printed version of a complaint tendered to the House on 23 January, although there is no record of it in *CJ*.

[10] For Ryves see Braddick, *God's Fury*, esp. pp. 282–4.

This carried a radical potential, however, in the possibility that new uses of established terms, or even entirely new vocabularies, might gain wide currency. For example, an essential charge of *The Interpreter* – that Parliament was acting tyrannously – was also used for a counter-purpose during the winter of 1642–3. Failure to win the war in autumn 1642 left Parliament's negotiating position no stronger than it had been in June 1642, and that raised fears that Parliament might conclude an easy peace. A number of pamphlets from December 1642 and the early months of 1643 had argued that in these circumstances Parliament would be deserting the people's interests and would itself have become tyrannical. In such circumstances the people could renounce the authority of parliaments since they were a threat to their interests.[11] This appropriation, a sense that the war was not about the defence of Parliament but the resistance to tyranny in any branch of government, rather confirmed *The Interpreter*'s case.

Of course, activists could not ignore the world of public print; indeed, it was crucial to political mobilization. In these public campaigns, particular cases became exemplary – loyalty and treason in Poole, Bristol, Hull or London were emblematic of the dangers to the nation as a whole, but also testament to the power of commitment to a godly cause.[12] *All the memorable and wonder strikinge mercies*, published the previous autumn, had consisted of eighteen engravings, a number of them recycled in later publications, which had narrated the liberation from popish threat. The majority of these engravings were of public scenes, the people as witnesses or actors in moments of their own liberation. Identifiable individuals were invariably agents of popish oppression. The title page placed this narrative in a millennial frame, with time on the left and truth on the right. Time was placed above a scriptural passage calling for patience in the face of God's wrath: 'In a little wrath I hid my face fro[m] the[e] for a moment but with everlasting kindnes will I have mercy on thee, saith the Lord thy redeemer' (Isaiah 54.1). Truth stood over the promise of redemption:

---

[11] David Wootton, 'From rebellion to revolution: the crisis of 1642/3 and the origins of Civil War radicalism', reprinted in Richard Cust and Ann Hughes, eds., *The English Civil War* (1997), pp. 340–56.

[12] For Poole, see Anon., *A True relation of a plot to betray the towne of Poole in the county of Dorset* (1643). There was a spate of publication about the deliverance of Bristol. For examples see Nathaniel Fiennes, *An extraordinary deliverance* (1643); Anon., *A full declaration of all particulers* (1643); I. H., *A briefe relation, abstracted out of severall letters* ([1643]); T. P., *Eben Ezer, as a thankefull remembrance of Gods great goodnesse unto the city of Bristoll* (1643); John Tombes, *Iehovah Iireh, or, Gods providence in delivering the godly* (1643). Hull and Beverley, of course, were famously delivered: see, for example, Anon., *More plots found out, and plotters apprehended* (1643). The revelation of the Waller plot in London was accompanied by a similar outpouring of pamphlets.

'I will mention the loving kindnesses of the Lord, and the praises of the Lord, according to all that the Lord hath bestowed on us and the great goodnesse towards the house of Israel which hee hath bestowed on them according to his mercies and according to the multitude of his loving kindnesses.' At the foot of the page was a millennial promise: 'And the fifth Angel poured out his viall upon the seat of the beast, and his kingdom was full of darknesse, and they gnawed their tongues for pain and blasphemed the God of heaven.'[13] The meaning of this redemptive history was of course open to doubt – who were now the blasphemers? – but one point at least is clear, that the people of Israel were actors in the drama of redemption.

Each side took advantage, but also suspected the effects, of this broad public participation and the associated news culture. *The Interpreter*, for example, had claimed that 'The Kings proclamations' now meant 'Printed papers, ballads, libels', while 'Lying pamphlets' were now the newsbooks, the 'True and perfect Diurnals, remarkable passes [sic] for all that desire to be truly informed, The Kingdomes weekly Intelligence sent abroad to prevent mis-information'.[14] Throughout the early months of 1643 Parliament had sought to prevent the publication of some of the king's proclamations, and the connections between particular Parliamentarians and the burgeoning newsbook and pamphlet industry is well attested.[15]

The need to persuade the public was never far from the minds of those negotiating a settlement, not least at the time of the Oxford Treaty. The MP Laurence Whitaker recorded the unease felt at the king's response to the first two articles of the propositions:

in all which their lordships delivered that there was fair and smooth language, but a denial to what we propounded and a censuring of our proceedings. So lest the people should conceive that the King desired peace and we are averse from it, they resolved this afternoon the committee of both houses should meet and consider some declaration to be published by way of answer to what we had received from his majesty.[16]

---

[13] *All the memorable and wonder strikinge parliamentary mercies effected and afforded to this English nation within this space of less than 2 years past A° 1641 and 1642* (1642), Thomason date 12 Sept 1642.

[14] Anon., *The Interpreter* (Oxford, 1643).

[15] *CJ, passim*; Joad Raymond, *The Invention of the Newspaper: English Newsbooks 1641–1649* (Oxford, 1996), esp. pp. 111–25, and, more generally, Jason Peacey, *Politicians and Pamphleteers: Propaganda During the English Civil Wars and Revolution* (Aldershot, 2004).

[16] *The Parliamentary Diary of Laurence Whitaker 3 October 1642–11 June 1647* (hereafter *Whitaker Diary*), transcript of BL, Add. MS 31116, in possession of the History of Parliament Trust, p. 115. I am grateful to Stephen Roberts for permission to consult

Parliament's cause was shifting and its definition in relation to respectable political languages or values had to be continually renegotiated as it was broadcast for the benefit of wider audiences.

Throughout the crisis precipitated by the Scottish rebellion polemicists had forced these issues but, as military parties formed, the definition of their respective causes in relation to this shifting polemical terrain was crucial and problematic in equal measure. In practice, too, the causes had to be continually constructed and reformed in the light of military and political imperatives: peace initiatives ran alongside military campaigning, each creating immediate but not necessarily compatible political needs. This instability of language threatened the solidity of the Parliamentary alliance, which was a dangerous thing both for war and peace efforts. There was a tender but unbreakable relationship between military mobilization and peace negotiations, something reflected in the centrality of calls for a cessation to the Oxford Treaty. Peace negotiations went alongside these escalations, offering both a reason for caution or, when they went badly, a demonstration of the imperative need to mobilize for war. In chronological perspective escalation and negotiation were contrapuntal.

IV

The continual shifting and redefinition of the causes cautions us against too rigidly defined categorizations of allegiance. However, during spring 1643, armed parties appeared in areas where previously that had been avoided – in Gloucestershire and Norwich, for example[17] – and it became increasingly difficult to avoid being labelled as a partisan of one side or the other. Following the passage of the Sequestration Ordinance in late March, the attribution of malignancy (which could result in property seizure) might attach simply to non-payment of taxes. Alongside the bishops, the definition of a malignant extended to those actively fighting for the king, opposing the Parliamentary forces, robbing or plundering those supporting Parliament, and those who had taken any oath or collected revenues for the king's army. But it also extended to those who

---

this transcript. This concern to persuade the public, as much as the king, lay behind the conduct of the 'paper war' the previous year, and the anxiety that the king 'came in with a reputation (among the people) of having long graciously sought peace' was an important factor motivating army politics in the run-up to the regicide too: Braddick, *God's Fury*, pp. 187–90, 558.

[17] A. R. Warmington, *Civil War, Interregnum and Restoration in Gloucestershire 1640–1672* (Woodbridge, 1997), pp. 43–50; John T. Evans, *Seventeenth-Century Norwich: Politics, Religion and Government, 1620–1690* (Oxford, 1979), pp. 119–28.

'have voluntarily contributed, or shall voluntarily contribute [to the royal coffers] not being under the power of any part of the Kings Army'.[18]

Naturally the space for neutrality was also closing. Peace petitioners in London were regarded as a fifth column, while the Commons moved quickly to scotch an attempted neutrality pact in the West Country. On 11 March Whitaker noted that men in Devon and Cornwall had 'made a treaty wherein they had bound themselves, by receiving the sacrament, to perform a protestation which they had framed to associate themselves together to join in a peace, wherein they meant also to take in the counties of Somerset and Dorset; that they would admit of no forces to be sent to there either from the King or Parliament'. The challenge was in part to parliamentary authority: 'this was done without the knowledge of the Earl of Stamford who commanded there in chief for the Parliament'.[19] Orders were immediately sent to the mayor and committee in Exeter to prevent a planned meeting on 14 March, and Mr Prideaux and Mr Nichol were sent 'in post to quench that association for a neutrality as had formerly been done in the counties of York and Chester'.[20]

The hardening of the parliamentary cause proved too much for some of its prominent supporters, and there were some notable changes of sides. In March, as Husbands's *Collection* took shape and Henrietta Maria was bombarded at Bridlington, Sir Hugh Cholmley left the parliamentary camp for the Royalists. He had taken control of Scarborough castle for Parliament, and in January 1643 had led a successful action at Guisborough. This taste of active warfare seems to have led him to revisit his commitments, however. He did not send men to support the Fairfaxes in the West Riding and defended that decision in print; when Henrietta Maria landed up the coast in March Cholmley changed sides.[21]

[18] *A&O*, I, pp. 106–17, quotation at 106.   [19] *Whitaker Diary*, p. 87.

[20] Ibid., pp. 87–8; see also Prideaux's reassuring report on p. 108. For the Yorkshire neutrality pact, which was also said to have been a challenge to parliamentary authority, see Anthony Fletcher, *The Outbreak of the English Civil War* (1981), pp. 389–91; Braddick, *God's Fury*, pp. 220–1. For Cheshire see Fletcher, *Outbreak*, pp. 385–7; John Morrill, *Revolt in the Provinces: The People of England and the Tragedies of War*, 2nd edn (Harlow, 1999), pp. 55–6. Fletcher corrects the account of Cheshire's 'third force' given in J. S. Morrill, *Cheshire 1630–1660: County Government and Society during the English Revolution* (Oxford, 1974), pp. 57–8. In Staffordshire the neutrality pact was agreed after Edgehill – perhaps as it became clear that it was going to be a war, not a single campaign: D. H. Pennington and I. A. Roots, eds., *The Committee at Stafford, 1643–1645: The Order Book of the Staffordshire County Committee*, Collections for a History of Staffordshire, 4th ser., 1 (Manchester, 1957), pp. xx–xxi. In Lincolnshire a 'snarling modus vivendi' had survived up until the eve of Edgehill: Clive Holmes, *Seventeenth-Century Lincolnshire* (Lincoln, 1980), p. 159.

[21] Jack Binns, 'Cholmley, Sir Hugh, First Baronet (1600–1657)', *ODNB*, XI, pp. 504–5. Sir Hugh Cholmley, *Nevves from Yorke* (1643), Thomason date January 18[?] 1643.

In defending himself from criticism during winter 1642–3 Cholmley made a number of arguments – about the local strategic position, as understood by him and his captains, and about the uncertain status of orders he had received from Fairfax – and he had also published the written advice of his captains. But even in a letter to the Speaker he sounded a little lukewarm, complaining that he was not trusted and that he could not get supplies or instructions for his better direction. As a result he asked to be discharged of his command.[22] In the course of his defence he stated his war aims:

> I did not seek this imployment, so I was not drawn into action by private ends, but out of desire to contribute my poore endeavours to the settling the truth of the Gospel, liberty of the Subject, and peace of the Kingdome, which I shall wish and heartily pray for, and that with as much honour as possibly may be to his Majesty. For if there be not a good understanding between him and his Parliament shortly, so that these unhappy distractions may be composed, to my judgement the Kingdome is in danger to bee ruined.[23]

Crucially, then, Cholmley was claiming that the point of the war was to preserve the peace – for him, by late spring 1643, that commitment pointed to a different allegiance.

This was consistent with the claims Cholmley made in his memoirs, for the benefit of his sons:

> I did not forsake Parliament till they did fail in performing those particulars they made the grounds of the war when I was first engaged, viz., the preservation of religion, protection of the King's person, and liberties of the subject; nor did I quite them then for any particular ends of my own, but merely to perform the duty and allegiance I owed my Sovereign, and which I did in such a way as was without any diminution to my honour either as a gentleman or a soldier.[24]

This was a reading of his obligations according to the Protestation and the oath of allegiance, but this latter point, about gentility and soldiering, is particularly important in understanding the memoirs, which give full advice about the private and public duties of a gentleman. The account of his Civil War actions comes amidst a fairly conventional story of youthful excess, debt and his emergence into public life following the death of his father. Cholmley's first public act was to lead attempts to extract money from his reluctant countrymen for the improvement of the harbour at Whitby ('I wish, with all my heart, the next generation may have more public spirit').[25] In response to pressure, he agreed to

---

[22] Cholmley, *Nevves*, A2v.   [23] Ibid.
[24] Nathaniel Cholmley, *The memoirs of Sir Hugh Cholmley* ([London?], 1787), pp. 67–8.
[25] Ibid., p. 51.

serve as a justice, taking on and vanquishing Sir Thomas Hoby, an old enemy of both his father and grandfather. He emerged from this the full figure of a gentleman: 'my father being dead, the country looked upon me as the chief of my family; and having mastered my debts, I did not only appear at all public meetings in a very gentlemanly equipage, but lived in as handsome and plentiful fashion at home as any gentleman in all the country, of my rank'. He kept a large household and good hospitality, and twice each week 'a certain number of old people, widows and indigent persons, were served at my gates with bread and good pottage made of beef, which I mention, that those which succeed may follow the example'.[26] As Cholmley explained it, in accounts written for crucial audiences, his Civil War behaviour was driven by the respectable values of a father of his country, and represented, in effect, an attempt to make sense of the extraordinary conditions of Civil War England in a conventional register.[27]

Cholmley seems to have enjoyed more success than other side-changers in affecting the judgement of posterity – for example Clarendon was far more convinced of Cholmley's integrity than of that of Sir John Hotham and his son, or of Sir Alexander Carew[28] – and Whitelock clearly agreed about Hotham:

This unfortunate gentleman had a good estate and interest, and was of a fair extraction in his country, yet his rough carriage, especially to his inferiors, his very narrow living, and the betrayal of the trust committed to him, rendered him so distasteful to all sorts of people, that his masters (for whom he had done so great service in resisting the king at his first coming to Hull) they now cast him off; his soldiers (who had fought for him) now chase him away from them, and his brother-in-law supplants him, and sends him with his wife and children prisoners to London.[29]

Crucial, here, was the plausibility of the claim to gentility, and therefore dependably honourable public commitments.

Uncertainty of allegiance led to an acute concern with plots and spies, denunciations of 'treasons' and valorization of conspicuous loyalty. A more active response was to promote oaths and covenants: fixity of purpose was crucial to fixity of allegiance, to the stability of the Parliamentarian mobilization. This seems to have been a consistent preference of Pym's, echoing the successful formula of the Scottish Covenanters, but

[26] Ibid., pp. 55–6.

[27] For further examples and fuller references see Braddick, *God's Fury*, pp. 297–302. See also, now, Barbara Donagan, *War in England 1642–1649* (Oxford, 2008).

[28] For Carew and the Hothams see Clarendon, III, pp. 235–6, 526–9; for his much more charitable view of Cholmley's 'conversion' see ibid., II, p. 468; III, p. 101 n.

[29] Bulstrode Whitelock, *Memorials of the English Affairs*, 4 vols. (Oxford, 1853), I, p. 206.

such initiatives tended in England to draw attention to the divisions which had no parallel in Scotland, at least at the point the National Covenant was signed. The move to associate counties in October 1642 had been tied to a proposal for 'a covenant or association that all might enter into', proposed by Pym 'with very great vehemence'. Local activists, however, had preferred to drop the mutual bond and proceed by way of taxation.[30] The lack of unity, in other words, forced Parliament to proceed by ordinance rather than covenant, and thereby, presumably, to increase the liability to fissure.

June 1643 saw another major, and divisive, attempt to stabilize allegiances around a fixed position: the Vow and Covenant and the formal constitution of the Westminster Assembly to discuss the church settlement, to define the reformation being sought. In March, following the collapse of the Oxford Treaty, and as Parliament took important measures to stiffen its military campaign, Charles had given some encouragement to the 'Waller plot', a plan to deliver London to him by stealth. It was discovered in good time, but the revelation was deliberately withheld until the Fast Day on 31 May, when news of the plot was immediately coupled to a new Vow and Covenant.

Like the Protestation it was designed to firm up the cause, and to sort the sheep from the goats. It summarized the national armed conflict as the result of 'a Popish and traiterous Plot, for the Subversion of the true Protestant Reformed Religion, and the Liberty of the Subject', which had given rise to 'a Popish Army . . . now on Foot in divers Parts of this Kingdom'. The best defence, it was now clear, was for 'all who are true-hearted and Lovers of their Country [to] bind themselves each to other in a Sacred Vow and Covenant'.[31] Opinion in London was divided, and an element of the Waller plot had been a proposal to carry out a census of Royalist sympathizers, parish by parish.[32] The Vow and Covenant offered a similar possibility, but the test was a stringent one. Those who

---

[30] Clive Holmes, *The Eastern Association in the English Civil War* (Cambridge, 1974), pp. 62–7. For Scottish unity see David Stevenson, *The Scottish Revolution 1637–44: The Triumph of the Covenanters* (Edinburgh, 2003 edn), and Margo Todd, *The Culture of Protestantism in Early Modern Scotland* (New Haven, 2002).

[31] *LJ*, VI, pp. 86–8. For the plot see Austin Woolrych, *Britain in Revolution, 1625–1660* (Oxford, 2002), pp. 257–8; Keith Lindley, *Popular Politics and Religion in Civil War London* (Aldershot, 1997), pp. 348–51; and Gardiner, I, pp. 144–9. For the protestation see Braddick, *God's Fury*, pp. 143–4.

[32] Lindley, *Popular Politics*, pp. 336–48; Braddick, *God's Fury*, pp. 252–61. Parliamentary escalation in the spring was more or less mirrored in a controversial initiative in London, co-ordinated from Salters' Hall and led by religious radicals, for 'a general rising': Lindley, *Popular Politics*, pp. 314–19; Robert Brenner, *Merchants and Revolution: Commercial Change, Political Conflict and London's Overseas Traders, 1550–1653* (Cambridge, 1993), esp. pp. 448–59; I am grateful to Tom Leng for pointing out this connection to me.

swore this oath renounced their own sins, and those of the nation, in the face of 'deserved the Judgements and Calamities that now lie upon' the kingdom. But they also swore 'That, in order to the Security and Preservation of the true Protestant Religion, and Liberty of the Subject, I will not consent to the laying down of Arms, so long as the Papists now in open War against the Parliament shall, by Force of Arms, be protected from the Justice thereof'. This was rather different from an abhorrence of the 'wicked and treacherous Design lately discovered'. However, the real test for many was that 'I do believe, in my Conscience, that the Forces raised by the Two Houses of Parliament are raised and continued for their just Defence, and for the Defence of the true Protestant Religion, and Liberties of the Subject, against the Forces raised by the King'. This implied that 'I will, according to my Power and Vocation, assist the Forces raised and continued by both Houses of Parliament, against the Forces raised by the King without their Consent'. Commands proceeding directly from the king were here contrasted with a higher obligation, since those who took the oath swore to 'answer at the Great Day, when the Secrets of all Hearts shall be disclosed'.

There can be no doubt that this now seemed a stiff test even for some of those who had actively supported the parliamentary war effort, let alone those on whose simple compliance the war effort had rested. Not the least of the problems was that the Vow and Covenant made no guarantee to protect the king's person; this was the subject of a separate Lords order that 'A short Declaration might be drawn up, and taken by their Lordships, the House of Commons, and the whole Kingdom, to declare their Loyalty to the King's Person, and His Crown and Dignity.'[33] Commitment to the war effort was here a godly duty in itself; all the questions about the resultant effects on the religion and liberty of the subject were not only begged, the answers were assumed. The Vow and Covenant fixed the cause, but at a point in advance of that reached by many of those on whose support Parliament's mobilization depended.

A short time later the Westminster Assembly was constituted to give shape to the Reformation: 'as yet many things remain in the Liturgy, Discipline and Government of the Church, which do necessarily require a further, and more perfect Reformation then as yet hath been attained'. In this history the cause was the completion, not simply the defence, of the Reformation. This was a more pressing problem, or urgent opportunity, since Parliament had declared that 'the present Church-Government . . . is evil, and justly offensive and burthensome to the Kingdome, a great impediment to Reformation and growth of Religion,

[33] *LJ*, VI, p. 87.

and very prejudicial to the State and Government of this Kingdome'. Abolished, this episcopal hierarchy should be replaced by 'such a Government... as may be most agreeable to Gods Holy Word'. But here practical politics intervened, since it was also important that the resulting settlement should be 'most apt to procure and preserve the Peace of the Church at home, and nearer Agreement with the Church of Scotland, and other Reformed Churches abroad'.[34]

There was an evident concern about the difficulty of undertaking this work in the full glare of a lively news culture: the Assembly's findings were to be delivered to the Houses, and were not to be divulged 'by Printing, Writing, or otherwise, without the consent of both or either House of Parliament'. This reflected a wider anxiety about printing, and the unlicensed divulgence of the secrets of state or divinity. Unlicensed and unlearned preaching or pamphleteering propagated error and encouraged zealous but ignorant speculation about fundamental truths. Here, too, June saw a crucial measure – the first of a number of attempts to re-establish press controls. Such control was necessary, in order to guard against 'the great defamation of Religion and Government'.[35] Prepublication licensing was re-established, then, two days after the Westminster Assembly had been constituted, and again by ordinance.

By June the need to fix the ideological cause behind military escalation had found expression in an attempt at a national Covenant and to define a national church settlement. Both were historically rooted, and sought a definition of the destination implied by the desire for reformation. Alongside these positive steps to define the parliamentary cause came attempts to shut down, or at least control, the public discussion that did so much to undermine these claims to legitimacy. These attempts to authorize and stabilize the cause, however, were not the end of the process – driven by military needs the escalation continued, it was legitimized with reference to these familiar arguments, and those terms continued to

---

[34] *A&O*, I, pp. 180–4, 12 June 1643.

[35] 14 June 1643, *A&O*, I, pp. 184–6. For the wider context see Michael Mendle, 'De facto freedom, de facto authority: press and Parliament, 1640–1643', *HJ*, 38 (1995), 307–32. There are two interesting points about these measures of censorship – they relate not only to things vended, but to other forms of publication; and they target tone as well as content. On the first point – that publication was not always intended for sale, and that political information circulated in print but non-commercially – see Jason Peacey, '"Scattered about the streets": Thomason's annotations and print ephemera', in Giles Mandelbrote and Jason Peacey, eds., *Collecting Revolution: The History and Importance of the Thomason Tracts* (forthcoming), and David Como, 'Sowing sedition and raising riot: pamphlets, placards and street-politics, c. 1635–1645' (unpublished paper; I am grateful to Professor Como for permission to cite this paper prior to publication); for the second point see Debora Shuger, *Censorship and Cultural Sensibility: the Regulation of Language in Tudor-Stuart England* (Philadelphia, 2006).

be contested. July brought the Excise, August the Solemn League and Covenant and a commitment to more radical iconoclasm, November the issue of a new Great Seal after months of hesitation and, on 20 December, there was a proto-Test Act: 'An Ordinance to disable any person within the City of London and Liberties thereof, to be of the Common-Councell, or in any Office of trust within the said City, that shall not take the late solemne League and Covenant.'[36]

V

The year 1643 was the first of the real war. The tense jostlings of the previous year had eventually led to a pitched battle at Edgehill, but that battle and its sequel at Turnham Green had proved inconclusive. Perhaps for the same reason the negotiations at Oxford were also inconclusive; the fighting had not shifted matters sufficiently one way or the other, and offered little reason to partisans to concede the territory laid out the previous summer. As negotiations failed, and a more concerted campaign opened, it became imperative to raise money and men for the war effort, and on the parliamentary side this led to significant escalation: the formation of regional armies funded by the assessment and, eventually, the excise; sequestration and penal taxation. All this was done by the authority of ordinance, an instrument decried in January by *A Complaint*. It was accompanied by pamphlet campaigns that attempted to define the cause more closely and lend it historical legitimacy, by the promotion of national oaths in support of the cause, and by drives for further reformation through iconoclasm campaigns. In mobilizing for war the cause was defined and redefined, with implications for the allegiance of those people on whom these calls were being made.

One of the key texts in defining the parliamentary cause as it stood in early 1643 was Edward Husbands's *Exact Collection*. Here was the battle for the ancient constitution, in which the king's advisers had scored a victory the previous summer. Its end point was the assessment – a compulsory tax levied by the power of ordinance. The case for defensive arms was a counterpoint to the necessity of constitutional innovation. This desire to fix the cause was understandable, but quickly outflanked by events, while such attempts to stabilize the parties offered hostages to fortune. Sir Hugh Cholmley defended his honour, for the benefit of his sons, by presenting his actions as consistent with the Protestation and the oath of allegiance. The *Exact Collection* was one of the key resources used by John Lilburne to shame the Parliamentarian leadership into more

---

[36] Braddick, *God's Fury*, pp. 296, 309–15, 323–4; *A&O*, I, p. 359.

effective action in defence of the rights of free-born Englishmen,[37] and there was a minor publishing industry advising on the compatibility or otherwise of the various oaths and covenants promoted during the 1640s and 1650s.[38] In 1647 the New Model Army published its own *Book of Declarations* explaining and justifying its intervention in politics; it was a point of reference in the debates before the General Council at Putney about what the army should do with its new-found role.[39]

Each exemplification of the cause, and each escalation, demanded a renewed commitment. Public support was constantly mobilized, in print and in action, through the imposition of the Vow and Covenant, or the performative politics attending, for example, the destruction of Cheapside Cross, the purgation of Somerset House or the burning of the *Book of Sports*. As *All the memorable and wonder strikinge mercies* made clear, the people of Israel were crucial to this both as witnesses and actors. Active campaigning had practical effects throughout the kingdom, and the language of well- and ill-affected clearly permeated village and borough politics.[40] Parliamentary and Royalist coalitions were created, however, against the background of rapidly shifting political arguments, in which partisans contested control of key terms and arguments before these wider public audiences. As they did so individual choices were reconsidered, and allegiances reassessed. An important but largely unconsidered legacy of materialist and progressive histories of the causes of the English Civil War has been a sense of the fixity of allegiance, and the correspondingly clear-cut view of 'side-changing'. In fact, of course, it may have been the cause that underwent a crucial change rather than the commitments of an individual.[41]

There is another point lurking behind this, about the creativity of the arguments of the Revolution. A common feature of Civil War argument

---

[37] Andrew Sharp, 'John Lilburne and the Long Parliament's Book of Declarations: a radical's exploitation of the words of authorities', *History of Political Thought*, 9 (1988), 19–44.

[38] David Martin Jones, *Conscience and Allegiance in Seventeenth-Century England: the Political Significance of Oaths and Engagements* (Woodbridge, 1999); Edward Vallance, *Revolutionary England and the National Covenant: State Oaths, Protestantism and the Political Nation, 1553–1682* (Woodbridge, 2005).

[39] Braddick, *God's Fury*, pp. 510–16.

[40] William Cliftlands, 'The "well-affected" and the "country": politics and religion in English provincial society, *c.* 1640–1654', unpublished Ph.D. dissertation, University of Essex, 1987.

[41] See, for an earlier example, S. P. Salt, 'Dering, Sir Edward, First Baronet (1598–1644)', *ODNB*, XV, pp. 874–80; Derek Hirst, 'The defection of Sir Edward Dering, 1640–1641', repr. in Peter Gaunt, ed., *The English Civil War* (Oxford, 2000), pp. 207–25; Jason Peacey, 'Popularity and the politician: an MP and his public, 1640–1644' (unpublished paper; I am grateful to Dr Peacey for permission to cite this paper prior to publication).

was to contest the historicization of any particular version of the cause by drawing attention to previous commitments which had been reneged upon, or to which partisans had failed to live up. But one further effect of the powerful but unanchored use of the rhetoric of anti-popery, or of an unfolding reformation, was that it allowed for the progressive revelation of the cause – as in Cromwell's famous assertion that religion (in the sense of liberty of conscience) was not the thing at first contended for.[42] This distinction, between attempts to fix the cause to a foundational text and a willingness to see it progressively unveiled, again points up the importance of the National Covenant, and then the Solemn League and Covenant, to the Scottish war. In Scotland divisions were expressed primarily over the interpretation of these foundational texts, and there were few claims beyond them. In England both those seeking the reformation of the spirit and those seeking the fundamental liberties of Englishmen claimed that this cause had not been the thing at first contended for, but had been progressively revealed in the course of the conflict. This was a liberating and creative possibility. It was also an issue that the Levellers wanted to have both ways on the first day of the Putney Debates – that the *Agreement* expressed what had been revealed to be the core of the battle for liberty, although part of the mechanism for that revelation had been the successive failures of actually existing political institutions to stick to their words, for which the grandees were criticized. Cromwell's insistence that army actions should be consistent with its previous declarations, while responding to earlier accusations about the army command's inconsistency, became by a kind of paradox an evasion of the purposes of the war as they now stood revealed.

The year 1643 was crucial in all these respects: it saw rapid escalation of the war effort, the crystallization of parties in localities which had hitherto resisted that, and a number of high-profile changes of allegiance. There was a marked polemical concern with plots and honour, treason and truth. This should prompt us to a more nuanced view of the parliamentary cause – how it was constructed and the ambiguities it presented. The imperative need for men and money led to an effort at mobilization which drew on diverse elements of the political culture, in ways that shifted quickly under the pressure of events. Much of this revolved around histories – narratives crossing the ground of recent events, which lent shape and direction to them. If the truly revolutionary consequences of this crisis lay in intellectual creativity rather than social-structural

---

[42] Cromwell's remark came in his speech at the dissolution of his first parliament in January 1655: W. C. Abbott, *The Writings and Speeches of Oliver Cromwell*, 4 vols. (Oxford, 1988), III, p. 586.

change, that has an important context in the need to legitimate the material demands of mobilization for war.[43] Escalation exposed the limits of
agreement that could be achieved around histories, particularly those of
English liberties and reformation. The resulting paralysis inspired some
radical attempts to transcend or escape history altogether, while Thomas
Hobbes and John Harrington grounded their political claims not in a
supposedly factual past but in counter-factuals. The central ambiguity
of the claim to see 'the first year of England's freedom by God's blessing
restored' – of the relationship of the cause to the history of liberty and
reformation – was present at the inception of the parliamentary military
campaign in the first year of the real war.

---

[43] Michael J. Braddick, 'Mobilisation, anxiety and creativity in England during the 1640s',
in John Morrow and Jonathan Scott, eds., *Liberty, Authority, Formality: Political Ideas
and Culture, 1600–1900* (Exeter, 2008), pp. 175–93.

7   Sacrilege and compromise: court divines and the king's conscience, 1642–1649

Anthony Milton

I

If historians are agreed in seeing religion as having been crucial to the politics of the 1640s, then they have tended to see the clergymen involved as being exclusively Parliamentarian ones. By contrast, the Royalist clergy in the 1640s tend to be depicted as passive sufferers at best, meekly retiring from the political stage, humbly providing spiritual comfort on scaffolds or in country houses. Rather than the outspoken and politically meddlesome Laudians of the 1630s, the Royalist clergy seem to be reduced to a meek pastoral role appropriate to those who have been politically defeated. This impression of a politically inactive clergy is understandable. After all, Charles in the 1640s had no clerical adviser remotely equivalent to William Laud in the 1630s and after May 1641 the king had no clerical privy councillor at all – a situation not seen since the sixteenth century.[1] The absence of clerical voices was encapsulated in early 1643, when the king arrived at a Privy Council meeting ready to put the case for *jure divino* episcopacy in response to a Scottish paper, but after heated opposition was persuaded not to do so.[2] Nevertheless, as we shall see, Royalist divines did not disappear from the scene, meekly accepting the dismantling of the established church. They preached, wrote, published and argued over the changes, constructing vigorous new defences of the existing church, and deploying a biblical rhetoric and outspoken providentialism that could match or even exceed that of Parliamentarian ministers.

Because Charles constantly foregrounded his religious concerns and the demands of his royal conscience, it often tends to be implied that we are dealing with the solitary king's irreducible inner convictions. Yet Charles would have been the first to observe that he needed his clergymen

---

[1] On the importance of the Privy Council during the war see R. Cust, *Charles I: A Political life* (Harlow, 2005), pp. 368–9.

[2] Edward, Earl of Clarendon, *The Life of Edward, Earl of Clarendon*, 3 vols. (Oxford, 1828), I, pp. 88–93 – cited in Cust, *Charles*, p. 369 n.

to ensure that the royal conscience was properly instructed: as he put it in his third answer to the Newcastle Propositions, a matter of conscience required that he be 'assisted with the advice of some of his own chaplains . . . and such other divines as shall be most proper to inform him therein'.[3] Political historians have increasingly recognized that Charles was not simply inflexible, but could be influenced and persuaded by those around him, much to the queen's alarm.[4] But there has been little attempt hitherto to recapture the advice that the king was receiving from his bishops and chaplains during these crucial years, when the extent of his room for manoeuvre in religious matters in particular was a pivotal consideration for the monarch, and a vital issue in the political process. Even if they could not aspire to the sort of influence on daily policy which Laud had exercised, court bishops and chaplains were acutely aware of the need to navigate the royal conscience through increasingly uncertain waters, as a series of treaty proposals posed a variety of threats to the survival of their church.

In this chapter I shall trace some of the arguments presented by Royalist clergy regarding the concessions that should and should not be granted by the monarch during the 1640s. My attention will be focused on those whom one might loosely label 'court divines'. This group includes bishops such as William Juxon, Brian Duppa, John Warner, Matthew Wren and Griffith Williams; court chaplains such as Richard Steward, Robert Sanderson, Gilbert Sheldon, Henry Hammond, Jeremy Taylor, Isaac Basire and Henry Ferne; and other divines present in Royalist Oxford, such as Gerard Langbaine and Edward Boughen. This was not a homogeneous group: while most of them had been close to the Laudian regime this was not true of them all, and some important differences of opinion sometimes emerged between them. But they were all anxious to find ways of arresting the decline in the church's fortunes, all hoped to influence the king in one way or another to this end, and some of them worked closely together. Sheldon and Hammond formed a particularly close alliance, while Wren referred on several occasions to

---

[3] Gardiner, *CD*, p. 313; John Evelyn, *Diary and Correspondence of John Evelyn*, ed. W. Bray and H. B. Wheatley, 4 vols. (1906), IV, pp. 189–90. We also know that Charles asked for copies of sermons previously preached before him by chaplains who were no longer able to attend him in person: Henry Hammond, *The Christians Obligations to Peace and Charity* (1649), sig. A3r. Section 24 of *Eikon Basilike* in which Charles insists on the importance of his chaplains' advice (*Reliquiae Sacrae Carolinae* (1658), III, pp. 185–93) was allegedly written by John Gauden, possibly with assistance from Brian Duppa (F. F. Madan, *A New Bibliography of the Eikon Basilike*, Oxford Bibliographical Society, new ser. 3 (1950), p. 131).

[4] E.g. C. Russell, *The Causes of the English Civil War* (Oxford, 1990), pp. 194, 206.

'our Tribe'.[5] What, then, were the principles that these divines were seeking to implant in the king's mind and conscience before as well as during the post-war negotiations over the future of the church? As I shall argue, we need to think of these divines not as mere cheerleaders for an existing Royalist position, but as people trying to make a pitch for what that Royalist position would be, seeking to address, instruct, warn and make demands on their own side. Not only was the survival of the Church of England as they knew it at stake in the negotiations, but they were themselves potentially liable to permanent exclusion from their ministry under terms proposed by Parliament.[6] They therefore had every reason to seek to influence the outcome of negotiations.

II

Even before the outbreak of civil war there had been a significant reforming assault on the church, with the Court of High Commission abolished and bishops excluded from the House of Lords, among other measures to which the king had assented. But subsequent peace negotiations revolved around seeking Charles's agreement to further reforms embarked on after the king had left the capital and to which Parliament was bound by the Treaty of Edinburgh, most notably the abolition of bishops and seizure of their lands. From the Oxford Propositions of 1643 onwards these were demanded by Parliament, and after 1646, when ordinances were finally passed abolishing episcopacy and the Prayer Book and alienating bishops' lands, Charles was required to assent to what was now a fait accompli.[7]

These were circumstances where court clergy could hardly be silent. There were two issues about which Royalist divines were particularly exercised – the abolition of episcopacy and the sale of bishops' and other church lands. But one matter should be dealt with first: the king's obligations arising from the coronation oath.[8] This issue had been raised by the king's Parliamentarian opponents – most publicly in Parliament's 'Third Remonstrance' of 26 May 1642, where it was claimed that the oath bound the king to pass all good laws submitted by Parliament, and to remedy by law any inconveniences in the kingdom. In order to highlight Parliament's partial reading of it, the full text of the oath was published in reply, revealing its important religious provisions. Not only did the king promise to keep 'the Laws, Customes, and Franchises granted to

[5] P. King, 'The episcopate during the Civil War, 1642–1649', *EHR*, 83 (1968), 523–37, at 535.

[6] Gardiner, *CD*, pp. 280, 301–2.   [7] Ibid., pp. 263, 268–9, 275, 291–2, 343.

[8] Richard Steward, *An answer to a letter written at Oxford* (1647), pp. 45–6. Cf. *A Vindication of Episcopacie* (1644), p. 46.

the Clergie, by the glorious King Saint Edward', but he had responded to a further episcopal admonition in unambiguous language:

> With a willing and devout Heart I Promise . . . that I will Preserve and maintaine to you [the bishops] and the Churches committed to your charge all Canonicall Priviledges, and due Law and Justice, and that I will be your Protector and Defender, to my Power, by the Assistance of God, as every good King, in his Kingdome, in Right ought to Protect and Defend the Bishops, and Churches under their Government.[9]

This part of the coronation oath had hitherto only been briefly touched on in an exchange between Sir Thomas Aston (in a treatise dedicated to Charles) and William Prynne in 1641.[10] But the argument that the oath bound the king not to make any concessions of clerical privileges was made more fully the following year in an anonymous and undated manuscript tract apparently composed soon after the king's response in which the oath had been printed.[11] Setting itself to assess 'Whither his Majestie may give his Royall assent to any Act of Parliament that tends eyther to the Ruine or diminucion of the present Clergy, Salvo Juramento?', the tract attributed central significance to the king's coronation oath in which Charles had bound himself to defend the rights of the clergy. The anonymous author argues that the oath necessarily binds the king 'untill it be remitted in an express forme either by the whole Clergy themselves . . . or by some body of Men, that represents the Clergy'.[12] This represented a novel and significant raising of the religious stakes on the Royalist side, implying that any further religious concessions by the king would do irreparable damage to his conscience and hopes for salvation. What makes the text particularly notable is that it appears to be the work of Richard Steward,[13] who as clerk of the closet and subsequently dean of the Chapel Royal was one of the king's closest religious advisers; Charles would later urge the Prince of Wales to 'take his [Steward's]

---

[9] Edward Husbands, *An Exact Collection of All Remonstrances* (1643), pp. 268–9, 290–1. This 'fifth question' was introduced into the coronation oath in the late fourteenth century: P. E. Schramm, *A History of the English Coronation* (Oxford, 1937), pp. 211–18; C. Wordsworth, ed., *The Manner of the Coronation of King Charles the First of England* (1892), pp. 23–4, 99, 114.

[10] Thomas Aston, *A Remonstrance Against Presbytery* (1641), ii ('A brief review of episcopacie'), p. 73; William Prynne, *The Antipathie of the English Lordly Prelacie, Both to Regall Monarchy and Civill Unity* (1641), pp. 514–15.

[11] BL, Add. MS 34312, fos. 1r–6r. This paper refers to the King's answer to the Lords and Commons' letter of 26 May 1642 as 'lately' published and makes no reference to a military conflict.

[12] Ibid., fos. 3v, 5v.

[13] The text is reproduced identically in Steward's *Answer*, pp. 46–52, apart from the word 'lately'.

advice, and give very much reverence to his opinion in every thing which concernes conscience or church affairs'.[14]

It seems very likely, then, that this more rigorous interpretation of the king's obligations towards the church and clergy was being made forcefully and directly to Charles during the Civil War by one of his closest clerical advisers. Charles would also have soon become familiar with the argument from the pens of his other clergymen. The oath was quoted in full – with the emphatic observation that this promissory oath could not be broken without the consent (which must not be a 'forced consent') of the bishops – in a semi-official anonymous volume *A Vindication of Episcopacie* that was published with the backing of the clerk of the closet (either Steward or his successor Sheldon) and Secretary Nicholas in 1644.[15] Similarly, Gerard Langbaine in his *A Review of the Covenant* (Oxford, 1645) argued that the king would be convicted before God of 'the foule crime of perjury' if he 'upon any suggested grounds of policy passe away their [the clergy's] Rights without their consent'.[16] The oath was published once again in full, with appropriate commentary, in Isaac Basire's *Sacriledge arraigned*, which was delivered before the king and 'published by His Majesties speciall command' in 1646.[17] The manuscript determination of the issue from 1642, with the full text of the coronation oath, was published in 1647, and the oath and its implications also found their way into a tract published by the bishop of Rochester, John Warner, in the same year.[18] Similar sentiments were expressed in 1647 by the divines of Oxford University,[19] in a text which was almost certainly the work of the king's chaplain Robert Sanderson – another divine whose opinions in matters of conscience Charles acknowledged to be of considerable importance to him.[20]

---

[14] *State Papers Collected by Edward Earl of Clarendon*, 3 vols. (Oxford, 1767), II, pp. 253–4, 261.

[15] John Bramhall, *The Serpent Salve* (1643), pp. 141–2; *Vindication*, pp. 28–31. See the draft of the *Vindication* in BL, Add. MS 34312, fos. 14–52, with the note by the anonymous author 'This tract I delivered to Dr. Bray [Laud's chaplain], who added nothing, but altred and transposed some things, and after shewed it to the Clerke of the Closett and Secretary Nicholas as his owne, by whose means it was afterwards printed.'

[16] Gerard Langbaine, *A review of the Covenant* (Oxford, 1645), pp. 62, 72–4. See also the discussion and quotation of the oath in *Certain disquisitions and considerations* (Oxford, 1644), pp. 12–13.

[17] Isaac Basire, *Sacriledge arraigned* (Oxford, 1646), pp. 97–100.

[18] John Warner, *Church-Lands Not to be Sold* (1647), pp. 25–9. Warner seems to have been thinking in the early 1640s about the king's religious promises in his coronation oath: see BL, Harl. MS 6424, fos. 102r–103v; Bodl., MS Eng. misc. b.193, fo. 178r.

[19] Robert Sanderson, *Reasons of the present judgement of the University of Oxford concerning The Solemne League and Covenant* (1647), pp. 12–13.

[20] Izaak Walton, *The Life of Dr Sanderson* (1676), sig. D7r; *ODNB*.

Most, if not all, of these were publications with which Charles was directly acquainted, and it seems clear that he was fully absorbing their message. At the Uxbridge negotiations, for example, the king's own directions to his commissioners spelt out quite clearly that he could not yield to a change of government by bishops because 'I hold my self particularly bound by the Oath I took at my Coronation, not to alter the Government of this Church from what I found it', even though his own commissioners expressed the view that he was willing to consider the question.[21] In the following year, in his private correspondence with the queen and public correspondence with the Covenanter Alexander Henderson, Charles insisted that his coronation oath prevented him from making any religious concessions that were to the detriment of the clergy, and specifically of the bishops.[22] He also followed Steward's insistence that only the Church of England itself lawfully and collectively assembled could free him from his oath.[23] In the surreal endgame of the Treaty of Newport negotiations in 1648 Charles once again swiftly raised the issue of his coronation oath to defend the clergy, and a separate day was devoted to an inconclusive discussion of the issue.[24] When in *Eikon Basilike* Charles invokes his coronation oath to defend the ecclesiastical government and revenues there is therefore no need to see this merely as an interpolation by his clerical editors – there is clear evidence that Charles also felt this way.[25]

The clergy's insistence on the inviolability of the king's coronation oath to protect the clergy was of course in part a way of bolstering the king's position in negotiations. But it is equally possible to see this as a direct threat to Charles of what awaited him if he dared to betray his church, for, as John Warner put it, 'what King, or Nation, will hereafter trust our King, who in breaking so just, and solemne an oath, as that at his Coronation, will rob his God, lose his faith, forfeit his soule, destroy a goodly flourishing Church, and utterly undoe them, who have hazarded all, thereby to keep loyalty, and a good conscience?' And it would not

---

[21] *Reliquiae*, II, p. 283.

[22] *Charles I in 1646: Letters of King Charles the First to Queen Henrietta Maria*, ed. J. Bruce, Camden Society 63 (1856), p. 27; *Reliquiae*, II, p. 311. See also the King's Answer to the Vote of No Addresses (ibid., II, p. 300).

[23] *Reliquiae*, II, pp. 324, 343.

[24] F. Peck, *Desiderata Curiosa*, 2 vols. (1779), II, pp. 388–9; Edward Walker, *Perfect copies of all the votes, letters, proposals and answers . . . that passed in the treaty held at Newport* (1705), p. 38. A paper of arguments concerning the oath – possibly prepared by John Glynne for his exchanges with Charles at Newport on 3 October – survives in Bodl., Ballard MS 45, fo. 11br.

[25] Where clerical editors may have been involved is in *Eikon*'s attempt to explain away Charles's earlier concessions on episcopacy within the terms of his coronation oath by having the king make the highly questionable claim that the bishops had specifically consented to the bill excluding them from parliament: *Reliquiae*, III, p. 53.

just be Charles who suffered from his perjury, since 'his wife, children, and posterity' would also be consumed.[26] When Saul broke his covenant with the Gibeonites, God punished the whole land for three years and destroyed almost all of Saul's posterity, but England should expect much worse afflictions if Charles 'after much consultation, long deliberation, and the many protestations (as I am informed) that it is against his conscience, violate so just, so holy an Oath as this'.[27]

III

This emphasis on the king's coronation oath was usually intended only as a supplement to arguments that it was impossible for the king's conscience to yield to the abolition of episcopacy. That episcopacy could never justifiably be abolished was a point insisted on with absolute clarity by many Royalist divines in the 1640s. The defence of episcopacy as *jure divino* had already been heightened under the Laudians, and was reasserted with particular vigour by Jeremy Taylor in 1642.[28] Royalist clergy were especially emphatic on this point because it was a consistent parliamentary demand that the king consent to their January 1643 bill abolishing episcopacy, a stipulation which was made even more inflexibly after Parliament's Solemn League and Covenant with the Scots the following September specifically required the abolition of church government by bishops. This was also an issue on which Charles himself had given the court divines cause for concern. The king's abandonment of episcopacy in Scotland met with increasingly direct criticism from English divines as Parliamentarians began to urge it as a precedent for the removal of English bishops.[29] Other concessions that the king had made in England against bishops' secular powers – most notably their exclusion from Parliament – also met with a troubled response and implicit criticisms from a number of court divines.[30]

The king's tendency to agree to concessions was all the more of a worry for court divines because they were conscious that many lay Royalists (including the king's councillors) were increasingly prepared to countenance the disabling – or even the wholesale abolition – of episcopacy

[26] Warner, *Church-Lands*, p. 27.   [27] Ibid., p. 28.

[28] A. Milton, *Catholic and Reformed* (Cambridge, 1995), pp. 454–70, 489–93.

[29] E.g. Steward, *Answer*, pp. 3, 18; Warner, *Church-Lands*, pp. 33–4; Bodl., Sancroft MS 78, p. 22; *Reliquiae*, II, p. 319.

[30] *Vindication*, p. 57; Edward Boughen, *Mr Geree's Case of Conscience Sifted* (1648), pp. 78–9; Bramhall, *Serpent salve*, pp. 20, 34–5; Griffith Williams, *The Discovery of Mysteries* (Oxford, 1643), pp. 26, 78–81; Henry Ferne, *Episcopacy and presbytery considered* (Oxford, 1644), p. 26; John Doughty, *The king's cause* (1644), p. 27.

as the price of a lasting peace. As Bishop Griffith Williams was complaining as early as 1643, such men were advising the king 'to purchase the peace of the Common-wealth with the ruine of Gods Church'.[31] By 1646 these men even included Secretary Nicholas, who reflected that the abolition of bishops would be regrettable, but was not to be compared with the abolition of monarchy.[32] In the face of this threat court divines embarked on a heightened defence of the institution of episcopacy. In 1644 *A Vindication of Episcopacie* warned that to abolish the episcopal order and ordination would be an act of formal schism from the universal church of Christ, would subvert the nation's fundamental laws, and would be against God's ordinance.[33] The following year, sensing the last chance of a possible settlement with Parliament in the Uxbridge negotiations, a number of royal chaplains (Steward, Sheldon, Ferne, Hammond, Benjamin Laney and Christopher Potter) offered a host of significant concessions on the practice of episcopal government, reluctantly accepting the necessity of what the king would term 'a regulated Episcopacy'.[34] But at the same time several of them published a new, emphatic series of broadsides against any Royalist suggestions that peace could be achieved by yielding to the parliamentary commissioners' demands that episcopacy be abolished altogether. Henry Hammond's *Considerations of present use concerning the Danger resulting from the change of our Church Government* was specifically aimed at those who believed that episcopal government was lawful, yet thought that to sacrifice it was not a change of religion, that it could be surrendered 'merely out of intuition of our own secular advantages'.[35] Hammond warned that abandoning episcopacy would be a work of 'practicall Atheisme'.[36] It is notable that Hammond set himself to oppose the charges that those who insisted on the need to preserve episcopacy simply preferred 'the interests of some inconsiderable men before the inconveniences and common wishes of all', and that it was only clergymen whose interests were concerned in the business. These were presumably the complaints being made in lay Royalist circles.[37] Similarly, Henry Ferne wrote a whole tract specifically against those who felt that episcopacy might be abandoned without prejudicing their religion and their devotion to the king's cause, in which he stressed that the abandonment of episcopacy would be against

---

[31] Williams, *Discovery*, pp. 2, 104.   [32] *Clarendon State Papers*, II, p. 308.
[33] *Vindication*, pp. 62–4.
[34] S. R. Gardiner, 'A scheme of toleration propounded at Uxbridge in 1645', *EHR*, 2 (1887); *Clarendon State Papers*, II, p. 275.
[35] Henry Hammond, *Considerations of present use concerning the danger resulting from the change of our Church Government* (1645), pp. 1, 3, 14–15.
[36] Ibid., p. 14.   [37] Ibid., pp. 1, 15–18.

religion.[38] Both works seem to have been published in January 1645, when the Uxbridge negotiations were at their height, as was Gerard Langbaine's *Review of the Covenant*, which also declared the extirpation of episcopacy to be 'in the highest degree sacrilegious, utterly against the Law of God'.[39] By 1646 the king's surrender to the Scots and receipt of Parliament's Newcastle Propositions made concessions on episcopacy a central political issue, and even though his court divines did not have direct access to their monarch after April, they would seem to have kept up the pressure to block the abolition of episcopacy through publications such as the reissue of Hammond's *Considerations*.

In the king's exchanges in 1646 with Henrietta Maria, and with his troika of Paris-based councillors Jermyn, Culpepper and Ashburnham, it is clear that Charles had acquired by this point an extremely high view of episcopacy, claiming for example that 'the whole frame of religion' rested upon the episcopal succession.[40] He told Henrietta Maria bluntly that yielding in this matter 'is a sin of the highest nature'.[41] Charles's letters to the queen also demonstrate that he had acquired the conviction that he had been punished by God for having taken away the bishops' votes in Parliament, and that while his upholding of episcopacy might regain God's favour, his abjuring of bishops would bring down further divine punishment.[42] When pressed by his counsellors to concede episcopacy, it is notable that the king appealed to the absent Steward, who may have been the source of some of these convictions of divine displeasure.[43]

Nevertheless, in the absence of his chaplains Charles still appears to have been vulnerable to making further concessions. It is interesting that by September 1646 the arrival of Will Murray, a groom of the bedchamber, seems to have prompted Charles to concoct a political compromise that involved the temporary suspension of episcopacy.[44] The king sought the approval of Bishop Juxon on the matter (allowing the bishop also to consult Duppa or Sheldon), applauding Juxon's worth and learning 'particularly in resolving cases of conscience', but Charles made it clear that he considered this 'compliance to the iniquity of the times' to be compatible with his coronation oath, 'considering how unable I am

---

[38] Ferne, *Episcopacy*, pp. 1, 27, 29.

[39] F. Madan, *Oxford Books*, 3 vols. (Oxford, 1895–1931), II, pp. 374–5; Langbaine, *Review*, p. 68.

[40] *Charles I in 1646*, pp. 26–7, 74, 83; *Clarendon State Papers*, II, pp. 242–4, 247–9, 255–6, 260–1, 264–5, 270, 273–5.

[41] *Charles I in 1646*, p. 7. Russell (*Causes*, p. 197 n.) notes that it is not clear whether these were views that Charles had had from the beginning of his reign, or were later developments.

[42] *Charles I in 1646*, pp. 80–1.   [43] *Clarendon State Papers*, II, p. 265.

[44] Cust, *Charles*, pp. 426–7.

by force to obtain that which this way there wants not a probability to recover'.[45] The suspension of episcopacy for three years would become a principal plank of the king's offers to Presbyterians thereafter – in his third answer to the Newcastle Propositions in May 1647, the Scots Engagement in December and the treaty of Newport in autumn 1648.[46] Clearly the court divines could not persuade Charles to abandon this concession, and yet (as we shall see) it could lead to the effective abolition of episcopacy, once its ambiguities were removed. Nevertheless, this royal consent to the suspension of episcopacy made it all the more important for the divines to ensure that the message that episcopacy must never be abolished continued to be made as forcefully as possible. It is notable that the emphatic defences of episcopacy by Taylor and Ferne were both republished in 1647, along with Steward's *Answer*, which insisted that episcopacy was a divine precept whose abandonment would be a greater sin than dispensing with the Lord's Day.[47] It is hardly a coincidence that the king's coronation oath became the subject of renewed pressure from court divines at this time.[48]

A related area of concern was the proposed alienation of bishops' lands – to which Parliament was bound by the terms of the 1643 Treaty of Edinburgh, and which was insisted on in subsequent parliamentary conditions.[49] Here was an issue where divines were able to invoke the evils of sacrilege, and to combine this with very direct threats of divine vengeance on the monarch, against arguments that this was an indifferent matter where 'Mistresse Necessity' dictated a flexible response.[50] The author of the *Vindication of episcopacie* claimed to be confident that Charles 'from his soule abhors the thought of so foule an Act' as to ruin his clergy in this way, which would expose him to the anathemas of donors and incur 'an everlasting blot of infamy', to say nothing of the divine vengeance that had in the past been visited on those who had seized church lands (including Henry VIII). Gerard Langbaine, writing in January 1645, was even more blunt: 'may we not feare that the Sacriledge of King Henries dayes cryes . . . loud for vengeance . . . And we never had any Solemne Nationall acknowledgment of it, or publique humiliation for it.' Any further alienation of church lands 'would be the ready way to bring upon us and our posterity all those fearful execrations with which

---

[45] *Clarendon State Papers*, II, pp. 265–7.
[46] Gardiner, *CD*, pp. 313, 329, 347; Walker, *Perfect copies*, p. 29.
[47] Steward, *Answer*, pp. 18, 24.
[48] It is not clear that the king had a view of any of these works. Steward's *Answer* was received by Thomason on 26 April, but the king renewed his offer of a three-year suspension of episcopacy the following month.
[49] Gardiner, *CD*, pp. 275, 292, 343.   [50] Steward, *Answer*, pp. 4–7.

those lands were at first devoted to God and the Church; and we should drink up the dregs of that bitter cup of Gods wrath and displeasure, of which, it is to be feared, our forefathers supped too deep'.[51] In the following year, as Parliament debated and passed an act alienating bishops' lands, this emphasis on God's providential judgement on past and present sacrilege rose to a fever pitch in Royalist discourse. A Latin sermon by Lancelot Andrewes warning of God's curse on the state for such sacrilege was translated and published, but the message was conveyed most strikingly by the layman Clement Spelman. Spelman published a new edition of his father Henry's *De non temerandis Ecclesiis* with his own 27-page preface which offers an extreme providentialist history of the divine vengeance that had been inflicted on those who had seized church lands, with detailed attention to the fates of the Norman kings and Henry VIII.[52]

This material seems to have had a profound impact on Charles at the time. Not only did it generate his fears of divine retribution if he were to grant the alienation of church lands, but it also encouraged his perception that the monarchy's current troubles reflected divine vengeance for the sacrilegious excesses of the Reformation for which Henry VIII had been all too culpable. This encouraged the further conviction that one way of regaining divine favour was to vow to make future amends for this past sacrilege. Clement Spelman later claimed that, after the king had read his book, Charles 'said when god pleased to restore him, he would restore his impropriacions to the church'. Around this time the king made a more formal promise to this effect, solemnly signing a vow on 13 April 1646 that if he were restored to his rights 'I will wholly give backe to his Church all those Impropriations which are now held by the Crowne; and what Lands soever I now doe or shall enjoy which have beene taken away eyther from any Episcopall See or any Cathedrall or Collegiate Church, from any Abbey or other Religious house. I likewise promise for hereafter to hold them from the Church under such reasonable Fines and Rents as shall bee set downe by some conscientious Persons, whome I promise to choose with all uprightness of Heart to direct Mee in this particular.' This was a vow extracted from Charles only days before he left Oxford and his court chaplains to surrender to the Scots. Sheldon

---

[51] *Vindication*, pp. 26–7; Langbaine, *Review*, p. 69.
[52] Lancelot Andrewes, *Sacrilege a snare* (1646), esp. pp. 20–2; Henry Spelman, *De non temerandis ecclesiis*, 3rd edn (Oxford, 1646), preface, sigs. b4v–c1v, c3v–c4v. See also Henry Spelman, *An answer to a question* (1646); Spelman, *An apology of the treatise De non temerandis ecclesiis* (1646); Spelman, *A larger treatise concerning tithes* (1647); Spelman, *Tithes too hot to be touched* (1647); Clement Spelman, *A letter from Utercht (sic)* (1648), p. 2.

would preserve a copy of the vow throughout the Interregnum.[53] Court divines and Charles himself continued to insist that to consent to the alienation of these lands would be a 'sin of the highest sacrilege' and would bring down the 'heavy curse' of earlier pious donors.[54]

IV

The royal conscience was engaged in a different manner when an alternative peace deal with the Independents was contemplated, and the legitimacy of a grant of religious toleration required clarification by the court divines.[55] Charles had been holding out the carrot of liberty of conscience to the Independents since at least 1644,[56] but this became more of a live issue in 1647, when the king was seized by the army. The Heads of Proposals were in crucial respects more palatable than earlier Parliamentarian proposals: although they required that Charles remove 'all coercive power, authority and jurisdiction of Bishops', they did not demand the abolition of bishops or of the Prayer Book.[57] The army also allowed the king access to his chaplains for the first time in more than twelve months. On 4 August his chaplain Gilbert Sheldon dispatched letters to a number of bishops and chaplains seeking their judgement on the question 'Whether, upon any necessity or exigence of state, it be lawful for a Christian prince, besides the religion established, so to tolerate the exercise of other religions in his dominions, as to oblige himself not to punish any subject for the exercise of any of them?'[58]

Rather than the court divines seeking to put a brake on the king's concessions, it seems clear that in this case Sheldon and Hammond were anxious to satisfy the king's conscience that this concession would be legitimate. The appeal for advice which the chaplains orchestrated sought to ensure a unanimously affirmative response as swiftly as possible, and

---

[53] Durham University Library, Cosin Letter Book 1B, no. 94; Bodl., Clarendon MS 27, fo. 130r; V. Staley, *The Life and Times of Gilbert Sheldon* (1913), pp. 40–3.

[54] Steward, *Answer*, pp. 25–32; Gardiner, *CD*, p. 329; Walker, *Perfect copies*, p. 86. See also, for example, Warner's treatise composed in consultation with Hammond and Sheldon: Bodl., MS Eng hist. b.205, fo. 2r. Thomason's copy of Warner's *Church-Lands* is dated 28 October 1647. On the background to the work's composition see Bodl., MS Eng. misc. b.193, fos. 22–5.

[55] For a more detailed discussion of these events, and of their parallel with an earlier approach to the Irish bishops, see my 'Coping with alternatives: religious liberty in Royalist thought, 1642–7', in Robert Armstrong and Tadhg Ó hAnnracháin, eds., *Catholics and Presbyterians: Alternative Establishments* (Manchester, forthcoming).

[56] *Clarendon State Papers*, II, pp. 180, 226–7, 244.   [57] Gardiner, *CD*, p. 321.

[58] Skinner's reply to Sheldon on 7 August mentions his letter having been sent on 4 August: H. Cary, ed., *Memorials of the Great Civil War in England*, 2 vols. (1842), I, pp. 329–30. For the replies of Ussher and Warner see ibid., pp. 334, 346.

bishops such as Morton and Wren, who wanted to take time over their responses and to insert qualifications, were simply sidelined.[59] By the end of August Sheldon had managed to secure an agreed response to the question, signed by six bishops and six royal chaplains, which stipulated that 'Although every Christian Prince be obliged by all just and Christian Wayes to maintaine and promote to his power the Christian Religion in the truth and purity of it, yet in case of such exigence and concernment of Church and State as that they cannot in humane reason probably be preserved otherwise We cannot say that it is unlawful, but that a Christian Prince hath in such exigence a latitude allow'd him, the bounding whereof is by God left to him.'[60]

Two of the signatories of the August declaration – Henry Hammond and Jeremy Taylor – seem to have been prepared to move further than the grudging position outlined in the declaration itself.[61] Hammond presented a non-coercive model of church discipline based on fraternal admonition in his *Five Propositions to the Kings Majesty and the Army, concerning Church-government* which seems to have been published at the same time that the king's question regarding toleration was sent out to the bishops.[62] Taylor had discussed the question 'Whether it be lawfull for a Prince to give toleration to severall Religions' in his *Liberty of Prophesying*, published just weeks before the king's similarly worded case of conscience, and had been emphatic that toleration of all opinions should be the norm, rather than a lawful exemption from punishment granted at a time of political exigency.[63] An even more radical response was composed by another royal chaplain who had not been approached regarding the August declaration, and who appears to have been somewhat distant from the other court divines. This was Michael Hudson, who had been a tutor to Prince Charles in the early 1630s and a royal chaplain and military agent in the 1640s, and who accompanied the king to Newark in April 1646 just prior to his surrender to the Scots. Anthony Wood reports that King Charles usually called Hudson '"his plain dealing chaplain",

---

[59] Bodl., Tanner MS 58b, fo. 456; Cary, *Memorials*, I, pp. 335–6; Bodl., Tanner MS 145, fos. 7–9.

[60] A copy of this statement signed by Ussher is in Bodl., Tanner MS 58B, fo. 460, dated 16 August 1647. A further copy is signed by Bishops Duppa, Prideaux and Brownrigg, along with the royal chaplains Sheldon, Sanderson, Richard Holdsworth, Hammond, Brian Walton and Jeremy Taylor. Yet another version (fo. 453a, and dated 28 August 1647) bears the additional signatures of Bishops Juxon, Piers and Warner.

[61] I discuss Hammond and Taylor in more detail in my 'Coping with alternatives'.

[62] Hammond's *Five Propositions* was procured by Thomason on 6 August 1647; its text is in fact lifted directly from Hammond's *Of Fraternal Admonition* (pp. 7–10) which had itself just been published (Thomason received his copy on 29 July).

[63] Jeremy Taylor, *ΘΕΟΛΟΓΙΑ ΕΚΛΕΚΤΙΚΗ. A discourse of the liberty of prophesying* (1647), §16.

because he told him his mind, when others would or durst not'.[64] In his dedication of *The Divine Right of Government* to the king in 1647, Hudson not only warned Charles of the danger of sacrilege (as other court divines had done) but accused the king directly of having committed this sin. In this case, however, the sacrilege lay in Charles having imposed forms of divine worship on those whose consciences would not allow them to observe such ceremonies, an even more extreme reading of the king's obligation to provide religious toleration.[65]

The problem with compromise on religious toleration, of course, was that Presbyterian opponents could claim that it showed a readiness on the king's part to grant that divine law could be compromised as a matter of political exigency, which should therefore legitimize further compromises on episcopacy and church lands. In reply, Steward had to emphasize that such toleration did not signify approval of divergent religions, 'but it meerely implies not to punish, which Kings may forbeare upon just reason of State'.[66]

V

In the event, however, Charles's flight and subsequent engagement with the Scots made further negotiation over the Heads impossible, and the question of the abolition of episcopacy once more came to the fore. While the king's coronation oath became the focus of a pamphlet debate between the Royalist Edward Boughen and the Parliamentarian John Geree in the middle months of 1648, it was in the negotiations at Newport in autumn 1648 that matters finally came to a head. At the beginning of the discussions the king rehearsed the familiar position: that his coronation oath obliged him not to undermine the clergy's interests, that the alienation of church lands was sacrilege and that it would be against his conscience to abolish episcopacy.[67] Nevertheless, over the following weeks Charles gradually but relentlessly surrendered the concessions over the church that he had supposedly been steeled to resist. By the beginning of November 1648 he had accepted the abrogation of the use of the Book of Common Prayer for three years even in his own chapel, and the abolition of deans and chapters and archbishops. He had also conceded that church lands already purchased might remain with their owners

---

[64] Wood, *Athenae Oxonienses*, III, p. 233 – cited in N. W. S. Cranfield, 'Michael Hudson (1605–1648)', *ODNB*.

[65] Michael Hudson, *The divine right of government* (1647), sigs. A2–A3r, pp. 148, 150–3, 156, 159. For a fuller discussion see my 'Coping with alternatives'.

[66] Steward, *Answer*, p. 19.

[67] Walker, *Perfect copies*, p. 38; Peck, *Desiderata*, II, pp. 387–9.

on ninety-nine-year leases, and that bishops could exercise no episcopal jurisdiction after their three-year suspension save that which was agreed by Parliament (and that – whatever form of church government might be agreed after three years – the bishops would never be permitted to ordain without the consent of presbyters). While he still refused to consent to the outright abolition of episcopacy, he had virtually granted it in practical terms; as Richard Vines pointed out, the bishops were 'in effect abolished'.[68]

Did this reflect the weakness of court divines? Some, such as Sheldon and Hammond, had been barred from attendance and others, such as Sanderson, who were there sometimes complained that they did not know the content of the king's answers.[69] Those court divines present were clearly active early on in drawing up the king's response to a paper submitted by the parliamentary commissioners' divines. Charles admitted that he had relied on his divines in composing this response because he acknowledged himself 'not to have absolute skill in what was sett downe in this his paper in every part of it'. His scruples were his own, but his divines had 'explained & enlarged them'.[70] But the scruples were then simply ignored as the parliamentary commissioners – who had no authority to negotiate – insisted that they had spent several days in debate about the king's 'Scruples and Doubts' and now bluntly demanded responses to Parliament's propositions.[71] In the face of repeated rulings that the king's replies were 'unsatisfactory', Charles made a series of further concessions. Anticipating 'how this will be iudged of abroad' by his fellow Royalists, Duppa could only appeal to Sheldon that 'whosoever seriously considers the kings present Condition, and ours at this time (who are merely passive in it) will forbear to censure us in that which we could not avoid'.[72] The reluctance with which Charles yielded to the concessions that were squeezed out of him may still reflect the continuing influence of his chaplains (and Charles himself privately confessed that his concessions were insincere and intended merely to buy time and to encourage laxity in his guard so that he could secure his escape).[73] Nevertheless, as the negotiations continued there were reports that some of Charles's divines were going beyond mere passivity and, recognizing the greater

---

[68] Walker, *Perfect copies*, pp. 64–5, 75–6; [Richard Vines], *His Majesties concessions . . . stated and considered* (1648).
[69] Lambeth Palace Library MS 943, p. 765: Sanderson to Sheldon, 23 Sept 1648.
[70] Walker, *Perfect copies*, pp. 43–8; Peck, *Desiderata*, II, pp. 390–1.
[71] Walker, *Perfect copies*, p. 48.
[72] Lambeth Palace Library MS 943, p. 763: Duppa to Sheldon, 10 Oct 1648.
[73] C. W. Firebrace, *Honest Harry* (1932), pp. 344, 345.

danger if an agreement were not reached, were urging the king to show greater flexibility. It was alleged in pamphlets that it was Duppa and Juxon who had been prominent in persuading the king to make further concessions. Some of the details are implausible; they had supposedly on their knees persuaded the king to alienate church lands – which Charles had not done at this point – while Juxon had allegedly declared to the king 'that he had seriously meditated upon the Originall Grounds of Presbytery, and found them consonant to the Word of God, and agreeable to the sacred Rules Ordained by the Apostles and Evangelists in the holy Scriptures'.[74] Nevertheless, it is possible that the two bishops were indeed adopting a permissive posture. In 1646 Juxon and Duppa had already effectively waived the proviso of the king's coronation oath. They had explained to Charles that his fixed resolution to uphold his oath 'gives you a great latitude to walke in, with safety of conscience, in your endeavours to that end (the rectitude of intention abating much of the obliquity in all actions)'. The king could compromise on episcopacy if he was thereby seeking to preserve and protect the church 'by the best ways and means you have now left you (which is all the oath can be supposed to require)'.[75] This opinion was shared by Jeremy Taylor – a royal chaplain consulted in 1647 but not physically present at Newport – although Taylor went further than most in also arguing that the alienation of church lands did not constitute sacrilege and would in fact be a prudent policy for the king to adopt.[76]

Nevertheless, there is scattered evidence of an attempt by court divines to arrest this wave of concessions. At the beginning of November Charles requested and secured leave for six more divines to attend him – Bishops Ussher, Brownrigg, Prideaux and Warner, and his chaplains Ferne and George Morley. Not only could Ferne and Warner be expected to reiterate their outspoken public attacks on the proposed abolition of episcopacy, but Morley (presumably acting under the instructions of Sheldon and Hammond) visited Matthew Wren in the Tower beforehand and offered to convey Wren's advice to the divines at Newport. Wren's intransigent response (which was also conveyed directly to the king at Charles's own request) was entirely predictable, and it is notable that as these new divines arrived at Newport Charles now stood his ground and claimed that he could not make any further religious concessions where his

[74] *A terrible thunder-clap for the Independent sectaries* (1648), p. 3; *Mercurius Pragmaticus* 24–31 October 1648. The latter claims that the crucial conference of the king with his bishops and clergy, in which Juxon satisfied Charles's scruples, took place on 24 October.

[75] *Clarendon State Papers*, II, pp. 267–8.

[76] Cary, *Memorials*, II, pp. 75–100 (original in Bodl., Tanner MS 57, fos. 468r–73r).

conscience was engaged.[77] Nevertheless, in a final statement of concessions on 27 November, the king agreed that episcopal power and ordination would be suspended until he and Parliament could agree on a future form of church government, and that legal title to church lands could be settled in the crown.[78] It was only the purge of Parliament and subsequent regicide that ensured that the final dismantling of the episcopal church did not proceed with effective royal approval.

VI

We know that many kingdoms and their kings have fallen because they spoiled churches . . . and destroyed their goods, and took them away from the bishops and priests . . . Wherefore they were neither strong in war nor firm in faith, nor did they come out victors, but . . . lost their kingdoms and lands and what is far worse the kingdom of heaven too; their inheritance was taken away from them.

This extract from a *capitulum* of Charlemagne was chosen to be placed in large type in a framed box at the beginning of the *Vindication of Episcopacie*, published in Oxford in 1644. The same quotation had been employed earlier by Richard Hooker (from whom this later author presumably took it), but in the context of the Civil War its threat of providential judgement on king and kingdom would have appeared a great deal more direct and immediate.[79] Bulstrode Whitelocke would later complain of the king's 'eager Divines about him' at Newport 'continually whispering matter of Conscience to him'.[80] But as the extract from Charlemagne demonstrates, they had already been whispering – and shouting – to him about conscience and sacrilege for a number of years.

Given the king's continuing tendency to vacillate and compromise, the image of Charles as the resolute committed defender of the church needs to be seen in part as an achievement of the court divines, not just in their manipulation of the text of the *Eikon Basilike* but also in their strengthening of his resolve in negotiations. Charles's famous remarks concerning the overwhelming importance of his conscience and his fears of divine judgement follow very closely the *dicta* that his clergy had been feeding him. Recent historians have noted that Charles's

[77] Peck, *Desiderata*, pp. 398, 403–4; Walker, *Perfect copies*, pp. 77, 82–3 (Brownrigg was subsequently barred). For Wren's exchanges with Morley and the king see Bodl., Sancroft MS 78, pp. 21–3.

[78] Walker, *Perfect copies*, p. 98.

[79] *Vindication*, sig. A1v; Richard Hooker, *Of the Laws of Ecclesiastical Polity, Book 5*, ed. W. S. Hill (Cambridge, MA, 1977), ch. 79 §15; *Capitula sive leges ecclesiasticae et civiles* (1588), fo. 271r.

[80] Bulstrode Whitelocke, *Memorials of the English affairs* (1682), p. 335.

characteristic negotiating technique was to establish in advance what was non-negotiable, to 'fix my negatives' (as he put it) – an approach which left little room for the 'constructive embracing of opportunities'.[81] However limited the influence of court divines on the talks themselves, they may have had a significant impact on the king's formulation of these preconceived 'negatives' which thereby shaped (and in effect torpedoed) wartime and post-war negotiations.

Nevertheless, the court divines did not have constant access to the king's ear; not only were there no divines on Charles's Privy Council, but none of them were admitted to his presence for over twelve months in 1646–7 and others were barred from his presence in 1648, while the king was always prone to change his mind and succumb to pressure from others. Moreover, Charles showed himself capable of making his own decisions – including in matters of conscience – in 1646 and 1647. It must also be emphasized that court divines were not always seeking to strengthen the king's inflexibility. Richard Steward had presented the matter bluntly in 1646: 'the only Option that seems left us now, is either to choose sinne or ruine; but yet (if well used) tis a condition glorious; a condition wherein all that noble Army of Martyrs stood'.[82] But there was also a logic to trying to salvage as much as possible from a desperate situation, and the instruction of conscience could also be a matter of providing practical and flexible solutions. Juxon and Duppa in 1646 and 1648, and Sheldon and Hammond in 1647, sought in part to salve the king's conscience so that necessary concessions could be made. However, at the Treaty of Newport, as Sean Kelsey has observed, Duppa was guiding the king towards concessions at precisely the same time that he was assisting in the creation of the image of the monarch inflexibly committed to the defence of the church in the text of *Eikon Basilike*, where Charles proclaimed his absolute obedience to the dictates of conscience and his abhorrence of Presbyterianism.[83]

The securing of the image of a monarch martyred for his defence of the church may thus have been a close-run thing. Nevertheless, there seems little doubt that the court divines had played very effectively the limited hand that they had been dealt in influencing the king's conscience. The king's remorse for the execution of Strafford has often been noted by historians. But he was haunted just as relentlessly by his fears that he had betrayed the clergy, and while he could no longer save Strafford he could still attempt to defend what remained of the

---

[81] Cust, *Charles*, pp. 395–6; Russell, *Causes*, p. 206.   [82] Steward, *Answer*, p. 53.

[83] S. Kelsey, 'The King's Book: *Eikon Basilike* and the English revolution of 1649', in N. Tyacke, ed., *The English Revolution c.1590–1720* (Manchester, 2007), pp. 155–6.

church. Walton recounts that Charles told his chaplain Sanderson that he felt so grieved at having consented to the abolition of episcopacy in Scotland (as well as Strafford's execution) that when restored to power 'he would demonstrate his Repentance by a publick Confession and a voluntary penance . . . barefoot . . . from the Tower of London, or White-hall, to St Paul's Church, and desire the people to intercede with God for his pardon'.[84] This may well be an apocryphal story, but there is plentiful evidence of Charles's profound sense of guilt over his ecclesiastical concessions, and his vow (preserved by Sheldon) to restore all crown impropriations to the church appears to be genuine. That Charles made such a solemn oath is a notable testimony to the effectiveness with which court divines had played on the themes of conscience, sacrilege and divine providence in the preceding years, and they would continue to do so until the king's death gave them their royal martyr. Not only did court divines help to shape the image of the royal martyr after Charles's death, but they may also have played an important role in supplying the king with some of the fatal resolve that frustrated a settlement and made his death inevitable.

[84] Walton, *Life of Sanderson*, sig. f1r–v.

8 Law, liberty, and the English Civil War: John Lilburne's prison experience, the Levellers and freedom

D. Alan Orr

I

The historical significance of the Levellers has been the subject of long-standing controversy. There is arguably no prevailing scholarly consensus on the Levellers and their role in the development of Anglo-American constitutionalism or the emergence of liberal democracy in the West. Historians and historians of political thought have portrayed them variously as proto-proletarian revolutionaries, proto-democrats, proto-liberals, ideologues of possessive individualism and, more recently, as advocates of a populist form of civic republicanism.[1] Liberals, neo-liberals, Marxists and neo-Marxists have obsessed over them, while revisionists have disparaged or dismissed them in their efforts to recast England's troubles of the mid-seventeenth century, not as an ideologically driven contest for sovereign power or a struggle for liberty, but as a catastrophic breakdown in a hitherto successfully functioning system of monarchical government.[2] Indeed, for the revisionism of the 1970s the significance of the Levellers lay largely in their insignificance. However, as the first popular political 'movement' to advocate the establishment of a written constitution, liberty of conscience, the extension of the franchise to all male heads of households and concomitantly the abolition of most property requirements, they remain an important object of historical enquiry.

---

[1] H. N. Brailsford, *The Levellers and the English Revolution*, ed. J. E. Christopher Hill (Stanford, 1961); Joseph Frank, *The Levellers: A History of the Writings of Three Seventeenth-Century Social Democrats: John Lilburne, Richard Overton, William Walwyn* (Cambridge, MA, 1955, repr. New York, 1969); M. A. Gibb, *John Lilburne the Leveller, a Christian Democrat* (1947); Pauline Gregg, *Freeborn John: A Biography of John Lilburne* (1961); C. B. Macpherson, *The Political Theory of Possessive Individualism, Hobbes to Locke* (1962), ch. 3; S. D. Glover, 'The Putney debates: popular versus elitist republicanism', *Past and Present*, 164 (1999), 47–80.

[2] See my previous discussion of this literature: D. Alan Orr, 'Sovereignty, supremacy, and the origins of the English Civil War', *History*, 87 (2002), 474–6.

This chapter addresses the writings of the Leveller leader John Lilburne (1614?–1657) during the mid to late 1640s. During this period Lilburne either wrote from his prison cell or under the imminent threat of arrest and imprisonment; for Lilburne, the experience of revolution was largely the experience of incarceration.[3] Situating his writings in this context, this chapter argues that Lilburne's continuing historical significance lay in the early articulation of what the late Sir Isaiah Berlin termed a 'negative' conception of liberty.[4] As the period of his imprisonment extended, Lilburne's view of liberty derived increasingly from the actual experience of being constrained behind prison walls. This view of liberty was more in keeping with that of Thomas Hobbes in his *Leviathan* (1651) than with that of the 'democraticall gentlemen' who, Quentin Skinner has argued, led the English Parliament down the path towards civil war.[5] For Lilburne liberty became less the 'republican' view of liberty as the absence of a condition of dependence on the will of another – a condition of slavery – than simply the absence of external physical impediment to act as he desired. This distinction is significant, because Skinner has identified this 'proto-liberal' conception of liberty as the mere absence of constraint more strongly with Royalist authors, including not only Hobbes, but also Griffith Williams, John Bramhall, Dudley Digges and Sir Robert Filmer. For these authors the condition of liberty bore no necessary relationship to the constitutional provision for self-government.[6] In contrast, for republicans such as John Milton, James Harrington and the sometime Leveller John Wildman, the provision for self-government, in which the representatives of the whole body of the citizenry exercised the sole law-giving power, was essential to the preservation of liberty. For republicans freedom was only possible in a free state where the citizenry remained subject only to their own collective wills.[7]

Furthermore, as his term of imprisonment lengthened, Lilburne increasingly appealed not to the sources of classical republicanism, but

---

[3] David Loewenstein, *Representing Revolution in Milton and his Contemporaries: Religion, Politics, and Polemics in Radical Puritanism* (Cambridge, 2001), ch. 1.

[4] Isaiah Berlin, 'Two concepts of liberty', in *Four Essays on Liberty* (Oxford, 1969), pp. 118–72; Quentin Skinner, 'A third concept of liberty', *Proceedings of the British Academy*, 117 (2002), 237–68; Skinner, 'Rethinking political liberty in the English Civil War', *History Workshop Journal*, 61 (2006), 156–70.

[5] Skinner, 'Third concept', 245–7; Quentin Skinner, *Hobbes and Republican Liberty* (Cambridge, 2008); Thomas Hobbes, *Leviathan*, ed. C. B. Macpherson (1985), ch. 21.

[6] Quentin Skinner, *Liberty before Liberalism* (Cambridge, 1998), p. 6; Skinner, *Hobbes and Republican Liberty*, pp. 149–57.

[7] Skinner, *Liberty before Liberalism*, chs. 1–2; see also Philip Pettit, *Republicanism: A Theory of Freedom and Government* (Oxford, 1997).

to the sources and authorities of the common law, or what Philip Pettit has characterized as 'traditional non-dominating institutions'.[8] With the continued, tyrannical sitting of the Long Parliament, and the failure to reach a consensus on a new *Agreement of the People* in December 1648, Lilburne appealed increasingly to the law of the land as interpreted, not by judges or parliament, but by a jury of his peers as judges of both law and fact.[9] Lilburne's experience of prolonged incarceration, therefore, led him to evolve a 'radical' or, more appropriately, 'populist' conception of what J. G. A. Pocock has termed the 'ancient constitution' in which the right to a jury trial was foundational.[10] To this effect, Lilburne drew heavily on the recently published writings of the late Chief Justice Sir Edward Coke (1552–1634) – the Long Parliament's 'own oracle' of the law.

Rather than offering a 'systematic unity', as Andrew Sharp has argued, Lilburne's writings of the mid to late 1640s reveal an ongoing, and sometimes subjectively reactive *process*, in which the immediate conditions of his imprisonment were critical to the development of his political thinking.[11] His experience of actually being constrained, combined with his increased exposure to common-law sources and his interaction with more formally trained fellow inmates, were all crucial to this process. During this time Lilburne developed a series of communicative

---

[8] Pettit, *Republicanism*, p. 89.

[9] For Lilburne and jury law-finding see T. A. Green, 'Conscience and the true law: the ideology of jury law-finding in the Interregnum', in T. A. Green, *Verdict According to Conscience: Perspectives on the English Criminal Trial Jury, 1200–1800* (Chicago, 1985), pp. 153–99; see also Annabel Patterson, 'For words only: from treason trial to liberal legend in early modern England', *Yale Journal of Law and Humanities*, 5 (1993), 389–416.

[10] J. G. A. Pocock, *The Ancient Constitution and the Feudal Law: A Study in English Historical Thought in the Seventeenth Century* (Cambridge, 1957, repr. Cambridge, 1987); Glenn Burgess, *The Politics of the Ancient Constitution: An Introduction to English Political Thought, 1603–1642* (1992); J. W. Tubbs, *The Common Law Mind: Medieval and Early Modern Conceptions* (Baltimore, MD, 2000); for the Levellers' relationship to the traditions of the common law see R. B. Seaberg, 'The Norman Conquest and the common law: the Levellers and the argument from continuity', *HJ*, 24 (1981), 791–806; Diane Parkin-Speer, 'John Lilburne: A revolutionary interprets statutes and common law due process', *Law and History Review*, 1 (1983), 276–96; Rachel Foxley, 'John Lilburne and the citizenship of "freeborn Englishmen"', *HJ*, 47 (2004), 849–74; and Martin Dzelzainis, 'History and ideology: Milton, the Levellers, and the Council of State in 1649', *Huntington Library Quarterly*, 68 (2005), 269–87. I prefer to use the term 'populist' rather than Janelle Greenberg's suggested term 'radical' in characterizing Lilburne's conception of the ancient constitution: Janelle Greenberg, *The Radical Face of the Ancient Constitution: St Edward's 'Laws' in Early Modern Political Thought* (Cambridge, 2001).

[11] Andrew Sharp, 'John Lilburne's discourse of law', *Political Science*, 40 (1988), 18–33; Sharp, 'John Lilburne and the Long Parliament's *Book of declarations*: a radical's exploitation of the words of authorities', *History of Political Thought*, 9 (1988), 19–44.

strategies centred on the activities of reading and writing aimed at securing the concrete goal of his release. These strategies involved not only engagement with the published authorities of the common law, specifically the writings of Coke, but also the activity of writing and the publication of a significant pamphlet literature in support of his cause.[12] The result was a conception of negative liberty firmly grounded in the received traditions and authorities of the common law.

II

During the mid to late 1640s John Lilburne was constantly in and out of prison. On 11 June 1646 he was summoned before the bar of the Lords to answer for his illicit printing activities, and was subsequently committed close prisoner first to Newgate and then to the Tower of London. He remained in the Tower until he was finally granted bail on 9 November 1647, shortly after the Putney Debates and the publication of the first *Agreement of the People*. His bail was revoked on 17 January and Lilburne was returned to prison for his role in organizing Leveller petitioning along with his new associate John Wildman shortly after a meeting at Wapping which both men had attended. He was not released until 2 August 1648, during the Second Civil War. In the aftermath of the regicide on 30 January 1649, his attacks on the legitimacy and legality of the Rump Parliament and the Commonwealth's newly established Council of State soon landed him back in the Tower after the publication of *The second part of Englands new chaines* on 24 March 1649. This controversial tract openly challenged the legality of the Rump Parliament's claim to 'Supreame Authority', and in particular the legality of its erection of a Council of State and a High Court of Justice for the 'judging and taking away of mens lives in an extraordinary way, as done for no other end, but make way for their own domination'.[13] Aside from a brief period of bail in July to visit his family, then ill with smallpox, he remained in prison until his treason trial by jury at the London Guildhall on 24–25 October 1649. On his acquittal, he and his confederates were released on 8 November 1649.[14]

---

[12] Loewenstein estimates that Lilburne produced over four-fifths of his corpus from behind bars: Loewenstein, *Representing Revolution*, p. 26; more generally see Jerome de Groot, 'Prison writing, writing prison during the 1640s and 1650s', *Huntington Library Quarterly*, 72 (2009), 193–215.

[13] E 548(16), [John Lilburne, Richard Overton and Thomas Prince], *The second part of Englands new chaines* (1649), in William Haller and Godfrey Davies, eds., *The Leveller Tracts, 1647–53* (New York, 1944), pp. 171–89 (quotation at p. 183).

[14] For details of Lilburne's life see Andrew Sharp, 'John Lilburne, 1615?–1657', *ODNB*.

During this period Lilburne became increasingly consumed with escaping the coercive apparatus of the state and discovering legal rules that would protect him from arbitrary interference with his person. Towards this end he deployed whatever political ideas came to hand, either from the established legal canons of the day or from contact with his fellow prisoners, most significantly the Welsh Royalist jurist David Jenkins, who 'strengthened his legalism with his friendship and example'.[15] While maintaining that his legal knowledge was still considerable before encountering the Royalist and that he remained 'the same man in principles' that he ever was, Lilburne also explicitly acknowledged his indebtedness to Jenkins in print, confessing that he had 'gained much . . . in the knowledge of the Law' from his fellow prisoner.[16] Through this contact with more formally educated prisoners and his own reading of common-law sources, Lilburne achieved during his long and frequent periods of incarceration a good standard of jailhouse lawyer. This was not the long years of study needed to develop the 'artificial reason' of the common lawyers, but a more haphazard, goal-directed process undertaken with the practical aim of securing his release. Lilburne's writings were frequently derivative; however, he remains significant in representing a pivotal moment in the development of the idea of liberty, when the traditions of the English law as the customary, unwritten rationality of the ages entered into an alliance with Leveller populism to fashion a common-law conception of negative liberty.

The main published resource to which Lilburne increasingly turned during his incarceration was the legal writings of Sir Edward Coke. James I had dismissed Coke from the bench in 1616; however, Coke remained a significant public figure, playing an active role in the parliaments of the 1620s and composing the four volumes of his *Institutes*, the first of which, his commentaries on Littleton's *Tenures*, appeared in print in 1628 as *The first part of the institutes of the lawes of England; or a commentarie vpon Littleton, not the name of a lawyer but of the law it selfe*. In 1632, on hearing that he was writing a book on Magna Carta, Charles I ordered Coke's papers to be seized; at his death in 1634 the remaining three completed volumes of Coke's *Institutes*, including the second *Institutes*, consisting of his commentaries on Magna Carta, remained in manuscript and out of

---

[15] Ibid.

[16] E 427(4), John Lilburne, *The peoples prerogative asserted and vindicated, (against all tyranny whatsoever)* (1648), p. 4; for Lilburne's association with Royalist prisoners in the Tower of London and the influence of Jenkins on his writing and his thinking see Gregg, *Freeborn John*, pp. 197–205; J. T. Peacey, 'John Lilburne and the Long Parliament', *HJ*, 43 (2000), 640–1; Parkin-Speer, 'John Lilburne', 282–6; J. W. Gough, *Fundamental Law in English Constitutional History* (Oxford, 1955), ch. 8.

circulation for the duration of the Personal Rule.[17] The Long Parliament made the recovery of Coke's lost writings a priority, and on 5 December 1640 the House of Commons appointed a committee to inquire after the late lord chief justice's papers and to investigate on whose authority they had been seized.[18] On 13 February 1641 the Long Parliament ordered that eleven seized volumes of Coke's papers, including the manuscripts of the second, third and fourth volumes of the *Institutes*, be restored to Sir Robert Coke, son of the late lord chief justice.[19]

Printed on the order of the Long Parliament, Coke's commentaries on Magna Carta appeared as *The second part of the institutes of the lawes of England: containing the exposition of many ancient and other statutes* in 1642; the remaining two volumes appeared in 1644 as *The third part of the institutes of the laws of England concerning high treason and other pleas of the crown, and criminall causes* and *The fourth part of the institutes of the laws of England concerning the jvrisdiction of the courts.*[20] Although Richard Helgerson has argued that these later three volumes never enjoyed the same degree of authority as the first volume, *Coke's Littleton*, their appearance did have a substantial influence on Lilburne and the development of his political thinking during the mid to late 1640s.[21] Lilburne was fulsome in his praise for the writings of the former chief justice, writing in spring 1648 that 'I heartily wish and desire that every man in England, that hath any spare money and time would buy them, and read, and study them, as the absolutest discoverers of the true mind of the Law of England.'[22] Lilburne's engagement with the *Institutes*, while at times highly selective, was significant, because Coke's writings were not exemplars of the language of natural law and natural right, commonly identified with Leveller thought, but instead appealed strongly to the authority of the common

---

[17] Kevin Sharpe, *The Personal Rule of Charles I* (New Haven and London, 1992), pp. 656–7.

[18] *CJ*, II, pp. 45–6.

[19] It would appear that Kevin Sharpe's contention that the papers 'never came to light' is somewhat erroneous: Maija Jansson, ed., *Two Diaries of the Long Parliament* (New York and Gloucester, 1984), p. 85; Sharpe, *Personal Rule*, p. 657.

[20] Sir Edward Coke, *The second part of the institutes of the lawes of England: containing the exposition of many ancient and other statutes* (1642); Coke, *The third part of the institutes of the laws of England concerning high treason and other pleas of the crown, and criminall causes* (1644); Coke, *The fourth part of the institutes of the laws of England concerning the jvrisdiction of the courts* (1644).

[21] Richard Helgerson, *Forms of Nationhood: The Elizabethan writing of England* (Chicago, 1992), pp. 91–2; D. Alan Orr, *Treason and the State: Law, Politics, and Ideology in the English Civil War* (Cambridge, 2002), pp. 21, 67–9, 128, 136, 156–9.

[22] John Lilburne, *The oppressed mans importunate and mournfull cryes to be brought before the barre of justice* (1648), p. 2. This pamphlet is dated 7 April 1648, a second edition appearing 18 April 1648; George Thomason did not possess a copy of this pamphlet.

law as immemorial custom handed down time-out-of-mind from England's ancient past.[23]

Misconceptions about the Levellers' relationship to the traditions of the common law have had a long history. Christopher Hill, in his original discussion of 'The Norman yoke', offered John Lilburne in particular as the exemplar of Leveller anti-Normanism – the belief that the existing English law was the illegitimate imposition of a foreign conqueror, William of Normandy, and that its imposition had somehow abrogated the existing English law. Hill argued that, while Lilburne may initially have cited the sources of the common law such as Magna Carta and Coke's *Institutes*, his experience in the courts over the course of the mid to late 1640s led him increasingly to the language of natural law and natural right.[24] In this interpretation, the political discourse of 'radicalism', with its attendant language of natural right and natural law, superseded the language of Coke and the common lawyers in Leveller political thinking. The Levellers concomitantly rejected the historical continuity of the common law from pre-Conquest times, making a decisive shift, in the words of Keith Thomas, from 'historic right to natural right'.[25]

Much of the evidence for Hill's interpretation derived from a June 1646 pamphlet entitled *The Just mans Justification*.[26] The pamphlet, an epistle to Justice Reeve of the Court of Common Pleas concerning a suit on behalf of Colonel Edward King lying against Lilburne in that court, made explicit reference to the 'Norman Yoke' set upon the English people at the time of the Conquest. Complaining of the common law's inaccessibility to the common man, and in particular of the continued use of Latin and law French in the courts at Westminster, Lilburne claimed that 'the greatest mischiefe of all, and the *oppressing bondage of England* ever since the *Norman yoke*, is this, [that] I must be tried before you by a law (called the Common Law) that I know not, nor I thinke no man else, neither do *I* know where to find it, or reade it; and how I can in such a case be punished by it I know not'.[27] Lilburne went on to argue

---

[23] Pocock, *Ancient constitution*, chs. 2, 3; see also Glenn Burgess, *Absolute monarchy and the Stuart constitution* (New Haven and London, 1996), ch. 6.

[24] J. E. Christopher Hill, 'The Norman Yoke', in Hill, *Puritanism and Revolution: Studies in Interpretation of the English Revolution of the Seventeenth Century* (1958), pp. 75–6.

[25] K. V. Thomas, 'The Levellers and the franchise', in G. E. Aylmer, ed., *The Interregnum: The Quest for Settlement* (1972), p. 64.

[26] E.340(12), John Lilburne, *The just mans justification, or a letter by way of plea in barre* (1646); Mark A. Kishlansky appears to have confused this pamphlet with E.342(2), *The just man in bonds, or Lieut. Col John Lilburne close prisoner in Newgate by the order of the House of Lords*, a work by William Walwyn published on 23 June 1646 after Lilburne's arrest and imprisonment: Mark A. Kishlansky, *The Rise of the New Model Army* (Cambridge, 1979), p. 316.

[27] Lilburne, *Just mans justification*, p. 11.

that, as a result of the Norman Conquest, the current practices in the law courts at Westminster were corrupted from their original pre-Conquest forms. He particularly complained about the continued use of Latin, a language that neither he 'nor one of a thousand of my native Country men' could understand, leading him to conclude that the form of current legal proceedings in the central courts flowed 'not from God nor his Law, nor the law of Nature and reason, no not yet from the understanding of any righteous, just or honest men, but from the Divell and the Will of Tyrants'.[28]

While eloquently narrated, and at times visionary, the pitfalls of recipe-card scholarship frequently marred much of Hill's work; the result was isolated fragments of quotation recorded thematically, and then cited out of context in order to produce an unsympathetic coherence that could be highly misrepresentative of authorial intent. As R. B. Seaberg has established, Lilburne actually distinguished between the substance of the common law which remained intact from before the Norman Conquest and the accretion of corrupt Norman procedures since the Conquest – most notably the use of Latin and law French as the languages of pleading and record.[29] While the '*Norman* rules' imposed by William I remained 'in the administration of the *Common Law at Westminster Hall*', Lilburne asserted later in the same work that common-law learning had survived 'after the making of *Magna Charta*', and that 'divers learned men in the lawes ... kept Schooles of the Law in the City of London, and taught such as resorted to them the Lawes of the Realme, taking their foundation from *Magna Charta* and *Charta de Forresta*'.[30] Reinforcing his assertion of the substantive continuity of the common law, Lilburne cited extensively not only from the historical writings of Samuel Daniel, but also more significantly from the *Proem* to the second part of Coke's *Institutes*.[31]

The House of Lords and in particular the earl of Manchester, who had been Lilburne's commander in the Army of the Eastern Association, were not pleased at the appearance of *The just mans justification*.[32] On 11 June Lilburne was summoned before the bar of the Lords to answer for his alleged libels and in *The free-mans freedome vindicated*, published

---

[28] Ibid.

[29] Seaberg, 'Argument from continuity'; see also more recently Dzelzainis, 'History and ideology', 279–85. Lilburne vehemently denied authorship of *Libertie vindicated against slavery*, which one of the warders of the Tower of London, John White, had mistakenly attributed to him: E 351(2), Anon., *Libertie vindicated against slavery* (1646); E 359(17), [John Lilburne], *Londons libertie in chains discovered* (1646), pp. 59–63; see also E 373(1), John Lilburne, *The oppressed mans oppressions declared* (1647), pp. 8–9.

[30] Lilburne, *Just mans justification*, p. 14.

[31] Ibid., pp. 13–14.   [32] Sharp, *ODNB*, 'John Lilburne'.

eight days later, he offered a narrative of his appearance and his replies to the Lords interrogations. Lilburne's legal case at this point was simple: he was a freeborn commoner in England, and because of that birthright, the House of Lords had no jurisdiction over his person in summoning him before their bar and arbitrarily imprisoning him contrary to chapters 14 and 29 of the Magna Carta. Lilburne disputed the Lords' right to command his appearance before them and appealed instead 'to the Barre and tribunal of my competent, proper and legall tryers and Judges, the Commons of England assembled in Parliament'.[33] In a later pamphlet narrating his appearance before a committee of the House of Commons in November 1646, Lilburne reinforced this argument, stating that 'their Lordships sitting by virtue of Prerogative patents, and not by election or common consent of the people; have (as Magna Charta and other good lawes of the land tell me) nothing to do to try me as a commoner whatsoever, in any criminall case, either for life, limb, Liberty or estate'.[34] Lilburne framed these arguments appealing not only to the law of nature but also to the notion of birthright: the right to judgment by a jury of his peers – commoners of his own condition – was a right conferred on him by the specific historical conditions of his birth as a freeborn commoner of England.

The initial conditions of Lilburne's imprisonment from the time of his arrest in June to his appearance before the Commons committee in November were extremely close. His prison experience during this time, simply put, was one of physical constraint, and this was reflected in his lack of literary production during the months of July, August and September.[35] By Lilburne's own account he was forced to communicate with his wife Elizabeth by shouting from his cell window in Newgate to her in the window of an adjacent building. Even this expedient was subject to extreme measures, with the clerk of Newgate, Henry Briscoe, threatening to board up Lilburne's cell window or have him moved to a cell with no window at all if he did not desist.[36] During this time Lilburne did not simply live under the threat of being deprived of his liberty. Instead he lived with the complete deprivation of his ability to do as he wished, whether that was writing in his own defence or enjoying the

---

[33] E 341(12), John Lilburne, *The free-mans freedome vindicated* (1646), p. 6; Thomason dates this pamphlet 23 June 1646 although the imprint is 19 June.

[34] E 362(6), John Lilburne, *An anatomy of the Lords tyranny and iniustice exercised upon Lieu. Col. Iohn Lilburne, now a prisoner in the Tower of London* (1646), p. 3; Lilburne dated this pamphlet 6 November.

[35] Seaberg, 'Argument from continuity', 798–9.

[36] *An anatomy of the lords tyrannie*, p. 6.

society of his wife and friends.[37] His condition was the complete negation of freedom and this experience of unfreedom would be deeply formative.

There were many problems with Lilburne's constitutional position as it developed over his initial period of imprisonment in summer 1646. *Floyd's Case* (1621) had definitively established that the House of Commons was *not* a court of record, and did not have the legal power to administer the oaths necessary for deposing witnesses. As a result, in instances of parliamentary judicature committees established for the taking of depositions, while they might include members of the lower House, also necessarily included representatives from the Lords. The provisions of Magna Carta to which Lilburne appealed instead pertained to the individual's right to be tried by a jury of peers – individuals of their own condition, whether lord or commoner. This was, of course, the birthright of all freeborn Englishmen as well as the king's Irish subjects, and *post nati* – Scots born after James I's accession to the English throne in 1603.[38] By the authority of Sir Edward Coke's writings, Lilburne was correct in the sense that, although the House of Lords had 'of ancient time' given judgment against those who were not of their condition, it had subsequently been enacted that 'hereafter no Peeres of the Realme shall be driven to give judgement on any others then on their Peeres according to the law'.[39] However, in spite of Lilburne's initial appeals to the Commons as his lawful triers, the lower House simply was not a court of record in a position to overturn the Lords' committal of him, enjoying only a limited jurisdiction over their own membership. Lilburne needed to go to law school, and the Tower of London became his inn of court.

Like any good jailhouse lawyer, Lilburne turned his attention to the legal arguments against his imprisonment. In this he was clearly aided by his contact with Jenkins and his exposure to Sir Edward Coke's writings. David L. Smith has characterized Jenkins as a 'constitutional' Royalist, a man strongly committed to the rule of law who had opposed monopolies and ship money during the 1630s.[40] In spite of their political differences, Jenkins and Lilburne were both victims of the Long Parliament and the Leveller and the Royalist had in common that they viewed

---

[37] Ibid., pp. 16–17.

[38] This privilege, notably, did not extend to foreign peers, who would be accounted commoners in England: see *Lord Sanchar's Case*, 9 Coke *Reports*, 117a–b; and my discussion of Maguire's trial in 1645: Orr, *Treason and the State*, pp. 160–1.

[39] Coke, 2nd *Institutes*, fo. 50.

[40] David L. Smith, *Constitutional Royalism and the Search for Settlement, c. 1640–1649* (Cambridge, 1994), pp. 234–7.

their ongoing imprisonment as contrary to law. They also undoubtedly feared that Archbishop Laud's fate – attainder by parliamentary ordinance – would soon become their own. However, while Jenkins was concerned with establishing constraints on the powers of Parliament in general and protecting the king's place in the constitution, Lilburne was more specifically concerned with establishing constraints on the Long Parliament in particular, until such time as permanent provisions for a self-governing commonwealth could be established under a new Agreement of the People. With a new Agreement in place, the present parliament would be dissolved and a new, uncorrupted representative body elected.

Jenkins in his *Discourse touching the inconveniencies of a long continued parliament* of June 1647 had already laid out many of the arguments that Lilburne would later utilize in attacking both the authority of the Long Parliament and its continued sitting.[41] Jenkins's principal target was the 'Act to prevent inconveniencies which may happen by the untimely adjourning, proroguing, or dissolving this present Parliament' of 10 May 1641, which had declared that the present parliament could not be dissolved (or even prorogued or adjourned) except by an act of parliament.[42] This, according to Jenkins, had created a 'perpetual parliament' – a thing contrary to both law and reason. Jenkins's arguments were subtle, and included, for example, an appeal to the language of the original writ of summons setting out limits on the powers of Parliament, confining them to the purpose for which Parliament was summoned. Jenkins, singling out the House of Commons in particular, argued that the Commons had no legal power to 'commit any man to prison, who is not of the said House, for Treason, Murder, or Felony, or any thing but for the disturbance of the publique Peace, by the priviledge of the whole body'.[43] The reason for this was that the writ of summons 'for them is onely *ad faciendum et consentiendum* to those things, whereof His Majestie shall consult and treat with his Prelates and Nobles, *et de communi consilio Regni* shall be there ordained, as appeares by the Writ'.[44] Furthermore, in keeping with the

---

[41] E 392(30), David Jenkins, *A discourse touching the inconveniencies of a long continued parliament* (1647).

[42] Gardiner, *CD*, pp. 158–9.   [43] Jenkins, *Discourse*, p. 6.

[44] Ibid. For the writs to which Jenkins refers see E 157(11), William Hakewill, *The manner of holding parliaments in England collected forth of our ancient records* (1641), pp. 24–6. Lilburne would also cite Hakewill: E 370 (12), [John Lilburne and Richard Overton?], *Regall tyrannie discovered: or, a discourse, shewing that all lawfull (approbational) instituted power by God amongst men, is by common agreement, and mutual consent* (1647), p. 97; contrary to David Wootton's opinion, I believe that this work was probably a joint composition of Lilburne and Overton and not the sole composition of the latter: David Wootton, 'Leveller democracy and the Puritan revolution', in J. H. Burns and Mark

precedents of the early 1620s and *Floyd's Case*, Jenkins asserted that the Commons had 'no power to examine any man' under oath independently of the Lords because they were not a court of record.[45]

However, the most powerful precedent that Jenkins invoked was that of Coke's report of *Bonham's Case* (1611) contained in his eighth *Reports*. This, of course, is the case that modern legal scholars associate with the development of the notion of judicial review now entrenched in US constitutional practice.[46] The case, dating from 1610 and first published in 1611, concerned a dispute between one Dr Bonham and the London College of Physicians, in which Bonham claimed that graduates of Oxford and Cambridge were legally permitted to practise medicine within the city of London without joining the college. The college, citing their letters patent of Henry VIII subsequently confirmed by act of parliament, vehemently disagreed, and took action against Bonham, first imposing a fine of £5, and then having him arrested and imprisoned when he continued to practise.[47] Coke, in ruling that Bonham had been falsely imprisoned, found that the college in making itself a judge in its own cause had violated a fundamental maxim of the common law. More famously, in his printed report he stated further that 'When an act of Parliament is against common right or Reason, or repugnant, or impossible to be performed, the Common Law shall controle it and adjudge this Act to be void; they are the words of the Law.'[48]

Citing *Bonham's Case*, Jenkins' *Discourse* argued that the statute made subsequent to the Triennial Act was void because it was both against common right and reason and impossible to be performed. A perpetual parliament, Jenkins argued, was against reason because it extended parliamentary immunities against lawsuits indefinitely, obstructing the rights of other subjects to recover debts and damages. Jenkins argued that 'The law of the land allowes no protection but for a yeare, to be free from suits ... but a Parliament perpetuall may prove a protection, not for a yeare, but for ever, which is against all manner of Reason.'[49]

Goldie, eds., *The Cambridge History of Political Thought, 1450–1700* (Cambridge, 1991), p. 426.

[45] Jenkins, *Discourse*, p. 7.

[46] Charles M. Gray, 'Bonham's Case reviewed', *Proceedings of the American Philosophical Society*, 116 (1972), 35–58; see also James R. Stoner, *Common Law and Liberal Theory: Coke, Hobbes, and the Origins of American Constitutionalism* (Lawrence, KS, 1992), ch. 3.

[47] Stoner, *Common Law and Liberal Theory*, p. 49.

[48] Coke, 8 *Reports*, 118a; Jenkins, *Discourse*, p. 2.

[49] Jenkins, *Discourse*, p. 3; see also E 393(39), John Lilburne, *Rash oaths unwarrantable* (1647), p. 27.

Furthermore, the statute was impossible to be performed because the death of the king would necessarily dissolve Parliament; because Parliament did not have the power to legislate a dead man back to life, the Long Parliament could not possibly make itself perpetual under the provisions of the statute.[50]

The same parliament-yoking arguments later re-emerged in many of Lilburne's pamphlets, especially in his post-regicide writings, when the seemingly limitless powers of the Rump Parliament and its outgrowth, the newly erected Council of State, emerged as an ominous threat to Lilburne and his confederates. His *Legall fundamentall liberties*, composed in prison and appearing in June 1649, reiterated many of the arguments which, mediated through his contact with Jenkins, he had appropriated from Coke's published works.[51] Writing in the aftermath of the trial of the king by a specially erected High Court of Justice and the establishment of the Commonwealth regime, Lilburne pursued a number of now-familiar strategies. As with Jenkins in 1647, his primary target was the act subsequent to the Triennial Act, forbidding the dissolution of the Long Parliament without its own consent. In attacking the 'tyranny' of the Rump Parliament, the developing pattern of appropriation is clear. Lilburne cited at length the same passage from *Bonham's Case* – the famous 'judicial review' passage – that Jenkins had previously deployed in attacking the Long Parliament in 1647.[52] He also appealed to the limitations set down in writ of summons in arguing that parliaments were 'principally called for the maintenance of the Lawe, and for the redresse of divers mischiefs and grievances that daily happen; and sutable [*sic*] to this are the ends contained in the Writs that summon them, and the intentions of those that chuse the Members and send them'.[53] Furthermore, because the king's writ was 'the Basis in law, and Foundation of this Parliament', his death had necessarily dissolved Parliament and the Rump's continued sitting was illegal.[54] 'I would fain know how it's possible for a Parliament to *confer or treat with King CHARLES now he is dead?*' asked Lilburne.[55] Furthermore, the act was 'repugnant' to the previous

---

[50] Jenkins, *Discourse*, p. 3.

[51] E 560(14), John Lilburne, *The legall and fundamentall liberties of the people of England revived, asserted, and vindicated* (1649); Thomason's date is 18 June for the first edition. Lilburne had of course previously used this argument.

[52] Lilburne, *Legall and fundamentall liberties*, p. 51.

[53] Ibid., p. 2; for an earlier example see E 411(21), John Lilburne, *The grand plea of Lieut. Col. John Lilburne* (1647), p. 7; the imprint is 20 October 1647, while Thomason's date is 25 October 1647. Significantly, Lilburne also cited in *The legall and fundamentall liberties* Coke 4th *Institutes*, fos. 9, 11, 37–9, 41–2.

[54] Lilburne, *Legall and fundamentall liberties*, p. 53.   [55] Ibid., p. 52.

Triennial Act, Lilburne argued, because 'how can every three years a *Parliament* be *begun* if this [Parliament] be *perpetual*?'[56]

Diane Parkin-Speer has argued that Lilburne, relying on Coke's report of *Bonham's Case*, 'applied rigorously the doctrine of judicial review of statute law, indeed applied it so vigorously that it became a weapon of the lay individual to evaluate whether a law was just or unjust, thus providing a theoretical justification for resistance to authoritarian government, whether revolutionary or traditional'.[57] These conclusions, linking Coke and subsequently Lilburne to a mature doctrine of judicial review, now appear overly ambitious. Insofar as they can be reconstructed, Lilburne's reading practices as he approached Coke's writings were not always rigorous, but were clearly selective, and directed towards not only the goal of securing his release but also that of improving the immediate conditions of his imprisonment. For example, on the issue of jailors' fees Lilburne, citing the second and fourth volumes of Coke's *Institutes*, argued that 'it is an abusion of the Law that prisoners . . . pay any thing for their entries into the Gaole, or for their goings out; that is the common Law; there is no fee at all due any Goalers whatsoever by the common Law'.[58] Elsewhere in the second *Institutes*, however, Coke stated with regard to unlawful imprisonment that 'If the Sherriffe, or Goaler retain a prisoner in Gaole after his acquittal, unlesse it be for his fees, this is false imprisonment.'[59] Coke's position was in fact much more complicated than Lilburne allowed, further revealing the sometimes haphazard nature of the Leveller's reading practices.[60] In reality, the late lord chief justice was probably more concerned with curbing abuse than altogether extirpating the practice of collecting jailors' fees.[61]

While relating Lilburne to a broader body of thought on competing conceptions of liberty, this chapter has also examined his writings in relation to the immediate circumstances of his imprisonment, his experience of unfreedom and, in particular, the reading practices that he developed as he approached the sources of the common law. Lilburne's reading and writing practices, his oral communication with other prisoners and the overall web of communicative strategies that he deployed in attempting

---

[56] Ibid., p. 47.   [57] Parkin-Speer, 'John Lilburne', 295.

[58] Lilburne, *Oppressed mans oppressions*, pp. 5–6 (quotation at p. 5); the citations from Coke are 2nd *Institutes*, fos. 74, 209, and 4th *Institutes*, fo. 41.

[59] Coke, 2nd *Institutes*, fo. 53.

[60] Anthony Grafton and Lisa Jardine, '"Studied for action": how Gabriel Harvey read his Livy', *Past and Present*, 129 (1990), 30–3; William Sherman, *John Dee: The Politics of Reading and Writing in the English Renaissance* (Amherst, MA, 1995), ch. 3.

[61] John Goodwin and his congregation appear to have come to Lilburne's rescue after his June arrest, as evidenced by a published letter thanking them for their support: E 400(5), John Lilburne, *Jonah's cry out of the whales belly* (1647), pp. 5–6.

to secure his release were all crucial to understanding the process of his political thinking during his period of imprisonment. For Lilburne, legal education was rough and ready; it was something that an ordinary citizen such as himself, literate but not learned, could achieve provided the law was printed in English. Coke's intended audience for the *Institutes*, written as they were in English, had been the Parliamentarians of the 1620s. These were men who were literate but not always learned in the ways of the common law, or comfortable with the legalistic jargon of law French which was the customary language of legal reporting until mid-century. For them there was none of the careful study over a lengthy period of years that Coke deemed necessary for the development of the 'artificial reason' that common-law jurists applied in making their judgements. Confined to the vernacular, and to the Tower of London, Lilburne developed a set of communicative strategies in his reading of Coke's published works for a very different purpose than that for which they were originally intended. In doing so, he fashioned a common-law conception of negative liberty.

III

In the 1980s, as part of a scholarly reaction against revisionism's perceived over-emphasis on the consensual nature of early Stuart political culture, Johann P. Sommerville resurrected the notion of long-term ideological causes for the English Civil War. In this interpretation the beginnings of deep and substantial ideological polarities were already evident by the start of the seventeenth century, setting the stage for conflict. Furthermore, these divisions would become even further exacerbated with the growing influence of an absolutist-leaning clerical estate that succeeded in gaining, first, the ear of King James I and then subsequently that of an even more sympathetic King Charles I.[62] In the 1990s Markku Peltonen argued that republican consciousness had already significantly developed during the seven decades prior to the outbreak of civil war, suggesting that Britain's republican experiments of the 1650s had deeper origins in English political culture.[63] More recently, Quentin Skinner has suggested that the 'democraticall gentlemen' who predominated in the Long Parliament had a recognizably republican conception of liberty that envisioned self-government as integral to the preservation of freedom.[64]

[62] Johann P. Sommerville, *Royalists and Patriots: Politics and Ideology in England 1603–1640* (1986; 2nd edn, Harlow, 1999).
[63] Markku Peltonen, *Classical Humanism and Republicanism in English Political Thought, 1570–1640* (Cambridge, 1995).
[64] Skinner, 'Third concept'.

The 1630s – a period in which Parliament did not sit – was a period of tyranny in which self-government stood in abrogation. With these arguments, the idea of long-term 'ideological causes' of the English Civil War, once consigned to the dustbin of Whig historiography, has re-emerged with a vengeance.

The notion of self-government, now closely identified with republican thought of the period, stood at the heart of Leveller political thinking. The call for a significantly broader franchise and frequent parliamentary elections in order to guard against what James Harrington would term the 'prolongation of magistracy' were hallmarks of their political programme.[65] The Leveller *Agreements* simply and concisely set forth blueprints for the reformation of the English constitution to form a self-governing commonwealth.[66] To borrow a phrase from J. C. Davis, the Leveller programme in this sense intended both to 'restore' and to acknowledge publicly what Mark Goldie has termed the 'unacknowledged republic' – the complex network of indigenous, self-governing local regimes through which the English effectively governed themselves. While hardly the deferential, consensus-oriented utopia that revisionist scholars presented in the 1970s and 80s, this highly decentralized, plural and complex constitutional order functioned relatively well, at least in the sense that there had been no conflict resulting in a full-scale civil war since the closing decades of the fifteenth century. However, by the mid-1640s the Long Parliament's development of an infinitely more oppressive military and fiscal apparatus than that of the Personal Rule had seriously undermined these traditions of local self-government.[67] This was when the Levellers emerged as a clearly identifiable group, as both defenders and advocates of these existing indigenous traditions of self-government.

John Lilburne's principal formative experiences, however, were less those of the unacknowledged republic, or those of a citizen participating in a self-governing commonwealth, than those of religious and political

---

[65] The Levellers, while rejecting the Harringtonian notion of 'equal' government, certainly agreed with him on the need for frequent rotation: James Harrington, *The Commonwealth of Oceana and a System of Politics*, ed. J. G. A. Pocock (Cambridge, 1992), pp. 8–42 (i.e. 'The first part of the preliminaries').

[66] I have addressed these issues elsewhere: D. Alan Orr, 'Constitutionalism: ancient, modern, and early modern in the *Agreements of the People*', in Philip Baker and Elliot Vernon, eds., *Foundations of Freedom: The Agreements of the People, the Levellers, and the Constitutional Crisis of the English Revolution* (Basingstoke, 2011).

[67] J. C. Davis, 'Afterword: reassessing radicalism in a traditional society: two questions', in Glenn Burgess, ed., *English Radicalism, 1550–1850* (Cambridge, 2007), pp. 356–8; Mark Goldie, 'The unacknowledged republic: officeholding in early modern England', in Tim Harris, ed., *The Politics of the Excluded c. 1500–1850* (Basingstoke, 2001), pp. 153–94.

persecution. His early political socialization consisted in being publicly flogged and locked up for a good stretch of time at the hands of a prerogative court in which there was no jury of his peers and defendants were customarily deposed under oath against themselves. Once he had been released from that prison, he again became a prisoner at the hands of the Royalists at Oxford. Then he became a victim, first of the Long Parliament, then of the Commonwealth, and then finally, after a period of exile, Oliver Cromwell's Protectorate. Quite simply, in the words of Thomas Hobbes, Lilburne during these periods of imprisonment was not free from 'opposition', or 'externall Impediments of motion'.[68] He was kept under lock and key.

Lilburne remained at this time a staunch advocate of self-government, identifying the right to the franchise in both local and parliamentary elections as a birthright of all freeborn Englishmen handed down time-out-of-mind since before the Norman Conquest and subsequently reconfirmed in Magna Carta.[69] He spoke the language of natural law and natural right, but he did so in the same breath as he spoke of native right and birthright. As a firm and vocal advocate of self-government, he was the primary author of *Foundations of freedom*, the second *Agreement of the People* published in December 1648, and he later played a major role in the Levellers' final *Agreement*, written, fittingly enough, from a cell in the Tower in late April 1649.[70] However, unlike the more republican John Wildman, who closely identified the idea of being 'at liberty' with the provision for self-government, Lilburne's views on the liberty of the subject were not nearly as closely intertwined with his views on the need to create – or re-create after the model of pre-Conquest conditions – a self-governing commonwealth.[71] For Lilburne liberty meant something far simpler and at the same time more complex and subjective. His experience of incarceration during the period 1646–9 taught him that parliaments, like kings, could become tyrannical; as a result, by mid-1649 the rule of law, as adjudged by a jury of peers, became his primary recourse.

Recent scholarship has once again made it fashionable to entertain the notion that Britain's military conflagrations of the mid-seventeenth

---

[68] Hobbes, *Leviathan*, p. 261.

[69] E 304(17), [John Lilburne], *England's birth-right justified* (1645), p. 33; also in William Haller, ed., *Tracts on Liberty in the Puritan Revolution*, vol. 3 (New York, 1934), p. 291; [Lilburne], *Londons libertie*, pp. 2–3, 14–16.

[70] Donald M. Wolfe, ed., *Leveller Manifestoes of the Puritan Revolution* (New York, 1944), pp. 293–303, 400–10.

[71] E 968(3), [John Wildman], *The Leveller: or the principles and maxims concerning government and religion which are asserted by those that are commonly called the Levellers* (1659).

century had long-term origins.[72] However, the intention here has been to demonstrate that the situation as it developed during the 1640s was far more complex, factionalized and ideologically messy than historians of political thought such as Sommerville, Skinner and Peltonen have hitherto allowed. Lilburne may have become a martyr for the Parliamentarian cause, and fought in the parliamentary armies, but he was hardly the kind of 'democraticall gentleman' who took the Long Parliament into war. He did not sit in the Long Parliament, the Short Parliament or any other parliament for that matter, and he would have been in his mid-teens at the calling of the most recent parliament prior to spring 1640. Most of what he knew about parliaments came from the books that he read, conversations with friends and fellow prisoners, being arraigned at the bar of the House of Lords and being interrogated before parliamentary committees. The prison experience was crucial to Lilburne's formation, because his experience of persecution at the hands of the Long Parliament and his exposure to more learned prisoners of differing political creeds led him to develop a common-law conception of negative liberty as simply the condition of non-constraint, or non-imprisonment, that was more in keeping with Royalist writers than with parliamentary apologists. It is often said that politics finds strange bedfellows. The same is true for political thought.

---

[72] For a recent example of this trend see Alan Cromartie, *The Constitutionalist Revolution: An Essay on the History of England, 1450–1642* (Cambridge, 2006).

9   On shaky ground: Quakers, Puritans, possession and high spirits

Tom Webster

I

The impact of the emergence of 'Quakers' on the contested field of religious orthodoxy and propriety in the 1650s, particularly when measured by the means of print exchanges, was considerable. While the 'actual' impact in terms of numbers is easily exaggerated, this should not lessen attention paid to the vicious negotiation of the arguments, portrayals and counter-portrayals. These negotiations made a crucial contribution to the process of identity among 'liberated' radicals, possibly those strongest in their denunciations of the Quakers and, to an even greater extent, the more plastic identity of the emergent group.[1] I intend to bring different light on this process using the lens of the discourse of possession, and what follows is a case study with the central concern of possession, of good or evil spirits, means of discernment and treatment, and the context-dependent apprehension and representation of physical and spiritual 'symptoms'. I have chosen this particular field for a number of reasons,[2] not least because the role of contested readings of possessions in the formation of early Quaker identity has been underestimated or under-explored. Certainly we have benefited from attention paid to the

---

[1] W. C. Braithwaite, *The Beginnings of Quakerism* (Cambridge, 1955), is still indispensable for context. Kate Peters, *Print Culture and the Early Quakers* (Cambridge, 2005) provides remarkably helpful ways into the disputes and the issue of identity. Indeed, I shall adopt her use of the term, hoping to avoid any suggestion of denominational history while also avoiding the obfuscations of 'the Children of Light' or 'people of the Lord', not least because the term 'Quaker', in the sense of 'those who are scornfully called Quakers', appears quite early and consistently in print: Peters, *Print Culture*, pp. 91–123, esp. pp. 106–7.

[2] Among them a personal one. Some twenty years ago I produced a lengthy and probably self-indulgent piece on Puritan fasting and prayer as a post-graduate student of John's. In the course of this I stumbled across John Darrell and his work with the possessed. At the time, I was wisely warned that too great a space given to this specific would take me away from the people, the place and the period of my thesis and to put it to one side for now. With different eyes, modified interests, hopefully more mature thinking and an undiminished appetite for the odd, I have returned to efforts to understand the experience and discourse of possession.

anti-popery and the witchcraft tropes in the literature against the early Quakers (not unconnected to possession), but focus on possession opens new windows which, I hope, will prove profitable.[3]

II

John Gilpin is the main character. An assessment of the ways in which the attacks and responses locked horns or, more importantly, had no accepted arena within which to lock horns, is revealing concerning the nature of the struggle. This will lead into an exploration of the ways in which these individuals became detached from their human selves, as it were, to become 'characters', almost anti-icons in the portrayals of the early Quakers and how possession became a recurrent theme, almost a given in the literature.[4] Gilpin had some relations with the Quakers in Kendal, but his experiences and separation provided the clerical and lay authorities with fuel for their denunciation. As George Fox later noted in his journal, 'And ye preists began to bee in a mighty rage att Newcastle & att Kendall: & uppe & doune in most countryes: & one Gylpin y^t sometimes come amongst us att Kendall who rann out & which ye preists made use of att times against us but ye Lords power confounded y^m all.'[5] While there is cause to question Fox's estimation of the complete success of the refutation, his account of the intensity and breadth of the dispute was no understatement.

This account is worth examining in detail, because it allows established elements of possession, sometimes modified by the new context, to be highlighted. The opening is Gilpin's attendance at a meeting where the main speaker was Christopher Atkinson. In Gilpin's own account he was encouraged to stop reading 'good Books', not to 'heare any Preaching Minister', or to remember any lesson from Scripture. Having read one pamphlet he returned to his bedchamber, where he began 'to tremble and quake so extremely, that I could not stand upon my feet, but was constrained to fall upon my Bed, where I howled and cryed (as is usuall

---

[3] Stephen A. Kent, 'The "Papist" charges against the Interregnum Quakers', *Journal of Religious History*, 12 (1982), 180–90; Ian Y. Thackray, 'Zion undermined: the Protestant belief in a popish plot during the English Interregnum', *History Workshop Journal*, 18 (1984), 28–52; Peter Elmer, '"Saints or sorcerers": Quakerism, demonology and the decline of witchcraft in seventeenth-century England', in J. Barry, M. Hester and G. Roberts, eds., *Witchcraft in Early Modern Europe* (Cambridge, 1996), pp. 145–79.

[4] This is part of a larger study broadening the materials used and the subjects addressed. The most conspicuous absence here is John Toldervey, a possessed man in Quaker circles who will be discussed elsewhere.

[5] Norman Penney, ed., *The Journal of George Fox* (Cambridge, 1911), I, p. 41, dated 1653.

with them) in a terrible and hideous manner'.[6] It should be noted that the interpolation 'as is usuall with them' generalizes from a single instance, a recurrent practice. As he lay awake he felt something 'lighting upon my neck, giving me a great stroke', descending down his body and entering him in the middle of his back. This was followed by an inner voice. After three days of waiting he lay face down in his garden and his hand started to shake, which he concluded was to be 'a figure of my spirituall Marriage and Union with Christ' (6). Then the voice returned, telling him that his sins were mortified and offering him anything he wanted (7). An hour later he went to another meeting, where Atkinson and John Audland were among the speakers.

While Audland was speaking, Gilpin was 'throwne upon the ground in the middest of the Company' where he remained all night, turning over and over, 'making crosses continually, with my Leggs one over the other', his hands moving as if he was writing on the ground which his inner voice told him '*did signifie the Writing of the Law within my heart*'. He then repeated the inner voice's words, '*Christ in God, and God in Christ, and Christ in thee*', a speech which he delivered 'in a strange manner, and with such a Voyce as was not naturally mine owne'. Both the involuntary physical contortions and the alien voice were among the expected symptoms of possession.

After quoting scripture, he obeyed the voice and rose to his feet, stooping as he was told he was to take up the cross. He went into the main street, followed by Audland and William Dodding. They asked him why he stopped outside a particular house, unbeknownst to Gilpin the home of a fiddler. Gilpin said, '*Whose house soever it be, Christ leads me hither, and hither I must goe*', and knocked, commanded by the voice to say '*Behold, Christ stands at the doore and knockes*'. He entered, took up the bass viol, played it and danced, without telling the witnesses of the internal exegesis his inner voice was providing for him (6–7).[7]

He was taken home, with Dodding refusing to leave him, Gilpin proclaiming as he went that '*I am the way, the truth, and the life*'. At home the same power 'cast me upon the ground, and caused me to make Circles round about the house with my hand' and then take up a stone which he perceived to be heart-shaped and held it up to the spectators, saying, '*Except you see signes and wonders, you will not beleeve*'. He threw the stone, crying, '*Loe, here is my heart of stone*' and, having been thrown upon

[6] John Gilpin, *The Quakers Shaken: Or, A Firebrand Snatch'd out of the fire* (Gateshead, 1653), pp. 4, 5. Hereafter, references will appear in the text.

[7] There is a possibility that this echoes William Sommers acting out his sins, particularly '*of dauncing, of Vyols and instrumenes, I being an apprentice to a Musitian*': Samuel Harsnett, *A Discovery of the Fraudulent practises of John Darrel* (1599), p. 117.

his back, the voice promised him two angels, whereupon two swallows came down the chimney, settling near him. He cried to them but they, understandably, did not approach, preferring to fly back up the chimney 'though both the doore and window were open'(9).

Two elements are noteworthy. The first is the explicit connection with the signs and wonders which were coming to be associated with the public presence of Quakers, thereby questioning their divine source. The second is less clear: the appearance of the swallows, while they prove not to be angels (and thus making the voice less trustworthy), bears a semblance to the familiars of a witch or perhaps the devils with which the familiars overlapped. That they used the chimney associates them with the liminal space of the house, a theme recurrent in stories of witches, made less ignorable by the emphasis Gilpin places on it in his text.[8]

Gilpin crawled out through the door and, having been carried back into the house, told one woman that she was wicked and had hindered the Lord's work, going on to draw a cross on the ground, standing on his head and leaping and dancing. Then he was cast down with the voice telling him that '*I had offended God in attributing that to my selfe, which was proper to Christ*', to which he responded by lying on his belly and licking the dust. This continued until the following evening, with Quakers coming and telling him to '*Be lowly, mind thy condition, and hearken to the voyce within*', leaving the reader aware of the irony, in that they can see the gap between this call and what the voice was actually saying, words to which Quakers had no access. Having sent them away, he stayed up alone, wondering whether the power was divine or diabolical, upon which he picked up a knife and held it to his throat, with the voice saying '*Open a hole there, and I will give thee the words of eternall life*'. He resisted the temptation and woke the following morning convinced that the power was diabolical, that

I was really possest with a Devill, which must be ejected; and in the morning I verily thought that a Devill went out of me, at which instant I roared very hidiously, crying, *Now is the Devill gone out of me*, at which instant, I and my Family, heard it thunder, (though none in the Towne besides, heard it) which made me thinke it was the Devill, *he being the Prince of the power of the Ayre* . . . .

He became convinced that he was now inhabited by the spirit of Christ and must undo what he had done the day before. He went out, wearing only his shirt, '*in Obedience to Christ*' and then insisted that he be carried

[8] Kenneth L. Carroll, 'Sackcloth and ashes and other signs and wonders', *Journal of the Friends' Historical Society*, 53 (1975), 314–25; Carroll, 'Quaker attitudes to signs and wonders', *Journal of the Friends' Historical Society*, 54 (1977), 70–84; Diane Purkiss, *The Witch in History: Early Modern and Twentieth-Century Representation* (1996), pp. 91–118.

back into the house, carried by four women as he had been the night before. He told the woman he had cursed that '*now Christ tels me that you are Gods servant*' and threw himself about on the bed, 'playing topsie turvie' before his teeth started to move and 'I thought I felt in my belly, a flowing up and downe, as of waters' (11–12). The sense of reversion continued (with the reader encouraged to accept the likelihood of perversion) with 'the Devils Angels' to be replaced with 'Christs Angels', 'whereupon I saw two Butter-flyes in the window'. He took one in his hand and swallowed it, placing the other at his throat, 'the power telling me, *it should enter in there*, saying, *nothing is impossible to them that beleeve*.' At this point he began to draw circles again and realized that it was still a diabolical spirit within him (12).[9]

This revelation was followed by a third assault, with a new spirit claiming to be Christ casting out the devil, 'after which, as I law [*sic*] on my bed all the members of my body fell a working as if the pangs of death had been upon me', with the power telling him that these were the pains of his new birth. He lay in this condition for a whole day and was told by the voice '*that I should worke wonders, and cast out Devils in his name*'. He was visited by two Quakers, George Bayly and John Braban, telling them that the devils had left and been replaced by Christ. Having been told by the voice that he was wearing a crown of glory but finding that his visitors could not see it, the voice told him that Bayly had a devil in him.

[T]he power told me he should *quake and tremble* which immediately he did: the power bade me speake to him *to fall flat upon the ground* which he did, and after a little space rose againe, and I asked him *whether the devil were gone out of him* (having been before perswaded by the power that I should cast him out) to which he gave me no answer but the power told me *that the Devill was ejected* ... (12–13)

He started to identify those in the company who had devils in them, confident that he could cleanse them. Once again he doubted the provenance of the voice, discovering that it was demonic and that his blasphemy had earned damnation. After a day spent telling his wife to raise their children in the fear of God, certain that the devil's abduction was imminent, in the evening he became convinced of deliverance and fell into 'a great agonie, and did sweat extreamely' throughout the night. He was relatively cheerful the following morning, although when a spirit told him '*that now the devil was finally cast out of me, and that the roome within me must not be left empty, but that Christ must come and have the whole, & sole*

---

[9] Cf. Purkiss, *Witch in History*, p. 139; C. L'Estrange Ewen, ed., *Witch Hunting and Witch Trials* (1929), p. 306.

possession, or else Satan would return and re-enter with seven other Devils worse then himselfe', he was wary, 'having be[e]n so often deluded'. The spirit persuaded him by recounting Gilpin's life, informing him that he would die in London in ten years' time and 'promising me prosperitie in the world' (13–14). He was told that he 'should lie (seemingly) dead', which he did until 'the power began first to move one of my legs, and then the other; after that my hands, and then my head, and at last my whole bodie'. He started to remove his spiritually polluted clothes. Discovering that he was no better, he realized that the latest spirit was also demonic. In his hopelessness, he finally understood why God had left him to the devil. In rejecting 'reading, hearing, prayer, &c.' he had become vulnerable to 'strong delusion', and the possession was God's 'just judgement' for other provocations, 'especially for rejecting the revealed will of God in his Word, and hearkning only to a voice within me; because what was spoken by it, was seconded by lying Wonders, of which God hath given notice in his Word, that so his people might not give credit to them, nor be deluded by them' (14–15).

This is to return to the opening of his account: he makes clear the causal connection between such neglect (supposedly encouraged by the Quakers) and vulnerability to the Devil. His conclusion is that any unprejudiced reader will agree 'that my quaking and trembling was of the devill' and invites such a reader to a broader conclusion: 'Many besides my self, have bin, and are in the like condition but few or none to whom the Lord hath manifested his Grace in such a manner as to my selfe' (16, misnumbered 15).

The primary printed response to Gilpin's account was by Christopher Atkinson. The focus is on understanding, on interpretation, which substantially changes the nature of the 'facts'. He starts by drawing attention to Gilpin's degeneracy before his conversion, with Bayly opening to him clerical failings and the mercy he had found in God's bringing him 'out of the customs, and fashions and traditions of men'. Gilpin made some progress, willing to 'testifie against the Priests' but, losing his guide, 'became voyd of understanding of the pure voice of God, which had called him out of darkness before into his light', and open to the Devil's deceits.[10] Atkinson never denied that Gilpin was possessed, but blamed the clergy and Gilpin's consequent failure to distinguish between divine and diabolical voices. Atkinson accepted the competition over the

---

[10] Christopher Atkinson, *The Standard of the Lord Lifted up against the kingdom of Satan, Or An Answer to a Book Entitled The Quakers Shaken, Written by one John Gilpin, with the help of the Priest of Kendal* (1653), pp. 5–6. Hereafter references will appear in the text.

possession of Gilpin's body, but effectively reversed the reading, leaving him still 'possessed with Legions, and reserved for everlasting fire'. This is perhaps at its most vehement when he deals with Gilpin's identification of Quakers as possessed and himself as freed: 'Oh thou Beast! Couldst thou seest the Devil in others, and not in thy self?' This places the emphasis on the ability to discern the spirits, with Atkinson sure of his superiority (2, 18).

Atkinson employed four illustrations to support himself. Prosperity was a deceitful promise, contrary to Christ's foreseeing of earthly troubles. His misapprehension of swallows as angels proved Satan to be his guide. The butterflies were plainly demonic as he was 'cast off' as fuel for Lucifer (21, 13, 16). For this to be convincing, of course, depends on the reader accepting that Gilpin has ultimately failed to escape the Devil, and the same ontological point applies to the last point about the possession. Gilpin blamed the Devil for his (and by inference others') trembling. Atkinson is dismissive.

> To any that have eyes thou liest open; was that the Devil that declared against sin and judgement, against sin in thee; was that the Devil that made the Devil in thee to tremble; when judgement was pronounced against sin in thee? will the Devil destroy his Kingdom? and I manifestly witness against thee that it was the Lord of Heaven and Earth, that made thee tremble before him and stoop; wo unto thee; it had been good if thou hadst never been born (23).

Perhaps the harshness of the final clause lay in the awareness that scriptural precedents are available for trembling by prophets and devils alike. The tract finishes with a petition from seventeen prisoners in Kendal in September 1653, calling upon the 'Magistrates, Preists and People' to turn their attention from prosecuting Quakers to punishing drunkards, adulterers and hypocrites and righting social injustice (24, 28, 31). For our purposes this adaptation, of the image broken forth from the author and, eventually, to become an icon in the argument, can be taken as an exemplum, to which we will return.

III

The place of possession in these relations broadens if we stay in the northeast. A response to *Saul's Errand*, a Quaker rebuttal of a petition to the Council of State, was part of the intention of Francis Higginson's *A Brief Relation of The Irreligion of the Northern Quakers*. He raises the spectres of Münster, and John of Leyden, and refers to Quakers as 'the turbulent Exorcists of *Germany*, redevive in England', and judges them more dangerous than Jesuits.[11] The suggestions become more concrete when he moves onto quaking. In their meetings, 'sometimes men, but more frequently Women and Children fall into quaking fits'. The fits involved swooning, swelling, foaming, purging 'as if they had taken Physick' and were ended with great roaring (15). His next task is to identify the source of this activity. Higginson accepts that some reckon that these 'Fits are meer feignnigs [*sic*], but others look upon them as reall passions'. He believes them to be 'Diabolical Raptures immediately proceeding from the power of Satan; if not from his Corporall Possession, or Obsession of the Parties so passive'. This is grounded in a total of ten proofs. These include Fox's evil eye, the precedent of Münster, the judgement of ministers, physicians 'and such as are able to judge' and the fits' similarity to that described in Mark 9.17–26. There is also the prediction of II Thess. 2.9 that such 'lying Wonders' will precede the coming of the Antichrist. Faking such fits is also unlikely because

It is an utter impossibility for any man, especially women, that never knew what belonged to Stage-playing, and young Children to feign such swoonings, tremblings, palsie-motions, swelling, foaming, purging, such great and horrid screechings, and roarings; yea common Modesty would restrain any man, or woman that are themselves, from such uncleanly Excretions as do often accompany these sordid Trances (16).

In addition, the Devil takes pleasure, with God's permission, in abusing bodies that are in his power. These are people 'who have forsaken the truth and true Worship of God, his Ordinances, Commandements, and are self-excommunicate', and so 'delivered up to Satan by God himselfe'. In particular, 'Women or Children, or those that have fasted long, . . . do most frequently fall into these Suprizals' (17).

At this point, he turns to the most orthodox of authorities, William Perkins. The first means of distinguishing between divine and diabolical trances is that 'Divine Ecstacies' tend to the furtherance of true religion, whereas these, in Higginson's reading, encourage 'the generall upholding of practises of ungodlinesse'. Second, the experiences are different, in that 'the Servants of God have all their Senses, . . . onely for a time the Actions and Operations are suspended and cease to do their duty'. On the other hand, 'in Ecstacies that be from Satan' reason is darkened and understanding obscured. Some have become 'furiously mad, and dyed in that madnesse', while that others 'have been and are strangely

---

[11] F[rancis] H[igginson], *A Brief Relation of The Irreligion of the Northern Quakers* (1653), 'To The Christian Reader'; see also pp. 12, 17, hereafter references in the text.

distracted' and retained 'the troubles and distempers of their heads, is too well known in these parts to be denyed'(18).[12] He concludes,

> That these and such like accidents especially that faculty which most of their Speakers have to cause their hearers fall into such Diabolicall Ecstacies above described, hath induced many understanding Christians to believe that these blasphemous hereticall Imposters are accompanied with the power and workings of Satan (20).

Although Higginson refers to Kendal twice (12–13, 30), Gilpin is absent both by name and as an anonymous example. Higginson's understanding of the likelihood of possession is very much the established orthodoxy. He stresses the vulnerability of women and children, and in England, despite exceptions, this was the expectation. In addition, the pessimistic prognosis along with the lessened sentience during possession was orthodoxy. This could cause problems with granting authenticity to Gilpin, partly in that he was adult and male, but also in that his testimony consisted of clear memories of internal visions, dialogues and unaccompanied activities. One of the consequences was a modification of the understanding of possession to accommodate these differences.

In Newcastle, a ministerial alliance was formed between Independents and Presbyterians against their common enemies, Baptists and Quakers.[13] This went beyond co-authored texts to determining the focus of the press in Gateshead. It is possible that at the heart of this was Thomas Weld, recently returned from New England, having been central in the Antinomian controversy. For our purposes, what is more revealing is his approach to stray sheep; Michael Winship refers to him as 'a particularly combative pastor' (surely a contradiction in terms) and he certainly had the spirit more of Boanerges, the son of thunder, than of reconciliation.[14]

The related perceptions, concerns and rhetoric become clearer if we take a brief look at the account of the Antinomian controversy that Weld co-wrote and published. Here, Weld held forth on the '*Jesuiticall dealing*' by which the Dissenters recruited the gullible, working first on women as they were '*the weaker to resist; the more flexible, tender and ready to yeeld*', hoping to use them '*as by an* Eve, *to catch their husbands also*'. Once '*these seducers*' had deluded such people by '*all these meanes and*

[12] Cf. William Perkins, *Discourse of the Damned Art of Witchcraft* (Cambridge, 1608), pp. 123–6, 222–34, 238–40, 246.
[13] For the context see Roger Howell, *Newcastle Upon Tyne and the Puritan Revolution* (Oxford, 1967), pp. 247–8, 254–8.
[14] Michael Winship, *Making Heretics: Militant Protestantism and Free Grace in Massachusetts, 1636–1641* (Princeton, NJ, 2002), pp. 70–1, 235–6, 306, 165–6.

cunning sleights' they were led to reject divine and civil authority. He was particularly harsh on their conviction that ministers '*must have dung cast on their faces, and bee no better than legall Preachers*, Baals *Priests, Popishs Factors, Scribes, Pharisees, and Opposers of Christ himselfe*'.[15] Each of these is familiar from the abuse traded with the Quakers. The same can be said of important elements and tropes in John Winthrop's account of the struggle to which this served as a preface. The court judged the fountain 'of all our distempers' to be Satan, drawing an explicit analogy with Münster.[16] There was a recurrent concern about uncontrolled testimony of the spirit, 'without concurrence with the word'; such spirits should be tested by the word of God, by scripture. In particular, one of the errors was that 'All Doctrines, Revelations and Spirits, must be tried by Christ the Word, rather then [*sic*] the Word of Christ', that is, by scripture rather than by the antecedent spirit that inspired the scripture.[17] Weld had a heightened sensitivity to the discerning of spirits and their provenance. As this is central to the appraisal of the difference between divine mystic vision and diabolical possession, Weld knew its polemical purposes as well as accepting its reality, and this may have played a role in its place in the controversy. At present this must remain no more than a suggestion, but it should be noted that Gilpin's *Quakers Shaken* found its first press in Gateshead. In addition, Weld's established tendency to draw clear lines in the sand in disputes may have assisted the tide of exclusion at the expense of any undertow of reconciliation in the fracas with the Quakers.

One of the first broader assaults on the Quakers following their initial impact on the region was *The Perfect Pharise[e]*, co-authored by Weld, Richard Prideaux, Samuel Hammond, William Cole and William Durant.[18] In the section asserting that spirits are not to be tested by scripture, the first point made is that if one speaks not according to the law it is to show that one lacks light; the second is that this withdraws the soul from God's judgement. This creates a vulnerability.

This is to open a gap unavoidably to all Satans delusions, as you may see by the short Relation of *Quakers shaken* in the case of *John Gilpin*; and we can no otherwise look upon this, then the very Hold Satan hath to keep this people under his delusions, by couzening them thus, to stop their eyes against the light, *John* 3.20.

---

[15] [Thomas Weld], 'Preface', in [John Winthrop], *A Short Story of the Rise, reign, and ruin of the Antinomians* (1644), n.p.

[16] [Winthrop], *Short Story*, p. 40; cf. Winship, *Making Heretics*, pp. 179–80.

[17] [Winthrop], *Short Story*, pp. 10, 13; see also pp. 36, 39.

[18] Thomas Weld, Richard Prideaux, Samuel Hammond, William Cole and William Durant, *The Perfect Pharise[e], under Monkish Holiness* (Newcastle, 1653).

Not only is the instance used as a ground on which to generalize, it also serves to question Quaker powers of discernment: 'how fully doth Satan pretend in the soul, to be an Angel of light? and wherein shall man distinguish?'[19]

Similar strategies are present when the tract moves on to practices. The characterization of 'quaking' is pointedly located.

> And for the manner of it, the trembling of all the parts of their body, grovelling upon the ground, foaming at the mouth, horrible noyse, running naked in the streets and markets, with other the like passions, are fully known; and the Narration of *John Gilpin* in print, will give any that desires more particular information, a full account.

The 'proper' scriptural precedents for 'trembling under Visions of the Lords Majesty' are accepted. However, 'we are fully convinced that the quakings of these men do not proceed from any such visions', primarily because for those who have 'been delivered out of their snares, it hath appeared to be a Diabolical delusion, as is convincingly apparent in the example of *Gilpin*'.[20] The net was widened to include all 'false Prophets' who have been 'under satanical extasies', such as Muhammad, John of Leyden, Bernhard Knipperdolling '& among the Papists, multitudes of examples of pretended raptures and extasies'.[21]

An alternative scriptural source for the interpretation of quaking is offered. Trembling can occur upon the sight of sin or due to the wrath of God. In the version of quaking given here, the latter category fits.

> For first, some of us do know, that very young Children have been under these extasies amongst them. Secondly, sense of sin never caused foaming, and running naked in the streets, that we do know of. Thirdly, by the narration of *Gilpin* you may clearly observe, that he was often under those quakings when he was purely possessed by Satan.[22]

Thus the value of quaking has been lessened by juvenile associations, and foaming has become an assumed element in all quaking and, by taking the single instance of Gilpin as evidential proof of the sources of all quaking, it becomes inherently Satanic.

James Nayler was called on to provide the riposte to Weld et al. Addressing the alleged refusal to test the spirits by scripture, Nayler shifts the means of measurement. It is not scripture per se that is to test the spirits, but the 'infallible spirit which is the Originall of all Scriptures' that should be used, the spirit of the letter of scripture, not the 'mere' letter itself of scripture. 'And by this spirit was the spirits tryed before the letter was; and all that are guided by the spirit of God, are the sons

---

[19] Ibid., p. 6.   [20] Ibid., pp. 41–2.   [21] Ibid., p. 42.   [22] Ibid., p. 43.

of God, and are one, and in one minde, and have one rule, and one Faith'. The ministers lack that one spirit, evinced by their wranglings over scripture, and are thereby disqualified from judging. Having built a greater authority, he turns to the use of Gilpin:

[I]t is no more then if the chiefe Priests should have called *Iudas* to have confuted Christ, and the rest of the eleven Apostles, which truth they owned and suffered for, though he denyed it, and consulted with the Priests to betray it, as *Iohn Gilpin* hath done now, who shall receive his reward, and you Priests also.[23]

The presence of Gilpin is implicit when Nayler turns to the subject of quaking. He accepts quaking and trembling, 'to which yee adde, *groveling upon the ground, and foaming at the mouth,* which are lyes and slandars of your owne inventing'. Effectively, the tract is dominated by throwing the accusations straight back at the antagonists: 'for calling *Devills and mad-men,* which ye cast upon us, that is your owne language'.[24]

Similar tactics are employed in the collective response to Nayler, with the addition of witnesses from Kendal along with the broadening of both assumptions and accusations. When it comes to dangers of abandoning the guidance of scripture as a measure of spirits, Gilpin reappears. His testimony is proof, and a partial reading of Atkinson is used to show that Gilpin's possession was accepted. Thus the reader can see 'what reason we had to say, this rejecting the *Scriptures* from being the tryer of Doctrines doth open an unavoydable gap to *Satans* delusions'. This allows a generalization that this 'is the strong hold of Satan, and the snare, with which he entraps them as he will'. He is, of course, present when they respond to Nayler's denial of the grovelling and foaming. 'Are they lyes and slanders? Was not *Iohn Gilpin* a *Quaker?*'[25]

Before moving on to the increased sensationalization and multiplication of the tropes of possession, it is necessary to attend to the increasingly vituperative tone of the texts on both sides – not that they had ever been affectionate. Without lacking in intellectual content, there is a greater degree of nay-saying. This is certainly not evidence of any loss of areas of contention or any limitation of creativity in abusive perception. As Nuttall observed in a crucial work, the apparently minimal but experientially huge and theologically critical distinction was between the Holy Spirit *in* or *behind/before* scripture. For Puritans, scripture was a restraint,

---

[23] James Nayler, *An Answer to the Booke called The perfect Pharisee under Monkish Holiness* (n.p., n.d.), pp. 16–17. Thomason dated it to 8 May 1654.

[24] Ibid., pp. 25–6, 29.

[25] Thomas Weld, William Cole, Richard Prideaux, William Durant and Samuel Hammond, *A Further Discovery of that Generation of men called Quakers* (Gateshead, 1654), pp. 74, 83.

a measure of the Holy Spirit; for the Quakers, scripture was an instance of the work of the Holy Spirit as they were themselves. Once this distinction was made, this matter was 'scarcely patient of logical resolution: to state position and counter-position was all that was possible'.[26] This gradual and possibly irretrievable loss of common ground fits into Michel de Certeau's understanding of mystic religion: 'the *schism* replaces *heresy*, which has become impossible'. Heresy depends on a dominant form with the capacity, both legal and intellectual, to have 'the power of naming *in its own discourse* a dissident formation and excluding it as marginal'. The 'schism' has two (or, in this case, more) positions each of which lacks the power to impose its criteria on the other. Hence it 'is no longer the case of an orthodoxy confronting a heresy, but of different Churches'.[27] It would be presumptive to impose the denominational model too tightly, but it would also be difficult to render a satisfactory means of measuring whether these phenomena were lying wonders or divine wonders that would satisfy both sides. When 'what happened' was agreed on, 'what it was' was no nearer to being resolved.

IV

I shall start with the continued appearance of Gilpin through time and in different forms of print, paying particular attention to the uses to which these forms were put and to modifications made to their stories. Recapitulations of his narrative appeared quite early in the newsbooks. In 1655 *The Weekly Post* provided such, with two pointed additions. Gilpin received direction to undo his service to Satan, 'whereupon he went into the street naked, where (in a vision) he beheld some of the Quakers dancing naked, others feasting, and some again greeting'. Once he was carried back in, he leapt about 'and immediately appeared a man without his head'. The first vision shows Quakers in a witches' sabbath. The headless man comes from the established images of departing devils in possession cases. The second addition recounts the threat of damnation adding Satan demanding his 'bond', presumably a covenant Gilpin had made, selling his soul to Satan. Gilpin refused, telling him that he had put it where Satan could not fetch it, in his Bible, between the pages containing Genesis 3:15, in which God grants the woman the ability to

---

[26] Geoffrey F. Nuttall, *The Holy Spirit in Puritan Faith and Experience* (Oxford, 1946), p. 157; cf. pp. 29–30, 42, 150–1, 154–9. Kate Peters convincingly suggests taking this further, particularly with reference to written and printed texts (*Printed Culture*, p. 30).

[27] Michel de Certeau, *The Mystic Fable, Vol. I: The Sixteenth and Seventeenth Centuries*, trans. Michael B. Smith (Chicago, 1992), pp. 18–19 (emphasis in original); cf. pp. 26, 98–9.

bruise the head of the serpent. This is followed by three instances of 'converted Quakers' back on the straight and narrow, each of which is approached by Satan, each of whom repulsed him with a single verse of scripture.[28] Samuel Clarke provided a version with particular emphases: Atkinson told his listeners to wait upon an inward light 'which (as he said) lies low hidden under the earth, *viz. The old man which is of the earthy earth*'. One of the Quakers told Gilpin that '*Christ was as man, had his failings, distrusted God, &c.*', and at the next meeting he was urged to take up the cross daily, 'saying, *Carry the crosse all day and it will keep thee at night*', Clarke taking the unheard voice and placing the words into the mouth of the Quaker. The cumulative effect is to make the Quakers rather weird and quaint, albeit in a naively heretical way, and to increase their culpability, or at least to make it more evident.[29] A similar tactic was employed in a shorter account describing meetings:

> sometimes one, sometimes more, fall into a great and dreadful shaking & trembling in their whole bodies, and all their joynts, with such risings, & swellings in their bellies and bowels, sending forth such shreekings, yellings, howlings, and roarings, as not onely affrighted the spectators, but caused the Dogs to bark, the Swine to cry, and the Cattel ran about, to the astonishment of al[l] that heard them.

Thus what formerly had been his symptoms became the 'artifices' by which Gilpin was drawn in.[30]

Gilpin's story was particularly popular in the yellow press. One version was largely taken from the original, although the later vision is less cruelly read, as simply dreaming of misled souls.[31] A much more vitriolic version (with a looser relationship with Gilpin's text) can be found in *The Devil Turned Quaker*. The account is prefaced by questions about Quaker ways of working, noting that animals were frightened by 'their roarings and howlings like Dogs', but that people were attracted to the freak show, only

---

[28] *The Weekly Post*, 17–24 April, 1655, No. 123; cf. *The Faithful Scout*, 20–27 April, 1655, No. 224.

[29] Samuel Clarke, *Mirrour or Looking-Glasse Both for Saints and Sinners* (1654), pp. 231–2. The narrative continues to p. 238 without substantial changes.

[30] *The Quakers Dream: or, The Devil's Pilgrimage in England* (1655), pp. 3–4. This piece reproduces the vision of the sabbath and the resistance to Satan of the converted Quakers in *The Weekly Post*. One is likely to be lifted from the other as the words are identical. *Quakers Dream* also attests to an explicit covenant with Satan, 'granting a Bond and Covenant', in a vision on Satan's appearance (3). The frontispiece is taken from *The Ranters Declaration* (1650), with the words in the speech bubbles changed. The account of the astonished animals, which is absent from Gilpin, seems to have been cut and pasted from Clarke's account of some Quakers in north Wales in 1653, or they share a common source: Clarke, *Mirrour*, p. 461.

[31] *The Quakers terrible Vision: or, the Devils Progress from the North of England, to the City of London* (1655), pp. 6–8, quoted p. 8.

to find that 'Sorcery' quickly 'bewitched' them. This leads into a jigsaw puzzle version of the narrative, with most of the incidents present in the original but in a different order. The additions have a clear purpose: Gilpin (who is never named) 'had been a great Professor of Religion for a long time, and a man of good parts' until he was 'bewitched by them'. Once he was possessed, the Quakers were so impressed with his antics that 'he soon became the chief among them'.[32]

The emphasis of *The Quakers Fiery Beacon* is more on the vulnerability of those converted by Quakers and on papist sympathies, possibly the guiding light of the Quakers. By removing the security of scripture and good ministry, foolish people are attracted by their performances.[33] The pamphlet 'proves' the Roman Catholic connections by crediting the authority of 'many learned intelligent Protestants' who have examined the symptoms and confirmed papist tutelage.[34] The author warns that it is not sufficient simply to rely on tracts like this to settle the battle over truth, as Quakers organize to rebut such honesty.

And to the end, they may not lose any of their Atheistical Proselites, several Letters are sent to remote places (which they term a fiery Beacon) to fore-warn them from being seduced, and prevent a falling off, as M[r] Gilpin did, who since his Conversion, having set forth a book, fully discovering their abominable wayes and practises, is now falsly branded for a licentious Liver.[35]

The third level of the process of detachment of argument from the fleshly individuals is when the symptoms and the issues involved become independent, a given part of the discourse. Some of the purposes will be familiar, but here there is sufficient confidence for them to be stated without the particular citation, thereby eliminating or at least lessening the arena for engagement. An early appearance can be found in *The Querers And Quakers Cause at The Second Hearing*, published in May 1653.[36] This ingenious tract consists of thirty queries to an unidentified Seeker from Yorkshire. The answers are irrelevant as the questions are all loaded, intended to foster disadvantageous associations with Quakers.

Similarly silent instances with a cumulatively effected conclusion appear in Donald Lupton's *Quaking Mountebanck*. The focus tends to be on physical manifestations of Quaker trickery. Dealing with quaking, foaming at the mouth is an assumed phenomenon and within two pages swoonings and bodily swellings have been added. The only possible

---

[32] *The Devil turned Quaker: Or, The Damnable, Devilish, and accursed Doctrines and Designes, of these desperate deluded, and deluding people; called Quakers* (1656), n.p.
[33] *The Quakers Fiery Beacon: Or, The Shaking-Ranters Ghost* (1655), p. 4.
[34] Ibid., p. 7.   [35] Ibid., p. 4.
[36] *The Querers And Quakers Cause at The Second Hearing* (1653), dated 20 May.

conclusion is that quaking can be equated with demonic possession.[37] This leaves the author the task of finding the causal element of the possession. He notes particular commotions during Fox's preaching, especially among women, mentioning two who 'were taken with their *Whyning yelping puppy-like Phrensical* fits' during Fox's 'confused *Babling*', and returns to people foaming at the meetings, raising the possibility of epilepsy, although it is not entirely clear whether this is an alternative explanation or a means of the enactment of the possession itself. To clinch the argument he brings in the story of ribbons and charms being distributed, resembling something like a bond between the zealot and the devil, a material register of the covenant that causes the possession.[38]

V

To draw broader conclusions requires stepping back from the stitches to appraise the tapestry. This is a matter of silent shifts in the reported symptoms and their moral assessment. Some continuity was necessary for the accusation to carry any weight. Thus the starting point is the quaking and trembling, but this needed to be built upon. Hence the foaming, paralyses and spasms, different from the 'regular' quaking in that such movements necessitated interpretation to gain some particular signification. A step further is taken in the occasion of extra-human strength, the appetite for self-harm and especially the 'swellings' and the movements within bodies that appear in hostile sources. Each of these was a required part of the curriculum vitae of any applicant for the post of 'possessed'.[39]

There are also a number of established symptoms that fall away unremarked on. 'Foaming mouths' were a poor substitute for the vomiting fits that characterized earlier possessions.[40] The most frequent expulsions were pins or feathers, but anything 'unnatural' was appropriate

---

[37] [Donald Lupton], *The Quaking Mountebanck Or The Jesuite turn'd Quaker* (1655), pp. 4, 5, 7, 10.

[38] Ibid., pp. 11, 15, 16–17, 19–20; cf. *The Quakers terrible Vision*, pp. 3, 4–5; *The Weekly Intelligencer*, 19–26 July, 1659, No. 12, 96; [John Denham], *A Relation of a Quaker, That to the Shame of his Profession, Attempted to Bugger a Mare near Colchester* (n.p., n.d.).

[39] Marion Gibson, *Possession, Puritanism and Print: Darrell, Harsnett, Shakespeare and the Elizabethan Exorcism Controversy* (2006); James Sharpe, *Instruments of Darkness: Witchcraft in England 1550–1750* (1996), ch. 8.

[40] This is not to say that 'foaming' was unprecedented, as it were. It appeared as a symptom of possession in John Darrell, *A brief apologie prouing the possession of William Sommers* (Middelburg, 1599), p. 9, and Anon., *A breife Narration of the possession, dispossession, and, repossession of William Sommers* (Amsterdam?, 1598). Rather more respectable backing can be found in Richard Bernard, *A Guide to Grand-jury Men* (1627), p. 49, and Mark 9.20.

as part of the authenticity test. There may be an echo of this in the occasional references to 'purging', but not more than echoes. There is a much more marked absence of the gift of tongues (although perhaps an echo in Fox's 'babbling') and in the sometimes lengthy performances of vices and virtues. Possibly as a consequence of the lesser attention paid to dispossession, there is a clear absence of arguments with demons, either between the godly and the devils or between the demons and the godly remnant of the individual possessed. In contrast to earlier accounts these tend to be solitary and much less of a public moral wrestling match than was expected. This is linked to a difference noted earlier, that these sufferers retained memories of their experience, in a sense making the sufferer more powerful, in that earlier symptoms were in need of an interpreter – religious, medical or sceptical – to identify what the symptoms were symptoms *of*.

Along with the different context comes a shifted sense of agency. In the most publicized cases, the possessed were often able to identify who had bewitched them. William Sommers, for instance, could claim an ability to identify many witches. Intellectually, witches were an unnecessary addendum, as Satan hardly needed the assistance of mere mortals to possess a vulnerable human. In more confrontational circumstances, especially where dispossession is less central, the identification of a culpable source or a culpable environment was attractive to writers hostile to the Quakers. Once the figure becomes generic and moves away from prodigal sons such as Gilpin, the line between bewitched and bewitcher becomes much more fluid. Once one was bewitched, enchanted or possessed, one was much more likely to become an agent of bewitchment. This brings the model closer to the New England experiences. North American and English witchcraft have tended to have separate historiographies. Thus when Carol Karlsen found a common ground shared by those accused of being possessed and those accused of witchcraft, it remained unremarked that this would have been unusual in an English context. It would be presumptuous to lay the blame on Weld or his colleagues returning from New England; it may be an import finding fertile soil or just a parallel development.[41]

The final point shares ground with Elmer's reading of the accusations of witchcraft directed at the Quakers, although it works in the opposite

---

[41] It is of interest that this association of recruitment, witchcraft and possession was also applied to Quakers in New England: Carol F. Karlsen, *The Devil in the Shape of a Woman: Witchcraft in Colonial New England* (New York, 1987), pp. 12–13, 135. William Sommers was accused of bewitchment but it was not among the charges brought against him: John Darrell, *A Detection of that Sinnful Shamful Lying and Ridiculous Discours, of Samuel Harshnet* (n.p., 1600), p. 32; Harsnett, *A Discovery*, p. 149.

direction.[42] We have encountered the broad-brush Quaker response to the pointillist accusations of possession; while Puritans could identify cases and generalize from (not always named) individuals, Quakers could counter with representations of the misguided ministry as generally a set of agents of Satan's possession. This broadened the terms of the debate and worked to the Quakers' advantage in the hectic push-and-pull of 1650s press campaigns. However, it rather diminished the place of the possessed individual in these debates. Ultimately it contributed to the generic accusations of 'enthusiasm', 'frenzy' and 'fanaticism' as a post-Restoration broad brush with which to tar all nonconformity. Ironically, the terms of abuse bandied about between the established radicals of the 1650s and the new kids on the block became terms of abuse that proved to be ecumenical in their target.

---

[42] Elmer, "'Saints or sorcerers'".

10   James Harrington's prescription for healing and settling

Jonathan Scott

James Harrington's *The Commonwealth of Oceana* (1656) has been intermittently famous since publication. Unlike other blueprints for a commonwealth, *Oceana* did not simply offer reasons for preferring a republic to monarchy. It furnished the first large-scale analysis, and explanation, of the collapse of the Stuart regime. Further, it made an unabashed claim to originality in Harrington's two great discoveries: of the principle of 'the balance of dominion' in the foundation, and the separation of 'dividing and choosing' in the superstructure. This knowledge might render a republic 'as . . . long-lived, as the world'.[1] By 1659 these arguments furnished the basis of a new political science, and satire.

Meanwhile interpretations of Harrington's text have diverged wildly. In the early 1940s *Oceana* stood at the heart of the celebrated 'gentry controversy'. In 1945, in a pioneering work by Zera Fink, Tawney's analyst of contemporary economic and social change became a 'classical republican'.[2] Building on this interpretation, J. G. A. Pocock made Harrington author of a 'Machiavellian meditation upon feudalism'.[3] Subsequently Harrington's classical republicanism has been depicted as Platonic, Aristotelian, neo-Roman, 'Virgilianized', Machiavellian or a synthesis of several of these elements mediated by Polybian constitutionalism.[4] Others have seen in him a utopian, a Stoic, a natural

---

[1] James Harrington, *Oceana*, in *The Political Works of James Harrington*, ed. J. G. A. Pocock (Cambridge, 1977), p. 321.

[2] R. H. Tawney, 'Harrington's interpretation of his age', *Proceedings of the British Academy*, 27 (1941), 199–223; H. R. Trevor-Roper, 'The gentry 1540–1640', *Economic History Review Supplements* no. 1 (Cambridge, 1953); Zera Fink, *The Classical Republicans: An Essay in the Recovery of a Pattern of Thought in Seventeenth Century England* (Evanston, IL, 1945).

[3] J. G. A. Pocock, *The Machiavellian Moment: Florentine Political Thought and the Atlantic Republican Tradition* (Princeton, 1975), p. 385; Pocock, *The Ancient Constitution and the Feudal Law* (Cambridge, 1958), p. 147.

[4] For Harrington as Platonist see Charles Blitzer, *An Immortal Commonwealth: the Political Thought of James Harrington* (New Haven, CT, 1970); Eric Nelson, *The Greek Tradition in Republican Thought* (Cambridge, 2004), ch. 3; J. G. A. Pocock, 'Introduction', in James Harrington, *The Commonwealth of Oceana and A System of Politics*, ed. Pocock (Cambridge,

philosopher and the author of a civil religion.[5] For still others Harrington's principal intellectual debt was to Hobbes, an engagement which has been used to problematize the idea of English classical republicanism.[6] In fact this diversity of interpretation reflects a key feature of Harrington's text: its deliberate, and strategic, multi-vocality. To understand why, we must relate *Oceana* to another intellectual agenda: that Interregnum argument concerning settlement to which the previously most important contribution had been Hobbes's *Leviathan* (1651).

Elsewhere I have explored this theme by analysis of *Oceana*'s Hobbes-indebted natural philosophy and metaphysics.[7] The focus here is on the political context in which Harrington formulated his intervention. This interpretation takes issue with those historians who have seen in Harrington a characteristic voice of republican opposition to Oliver Cromwell. In fact those voices belonged, in 1656, mainly to those commonwealthsmen (Marchamont Nedham, John Streater, Henry Vane, Arthur Haselrig) whose partisan agendas, among others, Harrington opposed. By contrast, *Oceana* was a holistic attempt to unite moderate commonwealthsmen,

---

1992), pp. xxii–xxiv. For his Aristotelianism, see Pocock, *Machiavellian Moment*, pp. 66–80; and James Cotton, *James Harrington's Political Thought and its Context* (1991), ch. 2. For his Machiavellianism, see Felix Raab, *The English Face of Machiavelli* (1964), ch. 6; and Pocock, *Machiavellian Moment*. For the Polybian synthesis see Fink, *Classical Republicans*, ch. 3; Pocock, *Machiavellian Moment*; and Blair Worden, 'James Harrington and *The Commonwealth of Oceana*, 1656', in David Wootton, ed., *Republicanism, Liberty and Commercial Society* (Stanford, 1994). For the neo-Roman Harrington, see Quentin Skinner, *Liberty before Liberalism* (Cambridge, 1998); for his 'Virgilianized republicanism', see David Norbrook, *Writing the English Republic: Poetry, Rhetoric and Politics 1627–1660* (Cambridge, 1999), pp. 357–78.

[5] J. C. Davis, *Utopia and the Ideal Society* (Cambridge, 1981), chs. 8–9; Alan Cromartie, 'Harringtonian Virtue: Harrington, Machiavelli, and the method of the *Moment*', *HJ*, 41 (1988), 987–1009; Jonathan Scott, *England's Troubles: Seventeenth-Century English Political Instability in European Context* (Cambridge, 2000), ch. 14; Mark Goldie, 'The civil religion of James Harrington', in Anthony Pagden, ed., *The Languages of Political Theory in Early-Modern Europe* (Cambridge, 1987), pp. 197–222.

[6] Raab, *Machiavelli*, ch. 6; Cotton, *Harrington*, ch. 4; Jonathan Scott, 'The rapture of motion: James Harrington's republicanism', in Nicholas Phillipson and Quentin Skinner, eds., *Political Discourse in Early Modern Britain* (Cambridge, 1993); Scott, 'The peace of silence: Thucydides and the English Civil War', in Miles Fairburn and W. H. Oliver, eds., *The Certainty of Doubt: Tributes to Peter Munz* (Wellington, 1996); Paul Rahe, *Republics Ancient and Modern, Volume 2: New Modes and Orders in Early Modern Political Thought* (1994), ch. 5; Rahe, *Against Throne and Altar: Machiavelli and Political Theory under the English Republic* (Cambridge, 2008), ch. 11; Arihiro Fukuda, *Sovereignty and the Sword: Harrington, Hobbes, and Mixed Government in the English Civil Wars* (Oxford, 1997); Glenn Burgess, 'Repacifying the polity: the responses of Hobbes and Harrington to the "crisis of the common law"', in Ian Gentles, John Morrill and Blair Worden, eds., *Soldiers, Writers and Statesmen of the English Revolution* (Cambridge, 1998), pp. 202–28.

[7] Scott, 'Rapture of Motion'; Scott, 'Peace of Silence'; Scott, *Commonwealth Principles: Republican Writing of the English Revolution* (Cambridge, 2004), pp. 162–6, 181–4, 285–92.

Presbyterians and Royalists: to overcome partisan division. This was to be achieved not simply by drawing on Royalist as well as republican sources and arguments. It was achieved by speaking systematically to Cromwell's own religious and political agenda. *Oceana* was, in short, not simply a work of opposition, but also of counsel, offering the Lord Protector, in place of the *Instrument of Government* (1653), a republican prescription for the realization of his ambition of healing and settling.

We may start with the secondary, but revealing, matter of biography. It was Nedham who preceded his career as a republican polemicist with an extended spell as editor of a Royalist newspaper. On this basis he has been vilified as a mercenary turncoat, a judgement which, while containing an element of truth, is less than the whole truth.[8] No one looks at Harrington in a similar light. Yet according to John Toland it was Harrington, not Nedham, who during the later 1640s served Charles I personally with 'untainted fidelity'. It was Harrington who 'vindicated . . . his Majesty's Arguments against the Parliament at *Newport* and . . . accompany'd him on the Scaffold'.[9] According to Aubrey, Harrington 'was on the scaffold with the King when he was beheaded; and I have oftentimes heard him speake of King Charles I with the greatest zeale and passion imaginable, and that his death gave him so great a griefe that . . . never any thing did goe so neer to him'.[10] This is, to say the least, an unusual résumé for 'a classical republican, and England's premier civic humanist'.[11] Yet it supplies a crucial context for the authorship of *Oceana*, the purpose of which was to diagnose the cause of the upheaval culminating in the regicide, and to make sure that it never happened again.

All republicans agreed that the government of a commonwealth consisted in the rule 'of laws and not of men'.[12] As Plato had explained, 'Where the law is subject to some other authority and has none of its own, the collapse of the state . . . is not far off; but if the law is the master of the government and the government is its slave, then the situation is full of promise.'[13] This insight was developed in Aristotle's *Politics*, along with an account of the moral purpose of political association to which English republican writing was indebted. From these sources English republicans derived a constitutional language which spoke of

---

[8] *The Character of Mercurius Politicus* (August 14, 1650), p. 1; Scott, *Commonwealth Principles*, pp. 14–15, 82–4, 241–7.

[9] John Toland, 'The Life of James Harrington', in *The Oceana of James Harrington . . . with An Exact Account of his Life* (1700), pp. xvi–xvii.

[10] John Aubrey, *Aubrey's Brief Lives*, ed. Oliver Lawson Dick (1958), p. 124.

[11] Pocock, 'Historical Introduction', in Harrington, *Political Works*, p. 15.

[12] Harrington, *Oceana*, in *Works*, p. 161.

[13] Plato, *The Laws*, trans. Trevor J. Saunders (Harmondsworth, 1975), p. 174.

government by the one, the few or the many.[14] This terminology was
deployed by Polybius, Cicero and Machiavelli to argue that these forms
should in some way be combined.[15] At the heart of classical republicanism a series of historians have discerned what they have described as the
Polybian notion of the mixed constitution. According to John Pocock,
and Arihiro Fukuda, this first burst on to the English political scene
in Charles I's *Answer to the Nineteen Propositions* (1642).[16] Yet far from
marking the arrival of a new, specifically republican perception, the publication of a mixed constitution analysis by the king's moderate advisers
more plausibly demonstrates that this analysis transcended the divide
between republican (or Parliamentarian) and Royalist. It was, that is to
say, contested real estate within a struggle for the status of legitimate
guardian of the ancient constitution.

Throughout the late medieval and early modern periods this language
of the mixed constitution had been deployed by writers as various as
Fortescue, Erasmus and Hotman to argue the case for legal, bounded,
or 'political' monarchy. By the mid-seventeenth century, the subsequent
republican argument ran, government which was moderate, mixed and
dedicated to the public good could no longer be provided by a monarchy which had become 'unnecessary, burdensome, and dangerous to
the...people'. One of Harrington's accomplishments was to reconfig-
ure this Aristotelian constitutionalism from its defunct mixed monarchy
framework into the shape of a now materially essential English republic. This was an attempt, in a Protectoral context, to acclimatize English
republicanism by giving it a more traditional, and mixed, constitutional
form.[17]

Within republicanism adherence to the doctrine of a mixed constitution was limited before 1653, and disputed between 1653 and 1660. By
far its most important adherent was Harrington, whose associates during
the 1640s were not other republicans, but moderate Royalists (like those
who had penned the *Answer*) and the king himself.[18] Moreover, even by
Harrington the invocation of Polybius was rare, and that of Plato, Aristotle and Cicero ubiquitous. In both *Oceana* and *The Prerogative of Popular
Government* (1658), Harrington gave as the sources for his definition of

[14] Aristotle, *The Politics*, ed. Stephen Everson (Cambridge, 1988), pp. 20–33.
[15] Machiavelli, *The Discourses*, ed. Bernard Crick (Harmondsworth, 1985), pp. 109–24.
[16] Pocock, *Machiavellian Moment*, pp. 361–6; Michael Mendle, *Dangerous Positions: Mixed
Government, the Estates of the Realm, and the Making of the Answer to the XIX Propositions*
(Birmingham, AL, 1985); Fukuda, *Sovereignty and the Sword*, chs. 1–2; Jonathan Scott,
review of Fukuda, *English Historical Review*, 115 (2000), 660–2.
[17] Scott, *Commonwealth Principles*, pp. 134, 141–3.
[18] Burgess, 'Repacifying the polity', relates the thought of both Harrington and Hobbes to
this intellectual background of 'constitutional royalism'.

'ancient prudence' as 'the empire of laws and not of men . . . Aristotle and Livy'. When Sidney made the same idea central to his *Discourses* he did so similarly with quotations from Aristotle's *Politics* and Livy's *History*.[19] Finally, as actually developed in *Oceana*, Harrington's doctrine of 'the balance' was not Polybian. In Polybius this had referred to a tripartite balance within the constitutional superstructure. In *Oceana* it became 'the balance of dominion', denoting the predominant ownership of property within a material 'foundation' on which the whole superstructure stood.

In England, as in the United Provinces, there were many republicans who regarded the mixed constitution as compromised by an element of the monarchy it sought to replace.[20] For some the best form was 'elective aristocracy', and Venice a powerful example in its support.[21] An alternative was the Machiavellian populism of both Nedham and Streater.[22] For Nedham the 'serene republic' was 'rather a *Juncta* then a *Commonweal*.'[23] Alongside Rome at its most popular, Nedham's other exemplar state was the unmixed democracy of Athens. So excellent was the work 'of *Solon* . . . [in] avoiding *Kingly Tyranny* on the one side, and *Senatoriall encroachments* on the other, hee is celebrated by all Posterity, as the man that hath left the only Patern of a *free state*, fit for all the world to follow'.[24]

The origins of Nedham's position lay in his earlier career as an anonymous, Lilburne-affiliated, Machiavelli-inspired Leveller pamphleteer.[25] Between 1651 and 1652 he pursued this democratic agenda against the oligarchical tendencies of Parliamentarians, and the tyrannical ones of army grandees. Following the dissolution of the Rump, the same argument was advanced by many commonwealthsmen against the Protectorate. On the eve of the first Protectoral parliament of September 1654

---

[19] Harrington, *Political Works*, pp. 161, 401; Algernon Sidney, *Discourses Concerning Government*, ed. Thomas G. West (Indianapolis, IN, 1996), p. 288; Sidney, *Court Maxims*, ed. Hans Blom, Eco Haitsma Mulier and Ronald Janse (Cambridge, 1996), p. 20.

[20] Eco Haitsma Mulier, *The Myth of Venice and Dutch Republican Thought in the Seventeenth Century* (Assen, 1980), pp. 125, 137–8; Jonathan Scott, 'Classical republicanism in seventeenth-century England and the Netherlands', in Martin van Gelderen and Quentin Skinner, eds., *Republicanism: A Shared European Heritage Volume 1: Republicanism and Constitutionalism in Early Modern Europe* (Cambridge, 2002), p. 67.

[21] *A Short Discourse between Monarchical and Aristocratical Government* (1649), pp. 11–16; John Cook, *Monarchy No Creature of God's Making* (1651), Dedication, p. 3; *A Perswasive to Mutuall Compliance under the Present Government* (1651), pp. 23–5.

[22] [Streater], *Observations upon Aristotle's first Book of Political Government* no. 5 (1654), p. 35.

[23] [Nedham], *Mercurius Politicus* no. 77 (20–27 November 1651), p. 1222; no. 86 (22–29 January 1652), p. 1368.

[24] Ibid., no. 71 (9–16 October 1651), pp. 1125–6; no. 73 (23–30 October 1651), p. 1158. This admiration of Athens found echoes in the Restoration writing of Neville and Sidney: Caroline Robbins, ed., *Two English Republican Tracts* (Cambridge, 1969), pp. 95–6; Sidney, *Discourses*, pp. 199–201.

[25] Scott, *Commonwealth Principles*, pp. 82–4, 156–8.

Streater's weekly newspaper *Observations upon Aristotle's first Book of Political Government* explained that it was characteristic of tyrants to forbid public speaking of the truth. Yet

> Those that represent a People, ought not to be daunted by the greatest Person or Forces under heaven... And it is their duties in those Councels, to set on foot debates of what is profitable and what is not profitable to the Commonwealth; of what is just, and what is unjust: They should rather sacrifice their lives, then condescend to any thing that is not for the good of the publike.[26]

In issue 10 of *Observations* there appeared a suspiciously topical account of the career of Nero, who first appeared on the public stage amid elaborate protestations of humility, professing himself a '*Laborious, and Painful Servant of the Commonwealth*', while courting the people and army. A few months later Oliver's speech dissolving this parliament included the statement: 'And for myself, I desire not to keep my place in this Government an hour longer than I may preserve England in its just rights.'[27] Thereafter, once Nero had 'ascended the *Meridian-line*' and become 'unlimmitted', he corrupted the 'souldiery... making use of them to be the keepers of the peace, [and] lay[ing] aside the people', before embarking on a spectacular career of 'lust, pride and cruelty'.[28]

In the parliamentary elections of 1654 and 1656 Cromwell faced vigorous republican opposition. When Sir Arthur Haselrig, Thomas Scot and others were '*violently kept out of the Parliament-house by armed men hired by the Lord Protector*' in September 1656, they published a *Remonstrance, [and] Protestation*.[29] A few months earlier had appeared R.G.'s *A Copy of a Letter from an Officer of the Army in Ireland*, which anticipated not only the historical analysis of Harrington's *Oceana*, but its key idea of an agrarian law.[30] In the style of Nedham earlier, and Sidney later, *A Copy of a Letter* was a work of Machiavellian interest theory extrapolating on the *Discorsi*'s assertion that the interests of kings or tyrants (which were the same) and republics were irreconcilable.

---

[26] *Observations Historical, Political and Philiosophical, Upon Aristotle's first Book of Political Government* no. 9 (June 1654), p. 58.

[27] Cromwell, speech of 22 January 1655 in *Oliver Cromwell's Letters and Speeches*, ed. Thomas Carlyle, 3 vols. (1857), III, p. 84.

[28] *Observations* no. 10, pp. 76–7.

[29] *To all the Worthy Gentlemen who are Duely Chosen... the 17 of September 1656* (Haselrig and Scot head the list of 98 signatures); *The Protector, (So called,) In Part Unvailed: By whom the Mystery of Iniquity, is now working* (1655); I.S., *The PICTURE of a New COURTIER drawn in a Conference, between Mr. Timeserver, and Mr. Plain-heart* (1656).

[30] Pocock, 'Historical introduction', pp. 10–12; Jonathan Scott, *Algernon Sidney and the English Republic* (Cambridge, 1988), pp. 115–16; R.G., *A Copy of a Letter from an Officer In Ireland, to His Highness the Lord Protector* (1656), pp. 8–9.

Reason of state in Kings and Tyrants, is to keep mankind poor and ignorant . . . point blank contrary to the . . . maximes of a Commonwealth, which is the nursery of vertue, valor, and industrie . . . The riches of the people in general, is the natural cause of destruction to all Regal States.[31]

Another attempt to influence the 1656 election was Nedham's *The Excellencie of a Free State.*[32] The purpose of this was to open 'the Eyes of the People' in the face of advice being given to '*his Highness to lay aside Parliament . . . and to lay a Foundation for absolute Tyranny, upon unbounded Monarchy*'. 'It is a pity, that the people of *England* . . . should be of such a supple humor and inclination, to bow under the ignoble pressures of an Arbitrary Tyranny, and so unapt to learn what true Freedom is.'[33] 'How came it to pass . . . that *Julius Caesar* aspired, and in the end attained [to] the Empire? . . . had not the Senate and People so long protracted the Power of *Pompey* . . . in *Asia*, and *Caesar* . . . in *Gallia*, *Rome* might have stood much longer in the possession of her Liberty.'[34] Fortunately, history showed that 'a People having once tasted the Sweets of Freedom, are so extreamly affected with it' that any such usurper must fear that 'upon the first opportunity' they will take their 'revenge'.[35]

Like Nedham's *Excellencie*, Harrington's *Oceana* appears to have been timed to coincide with the parliamentary elections of September 1656. However, owing to printing problems, exacerbated or caused by enquiries by the government, the work did not appear until October or November.[36] Like the *Excellencie*, and as the work of 'England's premier civic humanist', *Oceana* has been interpreted as an exemplary work of republican opposition.[37] Thus it is the view of Blair Worden that 'Although . . . *Oceana* . . . distances itself from the programme of the commonwealthmen, who want to restore the sovereign House of Commons, it is at one with them . . . in its detestation of Cromwell and of the expulsion of the Rump.'[38] This detestation manifests itself in Harrington's ironic representation of *Oceana*'s Lord Archon as a virtuous inversion of the real Lord Protector. In this role Lord Archon does everything for

---

[31] R.G., *A Copy of a Letter*, pp. 4, 5.

[32] Pocock, 'Historical Introduction', pp. 13, 34–7; Martin Dzelzainis, 'Milton and the Protectorate in 1658', in David Armitage, Armand Himy and Quentin Skinner, eds., *Milton and Republicanism* (Cambridge, 1995), p. 203.

[33] Nedham, *Excellencie*, Introduction, p. 4.

[34] Ibid., 'The Right Constitution of a Commonwealth', pp. 28, 30, 32, 64.

[35] Ibid., pp. 46–9.   [36] Pocock, 'Historical Introduction', p. 14.

[37] Ibid., pp. 6–42; Worden, 'James Harrington and "The Commonwealth of Oceana", 1656', in Wootton, *Republicanism*, pp. 82–138.

[38] Worden, 'James Harrington', p. 119. The argument is restated in Worden, *Literature and Politics in Cromwellian England: John Milton, Andrew Marvell, Marchamont Nedham* (Oxford, 2007), pp. 109–15.

the establishment of the nation's liberty which the Lord Protector had often promised, but conspicuously failed to do. It is certainly true that Harrington's work sought to offer what the bungling Lord Protector had failed to deliver. First and foremost, however, this was not that 'liberty' so beloved of the commonwealthsmen, but peace and settlement. '*We are disputing whether we should have Peace, or War: For Peace, you cannot have without some Government, nor any Government without the proper Balance: Wherefore if you will not fix this which you have, the rest is blood.*'[39]

It is not easy to detect Harrington's 'detestation of the dissolution of the Rump' in an account of that body likening it (using Hobbes's translation of Thucydides) to the Thirty Tyrants of Athens.[40] This was that 'government of Oceana ... consisting of one single council of the people, to the exclusion of the king and of the lords ... invested with the whole power of government, without any covenants, conditions, or orders whatsoever. So new a thing that neither ancient nor modern prudence can show any avowed example of the like.'[41] By contrast, *Oceana* defended the dissolution:

My lord general, being clear in these points and the necessity of some other course than would be thought upon by the parliament, appointed a rendezvous of the army, where he spoke his sense agreeable to these preliminaries, with such success unto the soldiery that the parliament was soon after deposed; and himself ... created, by the universal suffrage of the army, Lord Archon.[42]

That this tyranny of a few had now given way to a tyranny of one may have constituted another lost opportunity for settlement, but it was hardly a calamity in its own right. For Harrington, what gave unity to all of these failures was their epiphenomenal status. No politicians could solve the problem. For a solution it was necessary to see beneath the surface of such events to their material causes. This was the work of a lawgiver, who must also be, in Harrington's view, a natural philosopher. 'Policy is an art ... [and] Art is the observation or imitation of nature ... Some have said that I, being a private man, had been ... mad ... to meddle with politics ... My Lord, there is not any public person, not any magistrate, that has written in politics worth a button.'[43] Harrington's ambition to stand, to this extent, outside the immediate political context, was not simply that of a would-be political neutral. It was that of a philosopher, who wished like Hobbes to elevate politics from polemic to the status of civil philosophy.

[39] Harrington, *The Commonwealth of Oceana* (1656), pp. 113–14.   [40] Ibid., p. 49.
[41] Harrington, *Oceana*, in *Works*, p. 205.   [42] Ibid., p. 207.
[43] *The Examination of James Harrington* in *Political Works*, p. 858.

To understand Harrington's depiction of the Rump we must turn from the work of the commonwealthsmen, to that of the Protectorate's republican apologists. Fittingly the most important of these was Marchamont Nedham. In 1650 Nedham's appointment as propagandist for the new Republic, when he could otherwise have been hanged, reflected the Rump's view of the danger in which it stood from popular royalism (and perhaps also Levellerism). In 1654 we may take his commission to write the *True State of the Case of the Commonwealth* as evidence of the Protectorate's felt need to propitiate republican opinion. Now again Nedham defended 'the necessity and Justness' of the latest of 'several changes' and 'Alterations'.[44] Political forms were transitory and secondary ('being as the Shell to the Kernel'), and the alternatives facing the nation were worse. These included 'Anarchy and Confusion' on the one hand, or 'the *young Pretender*' fixed upon his 'private Interest' on the other.[45] In addition, however, there were now the disgruntled commonwealthsmen, 'who make it their business by cunning insinuations to draw away the hearts of the Well-affected . . . as if we had . . . introduced again that very thing, which was the great Bone of contention'.[46]

This, of course, was monarchy. Here Nedham's first important claim was that it was the Rump which had been on the point of betraying the nation's hard-won liberty, leaving the Army no choice but to intervene. 'Studious of Parties and private Interests, neglecting the publick', it had long delayed the '*Bill for a new Representative*', and only taken it up at the last minute, insincerely, 'to have had some . . . Pretext to thwart or scandalize that most necessary work of Dissolution'. Yet even 'admit that they had been real in their Intentions, for the putting a period to their own Authority (as was pretended)', constitutionally the Bill was flawed,

intending that the supreme authority should be lodged in *Biennial Parliaments*, and that they should have power to sit to make Laws, and govern from two years to two years successively . . . the evil consequences thereof . . . are discernable to every eye . . . the Supream Powers of making Laws, and of putting them in execution, were by that Bill to have been disposed in the same hands; which placing the *Legislative* and *executive Powers* in the same persons, is a marvellous In-let of Corruption and Tyranny: wheras the keeping of these two apart, flowing in distinct Channels, so that they may never meet in one . . . there lies a grand secret of Liberty and good Government.[47]

This was not Nedham's first visitation of the theme of separation of powers. The passage above quoted directly from *Mercurius Politicus* no. 109 of July 1–8 1652, in which this position was made compatible

---

[44] [Marchamont Nedham], *A True State of the Case of the Commonwealth* (1654), p. 6.
[45] Ibid., pp. 14, 49.   [46] Ibid., pp. 3, 8.   [47] Ibid., pp. 9–10.

with Nedham's advocacy of Athenian/Roman democracy by specifying that 'By the *Executive Power* we mean that Power which is derived from the other'; a capacity for 'the administration of Government in the execution of those Laws', not for sharing in their authorship.[48] In the *True State*, however, Nedham turned the same argument toward advocacy of a mixed constitution. Thus under the *Instrument of Government*, 'though the *Common-wealth* may now appear with a new face in the outward Form, yet it remains still the same in Substance, and is of a better complexion... then heretofore', in which the single person was 'not to exercise his Power by a Claim of Inheritance', but 'is *elective*, and that Election must take its rise originally and virtually from the People'.[49] That person shared his power both with a Council and with parliaments. This tripartite constitution, allowing for parliaments which were regular, but not perpetual, was proof against the tyranny of a single assembly, as well as of a single person. In short the *Instrument* had at last established a stable defence of the people's 'plenary... Liberty as Christians... against Anarchie and Tyranny', combining 'the Unitive vertue (but nothing else) of *Monarchy*... the admireable Counsel of *Aristocracie*... the industry and courage of *Democracie*'.[50]

It was Cromwell's 'great end... to wit, Healing and Settling', to defend the nation from both ungodly royalism and 'men of Levelling Principles'; to bring together moderates, 'judging this most likely to avoid the extremes of Monarchy on the one hand, and Democracy on the other'.[51] To serve this end, Nedham diluted his earlier unicameral commonwealth principles with the constitutional thought of moderate royalism. The status of Nedham's formulation as the regime's official position was underlined by the Protector speaking to his first parliament:

> I dare assert there is a just Liberty to the People of God, and the just Rights of the People in these Nations provided for, – I can put the issue thereof upon the clearest reason... For satisfaction's sake herein, enough is said in a Book entituled *A State of the Case of the Commonwealth*, published in January 1653[4].[52]

It is Worden's argument that, informed by hatred of Cromwell, Harrington's dedication of *Oceana* to him is ironic (it is 'an anti-dedication'), and his account of Lord Archon is an extended public joke at the Lord Protector's expense.[53] It is true that *Oceana*'s praise for the Lord Archon's 'lack of ambition in yourself', and 'virtues and merit' could have been read ironically, in the mode of Streater's earlier self-denying Nero. Unlike

---

[48] *Mercurius Politicus*, no. 109 (1–8 July 1652), pp. 1705–06.
[49] [Nedham], *True State*, pp. 28–9.
[50] Ibid., pp. 52–3.   [51] *Cromwell's Letters and Speeches*, III, pp. 20–1.
[52] Ibid., p. 84.   [53] Worden, '*Oceana*', p. 122.

Streater, however, Harrington never exposed the irony by descending to an account of its subject's actual wickedness. Unlike Streater's *Observations*, *Oceana* was not only directed at republicans but was also formally directed to the Lord Protector himself, praise for whose 'incomparable patriot[ism]' contrasted strikingly with Harrington's criticism of the Rump. Above all, what Worden's interpretation renders inexplicable is Harrington's political intention. Were his aspirations merely satirical and literary? This is not the impression given by any of his works, with their emphasis on implementable practicality.[54] Streater's intention, as his text made explicit, was the inculcation of insurrection. For Harrington insurrection was the disease and *Oceana* the cure. In fact we know from the evidence of the text, as well as from Toland, that *Oceana* was published with a serious political purpose, to be served most directly by enlisting Cromwell's support.[55]

This purpose was not to mock lost opportunities for settlement in the past. It was to achieve, in 1656, that settlement which had eluded the nation until that time.

The resulting rhetorical strategy was to show Royalists, commonwealthsmen and supporters of the Protectorate that they had nothing to lose from such a settlement, and everything to gain. As Toland recorded,

By shewing that a Commonwealth was a Government of Laws, and not of the Sword, he could not but detect the violent administration of the Protector... while the cavaliers on the other side tax'd him with Ingratitude to the memory of the late King... To these he answer'd, that... the Monarchy being now quite dissolv'd... he was... oblig'd as a good Citizen to... shew his Countreymen... such a Model of Government as he thought most conducing to their Tranquillity, Wealth, and Power: That the Cavaliers ought of all People to be best pleas'd with him, since if his Model succeeded, they were sure to injoy equal Privileges with others, and to be deliver'd from their present Oppression.[56]

Within the resulting exercise in multivocality, the voice to which least attention has been paid is its attempt to address the Lord Protector's own agenda. Yet what *Oceana* has to say to (rather than simply about) England's government in 1656 is both highly specific and fundamental to its purpose.[57]

For instance, his heroic work done, Harrington's Lord Archon tore himself from a senate with 'tears in their eyes' and 'retired unto a country

---

[54] See, for instance, Harrington, *Works*, p. 601.
[55] J. C. Davis, 'Equality in an unequal commonwealth: James Harrington's republicanism and the meaning of equality', in Gentles et al., *Soldiers, Writers and Statesmen*, pp. 229–42, at p. 230.
[56] John Toland, 'Life of Harrington', pp. xviii–xix.
[57] An important exception is Norbrook, *Writing the Republic*, pp. 363–74.

house of his, being remote and very private'. Recalling that in a speech to the first Protectoral parliament on 12 September 1654, Cromwell claimed to have begged, before the dissolution of the Rump, 'to have had leave to have retired to a private life', Worden takes this to be another savagely ironic juxtaposition of Cromwell's profession to his practice.[58] Yet another, more straightforward, reading is that Harrington's political intention in putting into the mouth of his Lord Archon the Lord Protector's own earlier words was to draw attention to *Oceana*'s claim to be furnishing Cromwell with the means for fulfilment of his own frequently stated ambitions. In relation to a work intended to appeal to many constituencies, and containing an element of counsel, even if Harrington believed Cromwell to be a hypocrite, all that this interpretation assumes is that he did not believe that the Lord Protector took that view of himself.[59]

Thus in another part of the same speech the Lord Protector had said of the *Instrument of Government*: 'The Gentlemen that undertook to frame this Government did consult divers days together . . . How to . . . give us settlement . . . I was not privy to their councils . . . [but] When they had finished their model in some measure . . . they became communicative.'[60] It is the most important fact about *Oceana*'s form, distinguishing it from all other republican works, that it is a 'model'. Of the 'four parts' of which the text is composed, 'The Modell of the Commonwealth', accounts for over 80 per cent of the work.[61] In his *Epistle to the Reader*, Harrington claimed to have been 'not yet two years about it'; that is to say, he began work shortly after promulgation of the *Instrument*. Partly for this reason he was deeply apologetic about the state of the text ('I am quite out of countenance at my worke'), which listed 159 errors. Yet while, therefore, 'the Discourses [that is, the other three parts of the work] be full of crudities . . . the Modell hath had perfect concoction'.[62]

In fact the thirty numbered 'orders' of the 'The Modell', dealing with similar electoral, political and military arrangements, are entirely explicable as a thought-through replacement for the half-baked *Instrument*'s

---

[58] Worden, '*Oceana*', pp. 122–3.
[59] Many similar points of interpretation cut both ways. In what Worden calls 'a deliciously ingenious passage' (*Literature and Politics*, p. 112), Harrington has Oceanic politicians 'lay violent hands upon' a Lord Archon seeking to retire. This is a reversal of the actual events of the dissolution. But it also dramatises *Oceana*'s claim to contain the formula for reversal of Cromwell's destructive relationship with England's political elite. These readings are not mutually exclusive. But without the latter it is hard to see what *Oceana*'s political purpose was.
[60] *Cromwell's Letters and Speeches*, III, p. 47.   [61] Harrington, *Oceana* (1656), p. 1.
[62] Harrington, *Oceana* (1656), printed for D. Pakeman, *Epistle*.

thirty-eight.[63] 'Shew me another intire Government consisting but of thirty orders . . . If you stir your hand, there go more nerves and bones into the motion; If you play, you have more Cards in the pack . . . [whereas] in a Commonwealth . . . where she is not perfect . . . every houre will produce a new Order.'[64] Yet such formal properties of the text, emphasized in the 1656 editions (of which there were two) by a Table of Contents in bold, disappear in the modern *Political Works*. The contents pages of this, while listing the seven chapter titles of the editor's 'Historical Introduction', do not list the chapter or section titles of Harrington's works. Within *Oceana*, Harrington's wide-spaced, large-font table of contents is rendered simply as a continuation of the small-font, single-spaced text of his 'Introduction'.[65] Similarly one would have no inkling from the modern edition that Harrington's orders were themselves distinguished from the surrounding text by black letter rather than roman type. As with the table of contents, type which was not roman becomes so. This editorial decision is defended as follows: 'The laws or "orders" of Oceana, both in the work of that name and as they reappear in *The Art of Lawgiving*, are printed in black-letter for pages at a time, and there seems no reason to inflict this on the modern reader.'[66]

In the seventeenth century black letter was the easiest type to read, and so the medium for public proclamations (such as the *Instrument*) and acts of parliament.[67] Deprived of the knowledge that Harrington presented these two works as dramatically contextualized sequences of promulgated law, how is a modern reader to understand their purpose? In addition to erasing what Harrington himself considered to be crucial features of *Oceana*'s structure, these changes have the effect of making it look much more like standard republican prose polemic than it was. Yet the formal features of Harrington's work, in addition to being unique, are inseparable from its claim to be not polemic but philosophy, and from that of 'The Modell' to offer not simply settlement, but one the 'perfection' of which may render it 'immortal'.

This is certainly the political context into which Harrington himself later placed his intervention.

Oliver . . . having started up into the throne, his officers (as pretending to be for a commonwealth) kept a murmuring, at which he told them that he knew not what

[63] J. P. Kenyon, ed., *The Stuart Constitution 1603–1688*, 2nd edn (Cambridge, 1986), pp. 308–13.
[64] Harrington, *Oceana* (1656), pp. 180–1.   [65] Pocock, *Political Works*, pp. vii–viii, 160.
[66] Ibid., p. xv.
[67] Keith Thomas, 'The meaning of literacy in early modern England', in G. Baumann, ed., *The Written Word: Literacy in Transition* (Oxford, 1986), pp. 97–131, at p. 99.

they meant, nor themselves; but let any of them show him what they meant by a commonwealth (or that there was any such thing) they should see that he sought not himself; the Lord knew that he sought not himself, but to make good the cause. Upon this some sober men came to me and told me: if any man in England could show what a commonwealth was, it was myself. Upon this persuasion, I wrote.[68]

Thus Harrington wrote not, like Streater or Henry Vane, to claim that Cromwell sought himself, but rather to show him what a commonwealth was, and that there *was any such thing*. In that 'art whereby my Lord Archon' subsequently 'framed the model of the commonwealth of Oceana' he was assisted by a Council of Legislators, who, in addition to ransacking 'the mines of ancient prudence', engaged in what falsely appeared to be a process of public consultation. This persuaded 'the people, who were neither safely to be admitted unto, nor conveniently to be excluded from' such a process, to believe that the Model was 'no other than that whereof they themselves had been the makers'.[69] Because for Harrington English parliaments had been part of the problem, rather than the solution, *Oceana* was not addressed, like the works of Streater, Nedham and Vane, to the people or to Parliamentarians. What was addressed to Cromwell was the formula for a 'perfectly equal commonwealth' to be enacted by a single lawgiver ('[W]heras a book or a building hath not been known to attain perfection, if it had not had a sole author . . . a commonwealth . . . is of the like nature') but in a way capable of conferring on it popular legitimacy.

As a 'model' *Oceana* continued a recent history of constitution-making associated with the army. Before the *Instrument* had been the Heads of Proposals (1647). This was an alternative to Parliament's Newcastle Propositions (1646), and it was responded to by three Leveller *Agreements of the People*. While railing against those 'of Levelling principles' the Lord Protector had asserted, 'As to the Authority of the Nation; to the Magistracy; to the Ranks and Orders of men . . . A nobleman, a gentleman, a yeoman; "the distinction of these:" that is a good interest of the Nation, and a great one!'[70] In *The Art of Lawgiving* Harrington derided the Levellers' *Second Agreement* as a recipe for 'downright anarchy'.[71] When *Oceana* described the 'mixture of . . . monarchy, aristocracy, and democracy' as 'the doctrine of the ancients', insisting that that 'only is good', this was juxtaposed to the doctrine of Hobbes, who 'is positive that they all are deceived, and that there is no other government in nature

---

[68] *The Examination*, in Harrington, *Works*, p. 859.
[69] *Oceana*, in Harrington, *Works*, pp. 208–9.
[70] *Cromwell's Letters and Speeches*, III, p. 21.   [71] Harrington, *Works*, p. 657.

than one of the three'.[72] Whereas Nedham and Streater had accentuated the anti-aristocratic bias already to be found in Machiavelli, in elucidating his own 'principles of authority' Harrington agreed with the Lord Protector, insisting, 'There is something first in the making of a *Commonwealth*, then in the governing of her, and last of all in the leading of her Armies . . . peculiar unto the Genius of a Gentleman.'[73]

In addition to its constitutional formula, *Oceana* spoke to most of the government's other concerns. Oceana was not simply a militarized polity, but society. For its citizen soldiers, divided into 'horse' and 'foot', military and political participation were intertwined. Creation of a citizen militia addressed an issue underpinning security and stability in terms recently identified by Parliament (a bill establishing a 'Select Militia' having passed in October 1656).[74] This was celebrated in the scriptural language characteristic of the Lord Protector's own army (and speeches). In the words of the Lord Archon,

My dear lords, Oceana *is as the rose of Sharon, and the lily of the valley . . . She is comely as the tents of Kedar, and terrible as an army with banners. Her neck is as the tower of David, builded for an armoury, whereon there hang a thousand bucklers and shields of mighty men.*[75]

Astonishingly, despite the book's title, Oceana's navy was not discussed. This contrasted strikingly with other celebrations of the republic's 'Arks of War . . . An hideous shole of wood-Leviathans' which had defeated the Dutch.[76] No feature of Harrington's text could have been more acceptable to the Lord Protector. There is abundant evidence to suggest that Cromwell's dissolution of the Rump had been particularly directed against members of the government whose management of a naval conflict had become increasingly successful, and expensive ('Oh Henry Vane!').[77] Writing later in exile one of those MPs, Algernon Sidney, said of the war 'they [the Dutch] were endangered and we destroyed by it'.[78] One possible explanation for Harrington's title relates to his later claim that the commonwealth was a ship. Another underlined

---

[72] *Oceana*, in Harrington, *Works*, p. 162.   [73] Machiavelli, *Discourses*, pp. 245–7.

[74] T. R. W. Kubik, 'How far the sword? Militia tactics and politics in the *Commonwealth of Oceana*', *History of Political Thought*, 19 (1998), 197–9.

[75] *Oceana*, in Harrington, *Works*, p. 333.

[76] Andrew Marvell, *The First Anniversary Of the Government under O.C.* in *The Poems and Letters of Andrew Marvell*, ed. H. M. Margoliouth, 2 vols. (Oxford, 1927), I, pp. 111–12.

[77] For the suggestion that Cromwell's jealousy of the navy was a factor informing the dissolution, see Scott, *Commonwealth Principles*, pp. 105, 260, 267–72.

[78] Sidney, *Court Maxims*, p. 171. Sidney's account of the dissolution quotes Cromwell as specifically blaming Vane. See Scott, *English Republic*, p. 102.

his claim to have identified the medium (a popular balance of dominion) in which Hobbes's *Leviathan* must swim.

In response to the recent military setback at Hispaniola, Oceana was a commonwealth for expansion. This mission was described, not in Machiavellian, but in godly and apocalyptic language:

A Commonwealth ... of this make is a minister of God upon earth, to the end that the world may be governed with righteousness. For which cause ... the orders last rehearsed are buds of empire, such as, with the blessing of God, may spread the arms of your commonwealth like an holy asylum unto the distressed world, and give the earth her sabbath of years or rest from her labours, under the shadow of your wings.[79]

Among the ancients it was neither Athens nor Rome which was Harrington's constitutional exemplar (as Venice was among moderns) but the Commonwealth of Israel (and secondly Sparta).[80] Concerning religious worship, again breaking with the commonwealthsmen, Harrington opposed the attempt to separate civil and spiritual government. Rather, he combined a national church, presided over by a state Council of Religion, with liberty for local 'gathered congregations' to meet separately. As Mark Goldie has noticed, 'Cromwell's church was a judicious marriage of congregationalist Independency and Erastian centralism. So was Harrington's.'[81] *Oceana*'s agrarian law was Harrington's principal contribution toward Interregnum (Christian humanist) social reform, whereby 'in giving encouragement unto industry, we [must] also remember that covetousness is the root of all evil'. Accordingly,

your commonwealth is founded upon an equal agrarian ... and if the earth be given unto the sons of men, this balance is the balance of justice, such an one as, in having due regard unto the different industry of different men, yet *faithfully judgeth the poor. And the king that faithfully judgeth the poor, his throne shall be established forever* [Proverbs 29:14]. Much more the commonwealth; seeing that equality, which is the necessary dissolution of monarchy, is the generation, the very life and soul of a commonwealth.[82]

Harrington's 'Model' applied itself to the reshaping not only of central but of local government. In his speech of 12 September 1654, Cromwell had claimed that his 'commission' came not only from 'Providence, in the sight of God', but from 'many Cities and Boroughs and Counties ... from the County General-Assizes ... all Justices of the Peace ... All the Sheriffs in England are my witnesses'. In pursuit of its 'ministry from

---

[79] *Oceana*, in Harrington, *Works*, p. 323.
[80] Harrington, 'The Preliminaries', in *Works*, pp. 174–86.
[81] Mark Goldie, 'The civil religion of James Harrington', p. 207.
[82] *Oceana*, in Harrington, *Works*, p. 322.

God' it was from the units of local government ('orbs', 'galaxies', 'tribes', 'tropics', 'hundreds' and 'shires') and their officers (justices of the peace, jurymen, coroners, high constables, lords high sheriff, lieutenants, custos rotulorum, phylarchs, conductors) that Oceana's power was conveyed as 'sap from the root . . . unto [all] the branches of magistracy or sovereign power'.[83]

Finally, Harrington's formula for healing and settling spoke directly to the government's security agenda, being proof against the sedition being fed by Royalists and Levellers/commonwealthsmen. This had resulted most recently in imposition of the major generals.[84] Alone among republicans Harrington denied a right to rebel. Much more effectively than Hobbes's *Leviathan*, an equal commonwealth deprived sedition of its interest and its power.

[A] government . . . attaining to perfect equality, has such a libration in the frame of it, that no man living can show which way any man or men, in or under it, can contract any such interest or power as should be able to disturb the commonwealth with sedition, wherefore an equal commonwealth is that only which is without flaw, and contains in it the full perfection of government.

Indeed,

Where the sovereign power is not as entire and absolute as in monarchy itself, there can be no government at all. It is not the limitation of sovereign power that is the cause of a commonwealth, but such a *libration or poise of orders, that there can be in the same no number of men, having the interest, that can have the power, nor any number of men, having the power, that can have the interest, to invade or disturb the government.*[85]

It was on this basis that *Oceana* proposed to admit Royalists to full citizenship. Among those to protest was Vane, for whom it was vital

in a Nation much divided in affection and interest about their own Government, none be admitted to the exercise of the right and priviledge of a free Citizen, for a season, but either such as are free born, in respect of their righteous principles, flowing from the birth of the Spirit of God in them . . . or else who, by their tried good affection . . . to . . . publick freedome, have deserved to be trusted with the . . . bearing their own Armes in the publicke defence.[86]

Yet Harrington's approach to the nation's 'divisions in affection and interest' was different. His target was all those 'parties into which this

---

[83] *Cromwell's Letters and Speeches*, III, pp. 50–1; *Oceana*, in Harrington, *Works*, p. 334; J. C. Davis, 'Political thought during the English Revolution', in Barry Coward, ed., *A Companion to Stuart Britain* (Oxford, 2003), p. 391.

[84] Davis, 'Equality in an unequal commonwealth', pp. 238–9.

[85] *The Art of Lawgiving*, in Harrington, *Works*, pp. 657–8.

[86] Vane, *Needful Corrective*, pp. 7–8.

nation was divided . . . temporal or spiritual'. 'To the *Common-wealths-man* I have no more to say, but that if he exclude any party, he is not truly such; nor shall ever found a *Common-wealth* upon the natural principle of the same, which is *Justice*.'[87] Thus

[T]he *Royalist* for having opposed a *Common-wealth* in *Oceana* . . . can neither be *justly*, for that cause, excluded from his full and equall share in the *Government;* nor prudently, for this, that a *Common-wealth* consisting of a party will be in perpetuall labour of her own destruction . . . [whereas] Men that have equall possessions, and the same security for their estates and of their liberties that you have, have the same cause with you to defend.[88]

In short, for Harrington the basis of political interest was material. 'Corruption . . . in manners' was 'from the *Balance* [of dominion]'. Whereas for other republicans success or failure depended on the moral qualities of citizens, for Harrington these were irrelevant. 'Give us good men, and they will make us good laws, is the maxim of a demagog . . . But give us good orders, and they will make us good men, is the maxim of a legislator.'[89] This must be understood in the light of Harrington's praise of '[Mr Hobbs'] treatises of liberty and necessity' as 'the greatest of new lights, and those which I have follow'd, and shall follow . . . as is admirably observed by Mr Hobbs . . . [the] will is *caus'd*, and being caused is *necessitated*'. It was on the grounds of a material natural philosophy derived from *Leviathan* itself that Harrington took exception to Hobbes's ridicule of the pretensions of Lucca to that 'LIBERTAS . . . written on the turrets of the city'. According to Hobbes, 'Whether a commonwealth be monarchical or popular, the freedom is the same.' Harrington responded that whereas in Turkey

the greatest bashaw is a tenant, as well of his head as his estate, at the will of his lord, the meanest Lucchese that hath land is a freeholder of both, and not to be controlled but by the law; and that framed by every private man . . . to protect the liberty of every private man, which by that means comes to be the liberty of the commonwealth.[90]

Quentin Skinner has drawn attention to this image as illustrating the emphasis placed by the neo-Roman understanding of liberty on independence from government by a will other than one's own.[91] Yet here Harrington spoke of the ownership, rather than tenancy, not only of one's head, but of one's 'estate'. As empire derived from the goods of fortune,

---

[87] Harrington, *Oceana* (1656), p. 46.   [88] Ibid.
[89] Quoted in Davis, *Utopia and the Ideal Society*, p. 123.
[90] *Oceana*, in Harrington, *Works*, pp. 170–1.
[91] Skinner, *Liberty before Liberalism*, pp. 85–6.

it was the purpose of an empire of laws 'to protect the liberty of every private man . . . of [even] the meanest Lucchese *that hath land*'. It was the sum of these 'private' liberties which 'comes to be the liberty of the commonwealth'.

Thus for Harrington the foundation for liberty lay not in the soul but in 'riches', on which men 'are hung, as by the teeth'; in an ownership of property widely enjoyed in Lucca, but not by the greatest bashaw in Turkey. *Oceana* dated 'The generation of the Common-wealth' to the early sixteenth century because not since then had the material basis for English monarchy existed ('wherefore the dissolution of the government caused the war'). Accordingly, *Leviathan*'s monarchical politics, far from offering a prescription for settlement, were a backward-looking recipe for future strife. It had been Hobbes's serious error to fail to pursue his natural philosophy to its political conclusion by identifying the material 'foundation' of government in England. Instead, *Leviathan*'s politics of the sword hung in the air 'as if by geometry', forgetting that 'this sword . . . without an hand . . . is but cold iron . . . The hand which holdeth this sword is the militia of a nation . . . an army is a beast that hath a great belly and must be fed; wherefore . . . without . . . the balance of property . . . the public sword is but a name or mere spitfrog.'[92]

Thus *Oceana* identified the underlying causes of England's political instability and fixed them. It secured the foundation by preventing any further change in the balance of dominion with an agrarian law. It secured the superstructure by separating debate from voting, so ending that destructive culture of democratic oratory which had been on show in English parliaments, as well as in ancient Athens.[93] The first of these was something the Protectorate had never even considered. The second involved a Venetian makeover of the Protectoral principle of separation of powers. Thus *Oceana*'s republican constitution was proffered, on the basis not of moral argument but of material necessity, determined by the balance of dominion. Amid the rip tide dragging the Protectorate back towards monarchy, *Oceana* sought to be the one republican alternative standing between the failing *Instrument*, and the looming *Humble Petition and Advice*.[94]

As the title of Vane's *A Healing Question* reminds us, *Oceana* was not the only republican act of Protectoral counsel. Yet it was the only one to make a systematic attempt to transcend party. Thus, like *A Healing Question*, *Oceana* spoke to the grievances of those alienated by the dissolution

---

[92] *Oceana* in Harrington, *Works*, p. 165.   [93] Scott, 'The peace of silence'.
[94] For a contrasting monarchical formula, see *A Copy of a Letter Written to an Officer of the Army by A true Commonwealths-man, and no COURTIER* (19 March 1656/7?).

of the Rump, providing for an end to Protectoral government and the re-institution of a republic. Unlike Vane, however, Harrington also spoke to the concerns animating the dissolution itself, subjecting the political process to constitutional controls, at once ferocious and irrevocable, making a restoration of monarchy, or any other self-destructive popular folly, impossible. In *A Discourse upon this saying* (1659), he elaborated:

Detest the base itch of a narrow oligarchy. If your commonwealth be rightly instituted, seven years will not pass ere your clusters of parties, civil and religious, vanish... The mariner trusteth not unto the sea, but to his ship. The spirit of the people is no wise to be trusted with their liberty, but by stated laws and orders; so the trust is not in the spirit of the people, but in the frame of those orders, which, as they are tight or leaky, are the ship out of which the people, being once embarked, cannot stir, and without which they can have no motion.[95]

With only thirty ingredients, and a twist, the most elaborate constitutional cocktail in English history was ready. Could the Lord Protector be persuaded to knock it back? Toland recorded:

[H]e did accordingly inscribe it to OLIVER CROMWEL, who, after the perusal of it, said... that what he got by the Sword he would not quit for a little paper Shot: adding... that he approv'd the Government of a single Person as little as any of 'em, but that he was forc'd to take upon him the Office of a High Constable, to preserve the Peace among the several Partys in the Nation, since he saw that being left to themselves, they would never agree to any certain form of Government, and would only spend their whole Power in defeating the Designs, or destroying the Persons of one another.[96]

Needless to say, it had not been *Oceana*'s intention to leave these parties to themselves. It would dissolve party into nation; and align private interest with the 'interest of mankind'. But if either the Lord Protector had not read the book, or having read it had failed to understand it, no modern scholar can be surprised. By the time Harrington began the process of issuing translations, explanations and simplifications, there being 'nothing in this world, next the favour of God, I so much desire as to be familiarly understood',[97] Cromwell was dead and the project of healing and settling was about to fall into other, post-republican hands.

---

[95] Ibid., pp. 737–8.   [96] Toland, *Life of Harrington*, p. xx.
[97] Harrington, *Valerius and Publicola*, 'To The Reader', in Harrington, *Political Works*, p. 782.

11 'The Great Trappaner of England': Thomas Violet, Jews and crypto-Jews during the English Revolution and at the Restoration

Ariel Hessayon

> *trepanner* (archaic): one who ensnares; an entrapper, decoy, swindler
> *Oxford English Dictionary*

I

On 24 February 1660 one Tobias Knowles – most likely Tobias Knowles (d.1669), pewterer of St Peter Cornhill, London, and afterwards a common councilman – gave evidence at the London sessions of the peace held in the Old Bailey. Knowles was charged with forging foreign coinage, a less serious offence than counterfeiting coin of the realm, which was a treasonous capital crime. He was to be declared innocent by a jury, but what is interesting for our purposes is that his testimony reveals details of a plot. Although Knowles's evidence cannot be regarded as entirely trustworthy because he sought to avoid implicating himself, a narrative can still be pieced together. In early spring 1659, accompanied by Thomas Violet (1609?–1662), a scheming goldsmith and possibly also his neighbour, Knowles claimed to have gone to '*Dukes-Place*' in London's East End. There the pair apparently entered the 'Synagogue of the *Jewes*' where they spoke with 'Mr. *Moses* their High-Priest' and some other unidentified Jews with whom Violet was apparently 'very conversant'.[1] These details can be substantiated. On 19 December 1656 a hitherto secret Jew of foreign origin called Antonio Carvajal (*c.*1596–d. 1659) had, following his endenization, signed a 21-year lease for a brick

It is with immense gratitude and deep respect that I offer this essay to my fellow Manchester United supporter, friend and mentor John Morrill. Earlier versions were read at a conference held at Birkbeck, University of London, at the School of Advanced Study and at seminars at the Institute of Historical Research and Trinity College Dublin. I would like to thank the participants for their helpful comments and suggestions. In addition, I have profited from the advice of Mike Braddick, Mario Caricchio, David Finnegan, Lorenza Gianfrancesco, Tom Leng, Michael Questier, David Smith and Brett Usher, but remain entirely responsible for any mistakes or shortcomings.
[1] Anon., *The Great Trappaner of England* (1660), pp. 1–3.

tenement on Creechurch Lane in the parish of St Katherine Creechurch. By March 1657 this structure was being converted into a synagogue.[2] Five years later another curious Christian visitor eager to learn Hebrew was granted admission on the sabbath after presenting a ticket to a porter. He compared the synagogue to a 'high built' chapel large enough to accommodate more than a hundred worshippers. Services were conducted upstairs away from prying eyes at street level, and to gain entry he had to pass through three doors, 'one beyond another'.[3] Moreover, Mr Moses can be identified as Rabbi Moses Athias (d.1666), Carvajal's cousin, who had arrived from Hamburg to lead the congregation.[4] Violet had previously discussed undisclosed business with these Jews, doubtless connected with choosing the designs of foreign coins. These seem to have been medals to commemorate the accession of Leopold I as Holy Roman Emperor in July 1658. According to Knowles, Violet intended to 'trappan' these Jews, claiming that the Council of State would reward him with half the Jews' assets if he caught them red-handed receiving 'a great quantity' of these unauthorized foreign coins. In other words, Violet – 'a Name too sweet for so foul a Carkass' – had set a trap for the Jews; one which pandered to prejudiced beliefs about Jewish criminality, particularly that Jews were guilty of counterfeiting and clipping coins.[5]

To ensure secrecy Violet allegedly threatened Knowles, saying that he would stab him the next time they met if he disclosed details of the deception. Evidently this did not deter Knowles from giving testimony at the Old Bailey which describes how Violet had instructed him to go to an unnamed tavern. There he would summon the Jews who would receive the newly minted foreign coins, at which point Violet intended to appear on the scene. Before Violet could spring his trap, however, Knowles claimed to have melted down the pieces. Even so, Knowles was still impeached by Richard Pight (c.1608–fl.1673), who, Knowles maintained, had given him permission to cast the coins.[6] An officer of the Mint (clerk of the irons and surveyor of the melting houses) in the Tower of London since July 1649 when Parliament granted him a patent, Pight reckoned he had been instrumental in discovering, apprehending and prosecuting eighty-six false coiners active across the country between 1650 and 1659.[7] Moreover, he had filed two indictments against Violet

---

[2] L. Wolf, 'Crypto-Jews under the Commonwealth', *Transactions of the Jewish Historical Society of England* (hereafter *TJHSE*), 1 (1895), 55–88, at 57, 59–60; W. Samuel, 'The first London synagogue of the Resettlement', *TJHSE*, 10 (1921–23), 1–147, at 20–1.

[3] Samuel, 'First London synagogue', 50–7.

[4] L. Wolf, 'The Jewry of the Restoration, 1660–1664', *TJHSE*, 5 (1908), 5–33, at 10–11.

[5] Anon., *Trappaner*, pp. 1, 3. [6] Ibid., pp. 3–5.

[7] *CJ*, VI, p. 252; *CSPD 1660–61*, p. 10; TNA, Mint 1/4, p. 2; E 178/6313; E 178/6589; HLRO, HL/PO/JO/10/1/284–5; *LJ*, XI, pp. 33, 53; William Henfrey, *Numismata Cromwelliana* (1877), pp. 34, 38–45.

for assault and battery at the London sessions of the peace and was in turn charged by Violet in January 1660 with abetting and assisting the counterfeiting of Dutch, Spanish and other foreign currency. Viewed in this light Violet's stratagem to ensnare the Jews thus appears as a minor aspect of a greater design: namely his attempt to supplant Pight and install himself, with the apparent backing of several members of the Council of State, as the Commonwealth's unofficial searcher and discoverer of false coiners. Exercising this authority would have enabled Violet, notorious for entangling his prey in a web of lies ratified by false testimony, to reap riches.[8]

As we follow Violet, an immigrant's son, from his alleged birth aboard ship – possibly crossing the English Channel – to his painful death, we shall see how his experiences of the Civil Wars, the Revolution and the Restoration enrich our understanding of these momentous events. At the same time the conjunction of shared mercantile interests, social networks and circumstances that partly entwine Violet's story with Carvajal's produces some unexpected parallels; both for different reasons were dissimulators, London inhabitants yet of foreign parentage and with extensive international contacts, on the margins or beyond the pale of 'Englishness'. Here, too, Violet's snares and plots enhance our knowledge of how London's visible Jewish community was perceived, as well as highlighting their undetermined legal status which made them collectively susceptible to extortion.

II

According to the anonymous author of *The Great Trappaner of England* (1660), a vitriolic pamphlet almost certainly issued in co-operation with London's Jewish community and attributable to Pight or one of his supporters, Violet was an unrepentant wicked dissembler:

a Common and most Horrid Swearer, a debauch'd Drunkard, especially upon Sabbath days, an Epicure and an abominable Lyer, and guilty of many other ennormous and Inhumane Crimes to the great Scandal of our Christian Religion especially amongst the *Jews*.[9]

This 'depraved and degenerating' man was born at sea – 'as though nature had ordained no Country should be burthen'd to own his Nativity, being Ingendred between a poor Dutch Fidler, and a Moorish Woman'.[10] He was the grandson of Rafell Vyolet of Antwerp and the son of Peter

---

[8] Thomas Violet, *To Supream Authority* (1660), pp. 2–8.
[9] Anon., *Trappaner*, p. 2. For Thomas Violet see Anita McConnell's entry in the *ODNB*, although this contains inaccuracies.
[10] Anon., *Trappaner*, p. 1.

Vyolett, an Antwerp-born musician who became a London citizen. His maternal grandfather William Dyamont was from Lucca in Tuscany. Thomas Violet was baptized on 5 December 1609 in the parish of St Mary, Whitechapel.[11] He was bound apprentice on 18 January 1622 to Timothy Eman (d.1638), goldsmith, for the term of ten years and made free of the Goldsmiths' Company on 25 February 1631. He bound his first and only apprentice in July 1631 and was described that year as a goldsmith living in Lombard Street.[12] On 18 May 1632 Violet was summoned before the wardens of the Company and, in an early indication of his vile temperament, charged with calling those who sat in Goldsmiths' Hall 'fooles & knaves'. His relations with the wardens deteriorated further when he was fined for refusing to attend their dinner the following year.[13]

Thereafter Violet was charged in the courts of Star Chamber and Exchequer with a number of offences, including the unauthorized export of gold and silver from the realm. He was imprisoned for several weeks in the Fleet, suffering, by his own account, domestic and foreign business losses before being pardoned in April 1634. In exchange, Violet initiated proceedings in Star Chamber against seventeen other individuals allegedly engaged in the unlicensed transportation of gold and silver. Among them were his former master and Sir John Wollaston, a common councilman who became Prime Warden of the Goldsmiths' Company and lord mayor of London; Wollaston was pardoned by the king on payment of a considerable sum, and would eventually take his revenge against Violet. Producing witnesses from abroad, paying their expenses as well as legal fees, and providing information – sometimes proven false – that led to convictions, Violet hoped to be rewarded with a share of the substantial fines initially totalling £24,100 imposed on his unfortunate victims.[14] Although he claimed to have spent £1,968 prosecuting these cases, Violet was not reimbursed by the crown. Instead, he was given the office for surveying, sealing, assaying and regulating gold and silver wire thread in September 1638.[15] Thereafter, allegedly worshipping

---

[11] Joseph Howard and Joseph Chester, eds., *Visitation of London*, Harleian Society, 15, 17 (1880–83), II, p. 314; LMA, P 93/MRY 1/1.

[12] Gs. Co., Apprenticeship Book, I, pp. 252, 305; Court Minute Book 'P' part 2, p. 538.

[13] Walter Prideaux, *Memorials of Goldsmiths' Company*, 2 vols. (1896), I, pp. 155, 161; Gs. Co., Court Minute Book 'R' part 2, fos. 104r–v, 164v, 205.

[14] *CSPD 1633–34*, p. 576; *CSPD 1636–37*, pp. 267, 402; Prideaux, *Memorials*, I, pp. 174–5; *CSPD 1637–38*, p. 153; *CSPD 1638–39*, pp. 132, 171–2; *CJ*, I, p. 107; HMC, *Fourth Report*, Appendix, p. 58; Thomas Violet, *Humble Declaration* (1643), pp. 6–16; Violet, *True Narrative* (1653), pp. 63–64; Violet, *True Narrative of Proceedings in Admiraltie* (1659), pp. 146–7; Violet, *Appeal to Cæsar* (1662), pp. 46, 49–50.

[15] *CSPD 1635–36*, p. 169; *CSPD 1637*, p. 312; *CSPD 1639*, pp. 419–20; Violet, *To the Kings Most Excellent Majesty* (1662), p. 8; Violet, *Two Petitions* (1661), pp. 1–3, 21.

Mammon rather than God, he was said to have enriched himself by impoverishing hundreds of artificers' families.[16]

All the same, the guilt of betraying his master (with whom he had lived nine years as an apprentice), fellow merchants and the Goldsmiths' Company weighed dreadfully on Violet. In the last week of his life he recalled that this was the 'first Great Cros' he had endured, and to dispel 'some great lies' determined to provide 'the truth' of this business. Claiming that the earl of Dorset had pressurized him into giving evidence at Star Chamber, Violet resolved 'to die' rather than become an informer. So he swallowed about a dram of mercury mixed in broth. His mother Sarah, however, found the porringer and discoloured silver spoon. Suspecting attempted suicide, she immediately sent for a neighbour, a doctor and an apothecary. With their care Violet recovered after about twenty weeks, attributing his survival to some strange extraordinary providential design.[17]

During the Civil War Violet was imprisoned first in Aldersgate Street and then the Marshalsea for refusing to aid the Parliamentarians financially, defaulting on his £70 assessment.[18] Following an exchange of prisoners on 25 December 1643 or thereabouts he became involved with Theophilus Riley, scout-master of the City of London, Colonel Reade, a '*Jesuiticall Papist*' and fomenter of the Irish Rebellion, and Sir Basil Brooke, a 'notorious *Papist*', in a '*seditious and Iesuiticall Practice and Designe*'. This plot was intended to divide the king's enemies by opening up a channel to negotiate a separate peace between Charles I at Oxford and the City, thereby setting members of London's governing elite eager for settlement against the more bellicose factions within Parliament, as well as alienating Parliament's Scottish allies.[19] On the discovery of the plot in early January 1644 Violet – disparaged as a 'most malignant . . . *Projector*', a 'broken Goldsmith, and a Protestant in shew' – was tried by a Council of War as a spy and committed to the Tower. His estate, consisting of the Essex manors of Battles Hall in Stapleford Abbots and Peyton Hall in Manuden, was seized and sequestered, while a debt due to him was assigned to someone else. Violet later maintained that £8,400 of his assets (subsequently revised to £11,000) were plundered. Despite petitioning, he remained imprisoned in the Tower for nearly four years – including 928 days spent in 'a dismal place, little better than a

[16] Anon., *Trappaner*, p. 1.   [17] TNA, Prob 20/2650.

[18] TNA, SP 19/37, fo. 91v; *CJ*, III, pp. 136, 353.

[19] *CJ*, III, p. 358; *LJ*, VI, pp. 369–70; VII, pp. 58, 60; *Kingdomes Weekly Intelligencer*, no. 38 (2–9 January 1644), 289–93; Anon., *A Cvnning Plot* (1644), pp. 3–4, 26–32; John Vicars, *Gods arke* (1645), pp. 118–21.

Dungeon'.[20] Once he was able Violet duly memorialized this fact, having it painted over the chimney to his room. Although mocked in a playful verse by fellow Royalist captive Sir Francis Wortley for setting down 'all the dayes' and swearing his 'injuries' were 'scarcely to be numbred', Violet's sense of misery had been so pronounced that 'being somewhat sicke in bodye' he drew up his will on Christmas Eve 1646. This included two bequests – one of £1,000 due upon several bonds, another of a £2,000 debt supposedly owed by the king – to the masters and governors of Christ's Hospital to be distributed as charitable loans to poor scholars.[21]

Following his release, probably during summer 1649, Violet begged Parliament for a pardon and the restoration of his sequestered estate. Lacking a conventional path of advancement through the Goldsmiths' Company's ranks, having supported the losing side in the Civil Wars, conspired with Catholics and with perhaps no other option for preferment, he became a turncoat. Pragmatically presenting himself as '*A true lover of his Countrey*', Violet set about publicizing both his expertise in catching unlicensed exporters of gold and silver ('*An old Deer-stealer is the best keeper of a Park*'), and his solution for reviving trade – which proposed imitating the United Provinces' mercantile practice.[22] Through this strategy he succeeded in obtaining the patronage of John Bradshaw, regicide and first president of the Council of State. Accordingly, Violet was instructed to present his papers to the recently established Council of Trade for their consideration. Published in a book entitled *The Advancement of Merchandize* (February 1651), printed by William Dugard with the Council of State's approval, these included several reasons for setting up free ports in the manner of Amsterdam, Livorno and Genoa, at which foreign merchants would have equal privileges with English natives. Some of Violet's arguments may have influenced Benjamin Worsley, secretary of the Council of Trade, as a few passages – particularly those concerning the decline of shipping passing through Dover and the arrival of immigrant merchant strangers – appear to have been incorporated in abbreviated form in Worsley's pamphlet *Free Ports, the Nature and Necessitie of them Stated* (1652), which was likewise printed by Dugard.[23] Violet's

---

[20] *CJ*, III, pp. 686, 692; *CJ*, VI, p. 550; Thomas Violet, *To the Right Honourable* (1647), brs.; *CJ*, V, p. 322; Violet, *True Discovery* (1650), pp. 14–15; Violet, *Two Petitions*, pp. 4, 16, 24.

[21] Francis Wortley, *A Loyall Song* ([1647]), brs.; Thomas Violet, *Petition Against the Jewes* (1661), p. 31; TNA, Prob 20/2650.

[22] Violet, *True Discovery*, title page, pp. 18, 62–3, 90; *CSPD 1650*, pp. 178–82, 292, 431, 454, 455, 473, 480; *CSPD 1651–52*, pp. 24–5.

[23] Thomas Violet, *Advancement of Merchandize* (1651), pp. 1–24; B[enjamin] W[orsley], *Free Ports* (1652), pp. 4, 8; Thomas Leng, *Benjamin Worsley (1618–1677): trade, interest and the spirit in revolutionary England* (Woodbridge, 2008), pp. 64, 68, 73–9.

further proposals concerning the East India Company and regulating gold and silver wire thread were also taken into account by Worsley.[24] In addition, Violet became associated with the corporation of moneyers in the Mint, who requested his help in rebutting a Frenchman's libels that the gold and silver coins they minted for the Commonwealth were of irregular size, badly designed and easily clipped.[25]

In December 1652 during the height of the first Anglo-Dutch war three ships, the *Samson*, the *Salvador* and the *St George*, were taken as prize goods near Ostend and brought up the river Thames. Laden with tobacco, wool and silver ultimately valued at £278,250, these vessels, together with several other ships, had seemingly embarked from the free port of Cadiz on 19 October bound for Amsterdam. As exporting plate from Spain without a licence was illegal, it was common practice for factors handling its transportation to protect the freighters' and owners' identities by using fictitious names or not revealing them in documents. Given this ambiguity the Spanish ambassador, Don Alonso de Cárdenas, pressed the Council of State on behalf of Philip IV for the return of what he insisted was rightfully his master's treasure. They in turn referred the matter to the High Court of Admiralty. At this point Violet intervened. Claiming to act on intelligence received from spies at Dover, he persuaded Bradshaw to grant him a warrant with the intention of gathering evidence proving that the *Samson*, the *Salvador* and the *George* sailed under a false flag; that although they professed to be from Hamburg they were actually freighting West Indian silver to enemy territory: the United Provinces.[26] Seizure of Dutch vessels or those carrying Dutch goods had been rising steadily for five years, with a corresponding increase in cases brought before Admiralty. Warning that this court, which had recently delivered 'quick judgments in such weightie businesses', was a 'dangerous Back-door' to the Commonwealth if the government did not remain vigilant, Violet urged several leading councillors – one of whom clamoured for continuing hostilities against the Dutch – not to let these prizes slip through the state's fingers.[27]

Repeating an earlier pattern of behaviour Violet delivered eighty-five witnesses for examination, most of them substantial merchants and their factors, hoping to recoup sizeable legal fees and assorted expenses (he

---

[24] Violet, *Advancement*, pp. 93–7; *CSPD 1651–52*, p. 441.

[25] *CSPD 1651*, pp. 231–4, 313–15, 460–1; *CSPD 1651–52*, pp. 23, 156–7; Violet, *Mysteries and Secrets* (1653); Anon., *Answer of Corporation of Moniers* (1653).

[26] *CSPD 1652–53*, pp. 15, 23, 47, 75, 233, 241, 398; Violet, *True Narrative*; Violet, *Proposals humbly presented* (1656), pp. 8–59, 70; Violet, *True Narrative of Proceedings in Admiraltie*; BL, Harleian MS 6034, fos. 1v–25v.

[27] Violet, *True Narrative*, sigs. a^{r-2}, b^r, pp. 38–40.

borrowed over £500 at interest, eventually inflating the figure to £1,500 costs) by being rewarded with either the restoration of his sequestered estate or £11,000 in compensation (the revised price he put on his plundered assets). In so doing Violet aroused the enmity of powerful forces: a pro-Dutch faction within the Council, their merchant allies, and agents of Archduke Leopold, governor of the Spanish Netherlands. After the Restoration he even attempted to turn this opposition to his advantage, shamelessly insisting that sowing divisions within Parliament and the Council of State, which supposedly culminated in Cromwell's dissolution of the Rump and Bradshaw's fall from favour, rather than naked self-interest had been his guiding principle all along. Whatever his real motives, the immediate outcome of the prosecution Violet initiated in the High Court of Admiralty was clear: the silver aboard the *Samson*, the *Salvador* and the *George* was unloaded and, according to his later accounts, taken on 29 April 1653 under armed guard to the Tower. There, over the course of almost a year, it was melted, minted and then distributed as coin to the army and navy, pumping huge amounts of money into circulation.[28]

Another intriguing aspect of this affair was the involvement of Jews and crypto-Jews. Hence, on the instruction of a Portuguese factor at Sanlúcar, the *Samson* was loaded at Cadiz with forty bars of silver that were to be consigned to his brother, 'a Jew dwelling in *Amsterdam*'.[29] Moreover, Antonio Carvajal was one of twenty-eight Dover factors for the Dutch merchants named as witnesses by Violet, giving his sworn testimony at Admiralty on 21 November 1653.[30] Violet indeed had previously recommended that the Council of State encourage Spanish silver merchants to transport their commodities via an English port such as Plymouth, and that they seek the advice of Carvajal and several other Dover factors in the matter.[31]

III

Carvajal was a major importer of silver from the West Indies and gold from Cadiz, as well as wine from the Canary Islands. He had been born overseas – probably Portugal – later trading mainly from Spain before departing for Rouen. Having lived in Rouen three years he arrived in

---

[28] Violet, *True Narrative of Proceedings in Admiraltie*, pp. 2, 15; Violet, *Appeal to Cæsar*, pp. 38–45, 53–54; TNA, Prob 20/2650.

[29] Violet, *Proposals*, p. 17.

[30] Violet, *True Narrative*, p. 38; M. Woolf, 'Foreign trade of London Jews in the seventeenth century', *TJHSE*, 24 (1974), 38–58, at 52.

[31] Violet, *Advancement*, p. 13.

England about 1635. Thereafter Carvajal exported a wide variety of goods including buckram to Corunna; woollens, ointment and whetstones to Rouen; gum to Bilbao; cloth and hats to Dunkirk; looking-glasses, knives, brushes and pewter to Terceira; canvas and hose to Madeira; and calico, taffeta and drugs to Venice.[32] He eventually settled in Leadenhall Street in St Katherine Creechurch, but did not attend church and was indicted for recusancy on 19 May 1640.[33] Even so, he contributed to a collection in aid of the Protestants in Ireland as well as paying his assessment.[34] On 14 March 1644 Carvajal petitioned the House of Lords on behalf of a Dutch merchant consortium, concerning the shipment of 300 barrels of gunpowder from Amsterdam to Dover that had been intercepted and appropriated for Parliament's use by the earl of Warwick.[35] Although Carvajal was prosecuted in the Lords in January 1645 for not going to church he later outwardly practised Catholicism, reportedly attending Mass daily at the residence of the Spanish ambassador, Cárdenas. There he stood godfather to a number of Catholic infants and had several of his own children baptised publicly, even if it seems that he remained 'a Jew in heart', adhering to Jewish law by having his sons circumcised privately at eight days old (Genesis 17:12).[36] Along with his two sons Alonso and Joseph, Carvajal was granted an endenization on 31 July 1655 which was subsequently confirmed by a patent.[37] This is significant, because Carvajal was to declare his Judaism publicly eight months later, during the investigation of António Rodrigues Robles (*c*.1620–d.1688).

On 13 March 1656 legal proceedings were begun against Robles, a wealthy merchant of Duke's Place, who was accused of being a Spanish national. As England was then at war with Spain the goods and property of enemy Spaniards were liable for confiscation. Robles countered that he was actually a Portuguese-born Jew from Fundão who had fled to Spain – possibly Seville or Madrid – with his family. There the Inquisition had murdered his father and tortured and crippled his mother. Robles, who at some point was 'cut across the face', escaped to the Canary Islands,

---

[32] John Paige, *Letters of John Paige*, ed. G. Steckley, London Record Society, 21 (1984), nos. 48, 51, 59, 60, 64, 81, 83, 84; L. Wolf, 'The first English Jew', *TJHSE*, 2 (1894–95), 14–46, at 16–18, 26, 45; Woolf, 'Foreign trade', 41–6.

[33] John C. Jeaffreson, ed., *Middlesex County Records (Old Series), III: 1625–1667* (1974), p. 147.

[34] TNA, SP 28/193; E 179/147/595; Prob 11/296, fo. 531r–v, pr. in Wolf, 'Crypto-Jews', 86–8.

[35] *LJ*, VI, pp. 378, 471; Wolf, 'First English Jew', 17, 24–5.

[36] John Bland, *Trade revived* (1659), p. 21; Violet, *Jewes*, p. 4; Wolf, 'First English Jew', 16, 27.

[37] Thomas Birch, ed., *Collection of State Papers of John Thurloe*, 7 vols. (1742), III, p. 688; Wolf, 'First English Jew', 45–6.

where he changed his name, professed to be a Catholic and worked as a custom house official in the port of Santa Cruz on Tenerife. Depositions by a number of witnesses, including a few Iberian Jews, revealed that Robles, who had been living in England for four or five years, was married to a Portuguese woman of the 'Hebrew nation and Religion' yet had also been seen attending Mass at the Spanish ambassador's house in London until about mid-November 1655. Furthermore, Robles was at that time uncircumcized; apparently after he was circumcized his foreskin was buried in accordance with Jewish custom, but his servant dug it up as a joke – much to Robles's displeasure.[38] This business forced other members of London's secret Jewish community out into the open because many either had Spanish origins or had resided there. Accordingly, on 24 March Carvajal and six other men, including Rabbi Menasseh ben Israel (1604–1657), who had arrived in London from Amsterdam the previous September 'to sollicit a freedome for his nation to liue in England',[39] petitioned Oliver Cromwell for permission to practise Judaism privately in their homes, to go about unmolested and to have a burial place outside the City of London. Cromwell referred this petition for consideration to the Council of State, which on 26 June returned it, apparently without recording the details or outcome of their discussion.[40]

Meanwhile evidence continued to be taken in Robles's case, and by mid-May he had his ships, merchandise and other property which had been seized restored to him. Nonetheless, the Admiralty commissioners decided that he was 'either noe Jew or one that walkes under loose principles, very different from others of that profession'.[41] Carvajal for his part was accused by a London merchant of ingratitude and hypocrisy:

[W]hen the War began with *Spain*, then he was neither Spaniard, Portugal, French nor Dutch, Italian nor Turk, but an Hebrew, a plain downright Jew, acknowledging he never was or would be a Christian, taking upon him the outward profession of Christianity only for safety, which now he needed no longer to make use of, being he could live in *England* a professed Jew.[42]

Depositions taken before inquisition tribunals in Lisbon in March 1659 and on the Canary Islands in March 1660 confirm that Carvajal threw off his disguise when 'the Protector Cromwell had broken the peace with Spain'. Thenceforth it was public knowledge that he adhered to the 'Law of Moses' in London, reportedly 'holding Jewish rites and ceremonies

---

[38] Wolf, 'Crypto-Jews', 60–8, 77–86; Lucien Wolf, ed., and trans., *Jews in the Canary Islands* (1926), pp. 178, 202–03, 204, 206–07, 213; E. Samuel, 'Antonio Rodrigues Robles', *TJHSE*, 37 (2002), 113–15.

[39] SUL, HP 4/3/2A; BL, Add. MS 4365, fo. 277v.

[40] *CSPD 1655–56*, pp. 237, 294–5, 316; Wolf, 'Crypto-Jews', 66–8, 76; Lucien Wolf, ed., *Menasseh Ben Israel's Mission* (1901), pp. lxxxv–lxxxvi.

[41] Wolf, 'Crypto-Jews', 86.   [42] Bland, *Trade revived*, p. 21.

in a back room of the house in which he lived' – presumably until the completion of the synagogue on Creechurch Lane.[43] Equally noteworthy was Violet's allegation that the 'great Iew' Carvajal had allegedly told him that the Jews planned to advance Cromwell £1,000,000 if he gave two thousand Jewish merchants and their families liberty to settle in England, where they would be endenizened.[44]

IV

About Christmas 1659 – just seven weeks after Carvajal's death – Violet outlined a new stratagem for extorting money from the Jews to Sir Thomas Tyrrell, formerly a commissioner of the Great Seal and soon to be a judge in the court of common pleas. Tyrrell, however, advised keeping it secret until the restoration of the monarchy. In June 1660, following King Charles's return from exile and his triumphant entry into London, Violet met Tyrrell again.[45] On Tyrrell's recommendation, Violet now presented his ploy to the Privy Council. Adopting an expedient alarmist tone and condemning the solemn observance of morning and afternoon services in the London synagogue as a 'great dishonour' and public scandal to the 'true Protestant Religion', Violet warned that 'multitudes of men and women' seeking after novelties in religion had become proselytes to Judaism. For rather than turning Christian, Jews had exploited religious discord to make converts. Furthermore, relying heavily on William Prynne's *A Short Demurrer to the Jewes* (1656) as well as legal records and precedents provided by Tyrrell, Violet denounced Jews as a cursed nation of blasphemous Christ killers, comparing their religious rituals to popish superstitions. He also raised the spectre of international Jewry, xenophobically stressing Carvajal's and his compatriots' Iberian background, censuring Jewish merchants for their cunning underhand tricks, and reproving Jewish tax-gatherers for sucking up wealth like a sponge. Accordingly, Violet proposed ensnaring London's burgeoning Jewish community within the 'Net of the Law', ransoming them to help pay off the national debt, and ultimately banishment.[46] On the morning of Friday 17 August he petitioned the marquis of Ormond, recently

---

[43] Arquivo Nacional da Torre do Tombo, Inquisição de Lisboa, Cadernos do Promotor no. 36, fo. 698, printed in *Academia das sciências de Lisboa. Boletim da segunda classe*, 4 (1911), 461–4; Wolf, *Jews in the Canary Islands*, pp. 176–7. I am most grateful to João Melo for locating and translating the former document.

[44] Violet, *Jewes*, p. 7; Wolf, 'First English Jew', 21.   [45] Violet, *Jewes*, pp. 7–8.

[46] Ibid., pp. 1–7, 8; cf. William Prynne, *Short Demurrer* (1656), pp. 50, 54, 57–8; L. Wolf, 'Status of the Jews in England after the Resettlement', *TJHSE*, 4 (1903), 177–93, at 181; Wolf, 'Jewry of the Restoration', 13.

appointed lord steward of Charles II's household and two other privy councillors, the earl of Southampton and John Lord Robartes, urging them to sign a draft warrant to apprehend the Jews of London and its suburbs – especially those dwelling in Duke's Place. As the Jewish sabbath was approaching, Violet urgently proposed sending thirty or forty soldiers to seize them at prayer and simultaneously secure their properties, money, jewels, merchandise and account books. With the seeming collusion of Sir Ellis Leighton, a courtier favoured by the duke of York, the Jews would then be transported under armed guard by boat to Chelsea College. Preying on fears of miscegenation, of Jewish seed adulterating Christian blood, as well as child poverty brought about by economic competition, Violet claimed to speak for all English merchants in the City and hoped to be rewarded with a tenth of any ransom if the Jews were not granted royal licence to remain in London.[47]

At the end of November a humble remonstrance concerning the Jews was addressed to the king. Echoing many of Violet's calumnies, giving credence to additional rumours and sharing similarities with his scheme if not writing style, it articulated the grievances of London merchants. Perhaps presented by Sir William Courtney, a member of the Convention Parliament, the remonstrance proposed empowering individuals to make inquisitions about the size, behaviour, wealth, habitations and economic activities of the Jewish community.[48] Two lists of London Jews that have been dated to winter 1660 suggest that some of this information was gathered, almost certainly to facilitate levying a tax, or imposing a fine, the seizure of goods, imprisonment or even banishment, had Charles II been swayed to follow one of these courses.[49] On 7 December the Privy Council, having read both a petition from the merchants and tradesmen of London calling for the expulsion of the Jews (probably delivered on their behalf by the lord mayor and aldermen of London) and another petition pleading for their continued residence signed by Carvajal's widow Maria and other prominent Jewish merchants, referred the matter on the king's instructions to Parliament. Ten days later the order was presented to the Commons, who postponed discussion 'touching Protection for the *Jews*' until the next morning.[50] Although any possible debate is unrecorded in the journals of the Convention Parliament (dissolved 29 December 1660), Violet was informed of developments by a London merchant, and hastily published *A Petition Against the Jewes*

[47] Bodl., MS Carte 31, fos. 17, 19.
[48] *CSPD 1660–61*, p. 366; Wolf, 'Status of Jews', 182, 188–92.
[49] BL, Add. MS 29868, fos. 15, 16, printed in Wolf, 'Jewry of the Restoration', 6–7.
[50] Wolf, 'Status of Jews', 186–88; *CJ*, VIII, p. 209; Wolf, 'Jewry of the Restoration', 28–9.

(January 1661). This proved, however, to be an ill-judged effort to gain royal and parliamentary favour.

Afterwards Violet, partly through the intercession of a former comrade in the Tower, Sir Lewis Dyve (1599–1669), continued regularly petitioning the king and Parliament with a number of proposals that would have offered him potentially lucrative employment if they came to fruition. These concerned remedying alleged abuses practised by the makers of gold and silver thread, regulating the Mint and customs duty, and enforcing the tariff on gold and silver exported by the East India Company. In May 1661, doubtless in recompense for risking his life serving Charles I and consequently enduring lengthy spells of imprisonment, Violet's model for regulating the customs was taken into consideration. Yet nearly eleven months later naught had transpired, prompting him to reflect bitterly that pinning his hopes on the turning political tide had yielded 'nothing but words'.[51]

On Saturday 5 April 1662 Violet orally declared his will, according to one version bequeathing his entire estate to his principal creditor Alexander Holt, goldsmith of Lombard Street, London, to whom Violet owed about £1,000 and without whose assistance he would have 'utterly perished and been undone'. As for his kindred, Violet had 'none that I care for' or who 'of late yeares' had obliged him to provide for them.[52] Little over a week later Violet journeyed to Windsor intending to persuade the dean and chapter there to grant him a reversion of the lease of lands in Great Haseley, Oxfordshire, belonging to Edmund Lenthall. Despite a purported letter from Charles II attesting to Violet's 'great sufferings and loses' during the Civil War, Violet obtained neither lease nor the £10,030 in compensation that he expected from Lenthall.[53] Believing that he had been defrauded, that he was the victim of broken promises, left with debts amounting to almost £2,000 and a number of creditors grasping for money, his debtors either unwilling or unable to pay him, despairing of being flung any moment into a debtors' prison where he would inevitably perish, Violet made 'a Roman Resolution': to die like a Roman and 'so put an end to all worldly troubles'. Consequently, on 16 April 1662, the day after returning home to St Peter Cornhill, London, he decided to 'truly state' his case in order to 'satisfie all the world of some remarkable pasedges of Gods Prouidence upon him'. Still hoping for a last-minute royal change of heart, yet haunted by the sad temptation

[51] *CSPD 1660–61*, pp. 271–2; *CSPD 1661–62*, pp. 12–13, 254; *Calendar Treasury Books 1660–67*, p. 178; Violet, *Two Petitions*; Violet, *Case of Thomas Violet* (no date = 1662); Violet, *To the Kings Most Excellent Majesty*; TNA, Prob 20/2650.
[52] TNA, Prob 20/2650; cf. Prob 11/366, fo. 377r.
[53] *CSPD 1660–61*, p. 249; TNA, Prob 20/2650.

of suicide, Violet contemplated the central events of his relatively long life.[54]

Foremost on his mind, as indeed it had been in many previous petitions, was the letter from Charles I to the lord mayor and aldermen of London dated 26 December 1643 that Violet had brought from Oxford 'when the Citty was in the hight of ther madnes'. Protesting his innocence, unrepentant, aggrieved, blaming Parliament's rage and the fury of some firebrands for his ruin, he consoled himself with the thought that God was the potter fashioning honour and dishonour out of clay vessels, bestowing preferment on Jacob and refusing Esau (Romans 9:13, 21). Next Violet recalled being questioned in Star Chamber in 1634. Invoking God as his witness, he rejected as a malicious falsehood the widespread accusation then current that he had voluntarily betrayed his associates to save himself. Violet's evidence was his attempted suicide and fortunate survival, envisaged as successfully overcoming a form of trial by ordeal through divine favour. There followed his failure to convince Parliament to restore his sequestered estate, which had forced Violet ever since to borrow at irregular intervals huge sums of money from several friends. After that came his involvement in the seizure of the silver cargo in the ships *Samson*, *Salvador* and *George*, together with associated manoeuvring in the High Court of Admiralty. Vowing that borrowing money he could not repay had wounded his soul, Violet then drew up a ledger showing his creditors and debtors. Continually vindicating his conduct, with an eye to his posthumous reputation, Violet's exercise in self-justification becomes thereafter increasingly repetitive and self-pitying, giving a powerful insight into his psychological disintegration. Thinking that he had been slighted and scorned, treated no better than a dog, that it would set a bad precedent if Charles II did not reward his faithful service and 'many sufrings' by seeing all his debts paid, Violet cited his own calamitous condition as a warning to posterity to serve God rather than trust in the promises of princes or great men. For the devil was a cunning sophist able through 'great craft' to make a man defer repentance of his sins. Thus Violet humbly implored Jesus to have mercy upon him, not to leave him alone for even a minute lest he commit the heinous crime of self-murder. But of the Jews whom he had intended to trap, blackmail, ransom and banish there was no mention.[55]

The following day Violet affirmed before witnesses that he hoped that the king would grant his petition.[56] Then at 1 o'clock on Sunday 20 April

---

[54] TNA, Prob 20/2650.
[55] TNA, Prob 20/2650; Staffordshire RO, Stafford, D(W) 1778/I/i/104.
[56] TNA, Prob 36/1.

1662 Violet poisoned himself. This time the consequences were fatal. Yet even in agony he continued writing, begging two qualities from Christ he himself had lacked in life – mercy and forgiveness:

> now the panges of deadth are on me I ask Christ Jeasus forgiuenes forgiue me mercie mercie sweet Jesuss Pray for me pray for me Interseed for me lett thy blud wyp away all my sines this great Cr[y]ing sine.

Thus the 'Great trappaner of England' died by his own hand.[57]

By early May rival claimants to Violet's estate had begun contesting the contents of his nuncupative will. Protracted legal proceedings ensured that the matter remained unresolved until mid-July 1663.[58] Meanwhile Violet was buried, in fulfilment of his wish, in the parish church of St Katherine Creechurch, possibly in the same vault where his mother and father lay interred.[59] Evidently the nature of his demise must have been kept secret, since Christian suicides were customarily denied both funeral rites and burial in consecrated ground.[60] Twenty-nine months earlier the great bell of St Katherine Creechurch had tolled to mark the passing of Antonio Carvajal, who had died on 2 November 1659 after an unsuccessful operation to remove what was most likely a kidney or bladder stone (Samuel Pepys had famously survived a similar procedure performed by the same surgeon). Carvajal was laid to rest in the newly acquired Jewish burial ground at Mile End. The synagogue he had helped to establish in Creechurch Lane opposite the Great Gate leading into Duke's Place was situated no more than one hundred yards from Violet's corpse.[61]

V

Notwithstanding the self-serving nature of much of Violet's evidence, his fluctuating fortunes during the English Revolution and at the Restoration are instructive. Indeed, constructing Violet's largely urban-based narrative illuminates not just his disturbed, ruthless character but the ways in which an individual could repeatedly fashion their identity and ostensibly change allegiance according to circumstance. Furthermore, it illustrates an unusual if hazardous route towards influence and prosperity,

---

[57] TNA, Prob 20/2650.

[58] TNA, Prob 20/2650; Prob 36/1; Prob 11/310, fos. 221v–22r.

[59] TNA, Prob 20/2650.

[60] Michael MacDonald and Terence Murphy, *Sleepless Souls* (Oxford, 1993), pp. 19–20, 48–9.

[61] Samuel, 'First London synagogue', 7–8, 20–1, 25; W. Samuel, 'Carvajal and Pepys', *TJHSE*, 2 (1935), 24–9.

together with affording glimpses of the complex interplay between civic and national politics, competing interest groups striving for control of republican commercial policy, the dilatory way in which Charles II dealt with his father's supporters, and unresolved religious tensions. In short, through Violet we see how someone on the margins of power attempted, with varying degrees of success, to attract patrons both by promoting the advantages of their specialist knowledge and, when necessary, eliciting sympathy through accounts of suffering and professions of constancy.

At a time when, as the work of historians of early modern London and its suburbs reminds us, an idealized sense of parochial community, emphasizing as it did values of neighbourliness, co-operation and charity, competed with the rival attractions of civic pageantry and ritual, guild affiliation and religious sentiment as the pre-eminent social bonds of a parishioner's life, Violet generally positioned himself outside these pivotal intersecting worlds. A London citizen who moved from one parish to another, at odds with his livery company, caring nothing for his kin except his mother and a cousin, rarely calling on his neighbours except when in need, but nonetheless capable of making charitable bequests, he inhabited a civic space we are unaccustomed to observing. Violet therefore alerts us to the more unconventional pathways trodden around the periphery of the City's notional boundaries by neither respectable householders nor vagrants but by something altogether different. Integrating these lives, which sometimes transgressed licit parameters, into our existing grand narratives of early modern London will contribute towards resolving disagreements about the dominant forces – structural stability or inherent tensions – driving the City's rapid transformation, extraordinary growth and governance.

Likewise, Violet's evolving persona manufactured on the one hand publicly through printed treatises, petitions, letters, lobbying and legal testimony, on the other privately through autobiographical recollections in manuscript, raises interesting questions about the nature of the early modern self – especially in the light of Stephen Greenblatt's pioneering study.[62] Indeed, enough is known about Violet to break down his identity into seven distinct components: ethnicity, nationality, age, gender, social class, political loyalties and religious beliefs. Ethnically Violet was perhaps unusual, as he may have been of mixed race, the progeny of a Caucasian father and perhaps very dark-skinned ('Moorish') mother. Regarding nationality Violet was English, although apparently born at sea. Besides, with a father and paternal grandfather from the Spanish

---

[62] Stephen Greenblatt, *Renaissance Self-fashioning* (Chicago, 1980).

Netherlands, an alleged 'Moorish' mother and Tuscan maternal grand-father, he must be placed at the edge of what constituted 'Englishness'. This acquires added significance when juxtaposed with James Shapiro's suggestion that one of the ways 'Englishness' was being defined during this period was by asserting what it was not, specifically that the notion was evolving at least partly in tandem with changing conceptions of what characteristics defined 'Jewishness'.[63] Turning to gender, there is no evidence that Violet married or sired children out of wedlock. All the same, it would be unwise to speculate about his sexual orientation or an off-putting personality disorder, given that marital union was dictated by considerations of 'good liking', status, wealth and religious sentiment rather than love. By contrast, Violet's perception of his standing within English society, together with the weight he placed on financial solvency as a way of retaining personal credit among his social equals and betters, is in keeping with Alexandra Shepard's findings about the links between economic self-sufficiency, honesty, responsibility and early modern concepts of manhood. This is borne out further by Violet's insistence that he had not squandered his money gambling but had earned instead a reputation for honouring his debts.[64] Again, as Michael MacDonald and Terence Murphy have shown, lost fortunes like Violet's and fear of destitution were a common motive for suicide, the instigation of the devil a formulaic explanation, while Roman precedents – particularly those justified by Stoic and Epicurean philosophy – informed Renaissance humanist and Protestant attitudes towards self-murder.[65]

Although he did not fight in the Civil Wars, Violet's allegiance was initially unquestionably to the king. An outmoded Marxist interpretation would doubtless view this as Violet acting in accordance with his class interest: affirming his social rank (the family was armigerous), safeguarding his valuable patent from Charles I to regulate gold and silver wire thread. Recently Barbara Donagan has suggested that Royalist allegiance 'seems to have been almost instinctive', emphasizing the strong element of personal loyalty involved as well as the desire of Royalists to uphold existing social norms, hierarchies and institutions. This, too, chimes with Violet's claims after the Restoration that duty required him to serve God, king and country; that Parliament and the City of London had ruptured the divine order by breaking God's laws.[66] Unfortunately, less is known of Violet's religious beliefs. His enemies

---

[63] James Shapiro, *Shakespeare and the Jews* (New York, 1996), pp. 4–5, 43–6, 167–93.

[64] Alexandra Shepard, *Meanings of Manhood in Early Modern England* (Oxford, 2003), pp. 186–92; TNA, Prob 20/2650.

[65] MacDonald and Murphy, *Sleepless Souls*, pp. 35, 42–60, 86–8, 260, 266–71.

[66] Jason McElligott and David L. Smith, eds., *Royalists and Royalism during the English Civil Wars* (Cambridge, 2007), pp. 4, 66–88; TNA, Prob 20/2650.

depicted him wearing a mask, as merely an outward Protestant, an ungodly sinner given to swearing, drunkenness, lying, sabbath-breaking, associating with Catholic plotters and other scandalous conduct. Here we see a striking correspondence with polemical representations of certain aspects of Cavalier behaviour. Moreover, Violet's suspected dissimulation resonates with Perez Zagorin's discoveries concerning widespread if divergent practices of deception throughout early modern Europe that enabled persecuted believers to hide their inner convictions.[67] Nevertheless, this image must be qualified by picturing Violet's death-bed plea to Jesus, whom, in an orthodox Protestant manner, Violet envisaged as mediator between God and man, atoning through the righteous shedding of his blood for humanity's sins.

The dissembler in religion had their counterpart with the Machiavel in politics. Here Violet cultivated a deserved reputation for excelling at 'fraud and feigned pretences'. Sir Lewis Dyve attested that he was 'able to put any shape and mould on himself to compasse his design', while many members of the Council of State reportedly thought him 'a sly and dangerous fellow', always presenting propositions that might 'bear double interpretations'. An immoral active 'instrument', he lived by 'shifts' and 'projects', tacking his sails in the shifting political winds but still occasionally unable to avoid floundering on the rocks.[68] Navigating these turbulent vicissitudes, the alterations in civic and national government, Violet's intrigues, lies and insinuations call attention to intricate, partly hidden dynamic personal relationships between agents, clients, patrons, friends and allies operating with varying degrees of cohesion on different scales at the core of political processes. Driven by ambition, avarice and enmity, the most dramatic moment of his early career – the plot to divide the king's enemies – has been integrated into Keith Lindley's account of popular politics and religion in Civil War London.[69] Similarly, Violet's attempt to ingratiate himself with the republican regime and participate in debates about the direction of its commercial strategy casts extra light on the Byzantine network of changeable alliances examined by James Farnell and Robert Brenner that underpinned the competing factions driving through anti-Dutch policies – notably the Navigation Act of 1651, which arguably precipitated the first Anglo-Dutch war – and anti-Spanish designs such as the expedition to attack the Spanish West Indies.[70]

[67] Perez Zagorin, *Ways of Lying* (Cambridge, MA, 1990).
[68] Violet, *Jewes*, pp. 20, 27, 32; Violet, *Appeal to Cæsar*, p. 54; Anon., *Trappaner*, p. 6.
[69] Keith Lindley, *Popular Politics and Religion in Civil War London* (Aldershot, 1997), pp. 247–8, 353–4.
[70] J. Farnell, 'The Navigation Act of 1651', *EcHR*, n.s., 16 (1964), 439–54; Robert Brenner, *Merchants and Revolution* (Princeton, NJ, 1993).

Commonwealth and Protectorate foreign policy, potential economic advantages and theological considerations – the necessity of converting the Jews before Christ's reappearance – also combined to create the necessary conditions in the face of widespread hostility to a debate about the readmission of the Jews to England. Modern scholarship, which is extensive, has tended to focus on Menasseh ben Israel's mission to Oliver Cromwell and the background to the Whitehall Conference of December 1655. Moreover, through a combination of hindsight and an understandable willingness to hold anniversary celebrations, 1656 is now widely trumpeted as an irreversible moment that marked the gradual informal readmission of Jews to England after a supposed absence of 366 years. While the so-called Resettlement was certainly a *de facto* if not *de jure* watershed, the tenor of this essay agrees with the direction of relatively recent work by David Katz, James Shapiro and Eliane Glaser among others in challenging the traditional optimistic, perhaps even convenient, picture of hitherto rootless persecuted aliens transformed through a strong current of Protestant philo-Semitism into grateful beneficiaries of a uniquely English form of religious toleration based on the peculiarities of common law.[71] In fact, it needs to be emphasized that there was no act of parliament, no proclamation from Cromwell, no order from the Council of State either welcoming Jews to England or changing their legal status as a community from aliens (foreigners whose allegiance was due to a foreign state) to denizens (foreigners admitted to residence and granted certain rights, notably to prosecute or to defend themselves in law and to purchase or sell land, but still subject to the same customs duties on their goods and merchandise as aliens). The only evidence we have suggests that publicly Cromwell remained undecided on the issue, even if, according to the Tuscan envoy Francesco Salvetti, he connived in permitting Jews to continue worshipping privately in their homes, a gesture consonant with the spirit of certain clauses of the *Instrument of Government* of December 1653, which had extended religious toleration to those Protestant sects that did not disturb the peace.[72]

Furthermore, by focusing on a comparatively neglected brief period in Anglo-Jewish history spanning the twilight of the English republic and the dawn of the Restoration, I have implicitly questioned the conventional chronological arrangement characteristic of several older grand narratives of Anglo-Jewish history: a broad-brush tripartite division into

---

[71] D. Katz, 'English redemption and Jewish readmission', *Journal of Jewish Studies*, 34 (1983), 73–91; David Katz, *Jews in the History of England* (Oxford, 1994), pp. 132–4; Shapiro, *Shakespeare and the Jews*, pp. 53–5, 60–2, 65–7; Eliane Glaser, *Judaism without Jews* (Basingstoke, 2007), pp. 1–3, 7–27.

[72] C. Roth, 'New light on the Resettlement', *TJHSE*, 11 (1928), 112–42, at 131, 141.

pre-Expulsion Period (mainly 1066–1290), Middle Period (1290–1655), and Modern Period (1656 to the present). Again, this is in keeping with a growing trend which favours integrating the crypto-Jewish and Jewish experience within English history rather than constructing an insular history of the Jews in England. It is also evident from the preceding account that with Cromwell's death on 3 September 1658, individuals professing their Judaism, both long-term residents and recent immigrants, were collectively vulnerable. No longer considered as under his personal protection they were once more exposed to full-blown prejudice which intermingled 'horrid' accusations revolving around the repulsive if familiar themes of deicide, blasphemy, blood, diabolism, magic and money.[73] Thus throughout 1659 London merchants trading with Spain voiced their complaints against Jewish competitors – these 'Horseleeches of every Commonwealth, State, and Kingdome' – by pamphleteering and petitioning; in one instance proposing to expel or banish them and appropriate their profits for the state's use.[74] As we have seen, Violet's traps and stratagems are of a piece with this clamour to push the Jews out through the door that Oliver Protector had tacitly opened, and close it shut behind them. Yet to appreciate fully the precarious position of London's tiny Jewish community at this time we must also be aware both of long-term developments stretching back to the legal issues surrounding the Expulsion of 1290 and of a variety of contexts. These include the fate of Jews in western Europe since the late fifteenth century; voyages of exploration and the European discovery of new lands; the invention of movable printing type and mass production of texts; the growth of biblical learning and rejuvenation of Hebrew studies; the Reformation and attendant dissemination of Lutheran and Calvinist teaching; the role of the Inquisition, especially in Iberia, in the Canary Islands and on the Italian peninsula; the use of agents to facilitate intelligence gathering and diplomacy; millenarianism and Judaizing (even in the absence of authentic Jews); debates about liberty of conscience and the treatment of religious minorities, notably Catholics and sectaries; English attitudes towards foreigners, especially Huguenots and other Protestant exiles; and financial markets, international trading networks and other economic issues.

While a detailed examination of Violet's machinations cannot transform our understanding of all the interwoven threads that, taken together, form the larger tapestry of this moment in Anglo-Jewish history – or for

---

[73] Wolf, *Menasseh's Mission*, pp. 107–22.
[74] Anon., *To the Right Honourable knights* (1659), brs.; [Richard Baker], *Marchants humble petition* (1659), pp. 9, 17, repr. in Wolf, 'Status of Jews', 186; Bland, *Trade revived*, pp. 2, 20–3.

that matter the English Revolution – it can nonetheless provide welcome texture. Indeed, the significance of an individual's life and thought to the historian can be measured in any number of ways. Violet's importance thus rests ultimately not so much on his achievements and failures, or on how many friends and enemies he made, or even on how many people read or owned his work,[75] but on what his experiences tell us about his times and the human condition itself. In this marriage of the particular with the general, this effort to tease out all the nuances from the extant sources and to integrate the conclusions within a wider whole we see, of course, a response to revisionism and its challenges.

---

[75] *Catalogus Librorum... Benjaminis Worsley* (1678), p. 98 no. 490; Giovanni Tarantino, ed., *Lo scrittoio di Anthony Collins* (Milan, 2007), p. 490 no. 10030.

12   The Cromwellian legacy of William Penn

Mary K. Geiter

I

William Penn, Quaker leader, Pennsylvania proprietor and political activist, spent his childhood years in the shadow of the English Civil Wars and the Interregnum, a period in which England was in the middle of a religious and political trauma so sweeping that its effects would be felt into the next century and across the Atlantic. To what extent those years informed his political and religious outlook is the main issue addressed in this essay. It argues that Penn was not only imbued with republican ideas from his formative years but was often at the centre of political and religious debates that carried over from the first half of the seventeenth century into and beyond the Restoration period. Also, this essay extends the discussion of his career with reference to the current historiography on the era of the Interregnum and the Restoration. For instance, when placed in the context of what historians have come to consider 'Atlantic history', Penn's colonizing activities in Pennsylvania add a dimension to what John Morrill has called 'the British problem'.[1]

II

Born into a family of means and influence, Penn seemed bound to play a significant part in English politics and society. His father, Sir William, was a prominent figure during the Interregnum and the Restoration, and on his death his son inherited a yearly sum of £1,500 in addition to estates in England and Ireland. While details of the young Penn's life during this time are sketchy, and there is very little extant correspondence between father and son, evidence does survive that suggests not only the esteem

---

[1] John Morrill, 'The British problem, *c.* 1534–1707', in Brendan Bradshaw and John Morrill, eds., *The British Problem, c.1534–1707: State Formation in the Atlantic Archipelago* (1996), pp. 1–38. For a recent discussion of 'Atlantic history' and a brief bibliography of the most salient contributions, see Mary K. Geiter and W. A. Speck, *A Dictionary of British America* (2007), pp. xviii–xx, 114–15.

in which William held his father, but Sir William's tremendous influence on his son's political and religious attitudes. Although at the time of his conversion to Quakerism, as Penn acknowledged, his father was in 'high wrath' against him, later recollections bear out the impact his father had on him. Penn was to write of his father,

> I had so little reason to doubt my father's constancy, 'tis true, he was actually engaged both under the parliament and king, but not as an actor in our late domestic troubles; his compass always steering him to eye a national concern, and not intestine wars, and therefore not so aptly their's (the parliament's), in a way of opposition, as the nation's. His service therefore being wholly foreign to these (domestic troubles) he may truly be said, to serve his country.[2]

The memorial to his father inside St Mary Redcliffe church in Bristol is a remarkable testimony to the esteem in which the admiral's wartime achievements were held by his pacifist son. That his father put the nation's interest ahead of his own was a sentiment that the son carried with him throughout his life, often, like his father, to his own detriment.

When war broke out in Ireland, Sir William saw his destiny in serving in the royal navy as part of the Irish squadron to protect that country from the threat of papist forces. His conviction was such that, in 1644, he refused his father's pleas for him to withdraw from public service and join the merchant navy, no doubt a more lucrative venture, saying,

> gold to me, in this, is dirt, 'tis the goodness of the cause that hath only put me on, and nothing whatsoever shall take off from the service I so cordially undertake and shall be so prodigal of my blood, that I shall think it very well spent and life to boot, for the maintenance of so good, so just, so pious a quarrel. And if ever God send peace, an honourable peace, peace and truth on this our nation, I may then, if I continue . . . think of the Levant voyage.[3]

His passionate reply clearly shows that, in Sir William's eyes, the war was, indeed, a religious one.

The role that religion played in the navy was, in some ways, of a practical nature. Adherence to a mixed polity, one which combined the defence

---

[2] Historical Society of Pennsylvania, William Penn Letterbook, 1667–1675, pp. 45–50, n. d., 1668? Cf. William Penn, *The Papers of William Penn*, ed. Richard S. Dunn, Mary Maples Dunn et al., 5 vols. (Philadelphia, 1981–6), I, p. 67.

[3] Penn, *Memorials*, I, pp. 93–4. For the Penn family's involvement with the Levant, see Mary K. Geiter, 'London merchants and the launching of Pennsylvania', *The Pennsylvania Magazine of History and Biography*, 121 (1997), 101–22, at 102, 110. There was a significant dissenting presence in the Levant trade. For a discussion of the influence of Nonconformity in trade and politics during the seventeenth century, see Gary Stuart De Krey, *A Fractured Society: The Politics of London in the First Age of Party, 1688–1715* (Oxford, 1985), pp. 77–89, 141–4. De Krey estimates that nearly 30 per cent of the Levant merchants were Dissenters.

of the Protestant religion, the privileges of Parliament, and prerogatives of the crown, was the focus of naval men such as Penn. The 1642 *Seaman's Protestation* illustrates this, but with a particularly strong sense of national interest. So, while it asserted the need to maintain the Protestant religion and acknowledged Charles I as king, it was the defence of the privileges of Parliament that caused it to be written. According to the *Protestation*, the 'happiness of this kingdome consists in their sessions'.[4] Thus, unlike the army which had to address domestic issues, the very distance and circumstances under which the navy operated caused it to concentrate its role away from faction and towards protecting the nation from foreign encroachment, no matter whether the country was ruled by a monarch or parliament. Thus, while the army concentrated on a civil war, for the naval forces the war extended beyond the internal political dispute. Sir William shared these sentiments and carried them with him throughout his life. He also remained true to the Protestant faith. So, although he was born and died Anglican, his attitude toward his faith was described as one where he adhered to the established church when he could, but 'his religion, was the Christianity of the Reformation, and he could find that when he could not find his church'.[5] When he became an Anglican once again is not known, but most certainly, he did so very early in the Restoration when he worshipped at St Mary Redcliffe. For Sir William, the transition back to a monarchy was also made smoother by his belief in Providence. Like Cromwell, he could view the failure of the 'Western Design' of 1655 in providential terms. The object of the expedition to the Caribbean, 'to wrest a horn from the head of the beast' by taking Hispaniola, was not realized. This could apparently only be explained in Cromwell's view as the shortcomings of God's instruments, in this case, Penn and Venables.[6] Likewise, the restoration of the monarchy could be seen as providential in terms of the failure of the Protector's successor to secure the Revolution.

A further clue to Penn's political and religious attitudes is provided by his family's link with Ireland. Penn claimed to have had his first intense religious experience at the age of twelve or thirteen. What this experience was based on is unclear, but we do know that during this time Penn was living with his family on their Irish estates.[7] A relatively unexplored

---

[4] *The Seaman's Protestation* (1642), as quoted in Penn, *Memorials*, I, pp. 17–19.

[5] Penn, *Memorials*, I, p. 94; J. D. Davies, *Gentlemen and Tarpaulins* (Oxford, 1991).

[6] Blair Worden, 'Oliver Cromwell and the sin of Achan', in Derek Beales and Geoffrey Best, eds., *History, Society and the Churches: Essays in Honour of Owen Chadwick* (Cambridge, 1985), pp. 135–6.

[7] Nicholas Canny, 'The Irish background to Penn's experiment', in Richard S. Dunn and Mary Maples Dunn, eds., *The World of William Penn* (Philadelphia, 1986), pp. 139–56.

relationship, which again has little in the way of documentary evidence, is that with his mother, who came from Kilrush, County Clare. Not much is known of her except that she lived in Ireland prior to going to London and marrying Penn's father. She had been married to Nicholas Vandershuren, a Dutch merchant, and was widowed in 1641 or 1642. Although the cause of Vandershuren's death is unknown, it occurred at the time of the Irish uprising, when Protestant settlers were attacked by Catholic insurgents and their lands taken.[8] Later, when Cromwell subdued the rebellion, Sir William and his wife petitioned for the return of her property and were compensated with land in County Cork as part payment for the admiral's service in the Irish Seas, as well as part restoration of his wife's property. The experience of living in Ireland after the Catholic rebellion and the subsequent massacres, which lost nothing in the telling, must have resonated with the son. Indeed it is, perhaps, through his mother and her experiences in 1641–2 that Penn's initial antipathy towards Roman Catholicism can be explained.

How far religious attitudes of the revolutionary years were carried over into the Restoration years is a subject of debate among historians. Recent work on the Interregnum and the Restoration has developed two conflicting contextual frameworks. One, inspired by the revisionist interpretation of early modern history, maintains that religion remained central to the political and social life of Restoration England. This interpretation emphasizes continuity from the 1650s to the 1660s. The other, in reaction to this, leans more towards the traditional view that saw the era as a more secular age than the revolutionary decades in the middle of the seventeenth century.[9]

Penn's career appears at first sight to uphold the revisionists' emphasis on continuity and the centrality of religion. A convinced Quaker who inaugurated a 'holy experiment' in his colony of Pennsylvania surely provides evidence for the notion that religious zeal did not fade with

---

[8] For this turbulent period in the history of Ireland, see especially Micheál Ó Siochrú, *Confederate Ireland, 1642–1649: A Constitutional and Political Analysis* (Dublin, 1999); Ó Siochrú, *God's Executioner: Oliver Cromwell and the Conquest of Ireland* (2008); Catherine Owens Peare, *William Penn* (1957), p. 11.

[9] Cf. Tim Harris, Paul Seaward and Mark Goldie, eds., *The Politics of Religion in Restoration England* (Oxford, 1990), with Alan Houston and Steven Pincus, eds., *A Nation Transformed: England after the Restoration* (Cambridge, 2001). This bald summary of the contrasting contextual frameworks of these two volumes rides roughshod over nuances in the approaches of the historians involved. Two even contributed essays to both collections. The second stresses that secularization is a more subtle process than is often assumed, and certainly does not consider religion to have become unimportant. Nevertheless the broad distinction between them is clear: in the first, religion remains central after 1660; in the second, politics and economics became as crucial.

the restoration of the monarchy. Certainly the tracts he wrote in 1668, immediately after his conversion, such as *Truth Exalted* and *Sandy Foundation Shaken*, display a degree of zeal bordering on enthusiasm. One in particular, *God's Controversy Proclaimed*, echoed the fanaticism of the Cromwellian era. In it he put words directly into the mouth of God, warning the nation that 'the time for making Inquisition for blood is come... Therefore Wo, Wo, Wo to the Murderer & the Oppressor, the Unclean Person & Drunkards, the Lyer & Swearer, the Prophan; & such as live in Vanity'. Where this anathema was thundered against people in general, Penn depicts God as having a particular aversion to 'all persecutors' and even to 'the professors of religion of all sorts within these isles; especially such as are scornfully called phanaticks or dissenters'.[10] Penn was probably in prison when he poured out his wrath in this tract and, significantly perhaps, he never published it. Nevertheless, he does appear to have been in a particularly apocalyptic frame of mind in the early 1670s. In September 1671 he wrote another tract warning the Dutch that God's wrath would be visited upon them if they did not mend their ways, and followed it up with another after the invasion of the United Provinces by the French in 1672, saying, essentially, 'I told you so.'[11]

By the mid-1670s, however, he became less enthusiastic and more pragmatic. His later works reveal a more secular side. Tracts such as *A Particular Account of Sufferings*, *Reasons why the Oaths Should not be made part of the Tests* and *Declaration or Test*, although pleading the case for the Society of Friends, really show a pragmatic slant when he argued the economic benefits that Quaker tradesmen bring to the nation. Penn was not only advocating these for his fellow Quakers, but for the dissenting community as a whole. This change in tone corresponds to the stylistic shift in religious discourse which Blair Worden identifies as the outcome of a growing dislike of enthusiastic rhetoric, as reason came to be seen as an ally rather than as an enemy of religion.[12]

Penn's adoption of a more pragmatic attitude reinforced his conviction that there had to be a political solution to the problem of religious persecution. Charles II's second Declaration of Indulgence offered a genuine respite to Dissenters, including Quakers, from prosecution under the penal laws. Penn took it on himself to upbraid magistrates who ignored

---

[10] Penn, *Papers*, I, pp. 184–91. As the editors observe, 'his language is Biblical, and almost Calvinistic in its reliance upon the harsh imagery of Isaiah and Ezekiel' (p. 184).

[11] William Penn Letterbook, pp. 1–3, 14.

[12] Blair Worden, 'The question of secularization', in Houston and Pincus, *A Nation Transformed*, pp. 20–40, at pp. 32–3.

it, and even to address Charles II to enforce it.[13] He also began to pre-
pare drafts of toleration bills to present to Parliament, presumably in the
event that the Cavalier parliament was dissolved and another one more
sympathetic were to be elected.[14] He even devised a form of agreement
between constituencies and their members delegating MPs to oppose
legislation that would compel conformity to the established church or
disturb any Dissenters in their 'quiet exercise of their consciences in that
way they sincerely believe God requires them to worship him in'.[15] In
short, Penn sought to achieve his religious objectives by secular means.

If Penn's religious writings reinforce the view that the Restoration era
was marked by increasing secularization, however, an examination of his
political aspirations substantiates the notion that there were major conti-
nuities as well as changes from the 1650s to the 1660s. Throughout his
life, Penn's connection to the revolutionary decades is seen in his political
and colonizing activities as well as in his religious activities. His friendship with Algernon Sidney, a republican soldier and Parliamentarian, was
close enough for Penn to support him in the exclusion elections of 1679
and 1680.[16] Sidney was a key influence on the first draft of Pennsylvania's constitution and a harsh critic of its final draft. After Sidney failed to
enter Parliament, Penn backed another former Cromwellian officer. The
governors Penn chose for his colony also illustrate a connection with the
republic with his choice in 1682 of his cousin, William Markham, who
had served in the navy during the 1650s, and in 1689 of John Blackwell,
who had been a captain in the Parliamentary army.

Three strands in particular connect Penn's activities to the
Cromwellian era. These are his commitment to religious toleration, his
constitutional experimentation and his interest in imperial expansion.

III

Penn experienced at first hand the treatment of Dissenters. In 1667, while
attending a Quaker meeting in County Cork, he was arrested and charged
with involvement in a riotous assembly. It seems to have been a baptism
by fire into the Society of Friends, for he became a Quaker around
this time. Similar episodes would be repeated in England, one in 1670
being of particular significance, since he was charged with fomenting
a riot that resulted in the famous Penn-Meade trial. However, whereas

---

[13] Penn, *Papers*, I, pp. 276–7, 283.

[14] Draft bills for toleration were to be presented to the Exclusion Parliaments. See Henry
Horwitz, 'Protestant reconciliation in the Exclusion Crisis', *Journal of Ecclesiastical History*, 15 (1964), 201–17.

[15] William Penn Letterbook, pp. 123–6.   [16] Penn, *Papers*, I, pp. 546–7.

the events in Cork served as an awakening for Penn where religious liberties were concerned, by the time of the Penn-Meade incident he had developed a fairly comprehensive view of the notion of civil liberty. The trial provided him with the opportunity to articulate his opinion that liberty of conscience was a civil right.

The trial is generally taken to have arisen from an alleged breach of the Conventicle Act, but the indictment made no mention of that statute. Instead, Penn and Meade were charged with breach of the laws against riotous behaviour, and Penn's defence lay in denying that their actions could be so construed: 'our meeting religiously to worship God in the street (through necessity, being by the soldiers kept out by the mayor's appointment or the Lieutenancy of our hired House) doth not contradict or any ways fall under the clauses of riot or rout in the statutes against Rioters etc.'. He claimed that the loss of their liberties or properties for lawful assembly was 'to prejudice the Government or good people of England that we claim as our birthright & inheritance, & as immutable foundations of the English Constitution'. In particular, it was 'destructive of the Great Charter'. While the trial was a milestone for freedom of speech and independence of juries, there was another aspect to it. Penn was asserting that the denial of the freedom of worship was an attack on liberty and property, and therefore an infringement of the rights of Englishmen. By reversing the charge of presiding over a tumultuous riot and challenging the legality of the indictment of holding an unlawful, seditious, and riotous assembly, Penn was acknowledging the primacy of the common law, as the court transcript shows. When he demanded by what law he was summoned, the recorder admonished him as 'an impertinent fellow', and lectured him that the law was unwritten and had to be studied for thirty or forty years to be understood. He ended his rebuke by asking Penn, 'would you have me to tell you in a Moment?'. Penn retorted, 'Certainly, if the Common-Law be so hard to be understood, it's far from being very Common; but if the Lord Coke, in his Institutes, be of any Consideration, he tells us, That Common-Law is Common Right, and that Common Right is the Great Charter.'[17]

In citing Coke, Penn was not just harking back to early Stuart precedents. He was also drawing on notions of liberty that were swirling about during the 1650s, so that by the time he was making his own observations on them they had become commonplace in political discourse. For Penn, civil liberties were at the forefront of his fight for religious liberties. We see this echoed in his works, *The Great Case of Liberty of Conscience*

[17] Penn-Meade Trial, 1670. Penn could not resist showing his erudition by citing his authorities: 'Confirmed 9 *Hen*. 3. 29. 25 *Edw*. I. 1. 2 *Edw*. 3. 8. *Cook Instit*. 2 p. 56.'

once more Debated and Defended (1670) and *A Perswasive to Moderation to Dissenting Christians* (1685). Moreover, both argued that persecution for religious beliefs was against reason and nature: 'Liberty of Conscience we ask as our undoubted Right by the Law of God, of Nature, and of our own Country.'[18] When he wrote the first tract, Penn was not prepared to go as far as encouraging inclusion of Catholics in office holding. However, by the time the second tract was written, changing political events caused him to take a softer line on civil liberties for them, too.

Penn's position accorded with arguments for religious toleration proposed after the Restoration, but they also followed Cromwellian precedents. Cromwell understood that toleration, and indeed liberty of conscience, was essential to peace and prosperity. His point of reference was the Netherlands, where religious freedom was shown to be conducive to a prosperous trading nation. Penn also uses the Netherlands for his model of toleration. Cromwell drew the line where liberty became incompatible with law, in terms of licentious behaviour and breaking of the laws of England. Liberty of conscience was a 'natural right', he said, but not one to be abused to the detriment of society.[19] Throughout his career, Cromwell hammered home the precariousness of persecuting people for their beliefs alone: 'For if these were but notions I mean these instances I have given you of dangerous doctrines both in civil things and spiritual, if, I say, they were but notions, they were best let alone.'[20] From this perspective, then, Cromwell was willing to entertain some toleration of Roman Catholics, perhaps on the Elizabethan principle of not making windows into men's souls. On the other hand, Cromwell drew the line at allowing Catholic involvement in English political institutions. This is not to say that he would not employ Catholics elsewhere. In the implementation of his imperial policy, he reinstated the Catholic Lord Baltimore, who had been deprived of his proprietorship of Maryland by the Rump. Baltimore's restoration was made on condition that he would promulgate legislation for the toleration of Protestants. An Act Concerning Toleration thus guaranteed the rights of Protestants in that colony.[21] Also, Cromwell himself undertook to tolerate Catholics in England as

---

[18] William Penn, *The Great Case of Liberty of Conscience* (1670). Compare Penn's view with Cromwell's address to Parliament on 3 April 1657, where he acknowledged that civil liberties of the nation were intertwined with religious liberty: Oliver Cromwell, *Oliver Cromwell's Letters and Speeches*, ed. Thomas Carlyle, 4 vols. (2005 repr.), IV, pp. 27–8; R. C. Richardson, ed., *Images of Oliver Cromwell: Essays for and by Roger Howell, Jr* (Manchester, 1993), p. 162.

[19] Cromwell, *Letters and Speeches*, III, p. 147.   [20] Ibid., p. 15.

[21] For a good treatment of Baltimore's position in England as proprietor of Maryland during this time, see John D. Krugler, *English and Catholic: The Lords Baltimore in the Seventeenth Century* (Baltimore, 2004), pp. 192–232.

a quid pro quo for Cardinal Mazarin's agreeing to relax the oppression of the Huguenots in France. There is an indication that distinctions were being drawn between 'papists', who were associated with popery and arbitrary power, and Catholics, who did not see a conflict in their allegiance to England and their religious adherence to the pope. This dichotomy continued into the Restoration.

Penn accepted the generally held view that the crucial difference between Catholics and the other persuasions was their allegiance to an external power, that of Rome. He made this clear in his *Seasonable Caveat Against Popery* in 1670 which was in response to a recycled tract, *An Explanation of the Roman Catholic Belief*, which had been presented to Oliver Cromwell in 1656. Later, in *One Project for the Good of England* (1680), he asked the question whether Catholics could be trusted when it was known that one of their tenets was not to keep faith with heretics. Therefore he asserted that the difference between papists and Protestants was political rather than religious. Penn claimed that he was an advocate of universal toleration, but the fact that *Seasonable Caveat* was first issued in Ireland, combined with his mother's experiences, may well explain, as previously noted, his initial reluctance to tolerate Catholics.

Penn firmly advocated a separation between the civil and religious spheres in *England's Present Interest Discover'd with Honour to the Prince and Safety to the People* (1675). While Catholics remained suspect politically, they could be afforded religious toleration. This distinction was picked up again in 1679, when he steered clear of opposition to Roman Catholics per se, but advocated punishment for those involved in the Popish Plot. He also called for the choosing of Parliament men who would 'maintain civil rights'. By 1685, with the accession of James II, Penn supported universal toleration to include men of the king's own religious persuasion in his *Perswasive to Moderation*, although he continued to distinguish between liberty and licence. However, the significance of this tract and its successor, *Good Advice to the Church of England, Roman Catholick, and Protestant Dissenter*, published the following year, is that Penn firmly places toleration on the foundation of English liberty. His seemingly changing attitude towards Catholics can be explained in terms of a changing political situation and an evolving and maturing philosophy. An overtly Catholic king was now on the throne, albeit one who did not enjoy good relations with the papacy. Penn was also aware of the move to consolidate the colonies under the crown. If followed through, this policy would deprive him of the proprietorship of Pennsylvania.[22]

---

[22] A Quo Warranto was issued against Pennsylvania in May 1686: TNA, PCR, 2/71, fo. 144v.

This cynical interpretation of his motives must be qualified, however, by stressing that Penn's philosophical maturation and the king's own philosophical leanings were not incompatible. This is particularly evident in Penn's active support for James's push to achieve liberty of conscience for Catholics and other Dissenters alike.[23] Only when James reversed his policy on toleration as a last-ditch attempt to secure Anglican support did Penn reverse his views on toleration for Catholics by publishing *Advice in the Choice of Parliament Men* in 1688.

Penn's philosophical maturation can also be traced back to his studentship under the leading Huguenot theologian, Moïse Amyraut, in Saumur in 1662. Amyraut was at the centre of the controversy between Protestant scholasticism and humanism. He claimed to have restored the philosophical link to Calvin over issues concerning grace and passive obedience. Although Calvin himself had preached the doctrine of passive obedience and non-resistance, Huguenots were split on this, particularly in response to the Massacre of St Bartholomew's Day in 1572 where some had asserted the right to resist. This led to a renewal of religious conflict in France which continued sporadically until 1628. The years of intermittent strife had witnessed a substantial decline in the strength of the Huguenot cause in France. Amyraut used his influence to reassert the Calvinist notion of non-resistance, thereby earning for his co-religionists a position of peaceful coexistence with the state, and persuaded Mazarin that the Huguenots had renounced the use of force against the regime. At the National Synod in 1628 Amyraut had affirmed Huguenot loyalty to the crown and his belief in the divine right of kings.[24] However, his views on universal salvation evoked accusations of Arminianism.

Amyraut's refutation of the English Independents' challenge to the divine right of kings was picked up by Penn during the Exclusion Crisis and the Glorious Revolution, when Parliament again challenged the crown. While he believed that Parliament could seek to bring the king, or the heir to the throne, back within the limits of the ancient constitution,

---

[23] For a discussion of Penn's political philosophy and activity during this period and his relationship with James II, see Scott Sowerby, 'Of different complexions: religious diversity and national identity in James II's toleration campaign', *English Historical Review*, 124 (2009), 29–52; Mary K. Geiter, *William Penn* (Harlow, 2000), pp. 59–63.

[24] Moïse Amyraut, *Discours sur la Souverainete des Rois* (1650); Brian G. Armstrong, *Calvinism and the Amyraut Heresy: Protestant Scholasticism and Humanism in Seventeenth-Century France* (Madison, 1969), p. 115. Penn's views were part of a larger religious controversy over Protestant scholasticism and Calvinistic humanism that raged across Europe during the seventeenth century. For a detailed discussion of the effects of this controversy on English politics see John Coffey, *Politics, Religion and the British Revolutions: The Mind of Samuel Rutherford* (Cambridge, 1997), pp. 12–121, 140–5. Amyraut's influence on Penn has been underestimated and requires further research.

Penn did not go so far as to support exclusion itself. This was the case during his involvement during the elections of 1679–80 when, although he backed Sidney as evidenced by his 1679 polemic, *England's Great Interest in the Choice of this New Parliament*, he believed, as Amyraut did, that religious dissent and support for the monarchy were not mutually exclusive. Combined with this and Penn's emulation of Amyraut's view on salvation, accusations of Socinianism and papist leanings were hurled at him. Penn defended himself, albeit somewhat provocatively, by acknowledging that he was a Catholic, 'tho not a Roman'.[25]

Penn hoped to revive what Cromwell failed to achieve, a long-lasting successful political and religious settlement, not in Britain but in Pennsylvania.[26] However, like Cromwell, who believed in the institution of parliament yet had problems in finding common ground with his parliaments, Penn found difficulties with his colonial assembly in reaching a consensus. The disputes between a proprietary party and its opponents became a commonplace of Pennsylvania politics during this period. Yet if there are similarities in their failure to establish political stability, Penn's quest for a stable religious settlement based on liberty of conscience was, unlike Cromwell's, to a large extent a success.

Penn's 'holy experiment' had many of the same hallmarks as Cromwell's proposals for religious liberty. He was seeking to establish a society tolerant towards religious diversity. Pennsylvania became a byword for the peaceful coexistence of sects that were deadly rivals elsewhere, not least in the mother country. Again like Cromwell, Penn operated from the assumption that fundamental law was essential to a stable society. To his mind, the fundamental laws, based on Magna Carta, rested on the notion of, and were synonymous with, English liberties. These liberties emanated from the idea of natural rights. Implied in this is the notion of civil rights. On several occasions Cromwell articulated these ideas in his speeches to the Protectorate parliaments. 'Liberty of conscience is a natural right', he said, warning his parliament that if they did not adhere to this principle they, too, would suffer persecution.[27] This sentiment was expressed in the James Nayler case, where Cromwell warned the House that Nayler's fate might well be theirs.[28] The barbaric punishment meted out to Nayler by the second Protectorate Parliament for his blasphemy in entering Bristol on a donkey, in imitation of Christ's

---

[25] William Penn to John Tillotson, 29 January 1686: Penn, *Papers*, III, p. 80. He went on to say that 'Our religions are like our hats . . . the only difference lies in the ornaments which have been added to thine.'

[26] Roger Howell, Jr, 'Cromwell and his parliaments', in Richardson, *Images of Oliver Cromwell*, p. 126.

[27] As quoted in Richardson, *Images of Oliver Cromwell*, p. 165.   [28] Ibid., p. 130.

entry into Jerusalem on Palm Sunday, was long remembered, particularly by Quakers. In April 1674 Penn was to admonish somebody who 'went into a singularity at ye Miscarriage of poor James Nailer'.[29]

IV

The Restoration did not include a written constitution, as did the Republic, but the idea was not forgotten. Colonial proprietors such as Penn composed constitutions that incorporated republican ideas. The Fundamental Constitutions of Carolina (1669) contained 'commonwealth' views held by the first earl of Shaftesbury and John Locke. Not quite a decade later, in 1676, Penn, along with Edward Byllings, wrote a document in the Concessions and Agreements of West Jersey which expressed similar ideas. In 1681 he was to embody republican concepts in his own colony's constitution so that it would serve as a colonial Magna Carta. The model for Pennsylvania's Frame of Government came from a number of sources: the Maryland constitution, John Locke's proposals on how Virginia's administration should work, and the fundamental constitution of Carolina. All except Maryland were influenced by former republicans who were familiar with the *Instrument of Government* implemented in 1653. The Frame itself evolved over two decades ending with the Charter of Liberties in 1701. The evolution of the document, through some twenty drafts during the period 1681–82, reveals an idealism that increasingly becomes honed by reality. The initial intention was to devolve as much power to the colonists as possible while limiting the power of the governor. The first draft clearly sets this out, where 'An Assembly shall be duely chosen by the Freeholders of this country to serve as their deputys to consult, debate, and resolve and in their names to consent to the enacting or abolishing of laws.'[30] By the time the final draft was completed, the legislative power had moved to the council and it was not until 1701 that the assembly regained that right.

The body of the constitution is often considered as essentially Harringtonian.[31] There are, indeed, links to James Harrington's *The Commonwealth of Oceana* which had been published in 1656 and dedicated to Cromwell. For example, both *Oceana* and the Pennsylvania constitution employed the secret ballot. Key to Penn's notion of a government was having a constitution based on fundamental laws. These were unchanging, emanating from the ancient constitution based allegedly

---

[29] William Penn Letterbook, pp. 118–21.   [30] Penn, *Papers*, II, p. 144.
[31] Mary Maples Dunn, 'William Penn, classical republican', *Pennsylvania Magazine of History and Biography*, 81 (1957), 138–56.

on Englishmen's rights. On establishing this precept, there were what he called circumstantial laws or temporary laws that could be changed given their place in time.[32] Likewise, Cromwell's speeches articulated the differences between things fundamental and circumstantial: 'The government by a single person and a Parliament is a fundamental!' he informed the second Protectorate Parliament; 'In every government there must be somewhat fundamental . . . Somewhat like a Magna Carta, which should be standing, be unalterable.'[33]

The basic structure in both the *Instrument of Government* and the first draft of the Pennsylvania Frame of Government was that government would take the form of a ruler or, in the case of Pennsylvania, governor, together with a council and parliament, or assembly as it was called in the colony. Although the constitution of Pennsylvania evolved into something more restrictive, Penn, like Cromwell, was less concerned with the style of government than that the government itself was based firmly on law. In the preface to the colony's constitution, Penn even echoes Cromwell's view on the relationship between government and religion: 'that Government seems to me a part of religion itself, a thing sacred in its institution and end'. And he repeats Cromwell's argument for necessities when it came to altering government: 'I do not find a model in the world that time, place, and some singular emergencies have not necessarily alter'd; nor is it easie to frame a civil government, that shall serve all places alike.'[34]

Criticisms of the Frame were made by Penn's republican friends Algernon Sidney and Benjamin Furly. They accused Penn of losing sight of natural rights, and observed that the last draft gave him more power than the ruler of Turkey – generally regarded as the most despotic of all.[35] Furly methodically laid out the differences between the original draft and its final version. Most notably, the provision for habeas corpus was eliminated, something that, ironically, Penn had called for during the Penn-Meade trial. Furly concluded with his preference for the first draft 'as being most equall, most faire, & most agreeing with the just, wise, & prudent constitutions of our Ancestors'. He was clearly shocked by Penn's apparent turnaround and wondered to Penn, 'Who has turned

---

[32] Edward Corbyn Obert Beatty, *William Penn as Social Philosopher* (Kessinger, 2008), p. 30. Penn employed this principle in 1703, when he told his secretary James Logan to stand for the fundamental rights in argument against the crown's attempt to interfere with the colony.

[33] Cromwell, *Letters and Speeches*, III, pp. 146–7 (Cromwell's second speech to the first Protectorate Parliament).

[34] Cf. the preface of the Pennsylvania Frame of Government with Cromwell's speech to the second Protectorate Parliament.

[35] Penn, *Papers*, II, pp. 124–5.

you aside from these good beginnings to [establish] things unsavoury &
unjust as fundamental to wch all generations to come should be bound?'[36]

Penn was sympathetic to their views, but he had to contend with a
group within the Privy Council who advocated centralizing the colonies
under the crown. Hence the clauses in the Frame that gave Penn absolute
power as proprietor were intended by the Privy Council to benefit those
advocates of central control at the expense of those in the colony who
were determined to use the assembly to defend, if not to expand, their
liberties. The counsellors allowed Penn more power because they felt that
they could control him. So the Frame moved from being a liberal document to become a more restrictive one in which power largely resided
in the governor and council. Later drafts circumscribed the power of
the assembly even more, due to the influence and final say of the Privy
Council. Nevertheless, Penn employed Harringtonian principles when
he made a third of the council rotate yearly. The whole assembly would
be up for election annually and the voting would be by secret ballot.
This was in keeping with Cromwellian views that parliaments should not
perpetuate themselves. As the Protector put it, 'that Parliaments must
not make themselves perpetual is a fundamental. Of what assurance is a
law to prevent so great an evil, if it lie in the same legislature to unlaw it
again? Is such a law like to be lasting? It will be a rope of sand, it will give
no security; for the same men may unbuild what they have built.'[37] Penn
stated that 'governments were like clocks', and that all they needed was
to be wound up and they would function like a machine. However, he
was also concerned that the governors should be moral agents, without
which good government could not exist. One way to accomplish this and
to avoid corruption was to prevent legislatures becoming perpetual. In
this, he was at one with Oliver Cromwell.

Penn's constitutional ideas extended from his colony to Europe. His
Essay on the Present and Future Peace of Europe, drafted in 1693, proposed
a federation of European powers. Partly as a response to the Nine Years'
War and an attempt at mending fences with the new regime of William
and Mary, the work is visionary, presaging a kind of European Union, if
not a United Nations. At the same time Penn seemed also to be looking
in the rear-view mirror. From its outset, homage is paid to Cromwell,
although somewhat critically, in order to argue that justice, not war, is
the procurer of peace.[38] Like Cromwell, Penn was not a subscriber to

---

[36] Penn, *Papers*, II, pp. 227–38.   [37] Carlyle, III, p. 147.

[38] Penn also references Cromwell in other tracts, such as *A Perswasive to Moderation* (1685),
where he critiqued Cromwell's reasons for aligning with France: 'O. Cromwell began,
and gave him the Scale against the Spaniard. The Reason of State he went upon, was the

the divine right theory; on the contrary, subjects should be involved in the law-making process. He arrives at this by outlining the transition from a state of nature to a civil society, and recognizes that a degree of coercion is needed because, 'so depraved is human nature, that without compulsion some way or other, too many would not readily be brought to do what they know is right or fit'.[39] The document also sets out a representative model in which 'deputies' from the various states would meet in a 'General Dyet, Estates, or Parliament'[40] in order to resolve differences that may arise between countries. The model for this was conceivably the merging of the English, Irish and Scottish parliaments into a single body at Westminster during the Cromwellian era. Just as the Scots and the Irish sent thirty members each to the first and second Protectorate parliaments, so the states of Europe were allocated a number of delegates to represent them in the Diet, although Penn admitted that he had made his calculations on a rough and ready basis. Unlike the Cromwellian precedent, however, there was no question of there being a European Protector in his scheme.

V

Penn's interest in a colonial venture was also part of his larger view of England's interests in the world. Like his father, Penn's compass was steering him to eye the national concern. The national concern, as in the 1650s, was geographic and economic expansion. Therefore Penn's participation in this arena was not just confined to colonial development in Pennsylvania, where he believed that God would make his colony 'the seed of a nation'.[41] His concern for England's greatness went further, with his vision of extending English influence to the Gulf of Mexico. Here again his outlook reflected Cromwell's imperial vision.

Although New England was a Puritan and Parliamentary stronghold during the Civil Wars, Virginia and Maryland were Royalist, the latter being a Catholic colony. By the end of 1650, following the beheading of Charles I, a commission was appointed by the Rump Parliament to tackle the Royalist colonial authorities. Virginia and Maryland, as well

Support of Usurp'd Dominion: And he was not out in it; for the Exile of the Royal Family was a great Part of the Price of that Aid: In which we see, how much Interest prevails above Nature. It was not Royal Kindred could shelter a King against the Solicitations of an Usurper with the Son of his Mother's Brother.'

[39] William Penn, *An Essay towards the Present and Future Peace of Europe* (1693), p. 9.
[40] Ibid., p. 11.
[41] Jean R. Soderlund, ed., *William Penn and the Founding of Pennsylvania* (Philadelphia, 1983), p. 53.

as Bermuda and the West Indian colonies of Antigua and Barbados, were brought under the control of the Rump. When Cromwell became Lord Protector, he extended the aim of regaining Royalist colonies in North America and the West Indies to capturing Spanish possessions in the Caribbean. His Western Design of 1655 aimed at seizing Hispaniola from Spain. Led by Sir William Penn and Robert Venables, English forces attempted to take the island but were repulsed. Although they were able to take Jamaica, the failure to take the more strategically important island, which would have posed a threat to the Spanish treasure fleets, was a major setback to Cromwell's ambitions in the West Indies.

Cromwell's Western Design, as we have seen, was inspired by his belief in Providence. Spain was, to his mind, England's natural and providential enemy dating back to Elizabeth's time. Furthermore, Spain was aiding the deceased king's son, recognized by his supporters as Charles II, in trying to retake the throne. Cromwell's primary interest, preventing the restoration of the Stuarts, influenced his decision to side with the merchants whose interest lay in the Caribbean over those who were trading with Spain directly. When the latter petitioned him not to go forward with the plan to send a force to the Caribbean, since it would be detrimental to their trade, which had expanded considerably since Elizabeth's reign, he responded by leaving the outcome to Divine Providence: 'Deus providebit'. When the expedition did not succeed as he had hoped, he believed that Providence had deserted him. Unfortunately for Sir William Penn, he became the scapegoat for the failure of Cromwell's Western Design and his service to the Protectorate effectively ended. He eventually retired to his Irish estates at Macroom, County Cork, but not before a stint in the Tower.

The younger Penn's world view reflected these Cromwellian projects when he proposed several ideas for extending England's influence overseas. His draft of *A Briefe and Plaine Scheame*, written in 1697, which recommended a union of the colonies, and his own Western Design, are reminiscent of earlier plans to extend English influence.[42] Also, his use of the word 'union' is important to understanding what was intended in these undertakings. During the 1650s, Cromwell included the Scots and Irish at Westminster, thus creating a British Commonwealth. He even revived an abortive proposal by the Rump Parliament that Holland and England form a union during the negotiations leading to the Treaty of

---

[42] *A Briefe and Plaine Scheame how the English colonies in the North parts of America may be made more useful to the Crown and on another's peace and safety with an universal concurrence* (1697) was the first of a two-pronged approach to securing the defence of the colonial mainland and eliminating illegal trade.

Westminster of 1654. Like the earlier attempt, this one foundered on the refusal of the Dutch to commit themselves to it. Had it succeeded it would not only have united the English with the Dutch Republic in Europe, it would also have involved the integration of their colonies, including New Netherland. So, not only was the Caribbean theatre being concentrated on, but Cromwell was also embarking on an imperial policy which included the North American mainland. Although the main aim of the treaty was to sideline the Stuarts, thus giving it an essentially European dimension in Cromwell's great scheme of things, his idea of union had a transatlantic dimension too. He recognized the necessity of creating a coherent defence against the French in that part of the world, while at the same time expanding England's interests. This dimension was picked up by the Stuarts. Charles II acquired New Netherland from the Dutch by force, giving it to his brother, the duke of York, as a proprietary colony. When the duke succeeded Charles as James II, he created the Dominion and Territory of New England. The Dominion was a military and political solution that aimed to come to grips with the need for colonial defence against the French, as well as getting to grips with the colonists themselves by enforcing the navigation acts.

Penn continued the idea of union in his *Briefe and Plaine Scheame*, which was also partly to offset the plan of the Board of Trade and William III to continue James's Dominion, and to address the issues of colonial defence against the French and the slack enforcement of the navigation acts. So, in one sense, Penn's vision for the colonies was more sweeping than Cromwell's, but their interests in furthering England's influence were the same.

Penn's own western design was also much broader in vision than Cromwell's, since it encompassed North America and the Caribbean as a geographical entity. It was also part and parcel of the British strategic aims in the War of the Spanish Succession with a commitment to obtaining Spain and its overseas possessions for the Habsburg claimant, Charles III. To achieve these aims would have meant removing the Bourbon claimant, Philip V, from Spain and its empire. Some acknowledgment of their help by Charles would almost certainly have involved territorial concessions to Britain. Consequently, Penn put forward two proposals to achieve this. One concerned the Caribbean, the other encompassed the whole of North America and even parts of Mexico.

The West Indian plan was to ensure access to Spanish possessions by British merchants. Penn's approach was to take the opportunity of the dispute over the Spanish crown to introduce a proposal that would secure what had hitherto been unattainable. In 1709, his *Memorial about the English Interest in the West Indias* laid out recommendations for securing

English shipping as well as ensuring freedom of the seas for peaceful nations. Although reminiscent of the vision of the 1650s, he advocated less aggressive measures, although he was not averse to encouraging force if required.[43] His proposals were among several that recognized the need to succeed where Cromwell had failed, but for Penn, there was, perhaps, a more personal motive. Although Pennsylvania was heavily dependent on trade with the West Indian islands, Penn was acutely aware of his father's failure in the Caribbean. Providence perhaps gave the son another chance to succeed where his father failed.[44]

The second proposal which Penn put to the duke of Marlborough, in 1709, was to drive the French from North America and extend British boundaries west and southwards to the mouth of the Mississippi and even to acquire the Yucatan peninsula.[45] If the English could gain control of this vast area, they would then control America.[46] For this, he recognized the possibility of the use of force on the Yucatan Peninsula to defeat the supporters of Philip V. In the end, Philip V's claim to the throne of Spain and its overseas possessions was recognized in the Treaty of Utrecht. Although the British mounted an expedition to take Quebec in 1711, it proved abortive. Indeed, Penn's strategic vision for expelling the French from North America was not realized until the Seven Years' War, fifty years after he proposed it.

The notion of Penn putting forward a strategic plan to the British commander-in-chief at the height of the War of the Spanish Succession seems curiously at odds with his image as a Quaker pacifist. Yet he had to be involved in schemes of imperial strategy as the proprietor of a large and vulnerable colony in North America. There was not only the aim of expanding England's territories, something that the Pennsylvania charter acknowledges. With that expansion came the question of how to come to grips with a growing empire.[47] The number of English colonies

---

[43] Cf. J. D. Alsop, 'William Penn's West Indian peace aims of 1709', *Journal of Caribbean History*, 19 (1984), 68–75. Alsop claims that Penn's peace initiative was limited in its objectives concerning the Caribbean. Geiter, *William Penn*, p. 139; BL, Add. MS 61366, fos. 179–82, 192 (William Penn to 'My Noble Friend [the Duke of Marlborough]', [May] 1709).

[44] There was even a rumour during this time that he was to be made governor of Jamaica: *Remarks and Collections of Thomas Hearne*, 4 vols. (Oxford, 1884–97), II, p. 217 (28 June 1709). Although Hearne mistakenly gave Penn a knighthood, like his father, he does identify him as the leader of the Quakers.

[45] BL, Add. MS 61366, fos. 191, 192.

[46] *Correspondence of Colonel Hooke*, ed. W. D. Macray, 2 vols. (1870–1), I, pp. 6, 8 (Memoirs of the Marquis of Torcy, 18 February 1703).

[47] Pennsylvania Charter, 1681: 'Whereas our trustie and well beloved subject William Penn Esquire sonne and heir of Sr. William Penn deceased out of a commendable desire to enlarge our English Empire and promote such usefull commodities as may be of benefit

acquired during the seventeenth century increased, with the acquisition of Jamaica, the Carolinas, New York, New Jersey and Pennsylvania. How to assimilate these territories into an English polity was an imperial problem. Morrill discusses this concern in his consideration of 'the British problem'. In his view the American colonies do not fit into this three kingdoms approach, which encompasses England, Scotland and Ireland. For example, comparisons drawn by some colonists and later historians between the American Indians and the native Irish break down.[48] A crucial difference was that the Indians were not regarded as subjects of the British crown, whereas the Irish were.[49]

While the American dimension does not fit neatly into the three kingdoms approach, nevertheless the colonies could be considered as an extension of the British problem. Although the charters were issued by monarchs describing themselves as kings of England, Scotland and Ireland – not to mention France – the colonies they created were dominions not of the three kingdoms but of the English crown. They thus raised questions of the relationship between the three kingdoms similar to those posed by the British problem. They were, after all, called plantations, a term which was used in Ireland and even in Scotland. Thus a direct analogy can be drawn between the North American colonies and the Ulster plantations populated by English and Scottish settlers. As Jane Ohlmeyer observes, 'Ireland, the Borders and the Highlands and Islands all served in some degree or other as "laboratories" of Empire'.[50] The colonies had seats of government comparable with Dublin, such as Philadelphia in Pennsylvania. Significantly, Penn referred to the area around Philadelphia as the Anglo-Irish referred to that around Dublin, as the Pale. He was well aware that the colonies were an integral part of a British context. Perhaps the most telling instance of this was when he prophesied that what James, duke of York, was up to in New York would be

---

to us'. Stephen Saunders Webb, 'The peaceable kingdom: Quaker Pennsylvania in the Stuart empire', in Dunn and Dunn, *World of William Penn*, pp.173–95. Webb uses the evolution of the granting of the Pennsylvania Charter to illustrate the transition from granting charters based on personal motives to recognizing the implications of a growing empire.

[48] Nicholas Canny, *Kingdom and Colony: Ireland and the Atlantic World, 1560–1800* (Baltimore, 1988); Morrill, 'British problem', pp. 12–14.

[49] Morrill, 'British problem', pp. 1–38. Compare Nicholas Canny, who points out that English colonial promoters under James I aimed at making Indians the king's vassals. Nicholas Canny, 'England's New World and the Old, 1480s–1630s', in Nicholas Canny, ed., *The Oxford History of the British Empire, Volume One: The Origins of Empire* (Oxford, 1998), pp. 148–69, at pp. 156–8. Penn, however, regarded the Indians not as subjects of the English crown but as independent agents with whom he had to negotiate.

[50] Jane H. Ohlmeyer, 'Colonization within Britain and Ireland', in Canny, ed., *Oxford History of the British Empire, Volume One*, pp. 124–47, at p. 146.

implemented in Britain when he became king. Just as the rule of the earl of Strafford in Ireland under Charles I had been cited as a precedent for what the king intended to impose on his English subjects, so James's arbitrary government of his proprietary colony was taken to be 'the schem & draught in litle of his admin[istrati]on of old England at large if the Crown should ever divolve upon his head'.[51] The problem for the English was how to establish a framework that would accommodate these differences, whether they were in Ireland or America.

The case of Pennsylvania demonstrates that the British government had learned lessons from earlier colonial experiments, and applied them in ways that were representative of the British problem. Each colony was independent from the other with cultural and sometimes linguistic differences. Before Penn acquired his colony, settlers from Scandinavia and the Netherlands inhabited the area. The arrival of English settlers increased this cultural complexity. Also to be considered were the Indians, whose own multicultural make-up added to the ethnic diversity. Moreover, in their case, the Charter made the expressed aim of reducing 'the savage natives by gentle and just manners to the love of civil society and Christian Religion'.[52] Prior to Penn's colonial enterprise, English colonial development posed problems with the native population. This was true from the outset at Jamestown to Bacon's Rebellion and King Philip's War. Therefore there was the issue of how to assimilate the other cultures into the English polity. Penn's approach was twofold, aimed at bringing some kind of imperial framework into effect.

His dealings with the Indians are well known, representing an attempt to come to terms in a peaceful way and yet with an eye to establishing English control through alliances. The Chain of Friendship was part of the strategy to secure the east coast for England. Partly to secure Pennsylvania's role in the fur trade, but also with an imperial dimension, the treaty with the ten kings and chiefs was an attempt to keep peace between their peoples and be bound by the laws of Pennsylvania, albeit while they lived near or among the Christian inhabitants. The Indians who entered into this agreement promised not to assist any other nation, whether they were Indians or others who were not friendly towards the English government.[53] The other approach was to naturalize the non-English population. Within a year of Penn's arrival in his colony, a bill entitled the Act of Union was passed, according to which all landowners

---

[51] William Penn, *The Case of New Jersey* (*c.*1680), p. 10.
[52] Pennsylvania Charter.   [53] Geiter, *William Penn*, p. 136.

in the colony had three months in which to swear allegiance to the king of England and obedience to Penn.[54]

VI

The career of William Penn sheds light on several problems posed by scholars investigating seventeenth-century British history. As we have seen, it tends to support the thesis that the second half of the century witnessed the growth of a secular outlook. Penn's initial religious enthusiasm cooled into a political pragmatism. He sought relief from persecution not only for Quakers but for all Dissenters, and even came around to extending it to Catholics and Jews. However, his ideological move towards full civil rights was piecemeal, partly because of the difficulty in coming to grips with what lay in the secular arena and what should remain in the spiritual realm.[55] This was very evident in his attitude to slavery. While a segment of the Quaker society was against it, noting that it was immoral, and possibly too worldly, Penn had a more guarded view, grounded in the reality of the political situation which he inherited when he became a colonial proprietor. Prior to his acquiring the colony, the European settlers already there owned slaves. The duke's laws of 1676 provided that Christians could not be kept in 'Bondslavery, villainage or captivity, except such who shall be judged thereunto by Authority'.[56] This left the door open to slaveholding.[57] Although the laws were superseded by the *Laws of Pennsylvania* when the colony was turned over to Penn, there was no effort, at least on his part, to abolish slavery, only to ensure that those in service be treated justly.[58] The proprietor, in fact, owned slaves himself and encouraged using them on his own plantation because they

---

[54] Penn, *Papers*, II, p. 337 (Document 97: Naturalization of Swedish Inhabitants, 11 January 1683). The Act of Union was passed on 7 December 1682.

[55] Penn tried to define this notion in Pennsylvania's *Body of Laws*, which said, 'And forasmuch it is principally desired by the Proprietary and Governor and the freemen of the Province of Pennsylvania and territories thereunto belonging, to make and establish such laws as shall best preserve true Christian and Civil Liberty, in opposition to all Unchristian, Licentious, and unjust practices (Whereby God may have his due, Caesar his due, and the people their due)' (7 December 1682).

[56] *Duke's Laws*, 22 September 1676.

[57] While the *Laws* do not single out blacks for enslavement, the fact that the duke of York was involved in the Royal African Company, a slave-trading enterprise, is indicative of his attitude towards slavery and perhaps explains this particular clause.

[58] *Laws of Pennsylvania*, p. 102, clause 29, 'That servants be not kept longer than their time', implies a distinction between indentured servitude and slavery; Benjamin Furly's critique of Pennsylvania's Frame of Government included advice on the manumission of slaves after eight years' service in that colony: Penn, *Papers*, II, p. 235. Apparently Penn did not take his recommendation.

were less problematic than indentured servants and because 'it were better they were blacks, for then a man has them while they live'.[59] Thus the 'holy experiment', if taken in the context of civil liberties, as well as liberty of conscience, was a qualified success. It can be said to have succeeded, however, as we have seen, in its realization of religious toleration. Penn's advocacy of it and its implementation in Pennsylvania realized an aspiration of Oliver Cromwell's for Britain.

Penn's imperial outlook reflected the expansionist vision of the Interregnum, encapsulated in Harrington's phrase that 'this is a Commonwealth for increase'. Indeed, his own conception of Pennsylvania as a commonwealth was a significant link with the Cromwellian era. Thus Penn's colony contained a strong dose of the republican spirit, if not of the good old cause.

---

[59] Penn, *Papers*, III: William Penn to James Harrison, 25 October 1685; William Penn to James Harrison, 27 November 1685; William Penn to James Harrison, 4 December 1685.

13 Irish bishops, their biographers and the experience of revolution, 1656–1686

John McCafferty

> God testifying of his gifts: and by it he being dead yet speaketh.
>
> Hebrews 11:4.

This verse from St Paul's letter to the Hebrews was only one of several scriptural texts that sustained the composition and publication of a growing number of funeral sermons and episcopal biographies in Stuart Britain and Ireland. The events of the 1640s and 1650s and the Restoration fused a long-standing tradition of writing about the English Reformation and its consequences with a debate about the legacies of the Civil Wars. During these decades the kingdom of Ireland experienced acute violence and vast transfers in landholding along ethnic and confessional lines. Its church as by law established endured attack and proscription, and then emerged as the defensive cornerstone of a hoped-for Protestant ascendancy.

Between 1656 and 1686 six printed and manuscript works commemorated the lives, deaths and publications of three Irish bishops, William Bedell, John Bramhall and James Ussher. Taken as a group they represent an evolving set of responses to tumultuous events worked out in the lives of individual church leaders. The series began with Nicholas Bernard's 1656 *The life and death of the most reverend and learned father of our church, Dr James Ussher.* This was a hugely extended version of a funeral sermon preached by Bernard at Westminster Abbey on 17 April 1656. William Bedell had died in early 1642, but his son and namesake's memoir, 'Life and death of William Bedell', was not composed until at least 1659.[1] Bedell's son-in-law, Alexander Clogie, wrote his *Speculum Episcoporum* in the mid-1670s.[2] In 1676 John Vesey, bishop of Limerick,

---

[1] The most accessible and best edition of both William Bedell junior and Alexander Clogie is E. S. Shuckburgh, ed., *Two Biographies of William Bedell* (1902). It contains a reference (p. 37) to Nicholas Bernard's *Certain discourses, viz. of Babylon (Rev. 18. 4.) unto which is added a character of Bishop Bedel* (1659).

[2] Thomas Wharton Jones, ed., *A True Relation of the Life and Death of the Right Reverend Father in God, William Bedell* (1872), p. 216; see also Karl Bottigheimer, 'The hagiography

prefaced Bramhall's collected works with a forty-three page work entitled *Athanasius Hibernicus or, the life of the most reverend father in God, John Lord Archbishop of Armagh*. In 1685 Gilbert Burnet marked the accession of James II and his own French exile with the *Life of William Bedell DD, bishop of Kilmore in Ireland*. This was a version of Clogie's earlier biography beefed up with correspondence and supporting documents. Finally, one year later, in 1686, Richard Parr's *Life of the most reverend father in God James Ussher . . . with a collection of three hundred letters* made it to press. Written over a span of three turbulent decades in British and Irish history these biographies have been singularly successful, in that both their tone and characterization of leading ecclesiastical figures have dominated all writing about the established church in Stuart Ireland.

It is important to locate these texts within a larger body of writing – encomiastic, controversial and historical – about their subjects and their churchmanship.[3] The deaths of Ussher and Bramhall occasioned John Quarles's *Elegie* (1656), Jeremy Taylor's *Funeral sermon* (Dublin, 1663) and Dudley Loftus's *Oratio Funebris* (Dublin, 1663). In addition, the Irish Articles of 1615, the Dublin convocation of 1634 and Laud and Wentworth's handling of the Irish church featured prominently in a roughly three-cornered pamphlet war between Nicholas Bernard, Hamon L'Estrange and Peter Heylyn.[4] At the close of the 1650s John Bramhall himself was moved to attack both Bernard and Heylyn for their treatment of his career during the 1630s.[5] Heylyn's own posthumously published biography of William Laud, *Cyprianus Anglicus* (1668), treated the Irish church through the lens of his subject and clearly

of William Bedell', in T. C. Barnard, D. Ó Croinín and K. Simms, eds., *A Miracle of Learning* (Aldershot, 1998), pp. 201–8.

[3] Jessica Martin, *Walton's Lives: Conformist Commemorations and the Rise of Biography* (Oxford, 2001), esp. chs. 1–3; John Spurr, '"A special kindness for dead bishops": the Church, history, and testimony in seventeenth-century Protestantism', *Huntington Library Quarterly*, 68 (2005), 313–34; Kevin Sharpe and Steven Zwicker, eds., *Writing Lives: Biography and Textuality, Identity and Representation in Early Modern England* (Oxford, 2008).

[4] Anthony Milton, *Laudian and Royalist Polemic in Seventeenth-Century England: The Career and Writings of Peter Heylyn* (Manchester, 2007), ch. 5; John McCafferty, *The Reconstruction of the Church of Ireland: Bishop Bramhall and the Laudian reforms 1633–1641* (Cambridge, 2007), pp. 108–11; Alan Ford, *James Ussher: Theology, History and Politics in Early-Modern Ireland and England* (Oxford, 2007), pp. 88–91, 233–4. One of these texts, Heylyn's *Respondet Petrus* (1658), had a significant afterlife and still merited a thirty-three page riposte written by James Tyrell, Ussher's grandson, appended to Richard Parr's *Life* almost thirty years after its own appearance: Parr, *Life of the most reverend father in God James Ussher* (1686), the appendix occurs after p. 101 and is separately paginated. *Respondet Petrus* was a riposte to Bernard's *Judgement of the late archbishop of Armagh* (1657).

[5] A. W. Haddan, ed., *The Works of the Most Reverend Father in God, John Bramhall*, 5 vols. (Oxford, 1842–5), V, pp. 81–5, where he takes issue with their characterization of his relations with James Ussher.

influenced the title, form and much of the polemical thrust of Vesey's *Athanasius Hibernicus*. So, as each of the six lives emerged between 1656 and 1686 it did so not only in the context of its historical moment but also in the context of the historical debate of the moment.

Because readers looked for explanation as well as edification, accounts of bishops in Ireland needed to say something about the 'Irish problem'. Accordingly, each of the three bishops had characteristics which permitted their lives to serve to illustrate points about the trajectory of English reformation in the island kingdom.

Bedell, the quasi-martyr, was the oldest, being born in 1571.[6] He had an impeccable godly education at Emmanuel College, Cambridge, which when coupled with his service in Sir Henry Wotton's embassy in Venice evoked a Jacobean springtime when it seemed (to true believers at least) that the Church of England model might go international. Viewed from the 1670s and 1680s this was an idyll which pointed to the realms of possibility opened up by a proper godly king. Bedell's Irish-language interests could be comfortably contained and deployed as an evangelical rebuke to Laudian laxism and Caroline toleration in 1630s Ireland.

Born in 1580, Ussher was no hidden gem like Bedell, but rather someone whose living reputation was very considerable. This rendered him hot property.[7] He offered godly integrity and immensity of learning which could be used to invest his more political stances, such as his loyalty to the crown, his role in Strafford's attainder or his defence of episcopacy either with tones of great solemnity or as emblems of the grim necessities forced on individuals by the Civil Wars. When yoked together with his Dublin birth, Ussher's international reputation gave fertile ground for speculation whether he was best understood as an instance of gold among the dross or as some harbinger of eventual Protestant triumph in Ireland. Finally, he was both prophet and sufferer.

John Bramhall, the youngest of the trio, was born in 1594. His very prominent role in church government in the 1630s made him attractive to those who wished to lay the blame for much of what happened during the Personal Rule at the door of one 'bad' bishop – William Laud. But it also made him equally attractive to those who wanted to cast him as the spiritual father of Anglican ascendancy in Ireland.[8] By the 1670s and 1680s Bramhall's own depiction of himself and Ussher as 'candles

---

[6] Karl S. Bottigheimer and Vivienne Larminie, 'Bedell, William (*bap.* 1572, *d.* 1642)', *ODNB*. See also Aidan Clarke, 'Bishop William Bedell (1571–1642) and the Irish reformation', in Ciaran Brady, ed., *Worsted in the Game: Losers in Irish History* (Dublin, 1989), pp. 61–72; and Alan Ford, 'The Reformation in Kilmore before 1641', in Raymond Gillespie, ed., *Cavan: Essays on the History of an Irish County* (Dublin, 1995), pp. 73–98.

[7] Alan Ford, 'Ussher, James (1581–1656)', *ODNB*.

[8] See Jeremy Taylor in Haddan, *Works of . . . John Bramhall*, I, p. lxxv.

in the levitical temple, looking one towards the other' had stuck fast as their paired lives became key to defenders of the Church of Ireland who battled with resurgent Catholicism and enduring Dissent.[9]

James Ussher died in 1656, John Bramhall in 1663 and William Bedell in 1642, in times respectively of burgeoning republic, restoration and civil war. Earlier (from 1634 to 1642) they were bishops of Armagh, Derry and Kilmore, operating together in the one ecclesiastical province during Thomas Wentworth's viceroyalty. They knew each other and all of them appear, in varying guises, in each of the six biographies. In Clogie's *Speculum episcoporum*, for instance, James Ussher appears as the 'famous Dr Usher, primate of all Ireland, that had heard great things of him [Bedell]'.[10] Some pages later he is, notwithstanding his fame and accomplishment, a hopeless procrastinator presiding over a broken system of ecclesiastical courts.[11] Clogie himself noted approvingly that Bramhall had, at Bedell's prompting, condemned the shambolic glebeland allocations of the Ulster plantation. Later on, though, Clogie gives a dark hint that John Bramhall narrowly escaped, due to the rebellion of 1641, arraignment for sodomy.[12] It is in this interplay of biographer, subject and interpretation that a set of evolving, often overlapping, responses to war and revolution can be discerned.

Each author (with the exception of Burnet) claimed direct personal knowledge of their subject. This had two functions. First, and obviously, it validated the author's claim to be a biographer by becoming part of the life story himself. Second, it allowed insertion of first-hand witness, reported speech, testimony of other contemporaries and 'authenticated' use of privileged materials such as diaries, letters and notes.[13] For these reasons their own biographies are of significance.

Nicholas Bernard met Ussher for the first time in 1624.[14] When he preached the funeral sermon in 1656 he was almoner to Oliver Cromwell.[15] Bernard's *Life* ends with a list of Ussher's writings, which has been viewed, quite correctly, as an attempt to establish a canon of

---

[9] Haddan, *Works of . . . John Bramhall*, V, p. 74.
[10] Shuckburgh, *Two Biographies*, p. 92.   [11] Ibid., pp. 117–18.   [12] Ibid., pp. 104, 150.
[13] At the same time, each author depicted 1641 and the ensuing wars as documentary holocaust and so the lives have, to varying degrees, an ancillary purpose of attempting some archival reconstruction – whether in Parr's three hundred letters or the letters, speeches and other material reproduced in the body of the text by Bedell junior, Bernard, Burnet, Clogie and Vesey.
[14] Probably at Emmanuel College, Cambridge. Nicholas Bernard, *The life and death of the most reverend and learned father of our church, Dr James Ussher* (1656), p. 40. Bernard was ordained by the primate in 1626, became his chaplain and went on to become dean of, first, Kilmore and then Ardagh. In Kilmore he clashed repeatedly with Bedell.
[15] Ciaran Diamond, 'Bernard, Nicholas (d. 1661)', *ODNB*.

Armagh's works.[16] Yet there was another impulse at work, and it was one that led all these biographers carefully to list, discuss, part reproduce or edit the works of their subjects. This is the sense in which the printed works of the subject are 'explicitly perceived as an afterlife'.[17] In this way the living witness of the biographer and the posthumous reputation of the works reinforce each other.

William Bedell was Bishop Bedell's eldest son and was ordained deacon by him in 1634. After his father's death he fled to England, where he died in 1670.[18] He pulls back from writing pure memoir and claims to base much of his evidence on 'Bedell's own letters'.[19] Alexander Clogie, a Scot, was ordained by Bedell in 1636 and became his son-in-law in 1637: 'my interest in him was very great from the year 1636 to the captivity of the land'.[20] Having officiated at Bedell's funeral, he fled to Dublin, left for England in late 1643 and eventually settled in Hertfordshire, where he lived on until 1698. *Speculum* was clearly intended for publication, is happy to offer direct witness, and also features an epilogue in 'deposition' form detailing Clogie's refugee journey from Cavan to Drogheda in spring 1642.[21] John Vesey insisted that his biography of Bramhall had been written at the behest of Michael Boyle, archbishop of Dublin and lord chancellor of Ireland.[22] He noted that he had only known Bramhall at the very end of the latter's life. Vesey had been archdeacon of Armagh in 1662, but was writing, in 1676, as bishop of Limerick.[23] This narrative life, which ends with a 'character' of Bramhall, is designed mainly as a preface to the works but also functions as a history of the Church of Ireland. Gilbert Burnet, as already noted, did not know Bedell, and so claimed his link through Clogie. He maintained that all he had done was 'the copying out [of] what was put into my hands'.[24] Like Ussher, Richard Parr was born in Ireland, at Fermoy, Co. Cork. The

---

[16] Bernard, *Life and death*, pp. 121–3.   [17] Martin, *Walton's Lives*, p. 90.

[18] Wharton Jones, *A True Relation*, pp. 226–39. He became minister at Rattlesden, Suffolk, in 1644.

[19] Shuckburgh, *Two Biographies*, p. 23. He offered his work as 'reparation ... for the hard entertainment the world gave to this bishop while he lived' and for 'the imitation of others': ibid., p. 1.

[20] Ibid., p. 79.   [21] Ibid., pp. 210–13.

[22] John Vesey, ed., *The works of the Most Reverend Father in God, John Bramhall ... collected into one volume, in four tomes: to which is prefixt, the authour's life: and in the end is added (for the vindication of some of his writings) an exact copy of the records* (Dublin, 1676), epistle dedicatory.

[23] S. J. Connolly, 'Vesey, John (1638–1716)', *ODNB*.

[24] Gilbert Burnet, *Life of William Bedell DD, bishop of Kilmore in Ireland* (1685), sig. bv. In 1685, the translation of the Old Testament into Irish on which Bedell had been working was also published, as *Leabhuir na Seintiomna or the books of the Old Testament translated into Irish by the care and diligence of Doctor William Bedell late bishop of Kilmore in Ireland and for the publick good of that nation.*

two men met in Oxford in 1642, and Parr served as the primate's chaplain until 1655.[25] His life offers first-hand witness, private conversations and selections from private notebooks and diaries in addition to the letters. In each case, then, the polemical or explanatory thrust of the work is founded on a premise of authenticity, intimacy and privileged access.

This pervading sense of 'insider' information in a cluster of episcopal lives composed in slightly varying but broadly similar formats by English, Scots and Irish-born writers explains how they became so standard that the new biographers and editors who appeared in the nineteenth century as part of the ferment caused by the Oxford Movement and looming Irish disestablishment chose the same subjects. The *Library of Anglo-Catholic theology* reissued Bramhall's works from 1842 to 1845.[26] Charles Elrington created a definitive new biography as a preface to a seventeen-volume edition of Ussher's works published from 1847 to 1864.[27] Eighteenth-century reprints of Burnet gave way to H. J. Monck Mason's admiring 1843 biography.[28] There was also a print edition of Clogie in 1862, and an 1873 edition of Bedell junior with a large antiquarian apparatus. Finally, in 1902 Cambridge University Press published an edition of both lives of Bedell.[29] In the twenty-first century the three bishops maintain their gravitational pull. Bedell was the subject of a short biography published in 2001 focusing on his Irish translations.[30] Then, in 2007, Ussher received a full-length biography and Bramhall a biography to 1641. In the same year there was also a substantial, partly biographical study of Bramhall and Hobbes and a dual, theologically focused, biography of Ussher and Bramhall.[31]

---

[25] Richard Parr, ed., *Life of the most reverend father in God James Ussher . . . with a collection of three hundred letters* (1686), p. 6. Loyal to the king, Parr was vicar of Camberwell, Surrey, from 1653 until he died in 1691. Alan Ford, 'Parr, Richard (1616/17–1691)', *ODNB*. Ford notes that Parr had 'considerable difficulty in getting the book past the censors. Faced with a considerable delay he appealed to Archbishop Sancroft, but eventually had to make a series of cuts, removing offending passages.'

[26] A. W. Haddan, ed., *The Works of the Most Reverend Father in God, John Bramhall*, 5 vols. (Oxford, 1842–5), although they omitted Vesey's *Athanasius*.

[27] C. E. Elrington, *The Whole Works of . . . James Ussher*, 17 vols. (Dublin, 1847–64).

[28] H. J. Monck Mason, *The Life of William Bedell, D.D., Lord Bishop of Kilmore* (1843).

[29] For a full account and discussion of the publishing history, see Karl Bottigheimer, 'The hagiography of William Bedell', in T. C. Barnard, D. Ó Cróinín and K. Simms, eds., *A Miracle of Learning* (Aldershot, 1998), pp. 201–8.

[30] Terence McCaughey, *Dr Bedell and Mr King: The Making of the Irish Bible* (Dublin, 2001).

[31] Ford, *James Ussher*; McCafferty, *Reconstruction*; Nicholas Jackson, *Hobbes, Bramhall and the Politics of Liberty and Necessity: A Quarrel of the Civil Wars and Interregnum* (Cambridge, 2007); Jack Cunningham, *James Ussher and John Bramhall: The Theology of Two Irish Ecclesiastics of the Seventeenth Century* (Aldershot, 2007).

Most of the nineteenth-century and all of the twenty-first-century authors just mentioned have been concerned to produce scholarly work which further contextualizes and interprets the lives and careers of their subjects. As a result these Irish Protestant lives have become, in the main, source materials decoupled from the contours and trajectories of their composition and dissemination.[32] In a recent article Kevin Sharpe and Steven Zwicker discuss changing fashions in biographical writing and note an interesting effect: 'civil war and revolution not only and inevitably wrote and rewrote lives as texts of party and cause, they fashioned a desire, an appetite and market for lives, old and new, a market which printers and publishers rushed to satisfy'.[33] The six episcopal lives under consideration were, in part, creatures of the market and so offered a combination of rewriting and familiar staples which both enticed and reassured their readership. Episcopal lives drew from many roots – Plutarchan, Erasmian and Lutheran, the funeral sermon and the encomium. Above all, and in common with most early modern life writing, they had exemplary purpose, as Nicholas Bernard told the reader at the very outset: 'the writing of the lives of holy and eminent men departed are for us surviving (as a father saith) *veluti speculum, exemplum, condimentum*, as a glass to trim our lives by, a copy to improve our hands, a sauce to sharpen our tastes of the heavenly gift in them: by which, as after a manner, the persons themselves live with us after their deaths'.[34] His 'father', adroitly enough, is Bernard of Clairvaux writing at the beginning of his life of St Malachy of Armagh, Ussher's eleventh-century predecessor. While these men are worthy of imitation their own virtues are innate, are manifested in childhood and remain constant throughout their lives.[35] Such apparent flaws as a hot temper can be rationalized and even celebrated as zeal or disgust for vice.[36] Yet all bishops are pushed through the strainer of 1 Timothy 3. Wherever the three Irish bishops lay, or were deemed to lie, on the ecclesiological and theological spectrum, their varied biographers are careful to make them husbands of one wife, heads of godly households, free yet sober in conversation, grave countenanced, plain in dress and diet, careful in their choice of ministers.[37] On top of

---

[32] Some critique of the lives as source material has been attempted, most recently in Cunningham, *James Ussher*, pp. 20–2; Ford, *James Ussher*, pp. 227–30; McCafferty, *Reconstruction*, pp. 108–12.

[33] Sharpe and Zwicker, *Writing lives*, p. 19.   [34] Bernard, *The life and death*, sig. A3, r–v.

[35] Bernard, *The life and death*, pp. 23, 31, 105–6; Parr, *Life*, p. 3; Shuckburgh, *Two Biographies*, p. 4; Martin, *Walton's Lives*, pp. 43–5.

[36] Martin, *Walton's Lives*, p. 62; Parr, *Life*, p. 80.

[37] See inter alia, Bernard, *The life and death*, pp. 57, 58, 84–5; Shuckburgh, *Two Biographies*, pp. 17–19, 71, 106, 107, 108, 155; Parr, *Life*, pp. 79, 85–6, 87–8.

all this they are 'dead bishops'.[38] Beginning with Luther's own demise, much weight was placed on proper deathbed deportment, valediction and blessings in pursuit of an assurance that the Protestant divine was saved.

Bernard's Ussher slips away privately, contritely, without much fuss, having expressed a wish to die like William Perkins.[39] The state funeral which follows emphasizes his non-partisan stature. This was not enough for Richard Parr, who could not overturn Bernard's well-established narrative, but who also offered a near-deathbed in St Donat's, Glamorgan, in 1645. Here Parr enters into a set of conversations with the archbishop which touch on three of the dominant motifs of the life – condemnation of rebellion, the primate's ingrained scholarliness and his visceral royalism.[40] This then freed Parr to treat Ussher's actual death and funeral as an opportunity to attack the parsimony and duplicity of Oliver Cromwell.[41] William Bedell also had his death adjusted according to taste. His son states that his father was reduced to 'panting' and said succinctly, 'Be of good cheer, be of good cheer: whether we live or die, we are the Lord's.'[42] Edifyingly simple, but not sufficient for Clogie, who gives a deathbed speech created from a dense weave of scripture, creed and spiritual testament.[43] In every text, then, dying, death and the funeral are just as much an executive summary of the written life as they are the end point of the 'real' life.

The life and death of each bishop also functions as an argument for episcopacy. Besotted with the ancient church and its fathers, Bedell, Bramhall and Ussher and their biographers fashioned a lineage for themselves which gave their lives a three-dimensional pedigree – scriptural, patristic and reformed.[44] Ussher is paired with or compared to Samuel, Peter, Paul, Athanasius, Augustine, Patrick, Malachy, Richard Fitzralph and William Perkins;[45] Bedell to Noah, Moses, Elijah, Jeremiah, David, Daniel, Caleb, Augustine, Calvin and Zwingli;[46] Bramhall to Aaron, Abiathar, Daniel, Elisha, Paul, Athanasius, Augustine, Aquinas, Richard Fitzralph and Cranmer.[47] In this way the author places the subject in a cloud of witnesses that transcends space and time. This, in turn,

---

[38] Spurr, '"A special kindness for dead bishops"', 313–34.

[39] Bernard, *The life and death*, p. 110.   [40] Parr, *Life*, pp. 60–2.

[41] Ibid., pp. 78–9.   [42] Shuckburgh, *Two Biographies*, p. 73.

[43] As with Ussher's public funeral, Bedell's corpse's treatment at the hands of the Irish testifies to his saintly stature: Shuckburgh, *Two Biographies*, pp. 198–202, 204–6.

[44] Bernard, *The life and death*, pp. 29, 42; Parr, *Life*, pp. 12, 96, 98; Shuckburgh, *Two Biographies*, p. 3; Vesey, *The works*, sig. f2r, nr.

[45] Bernard, *The life and death*, pp. 3–4, 8, 22, 34, 35, 38, 40, 110–13; Parr, *Life*, p. 80.

[46] Shuckburgh, *Two Biographies*, pp. 92, 100, 106, 124, 155, 175, 188, 196, 203.

[47] Vesey, *The works*, sig. f3r, k1v, m1v, nr, n1v, p1v, qr.

heightens the significance of the individual life when placed in the more messy context of its own time and that of the biographer.[48]

The three bishops are dead men speaking through the mouths of their biographers. They speak on various dates of composition and publication. So while appreciation of the generic qualities of the biographies exposes the dangers of reading them as plain source material, a consideration of the works in their chronological sequence opens up further perspectives. Bedell, Bramhall and Ussher served together, as already noted, in the 1630s, yet the first Irish bishop of their cohort to 'speak' through a posthumous work was John Atherton, bishop of Waterford and Lismore, hanged for sodomy in December 1640. Nicholas Bernard's *Penitent death of a woeful sinner* (Dublin, 1641) was written at Ussher's request as a riposte to an anonymous lurid verse sketch which depicted Atherton as a crook and insatiable sex monster.[49] *Penitent death* is a plea for episcopacy despite the sins of one bishop and because of the virtues of another. As Bernard fawns over Ussher in the dedication, 'your own picture by which, if others in this age had been drawn, I believe the office had never been so much as questioned'.[50] Atherton only comes to true confession when he acknowledges that his sins as hierarch – law business, aggressive jurisdiction, convocation demeanour – are as great as his fleshly sins.[51] Bernard's message is simple. It is that while 'proper' episcopacy could have prevented turmoil, 'disordered' episcopacy hastened it. Bernard's *Life and death* was *Penitent death*'s direct descendant and is the text to which all other five lives refer without fail. It was the only one to retain a sermon form.[52] It maintained, quite conventionally, that its subject was a living sermon, but James Ussher is not just another bishop.[53] He is a prophet. Once ordained, he speaks, predicting in 1601 a chastisement forty years later. Once released his prescience grows and grows, and the bishop sees all.[54] This trait not only underscored the centrality of war

---

[48] Accordingly, great care was taken in choice of associate for each subject. For example, Parr connected Ussher to Henry Hammond and others whose importance was only manifest in a Restoration retrospect: Parr, *Life*, pp. 49, 64. Occasionally the historical record required adjustment for auctorial reasons. Nicholas Bernard omitted Ussher's provision to the see of Carlisle in 1642 and Charles I's execution in its entirety. Richard Parr erased Ussher's more godly English contacts. Bedell junior pared down his father's Venetian years to the bone, and Alexander Clogie did the same for Bedell's provostship of Trinity College Dublin.

[49] *The life and death of John Atherton lord bishop of Waterford ... who for incest buggery* (1641); Peter Marshall, *Mother Leakey and the bishop* (Oxford, 2007), chapters 4 and 5.

[50] Nicholas Bernard, *The penitent death of a woefull sinner* (Dublin, 1641), sig. ¶ 1v.

[51] Bernard, *The penitent death*, pp. 15–17, 27–8; McCafferty, *Reconstruction*, pp. 154–5.

[52] The biography is bracketed by an exegesis of 1 Samuel 25, i, and a final blessing.

[53] Bernard, *The life and death*, pp. 16–17; Martin, *Walton's Lives*, p. 24.

[54] Bernard, *The life and death*, pp. 64, 66, 89, 90.

and rebellion to this life but also meant that Ussher's positions on church government, the Prayer Book, toleration and other matters were covered in a mantle of prophecy. In Bernard's primate the distinction between opinion and prediction is deliberately collapsed.

The sin alleged to have prompted divine retribution in 1641 was one of toleration. For Ussher recusancy was a family affair, since his uncle Richard Stanihurst and, according to Bernard, his own mother had opted for the Roman communion. The account of Ussher's stand against limited toleration in 1626 is immediately prefaced by Bernard's vignette of his domestic piety. In confessionally divided Dublin, Ussher has chosen to make Protestantism his real home. Accordingly, Bernard is at pains to locate the moment of his 'serious' conversion at just ten years old.[55] Ussher's reformed credentials are enhanced by the kin from whom he has separated. His academic forays to England are also a means by which the author can situate him in a particular branch of the Protestant family. There is, for example, a deathbed visit to Christopher Goodman and arduous conference preaching to Essex ministers.[56] This firmly stamps the primate with a nostalgic Jacobethan mark borne out in Bernard's return to a familiar theme. Having praised Ussher's 'moderation, meekness, humility, ingenuity', he then fused character with creed by suggesting that his man's expedient of 1641, a scheme for modified episcopacy, could have saved the day.[57]

William Bedell the younger's 'life and death' was influenced by reading Nicholas Bernard.[58] If Bernard's Ussher was a prophet, then Bedell's Bedell was a preacher. The account of his pulpit style, of his scriptural study and of his theological opinion given towards the start of the work serve to establish the key themes for this life.[59] 'His voice was but low, his action little: but the gravity of his aspect very great.'[60] The entire text is replete with assertions of Bedell's quiet authenticity, of instances where great men eventually take note and bend to his opinions.[61] His life, like his homilizing, is understated but effective. As the narrative progresses towards a martyrdom, the prominent and powerful heed the bishop less and less and his own destruction becomes emblematic of the failure of

---

[55] Ibid., pp. 24–5, while reading Perkins.   [56] Ibid., pp. 42, 54.

[57] Ibid., p. 105. This is neatly complemented by an apocalyptic hint that Ussher as hundredth archbishop of Armagh might well be last.

[58] He had planned as early as 1643 to pen an account of his father's 'courteous usage' at the hands of the Irish rebels: William Bedell to Samuel Ward, 12 June 1643, Wharton Jones, ed., *A true relation of the life and death*, pp. 229–31.

[59] Shuckburgh, *Two Biographies*, pp. 6–8.   [60] Ibid., p. 6.   [61] Ibid., p. 35.

Charles I and his courtiers to read the signs of the times.[62] Only just over one third of the text is given to the years 1571–1629, so that the great bulk of it is concentrated on the final thirteen episcopal years of his life. The themes selected by the younger Bedell for the pre-Kilmore years are chosen to heighten the sense of unity in the life. For instance, the perfunctory account of the Venice years reads as an apprenticeship for Ireland – 'a singular opportunity to become acquainted with the mysteries of papal iniquity' – while simultaneously learning a new language.[63] There is also the heady prospect of persuading Catholic clerics who are *naturaliter* Protestant to give up the error of their ways.[64] Translation and conversion go on to become the bijou triumphs of the failure that was Kilmore diocese in the 1630s. In the same way Bedell's early clash with Bishop Jegon of Norwich prefigures his contretemps over jurisdiction with Ussher and his own chancellor Allan Cooke. That latter incident gives rise to one of the author's rare recourses to a scriptural parallel: 'no man stood with me but all men forsook me'.[65] Otherwise the life virtually eschews scriptural and patristic allusion. This may well be a deliberate strategy in a life whose dominant theme is of a brave man isolated against the odds, in which Bishop Bedell, like his grandfather the Marian exile, professes his evangelical faith overseas.[66] Even the apparently respectful demeanour of the Irish rebels at his funeral further isolates him as the only Englishman to be so treated.[67]

Clogie's Bedell is less suffering servant and more *speculum episcoporum*: 'this good, evangelical and primitive bishop'.[68] This was a much longer and, through Burnet's edition, a vastly more influential work. As with Bedell junior, the early years set the tone, but here the Venice section is much more extensive. William Bedell is presented as an antithesis to the apostate James Wadsworth, chaplain at the Madrid embassy.[69] There is a richer harvest of converts and Clogie enters into much greater detail

---

[62] Ibid., p. 30.   [63] Ibid., pp. 8, 13.

[64] Most of the brief account of Venice is given over to a story of Jasper Despotine, Bedell's sole Italian convert: ibid., pp. 10–12.

[65] 2 Timothy 4, xvi: Shuckburgh, *Two Biographies*, p. 51.   [66] Ibid., pp. 1–2.

[67] Ibid., pp. 56–75.   [68] Ibid., p.124.

[69] Wadsworth's career ended in his conversion and consequent employment as English tutor to the Infanta. Clogie rounds off his account of the Venetian embassy with the observation that Bedell's epistolary prowess had convinced Wadsworth's son to return to the Church of England. Bedell published his correspondence with Wadsworth as *Copies of certain letters which have passed between Spain and England in matter of religion* (1624): Shuckburgh, *Two Biographies*, p. 89. See also James Wadsworth junior, *The English Spanish pilgrim* (1629), p. 78.

about Bedell's activities as translator, linguist and controversialist.[70] In the Kilmore section, direct comparisons are made between the Italian and Irish translation and conversion projects.[71] Repeated emphasis is placed on Bedell's treatment of his fellow ministers as *synpresbyteri*, which is in part another instance of nostalgia for an idealized Jacobean church, but also serves as the linchpin for a scene in which John Adamson and other Edinburgh ministers, 'great sticklers for the Scottish covenant', declare, 'What have we done? If the king will give us such bishops as this, we will beg them on our knees of him and receive them with all our hearts.'[72] So, as with Ussher, Bedell is presented as one who could have saved the day with courteous, modified episcopacy.

Yet it is reform of the Irish, not the Scots, which lies at the very heart of this text. Clogie opts for a large historical canvas, pointing to efforts of the fourteenth century to civilize the Irish 'in speech and apparel'. His Irish are the barbarian thralls of 'idolatrous priests'.[73] Bedell is the one who attempts to dispel that ignorance through use of their own tongue and in doing so evokes hostility and envy.[74] He is eulogized for his efforts in a unique fusion of Isaiah 57:7 and article twenty-four of the Thirty-Nine Articles: 'whose feet were shod with the preparation of the gospel of peace and thereby made so beautiful upon the Irish mountains, in bringing good tidings of good things and publishing salvation unto them by the scriptures to be read and understood in their own language'.[75] Clogie's intense use of parallel and comparison became even more elevated as he moved into his account of the 1641 rebellion. Here disaster is not presaged by signs and wonders but driven by a political cycle which he declares has resulted in the destruction of plantations every forty years – which is itself a nice variant on Ussher's prophecy.[76] Bedell himself, of course, had noted the signs and, equally predictably, no one had paid him any heed.[77] Then, having given an account of the October 1641 plot to seize Dublin Castle, the trajectory of the rebellion and a lavish deathbed scene, Clogie took his most ambitious encomiastic step. Cranking up from a restatement of Bedell's antipopery, he drew a direct comparison between Jesus Christ's ministry in and to Galilee with William Bedell's ministry in and to Ireland. In this closing flourish, Bishop

---

[70] Clogie incorrectly put his subject *in situ* during, rather than just after, the Interdict crisis, and, again incorrectly, has Marco Antonio de Dominis, archbishop of Spoleto, travelling to England with Bedell: Shuckburgh, *Two Biographies*, p. 87. De Dominis did not leave Italy until 1616 whereas Bedell returned home in late 1610 or early 1611.

[71] Shuckburgh, *Two Biographies*, pp. 132–3.   [72] Ibid., pp. 100, 110–13, 162.

[73] Ibid., p. 124.   [74] Ibid., pp. 125–6, 129, 134.   [75] Ibid., p. 131.

[76] Ibid., pp. 124, 167–8.   [77] Ibid., pp. 98, 100.

Bedell hovers between being an *imitatio Christi* and an *alter Christus* for Ireland.[78]

John Vesey's *Athanasius Hibernicus* evokes an exiled defender of orthodoxy, and veers sharply away from the intense personal engagement of Clogie. Written about the same time, it is a very different work. Vesey's acquaintance with Bramhall was limited, and probably happened about the time that the archbishop had suffered the first of a series of strokes.[79] The biography was published in the wake of the refusal in 1673 of James, duke of York, to take communion and just a year after the rebuilding of St Paul's had commenced.[80] This was a brittle time for the Church of England, whose public ascendancy was shot through with anxiety about a future threat from Catholicism and a present threat of toleration for dissent. It is not surprising, then, that Vesey introduced Bramhall by locating his birth (1594) in a providential framework in which recent defeat of the Armada was followed by increased threat from Protestant dissent.[81] The entire biography is saturated with jittery and defensive statements which, in turn, are connected to a broader reformation history of Britain and Ireland. When discussing Bramhall's intensive campaign for recovery of temporalities during the 1630s and 1660s, Vesey leaps back to condemn 'the mercenary doctrines' of the medieval church and leaps forward to suggest a new scheme for leasing church lands.[82] In a similar way the Irish rebellion of 1641 does not stand alone as a pre-eminent catastrophe, as in the previous lives, but is more tightly bound up with turmoil across all three kingdoms. This recurring eclipse of the subject by wider history is a strong indication that Vesey imitated more than the title of Heylyn's *Cyprianus Anglicus*. *Athanasius Hibernicus* itself often reads like a case for the defence, as Vesey repeatedly noted that his subject 'stands accused' or is 'subject to censure'.[83] In response, perhaps, to the type of criticisms levelled in *Penitent death*, Bramhall's legal and administrative acumen is carefully tied to his zeal for the Church of England, pastoral

---

[78] Ibid., p. 209.

[79] Vesey says that he wishes that his predecessor William Fuller, who had recently been transferred to Lincoln, had written his proposed biography of Bramhall: Vesey, *The works*, sig. f*r*. John McCafferty, 'John Bramhall's second Irish career, 1660–1663', in James Kelly, John McCafferty and Ivar McGrath, eds., *People, politics and power* (Dublin, 2009), pp. 16–27.

[80] John Spurr, *The Restoration Church of England* (New Haven, 1991), pp. 69–73.

[81] He made the tart observation of the 1590s that: 'I do not believe that these parties did then act by concert, though of late (if reports be true) some overtures have been made whereby the different interests of Herod and Pilate might be so far accommodated by a mutual indulgence that the Church of England might expect in a short time to have been crucified between them': Vesey, *The works*, sig. f*r* – f*v*.

[82] Ibid, sig. h*v*, p*r*.   [83] For example, ibid., sig. f1*v*, q*r*.

concern and fearless pursuit even in the face of the most powerful of the church's rights and properties.[84]

In his 1663 funeral sermon, Jeremy Taylor had made much of the confirmation of the 'Dukes of York, and Gloucester and the Princess Royal' by the exiled Bramhall.[85] By 1676 this was not the happiest image, but Vesey's general debt to Taylor is considerable, and he borrowed the latter's theme of defence of unity of the Church of England with great gusto. The Church of Ireland, Vesey explained, had under Elizabeth and James been so provoked by 'Romish fishers' that it had become a little 'sour and Calvinistical'.[86] This concern to locate John Bramhall at a judicious median point, 'the pattern of primitive antiquity', neatly marries an understanding of the Civil Wars as an outworking of faction with Vesey's own High Church leanings.[87] Repeated insistence on unity did raise the tricky old question of Ussher. There was little point in denying that the 1634 convocation had caused some friction between the two bishops, but in concluding the life with a reflection on the primatial pair Vesey made a final claim to unity within acceptable bounds of diversity: 'primate Usher his immediate predecessor was very famous in his generation, and Primate Bramhall no less. The memory of both these learned prelates will never die; their learning was not altogether in *eodem genere*; but both very extraordinary in their way.'[88]

Because it is an intermittently glossed version of Clogie there is little distinctive about Gilbert Burnet's *Life of William Bedell*. The interest here lies in the preface, in which Burnet explains the purpose of this project. It is all about episcopal office. The entire preface is a paean to bishops – in the early church, in the Catholic Church, in contemporary France. Then there are quick character sketches of Patrick Forbes of Aberdeen, William Forbes of Edinburgh, Andrew Boyd of Argyll and Patrick Scougal of Aberdeen.[89] Bedell and Clogie themselves only make an appearance on page 29 of a thirty-three page preface. Running to a total of almost 400 pages, Burnet's 'bare and simple relation of his

---

[84] Ibid., sig. f1*r-v*, k*v*.   [85] Haddan, *The works of . . . John Bramhall*, I, p. lxx.

[86] Vesey, *The works*, sig. i1*r*.

[87] Ibid., sig. o1*r*, and also c2*r*, h*r*, m*r*. See also D. W. Hayton, 'The High Church Party in the Irish convocation, 1703–1713', in H. J. Real and Helgard Stover-Leidig, eds., *Reading Swift* (Munich, 1998), pp. 117–40. This is further reflected in the tripartite division of the edited works under the labels 'against Romanists', 'against sectaries', and 'against Mr Hobbes'. Hobbes in this instance represented for Vesey the philosophical embodiment of revolution.

[88] Vesey, *The works*, sig. q*v*.

[89] In the case of Bishop Boyd, Burnet mirrored Clogie's contention about Bedell: 'some of the severest of them have owned to me that if there were many such bishops, they would all be episcopal': Burnet, *Life of William Bedell DD*, sig. a4.1*v*.

life' made Bedell's reputation. It was translated into French in 1687 and republished in English in 1692 and again in Dublin in 1736 and 1758. At the close of the life, Burnet excised Clogie's great flourish and replaced it with a prayer more suitable to his purpose and the concerns of a Church of England in the realm of a Catholic king, 'that all differences about lesser matters being laid down, peace and truth may again flourish, and the true ends of religion and church government may be advanced, and instead of biting, devouring and consuming one another, as we do, we may all build up one another in our most holy faith'.[90]

Coming thirty years after Nicholas Bernard, Richard Parr's *Life of . . . Ussher* was published in the tense atmosphere immediately preceding Richard Talbot's appointment as Catholic lord deputy of Ireland. Parr lost no time in attacking Bernard for omissions that he suggested were a combination of forgetting and anxiety about the likely reaction of the Cromwellian authorities. He also took exception to some of the content of Burnet's *Life*.[91] He was here to set the record straight. Liberally sprinkled with, as already noted, direct quotations and apparent extracts from Ussher's private papers, this volume of life and letters moulded the archbishop of Armagh into a new shape. Like Vesey, Parr placed his man at the centre: 'nor was his care confined only to the conversion of the ignorant Irish papist, but he also endeavoured the reduction of the Scotch and English sectaries to the bosom of the church'.[92] He deleted Ussher's godly English connections and presented the scheme for modified episcopacy as dire necessity which sprang into existence only in 1648.[93] The primate's 1631 history of predestinarian controversy, *Gotteschalcus*, is pressed into service to explain that he believed that 'men should not dogmatize in these points'.[94] This monitory note about Protestant faction fighting is immediately followed by Parr's observation that at about this time the 'Romish faction' was growing 'very prevalent'.[95]

Parr's Ussher is a royal bishop who was on intimate terms with James I and Charles I.[96] His sermons before the king during the Civil War are lovingly detailed.[97] The execution of Charles I becomes a central moment of the text, prostrating Ussher both spiritually and physically.[98] Here, the archbishop is a prophet only in a very minor key, and treatment of

---

[90] Burnet, *Life of William Bedell DD*, p. 234.   [91] Parr, *Life*, preface, p. 2.

[92] Ibid., p. 39.   [93] Ibid., p. 66.   [94] Ibid., p. 37; McCafferty, *Reconstruction*, p. 90.

[95] Parr, *Life*, p. 38.   [96] Ibid., pp. 17–18, 24, 26, 38–9.

[97] Ibid., pp. 49, 57, 69. Ussher is also brought into association with William Laud, who had dropped below view in Bernard's *Life*: Parr, *Life*, p. 40.

[98] Parr, *Life*, pp. 71–3. Parr stops short of saying so but hints strongly that Ussher began to go into irreversible decline after 1649.

Ussher's great prediction of 1641 is perfunctory.[99] His gift for foretelling is only deployed once again after Charles has been beheaded, in order to predict the downfall of Oliver Cromwell.[100] He is Augustine rather than Samuel.[101] While toleration is still the sin that sparked off 1641, its child, rebellion against the crown, is *the* manifest evil and so Ussher condemns it regularly.[102] This life also attempts a definitive account of one of the foremost scholars of the seventeenth century in its copious references to books, manuscripts and libraries and the lengthy treatment of each publication. There are purposes here beyond the descriptive. Parr dismissed Nicholas Bernard's *Judgment* as an inadequate treatment of the archbishop's intellectual profile and as a work of hearsay with no provable documentary foundation.[103] The aim here, as elsewhere in this work, is to prise the primate out of the immediate controversies and disputes of the 1640s and 1650s, and to stress his international standing and the lasting quality of his scholarly work.[104] Parr's account of the fate of Ussher's library is also a mini-history of the end of the Cromwellian regime. The books, his relics, having been purchased by the army are then transferred by Charles II to the library of Trinity College.[105] In this way, although dead, Ussher shares in the glorious restoration. As with Vesey and Burnet, the contemporary application of the life is spelled out at the very close: 'for the confutation of the adversaries of our religion, and the conviction of all those who clamour against the doctrine, government and godly worship in the Church of England'.[106]

The death dates of the three bishops read like the beginning, middle and end of one phase of what John Morrill has dubbed England's wars of religion. These six lives, with their varying emphases, functions and pre-occupations, represent overlapping reflections on that experience. Each author attempted to engage with all the uncertainties of his own times through his dead bishop, and as a result there is a discernible shift over time from Protestant hagiography to more institutional, constitutional lives. Yet with change also goes consistency, as each life remains in a familiar exemplary framework. Each life balances its subject between two polemical poles of popery and Protestant faction as particularly under-stood in terms of Ireland's sixteenth- and seventeenth-century experi-ences. In this way the lives reveal the gradual working out of an Irish Anglican sensibility, because, when viewed together, they capture an important and often overlooked time when the Irish rebellion was the fulcrum on which Irish Protestant identity rested. The Williamite wars

---

[99] Ibid., p. 9.   [100] Ibid., p. 73.   [101] Ibid., p. 80.
[102] For example, ibid., pp. 57, 61, 65.   [103] Ibid., p. 94.   [104] Ibid., pp. 95–100.
[105] Ibid., p. 102.   [106] Ibid., p. 103.

would change that for ever. These six lives were completed in a chrono-logical arc stretching from the middle of one revolution to the cusp of another. For contemporaries these were decades of uncertainty, trouble, dislocation and, not infrequently, sheer terror. In many respects these episcopal memorializations offered key reassurances. They reiterated that rebellion was the inevitable outcome of Irish incivility and papistry inter-acting with culpable toleration and botched plantations. They presented Church of England episcopacy as a safe path between the extremes which had caused civil war in Britain. The character, the innate virtues, of each bishop purported to offer a moral compass for confused consciences. Yet the particular interest of this set of lives lies in the points where aucto-rial attempts to marry personality and principle failed. In their backward glance over the lives of their subjects, the biographers provided familiar landmarks but could never filter out the tensions, anxieties and debates of their own day. Their very insistence on depicting their chosen bishops as exemplars of unity, piety, moderation and primitive episcopacy whose lives were played out in a discernible moral framework actually serves to highlight the traumatic uncertainties of the revolutionary years in the three kingdoms. Individual experience, no matter how well contextual-ized or how brilliantly articulated, can do no more than offer partial, if often vivid, insight. That is both the sweet allure and bitter aftertaste of life writing. It is why these six works were composed and it is why they are still read.

14 Religion and civil society: the place of the English Revolution in the development of political thought

Glenn Burgess

I

John Morrill brought his seminal essay on 'The religious context of the English Civil War' to an end with a flourish: 'The English Civil War', he concluded, 'was not the first European revolution: it was the last of the Wars of Religion'.[1] A decade after the words were first written, John expressed some regret that the essay had not been thought out as well as he would have liked, and had misled others about the position he held.[2] He focused particularly on the perennial difficulty of separating the religious from other contexts and causes. His flourish was not intended to claim that the Civil War was only about religion, although, as with other early modern religious wars, 'religious poles are the ones around which most other discontents formed'. But the underlying issue remained that of separating religion from other things:

There are no historians nowadays who would deny that religion was *an* important dynamic within it [the Civil War]. But many would suggest that the use of the term 'religion' itself is unhelpful . . . [R]eligion is so interpenetrated into every aspect of early modern thought, that to say that it is the religious aspects of their thought that matters in making and shaping the conflict is a tautology.[3]

These thoughts of John Morrill are the starting point for the present essay: how can the interpenetration of religion into all of early modern thought be teased apart for analysis? Is it meaningful to talk about a war of religion in a world in which politics and religion were so difficult to separate? In partial answer to these questions, I would suggest that we might approach the matter by asking how early modern thinkers themselves understood the relationship between religion and (in this case) political thought. From this perspective, the idea that the Civil War might be a war of religion is used less as a historian's retrospective judgement on

---

[1] John Morrill, *The Nature of the English Revolution* (Harlow, 1993), p. 68.
[2] Ibid., p. 34.   [3] Ibid., pp. 36–7.

270

its causation or dynamics, and more as a possible label for some positions advanced in the contests over the meaning of events that engaged contemporary participants and observers. I explore in this essay different ways in which the interaction of the political and the religious dimensions of events were conceptualized by those who lived through them. They were, of course, perfectly able to make distinctions between the temporal and the spiritual, between the demands of churches and of civil authorities, between the commands of gods and of kings. None of those distinctions is precisely a distinction between religion and politics; all of them, though, can help us to understand the degree to which, for contemporaries, the Civil War might or might not have been seen to be about religion. In taking this approach we can see, too, that the idea of a 'war of religion' would have been as contestable for them as it is for us, and that the very act of attaching meaning to events was itself a polemical strategy.

It is tempting to understand some of what will emerge in the course of this essay as evidence of a process of secularization. This process is supposed to have separated out religion from politics, and left the latter to be guided by secular considerations.[4] It is possible to question directly whether secularization of this sort occurred at all within the early modern period. The English Revolution, it might be said, had the effect of clarifying the relationship between the demands of individual conscience and those of public authority; it did not necessarily secularize people's understanding of public authority. Indeed, public authority was wielded by churches as well as by states. It remained the case after 1660, as it had been before 1640, that the established character of the Church of England inevitably gave the church an important place in the sphere of politics as well as in the sphere of religion; it remained the case through the eighteenth century that different idioms of political discourse were attached to different denominational groups, and that confessional identity was a key to understanding the varieties of political argument; it remained the case, for many at least, that politics itself could not be understood without reference to God or to providence.[5] That is as true for John Locke, who undoubtedly carried forward some of the legacy of the English Revolution, as it was for Archbishop Laud in the 1630s. Secularization, on this view, is an unhelpful concept.

---

[4] A standard account is C. John Sommerville, *The Secularisation of Early Modern England: From Religious Culture to Religious Faith* (Oxford, 1992), esp. ch. 1, ch. 9, pp. 149–53; a valuable meditation on the subject is Blair Worden, 'The question of secularisation', in Alan Houston and Steven Pincus, eds., *A Nation Transformed: England after the Restoration* (Cambridge, 2001), ch. 1.

[5] These formulations owe much to J. C. D. Clark, *English Society 1660–1832*, 2nd edn (Cambridge, 2000), esp. the introduction and ch. 1.

Be that as it may, my reasons for not casting this essay as a study of the secularizing effects on political thought of the English Revolution are rather different. The approach advocated here is rooted in the assumption that 'secularizing' arguments are very often moves in a game and not necessarily part of a long-term process. In other words, the characterization of events and the development of arguments in ways that look 'secular' often occur for local argumentative or polemical reasons, and need not be understood as indicating an underlying secularism of outlook. There is enormous complexity and subtlety to the ways in which early modern people conceptualized the interpenetration of religion and politics. In the end, much depended on the way in which God was thought to command and communicate with his human creation, but because the channels included both the natural and the supernatural, there was plenty of scope for playing alternative 'secular' and 'religious' views against one another without challenging underlying assumptions about the fundamental reliance of human politics on religion. Secular 'moves' do not have to amount to secularization. It *may* be that many moves like those explored below add up in the long term to a process, but that is a possibility that there is no need to pursue here.

In exploring these matters, I shall construct an argument that links together four case studies, each focused on one individual. The case studies can never 'prove' the validity of the argument. But they might make us aware that history is the sum of the intersecting moves made by individuals, and that looking beneath what might seem to be processes helps us to appreciate the variety and complexity of the individual thoughts and actions from which processes were constituted (and are constituted, by historians).

II

Even for those who might seem most obviously likely to understand the English Revolution as a war of religion, like the Puritan minister Stephen Marshall, things were rather more complicated. If ever there was a Puritan revolution, Marshall would seem its ideal promoter.[6] As one of the five men who wrote under the pseudonym 'Smectymnuus', Marshall threw himself into the campaign against *jure divino* episcopacy from February 1641.

---

[6] Not surprisingly, he figures prominently in William Haller's *Liberty and Reformation in the Puritan Revolution* (New York, 1955), as in Stephen Baskerville's *Not Peace but a Sword: The Political Theology of the English Revolution* (1993).

A graduate of Emmanuel College, Cambridge, Stephen Marshall was from about 1625 vicar of Finchingfield in Essex. He seems to have conformed sufficiently – but only just sufficiently – to avoid trouble under Archbishop Laud. Nathaniel Brent described him to Laud as 'a dangerous person but exceeding cunning. No man doubteth but that he hath an inconformable heart, but externally he observeth all . . . He governeth the conscience of all the rich puritans in those parts and in many places far remote and is grown very rich.'[7] There is certainly no doubting Marshall's involvement with Puritan networks in Essex and Suffolk, and by 1640 he was working closely with the important Puritan patron and lord-lieutenant of Essex, the earl of Warwick. Thereafter, he remained a key player on the parliamentary side, Clarendon remarking that 'the archbishop of Canterbury had never so great an influence upon the counsels at Court as Dr [Cornelius] Burgess and Mr Marshall had then upon the Houses'.[8] In 1640 Marshall was one of the first two men appointed to preach to the Short Parliament on a fast day; on 17 November he delivered one of the first two fast-day sermons preached to the Long Parliament, and was to deliver a total of thirteen sermons to that body by 1653, including one to the Lords on the day following the execution of Charles I.[9]

The very titles of Marshall's Fast Sermons take us to the core of Puritan concerns in the 1640s: *A Peace Offering to God* (7 September 1641), *Reformation and Desolation* (22 December 1641), *Gods Master-Piece* (26 March 1645), *Emmanuel: A Thanksgiving-Sermon* (17 May 1648). These were sermons on public affairs, on the desperate need for reformation, on God's displeasure with England's failings and the ways in which that displeasure might be assuaged, through fasting, prayer and repentance, on the need to take a stand and support God's cause against its enemies. Marshall through his sermons constructed the English Revolution as an act of reformation, necessary to complete the work that had begun and stalled under the Tudors and had then been undermined by Charles I and Laud. The drama playing on the English stage was a religious one, and the Civil War, in John Morrill's phrase, was England's (or at least Marshall's) 'war of religion'.

Much the most famous of Marshall's Fast Sermons was preached on 23 February 1642. Clarendon can be left to tell the story of 'Mr Marshall,

[7] Tom Webster, 'Marshall, Stephen (1594/5?–1655)', *ODNB*, drawing also on the original *DNB* article of 1893.
[8] Clarendon, I, p. 401.
[9] John F. Wilson, *Pulpit in Parliament: Puritanism during the English Civil Wars 1640–1648* (Princeton, NJ, 1969), pp. 109–10.

who from the 23rd verse of the 5th chapter of Judges, *Curse ye Meroz, said the angel of the Lord; curse ye bitterly the inhabitants thereof, because they came not to the help of the Lord, to the help of the Lord against the mighty*, presumed to inveigh against, and in plain terms to pronounce God's own curse against, all those who came not with their utmost power and strength to destroy and root out all the malignants who in any degree opposed the Parliament.'[10] One needs, perhaps, to be a little careful. The sermons were not always as explicit as Clarendon or as many historians have suggested, yet there is no doubt that those who heard *Meroz Cursed* – and after its initial outing, Marshall preached it elsewhere some sixty times – could hear it as a call to arms in a religious war, a crusade even. The Parliamentarian soldiers captured at the siege of Brampton Bryan referred directly to Marshall's sermon in claiming that 'they did but *help God against his Enemies*'.[11] It is easy to see why. Marshall's condemnation of the neutrality of Meroz was cast in bloody terms. God's work required commitment, he argued, turning now to Jeremiah 48:10: 'Now what was the worke which was to be done? The next words will tell you, *Cursed is every one that withholds his hand from shedding of blood*... [H]is work was to go and *embrew* his hands in the *blood of men*, to spill and *powre* out the *bloud* of *women* and *children*, *like water* in every street... if he go not through with the work: he is a cursed man, when this is to be done upon *Moab* the *enemy of Gods church*.'[12] It is possible to argue that Marshall was not intending this literally, but it is equally possible to suggest that those who heard him cared little for his intentions or qualifications.

The example of Marshall would seem straightforwardly to suggest that for many of those who experienced it, the 'English Revolution' was above all a war of religion, intended to reform England and return it firmly to God's cause. As the 1640s continued, the religious character of events became increasingly apparent, as Cromwell and his fellows searched for signs of God's providence, and struggled to inform their consciences; as radical millenarian ideas began to flourish and form the intellectual foundation for individuals and sects expecting the world to be turned upside down; as the Westminster Assembly produced and Parliament implemented plans to replace the episcopal Church of England with a presbyterian church; and as many of the godly sought to free their consciences from the discipline of secular authority.

[10] Clarendon, II, pp. 320–1.
[11] Glenn Burgess, 'Was the English Civil War a war of religion? The evidence of political propaganda', *HLQ*, 61 (1998), 173–201, at 173–4.
[12] Stephen Marshall, *Meroz Cursed* (1642), pp. 10–11. It is worth comparing the earlier version, printed in 1641, 'not by the Author' (presumably from listening notes), as *Meroz Curse*, preached 2 December at St Sepulchre's, London.

Notwithstanding all of this, Stephen Marshall, writing at the very beginning of these events and developments, sounded a very different note in some of his other writings, in particular his defence of Parliament's war against the king, *A Plea for Defensive Arms* (1643). In that work, Marshall accepted without reservation the standard Christian view that the true faith could not and should not be defended or spread by violent means. Under persecution, the primitive church rightly resorted only to prayers and tears. So, was Parliament fighting a war of religion or not? The answer was 'yes' – but it was not a straightforward yes. Marshall defended the war primarily on legal and constitutional grounds. He made the general point that every place was different. '[T]he power of Magistrates in one Countrey differs from the power of Magistrates in another Countrey, and how the duty of Subjects differs in each, must be found only in the Laws of the respective places.'[13] Among the things that Marshall found in the laws of England was the principle that 'Religion was established by Law', thus giving the English a particular legal right to defend religion against the errors of their own king.[14] In the same way, the early Christians had acquired this right to defend their faith by force only when the church was legally established in the Empire by Constantine.

In making this argument Marshall introduces a theme that will occupy me for the remainder of this essay. Although his sermons leave no doubt about the religious character of the English Revolution, his political writings are thoroughly legalistic, and allow religion to be defended by force only when there is constitutional provision for this to happen. It is impossible to know for sure why Marshall argued in the way that he did; but three explanations do seem plausible. First, he might have been trying to *extend* support: religious arguments tended of their nature to have only sectarian appeal; but arguing that Charles I had to be resisted in order to protect the laws and legal rights of Englishmen extended the appeal of the message beyond sectarian boundaries. Second, Marshall might have been trying to *legitimize* the cause by appealing to positive law. For many at this time 'politics' as such scarcely existed: there was law and there was religion, and between them they gave all the political guidance needed. But what was the relationship between law and religion? Marshall's attempt to provide a legal argument perhaps betrays anxiety that religious grounds alone were not sufficient to legitimize political actions of the sort found in the 1640s. Furthermore, to resist without legal grounds risked bringing discredit and scandal on the godly by making them look like the

---

[13] Marshall, *A Plea for Defensive Armes* (1643), p. 4.   [14] Ibid., p. 20.

propagators of disorder.[15] Finally, Marshall might have been trying to *control* the anti-Royalist forces. Dangers lay in defending revolution entirely in terms of the rights of the zealous to fight in God's cause. How could such a war be governed, controlled and organized by legitimate authorities or by social elites? What was to prevent any Tom, Dick or Harry from deciding that religious inspiration justified his attack on parliament or landlord, minister or master? Religious zeal was a powerful motivating force, but a dangerous one. Its effects were hard to control. But Marshall's legal argument was one that left Parliament firmly in control because it possessed, in his view, the undoubted constitutional role, as the highest court in the land, of defending law and liberties against an errant king.

Marshall's legal arguments were not 'secular': they were still clearly intended to defend a war of religion, but one in which religion was established by law and possessed as a legal right. Nonetheless, these arguments reveal things that could impel people, even those deeply involved in a zealous cause, to develop arguments that mitigated the consequences of their own zeal. Moving forward to examine ideas expressed by Henry Ireton late in the 1640s, we are in a world in which the difficulties of controlling the zealous and enthusiastic have become considerably more acute.

III

Henry Ireton rose from being a jobbing local attorney to become Commissary-General of Parliament's New Model Army and son-in-law of Oliver Cromwell. From 1647 he was the army's most significant political writer, and the author of the November 1648 *Remonstrance* that made a clear break between the Parliament, which having defeated the king twice wished nonetheless to persist in negotiating a settlement with him, and the army, which had had quite enough of Charles Stuart, 'that man of blood', and was determined to call him to account. Ireton was to sign Charles's death warrant, and then to die of fever in 1651 during the still-controversial conquest of Ireland by the New Model Army.

Ireton is an important political thinker, although his ideas have received less attention than they deserve. The prevailing view sees him as a godly Puritan, which he undoubtedly was – a man 'at all times animated by the

---

[15] Alternative ways of linking religious and legal justifications, based on ideas of covenant, are explored in Edward Vallance, 'Preaching to the converted: religious justifications for the English Civil War', *HLQ*, 65 (2002), 395–419; Vallance, *Revolutionary England and the National Covenant: 'State Oaths', Protestantism, and the Political Nation, 1553–1682* (Woodbridge, 2005).

vision of a godly commonwealth';[16] yet he was also greatly concerned –
in ways very similar to Thomas Hobbes, the greatest political writer of
the English Revolution – to *counteract* the dangers of religious zeal.

The best evidence for this is in the Whitehall Debates, intended to
revise the Levellers' second *Agreement of the People* into a form that the
army would recommend to Parliament as a constitution for England
after the end of the Stuart monarchy. The discussions are well recorded
only for a single day (14 December 1648). I would not claim that
Ireton was a 'secular' thinker, but rather that he was impelled in these
debates, whatever his godliness and whatever degree of religious motivation might have led him to join and command Parliamentarian forces, to
construct a political world immunized against the instability generated
by religious enthusiasm. There was no shortage of such enthusiasm in
the Whitehall debates. Joshua Sprigge – an Independent minister who
was soon to oppose the regicide, but who had come to think that millennial change would transform the spirits of men, rendering institutional
change unnecessary – insisted that since God has 'thus taken us apieces'
and 'brought forth the government of the sword', it was necessary to
wait, allowing God to act. Men do not have the power to settle things
with their Agreements of the People. 'God will bring forth a New Heaven
and a New Earth [Revelation, 21:1].' In the meantime the only thing to
do was 'restrain the magistrate' so that he could not persecute God's
people.[17] Hold back the civil sovereign; give the godly their head.

Ireton did not agree. Unlike the godly enthusiasts, he was troubled by
the consequences of tolerating the excesses of the godly. Through a series
of interventions in the debate, he constructed a thoroughly Hobbesian
position. It was built on three key points.

First, like Hobbes, he emphasized that the central political value, which
governments existed to maintain, was peace. There were those who saw
liberty (religious or civil) rather than peace as the chief end of government. They were wrong. On the contrary,

the necessary thing, that which *necessarily* leads all men into civil agreements or
contracts, or to make commonwealths, is the necessity of it for preserving peace.
Because otherwise, if there were no such thing, but every man left to his own will,
men's contrary wills, lusts and passions would lead every one to the destruction
of another, and to seek all the ways of fencing himself against the jealousies of
another.[18]

[16] Ian Gentles, *The New Model Army in England, Ireland and Scotland, 1645–1653* (Oxford,
1992), p. 288. See more expansively David Farr, *Henry Ireton and the English Revolution*
(Woodbridge, 2006).
[17] A. S. P. Woodhouse, ed., *Puritanism and Liberty*, 2nd edn (1951), pp. 134–6.
[18] Ibid., p. 130 (emphasis in original).

Second, like Hobbes, Ireton then asserted that the power that government had was related to its need to preserve the peace, and did not extend to consciences which were immune from it:

All civil power whatsoever, either in natural or civil things, is not to bind men's judgments. The judgment of the Parliament is the supremest council in the world, [but] cannot bind my judgment in anything, and whether you limit it to civil things or natural things, the effect of that power is that he hath not power to conclude your inward, but [only] your outward man; the effect of all is but the placing of a power in which we would acquiesce for peace' sake.[19]

It was therefore particularly important, third, to be clear about what it was that peace required. Here Ireton decisively broke with the views of many of the godly. Even if it was accepted that the civil magistrate was given 'a trust to them for the outward man, and with acquiescence but for peace' sake', it still remained necessary to decide explicitly whether 'it be fit for us to commit a trust . . . for this purpose, concerning spiritual things as concerning civil things'.[20] That is to say, should the civil magistrate be able to punish the outward man for religious offences? (Conscience, the inner man, did not, of course, come into it.)

Ultimately, Ireton answered that question affirmatively. He argued that man's duties to God, his spiritual duties, were not revealed purely in the Christian revelation. They were understood by all men through natural reason, and thus could be controlled and restrained at all times. The decalogue was not simply a set of revealed laws, or God's positive commands to his peculiar people: parts of it were embedded in the law of nature itself, and the commands known to all human peoples. So Ireton's position here was again Hobbesian rather than Mosaic: blasphemy, idolatry and atheism were to be punished because the sovereign enforced the law of nature, not because he was the mediator of specific divine commands.

The paramount importance of maintaining peace, guidance on which matter was provided by the laws of nature, meant that no magistrate could afford to grant immunity to all spiritual or religious matters. In his elaboration of these points, the parallels with Hobbes accumulated, reminding us that so many of the developments that constitute part of the legacy of the English Revolution cross our usual categories. Royalists, Parliamentarians, Puritans, radicals – all can be made to appear progressive or reactionary, liberal or authoritarian. Ireton, while denying again that magistrates could punish 'any man for his conscience', went on to say that the real question was '[w]hether you shall make such a provision

---

[19] Ibid., pp. 130–1.   [20] Ibid., p. 131.

for men that are conscientious, that they may serve God according to their light and conscience, as shall necessarily debar any kind of restraint on anything that any man will call religion'. Do we wish to allow men 'to practise idolatry, to practise atheism, and anything that is against the light of God'? If you do not allow the magistrate to regulate the public face of religion, then you cripple his capacity to preserve peace and order. What bothered Ireton was that the magistrate might be prevented from restraining 'anything which men will *call* religion'.[21] One can almost hear the sardonic, sarcastic voice of Hobbes in that. Both men agreed that there was enormous risk in giving immunity to men's actions whenever they cared to invoke conscience in their defence. Ireton might have been godly, but he was, in a sense, a godly Hobbesian, unlikely as such a creature might seem.[22]

There was nothing secular about Ireton's position. Far from it: he recognized the importance of religious discipline, of public control over religion, for the peace and stability of civil society. This is a different version of the interpenetration of religion and civil society from that of Stephen Marshall, resting on a perception that religious zeal was indeed at work in the world, but could if untamed prove dangerous. Equally, a broadly similar conclusion was reached by Hobbes and the other great theorist of the 1650s, James Harrington. The former emphatically endorsed the control of the civil sovereign over *all* public matters of faith and religious worship, even designating the civil sovereign the chief pastor of the community over which he ruled. But Hobbes also agreed with Ireton that the inner man was immune from coercion, and went so far as to affirm in *Leviathan* (1651) that

There is another error in their [the scholastics'] civil philosophy... to extend the power of the law, which is the rule of actions only, to the very thoughts and consciences of men, by examination and inquisition of what they hold, notwithstanding the conformity of their speech and actions... [T]o force [a man] to accuse himself of opinions, when his actions are not by law forbidden, is against the law of nature.[23]

Similarly, the republican theorist James Harrington summed up his ideas in a late work as requiring a 'national religion', made up of 'a popular clergy, of the Scriptures (or of some other book acknowledged divine), with a directory', and 'a council for the equal maintenance both

---

[21] Ibid., pp. 143, 146.
[22] Richard Tuck has explored some of the things that might help to explain this pattern, but does not use much of the Whitehall debates: see his *Natural Rights Theories* (Cambridge, 1979), ch. 7; and *Philosophy and Government 1572–1651* (Cambridge, 1993), ch. 6.
[23] Thomas Hobbes, *Leviathan*, ed. Edwin Curley (Indianapolis, 1994), p. 466.

of the national religion and of the liberty of conscience'.[24] Elsewhere, he suggested that the council of religion should ensure that religions, including the national, were non-coercive, but should not allow toleration to Jews or 'idolatrous' groups. Some policing of the unacceptable was still needed.[25] This state council would act both as religious authority in the national church (in consultation with the universities), propagating a kind of republican 'civil religion', and as an umpire in disputes over toleration. In Harrington as in Hobbes, Ireton and others, there is a shared perception (a) that the state must control and police religion; (b) that in different ways religion was essential to political peace and order, and the state should provide for the religious needs of its subjects; and (c) that the state must take the danger of religious enthusiasm away by two means, controlling public provision and maintaining some degree of toleration for 'safe' beliefs.

IV

Hobbes was, of course, a Royalist, at least for some of the time, although one whose religious views, when they became known after the publication of *Leviathan* in 1651, were profoundly shocking to many other Royalists, most of whom were very traditional defenders of the Church of England.[26] But there were Royalists capable of sharing some of Hobbes's perspectives, and they were pushed into them by the same imperative driving so many others: the need to protect the peaceful existence of civil society from the dangerous consequences of religious enthusiasm. An example is Jasper Mayne, who was, in many respects, a typical Royalist.[27] He was a sort of absolutist, arguing that subjects had no rights whatsoever against their kings, and even suggesting that they had surrendered their liberty of person and their property to monarchs. Like many, though, he tempered this a little by recognizing that laws had grown up to

---

[24] James Harrington, *The Commonwealth of Oceana and A System of Politics*, ed. J. G. A. Pocock (Cambridge, 1992), p. 285.

[25] Ibid., pp. 126–7. See further Mark Goldie, 'The civil religion of James Harrington', in Anthony Pagden, ed., *The Languages of Political Theory in Early-Modern Europe* (Cambridge, 1987), ch. 9.

[26] There has been a lot of interesting work on Hobbes's religious ideas, especially the claim that he was an Independent, advanced in Jeffrey R. Collins, *The Allegiance of Thomas Hobbes* (Oxford, 2005). A way in to many of the recent debates can be found through the essays in Patricia Springborg, ed., *The Cambridge Companion to Hobbes's Leviathan* (Cambridge, 2007).

[27] See my fuller account in Glenn Burgess, 'Royalism and liberty of conscience in the English Revolution', in John Morrow and Jonathan Scott, eds., *Liberty, Authority, Formality: Political Ideas and Culture, 1600–1900: Essays in Honour of Colin Davis* (Exeter, 2008), ch. 1.

moderate the excesses of kings, although these laws were rather alarmingly described as '*Figures* in the *Dust* . . . [at] the *Mercy* of the next *Winde* that blowes'.[28] Less typical was Mayne's consideration of whether religion could be a just cause of war or revolution.

Mayne began his answer to this question with a consideration of the opinion of Grotius that if there was found a nation of atheists, it would be legitimate to use force 'to banish them out of the *World*' because religion was essential to the maintenance of human societies. Laws fostered sociability by punishing men for their *actions*, but religion was needed to bind men's consciences to the requirements of sociability.[29] Grotius was concerned especially with those opinions that denied that God would punish men for sin, whether they also denied his existence or not, and cited the case of Diagoras of Melos and of the Epicureans, 'who were expelled and banished all Cities that had any Regularity and good Manners amongst them'.[30]

Mayne was none too persuaded by this, because he could see that atheists might be capable of sociability. What this implied was that religious faith was not indisputably necessary for social and civil order, a position that in the context of the 1640s had pacifying implications, because it made possible the argument that the stability of the political world required a common human civility and not a divisive religious zeal. Here is Mayne's careful exploration of the subject:

Though I shall grant the saying of *Plutarch* to be true, that *Religion* . . . [is] one (nay one of the firmest) *Bonds* of *Society*, and *supporters* of *Lawes*, yet I have not met with any *demonstrative* Argument, which hath proved to me, that there is such a necessary dependance of *Human society* upon *Religion*, that the Absence of the *One* must inevitably be the Destruction of the *other*. If it be, this is most likely to come to passe in the *State*, or *Commonwealth*, which is of this opinion among themselves; Not in a forraigne *State*, or *Common-wealth* which is not. But since 'tis possible that a Countrey of *Atheists* may yet have so much *Morality* among them, seconded by *Lawes* made by common agreement among themselves, as to be a *People*, and to hold the society of *Citizens* among themselves, And as 'tis possible for them, without *Religion*, so farre, for meere *utility* and *safeties* sake, to observe the *Law* of *Nations*, as not to wrong or injure a *People* different from themselves, so where no *civill wrong*, or *injury* is offered by them to another *People*, but where the *morall Bonds* of *Society*, and *commerce*, though not the *Religious*, of *Opinion*, and *Worship*, are unbroken by them, for the *People* not injured to make *Warre* upon them, for a *feard, imaginary consequence*, or because, being *Atheists*,

[28] Jasper Mayne, *Ochlo-machia: Or, The People's War* (Oxford, 1647), pp. 11–12.
[29] Mayne, *People's War*, pp. 22–4.
[30] Hugo Grotius, *The Rights of War and Peace*, ed. Richard Tuck, 3 vols. (Indianapolis, 2005), II, p. 1038 [II.xxXLVI].

'tis possible that their example may spread, is an Act of *Hostility* which I confesse I am not able to defend.[31]

From the point of view of social utility, one religion might be as good as another, for even '*Idolatry*, though it be a *false Religion*, is yet as conservant of *Society . . . as if't were true*'.[32] The principle that it 'would be unreasonable to make *Warre* upon mens *persons* for the reception of a *Doctrine* which cannot convince their minds' applied to all faiths, even the true one, because it had at least some dependence on non-rational and supernatural claims.

> In short, some things in the *Excellencyes*, and *Height* of the *Doctrines* of Christian *Religion* being no way *demonstrable* from *Human principles*, but depending for the *credit*, and *evidence* of their *truth* upon the *Authority* of *Christs miracles*, conveyed along in *Tradition*, and *Story*, cannot in a *naturall* way of *Argumentation* force *assent*. Since, as long as there is such a thing in men, as *liberty* of *understanding*, all *arguments*, even in a *Preaching*, and *perswasive* way, which carry not *necessity* of *demonstration* in their *Forehead*, may reasonably be rejected.[33]

The lesson was the folly of compelling others to assent to one's own understanding of religious demands. In religion, one could persuade and argue, but Mayne concluded that in civil societies the power and authority needed to ensure peace could only be civil power. Civil power was, indeed, all the power that there was: churches possessed only a spiritual capacity.

We again see, and this time in Royalist not Parliamentarian circles, the perception that religious enthusiasm must be contained and human societies protected from its destabilizing potential. Royalists like Mayne could, more unproblematically than the Puritan-Parliamentarian, admit that it was religious enthusiasm that had got England into the mess of the 1640s and fuelled the rebellion against Charles I; but, nonetheless, Mayne's response to the problems posed by the religious war through which he was living carried implications for religion in general, not just for enthusiastic religion. It is startling that this explicit willingness to contemplate a society of atheists in mid-seventeenth-century England comes from the pen of a Royalist clergyman. It is an extreme attempt to clarify the public role of religion and its control by public authority, and to undermine the effects of personal zeal by depriving the inner man, the conscience, of a public voice or agency. The case of Mayne makes it startlingly plain that the most 'advanced' and 'liberal' opinions were not

---

[31] Ibid., pp. 24–5.   [32] Ibid., p. 26.

[33] Jasper Mayne, *A Sermon against False Prophets* (1647), p. 16. (There are two printings of this pamphlet with different paginations.)

necessarily to be found among the supporters of Parliament, and that the compulsion to unpick the dangerous interpenetration of religion and politics could manifest itself in surprising ways.

V

After the Restoration of the Stuart monarchy in 1660 the events of the English Revolution continued to haunt the political imagination. The 1660s and 1670s saw the building of a confessional state by the Anglican gentry, determined never again to see the destructive might of religious zeal unleashed. But this effort undermined itself: the more nonconformity was separated from the Anglican church-state, the greater the need for that church-state to preserve its stability by some accommodation with the existence of 'separated nonconformity'.[34] The settlement of 1688–9, and its aftermath through to 1707, achieved a remarkable balancing act, ensuring the perpetuation of an Anglican church-state (and ensuring the loyalty of the monarchy to the Anglican establishment – no small achievement) at the cost of a limited toleration for Protestant dissent.

This arrangement can only be understood as a legacy of the English Revolution, and in the debates and arguments that occurred between 1660 and 1688 we can see a struggle for control over that legacy. What lessons were to be derived from the horrors of religious civil war that had torn apart the nation and subjected it to the military authority of an upstart minor gentleman? Or, perhaps, depending on your point of view, how could the Nonconformist reconcile his duty to God and his duty to man – how could he advocate a religious freedom for himself that would not become a political anarchy for all?

One man who wrestled with these questions more productively than most was John Locke. In his engagement with other writers, most notably Samuel Parker – bishop of Oxford after 1686, thanks to his support for the religious policies of James II – Locke can be found engaging in a protracted argument about the legacy of the English Revolution.[35]

Parker was, some of the time, a Hobbesian, although like most Hobbesians keen to distance himself from a man with a dangerous reputation

---

[34] Clark, *English Society*, p. 319.
[35] On Parker see Gordon Schochet, 'Between Lambeth and Leviathan: Samuel Parker on the Church of England and political order', in N. Phillipson and Q. Skinner, eds., *Political Discourse in Early Modern Britain* (Cambridge, 1993), pp. 189–208; Schochet, 'Samuel Parker, religious diversity and the ideology of persecution', in R. D. Lund, ed., *The Margins of Heterodoxy: Heterodox Writings and Cultural Response, 1660–1750* (Cambridge, 1995), pp. 119–48.

for atheism (and worse).[36] Throughout his life, Locke shared with Parker and other Hobbesians a perception that the highest political value was peace: the centrality of this view in political thinking, and its victory over views that suggested that peace might need to be sacrificed in the pursuit of other, perhaps godly, values, was itself a chief legacy of the Revolution, and one shared across many boundaries. In his notes on Parker's *Discourse of Ecclesiastical Polity* (1669) Locke can be seen agreeing with the basic point, while disagreeing with Parker's account of its implications. Here is Parker:

The peace and tranquillity of the commonwealth, the prime and most important end of government, can never be sufficiently secured, unless religion be subject to the authority of the supreme power, in that it has the strongest influence upon human affairs.

And here is Locke's question:

Whether this proves anything but the magistrate's business being only to preserve peace, those wrong opinions are to be restrained that have a tendency to disturb it (and this is by every sober man to be allowed)?[37]

Parker argued, in ways that might remind us of Ireton, that religious matters could not be excluded from the authority of the civil magistrate, for this could result in a damaging clash of 'contradictory commands': 'Seeing no man can be subject to contradictory obligations, 'tis by consequence utterly impossible he should be subject to two supreme powers', one civil and one ecclesiastical. Locke's comment on this gets us to the heart of the subject:

The end of government being public peace, 'tis no question the supreme power must have an uncontrollable right to judge and ordain all things that may conduce to it, but yet the question will be whether [religious] uniformity established by law be . . . a necessary means to it.[38]

It was agreed, then, that religion must be subject to public control where the demands of maintaining peace were concerned; but it was clearly not agreed precisely what degree of interference in religion was thus justified. Parker was a theorist of intolerance; Locke of tolerance; but they shared at one level a common judgement that if religious belief compromised the requirements of peace, then it was subject to civil control.

Locke changed his mind about the degree to which religious belief should be interfered with by the state. At the Restoration, Locke was

---

[36] Jon Parkin, 'Hobbism in the Later 1660s: Daniel Scargill and Samuel Parker', *HJ*, 42 (1999), 85–108.

[37] John Locke, *Political Essays*, ed. Mark Goldie (Cambridge, 1997), pp. 211–12.

[38] Ibid., p. 213.

twenty-eight years old, and a fellow of Christ Church, Oxford, where he lectured in Greek, rhetoric and moral philosophy. His earliest responses to the English Revolution are hard to reconstruct. Comments on Quakers made before the Restoration suggest that he was dismissive of the claims of radical religion, and worried by its consequences.[39] In a letter of 1659 to Henry Stubbe, Locke expressed his regret that Stubbe's *Essay in Defence of the Good Old Cause* (1659) had not extended its defence of toleration to include accounts of recent Dutch, French and Polish practices, noting that

> when you have added the authority of dayly experience that men of different professions may quietly unite . . . under the same government and unanimously cary the same civill intrest and hand in hand march to the same end of peace and mutuall society though they take different way towards heaven you will adde noe small strength to your cause and be very convinceing to those to whom what you have already hath left noething to doubt but whither it be now practicable.[40]

Whether or not Locke was persuaded even to this point may be doubted; but at the very least it seems reasonable to conclude from this that he remained doubtful of the practicability of toleration.

Certainly, by the time he wrote his two *Tracts* in 1660–1 Locke's views had hardened into a position not far removed from that of Hobbes or Parker, that potentially the sovereign's control over religion was very extensive. By late 1667 he was already defending the tolerationist principles that were to receive fuller expression in his *Letter Concerning Toleration*, written in exile in the Netherlands in 1685. Locke never abandoned his basic acknowledgement that peace was the paramount political goal; but he did change his mind in two crucial ways about how peace was to be achieved. First, he argued in 1660–1 that it was the people and not their rulers who posed the greatest threat to peace, declaring that 'the multitude . . . are as impatient of restraint as the sea, and [their] . . . tempests and overflows cannot be too well provided against'. Rhetorically, he asked,

> Whence is most danger to be rationally feared, from ignorant or knowing heads? From an orderly council or a confused multitude? To whom are we most likely to become a prey, to those whom the Scripture calls gods, or those whom knowing men have always found and therefore called beasts?[41]

Locke admitted that his position left the magistrate effectively unlimited in his power to tax, to imprison and so on, but, he added, 'these

---

[39] John Locke, *Selected Correspondence*, ed. Mark Goldie (Oxford, 2002), pp. 5–7.
[40] Ibid., p. 12.
[41] John Locke, *Two Tracts on Government*, ed. Philip Abrams (Cambridge, 1967), p. 158; Locke, *Political Essays*, p. 39.

are inconveniences whose speculation following from the constitution of polities may often fright but their practice seldom hurt the people'.[42] By the 1680s Locke was explaining away the inconveniences of the opposite doctrine. In his *Two Treatises* he developed a theory of the 'dissolution of government', those words expressing the idea that revolutions were not caused by the violence of an inconstant multitude, but by the ways in which the misgovernment of rulers dissolved government and left the people in a state of nature, where they might need to rely on violence to protect them. In saying this Locke was shifting from one view of the legacy of the English Revolution – that expressed by Parker – to another. The phrase 'dissolution of government' takes us back to the very core of the political thinking of England's war of religion. On 20 May 1642 the Lords and Commons had declared that 'it appeares that the King (seduced by wicked Counsell) intends to make warre against the Parliament... That whensoever the King maketh warre upon the Parliament, it is a breach of the trust reposed in him by his people, contrary to his oath, and tending to the dissolution of this Government.'[43]

Second, Locke changed his assessment of the consequences of religious diversity. In 1660–1 he acknowledged that 'almost all these tragical revolutions that have exercised Christendom' were caused by religion, at least in the sense that 'there hath been no design so wicked which hath not worn the visor of religion, nor rebellion which hath not been so kind to itself as to assume the specious name of reformation'. This readily became an argument for the sovereign's right to restrict tightly the latitude of religious freedom enjoyed by his subjects. The sovereign, as 'guardian of the peace', had to intervene in matters of the faith.[44] But this view was abandoned. By 1667 Locke was arguing that religious differences among people served only 'to divide and subdivide [men] into so many little bodies, and always with the greatest enmity to those they last parted from or stand nearest to, that they are a guard upon one another, and the public can have no apprehensions of them'.[45] In the mid-1680s, in the *Letter*, Locke affirmed more emphatically that

It is not the diversity of Opinions, (which cannot be avoided) but the refusal of Toleration to those that are of different Opinions, (which might have been granted) that has produced all the Bustles and Wars that have been in the Christian World, upon account of Religion.[46]

[42] Locke, *Two Tracts*, pp. 157–8; Locke, *Political Essays*, pp. 38–9.
[43] *The Votes of Both Houses of Parliament, the 20 of May 1642* (1642), pp. 1–2; *CJ*, II, 20 May 1642.
[44] Locke, *Two Tracts*, pp. 160–1; Locke, *Political Essays*, pp. 40–2.
[45] Locke, 'Essay', in John Locke, *Political Writings*, ed. David Wootton (Harmondsworth, 1993), p. 198; Locke, *Political Essays*, p. 149.
[46] John Locke, *A Letter Concerning Toleration*, ed. James Tully (Indianapolis, IN, 1983), p. 55; Locke, *Political Writings*, p. 431.

The *Letter* did continue to affirm the view that the sovereign could restrain any doctrines harmful to peace, but Locke now appreciated that religious diversity sapped rather than enhanced the disruptiveness of religion, and that therefore toleration was more compatible with peace than was intolerance.

We should not interpret Locke's thought of the mid and late 1680s, his theory of toleration or his theory of civil politics, as secular, for at least two reasons.[47] First, his civil politics, as expressed in the *Two Treatises*, was fundamentally rooted in a reading of the relationship between God and man. All men were God's creatures, and as such remained the property of their maker. God had entrusted to each individual some rights over themselves. It followed from this that anything that infringed a person's limited self-ownership – assuming that that person had not broken the commands of the law of nature – was a usurpation of God's ultimate ownership. The only way in which authority over others could be acquired was with their consent. But God also retained in his own hands some things, including authority over consciences, so that not even with his or her consent could authority over the conscience of another be acquired.[48] This was a view of politics rooted in a sense of the ways in which God's authority structured the political domain.

Second, the theory of toleration that Locke built on this foundation tended to undermine its own strict division between civil matters and matters of conscience. As already indicated, he was compelled to accept that where religion did have political consequences (Islam, Catholicism) it might be persecuted. He made little of the point, but it was never lost. He also undermined in other ways his own account of the civil peacefulness of religious belief. What, he asked, might happen if men *were* persecuted? Surely care for their soul came before public peace? Locke continued, a little cryptically,

There are two sorts of contests among men; the one managed by Law, the other by Force: and these are of that nature, that where the one ends, the other always begins. But it is not my business to inquire into the Power of the Magistrate in the different Constitutions of Nations. I know only what usually happens where Controversies arise, without a Judge to determine them. You will say then the Magistrate being the stronger will have his will, and carry his point. Without doubt. But the Question is not here concerning the doubtfulness of the Event, but the Rule of Right.[49]

---

[47] See more generally Jeremy Waldron, *God, Locke, and Equality: Christian Foundations in Locke's Political Thought* (Cambridge, 2002); and the debate on this interpretation in *Review of Politics*, 67 (2005), 405–513.

[48] John Locke, *Two Treatises of Government*, ed. Peter Laslett, 2nd edn (Cambridge, 1967), II, p. ii. §6–9, pp. 288–90.

[49] Locke, *Letter*, p. 49; Locke, *Political Writings*, p. 424.

The effect of this threat of force is surely to undermine Locke's careful attempt to stress the peacefulness of sectarianism. Certainly, it was persecution that might spark off violence; but could a ruler be sure that groups would never *feel* persecuted (perhaps wrongly)? Might it not be better, after all, to insist on uniformity, so the risk of violence never arose? Religious freedom was, for Locke, a natural right, and could be defended as such. That merely shifted the ground for religious violence; it did not abolish it. Locke *could* not abolish it while continuing to acknowledge the possibility of a clash between civil and religious duties. It was left to others to try to mitigate the effects of the doctrine. Gilbert Burnet, in a very Lockean defence of opposition to James II, wrote that 'It is indeed clear ... that the *Christian Religion* as such, gives us no grounds to defend or propagate it by force.' But, just like Stephen Marshall in 1642, Burnet could add:

> But if by the Laws of Government, the *Christian Religion*, or any form of it, is become a part of the Subject's *Property*, it then falls under another consideration, not as it is a *Religion*, but as it is become one of the principal rights of the *Subjects*, to believe and profess it: and then we must judge of the Invasions made on that, as we do of any other Invasion, that is made on our *Rights*.[50]

Religion could be defended in the same way that property rights could be defended.

Locke was by no means an architect of the settlement of 1688–9 which followed the departure of James II; he was more politically subversive and more religiously inclusive than the cautious men who assisted William III to the throne. But he shared one thing with many of these men: an awareness that Protestant dissent was more safely anchored to political peace by toleration than by persecution. This was one of the legacies of the English Revolution, albeit, as we have seen, a contested one.[51]

VI

Four men – a Puritan minister who denied the consequences of his own zeal, a godly army commander who sought to mitigate the zeal of others, a Royalist clergyman whose alarm at the horrors of religious war led him to imagine a society existing altogether without religion, and a famous

---

[50] Gilbert Burnet, *An Inquiry into the Measures of Submission to the Supream Authority* [1688], in Joyce Malcolm, ed., *The Struggle for Sovereignty: Seventeenth-Century English Political Tracts*, 2 vols. (Indianapolis, 1999), II, p. 5.

[51] It is also an enormous subject, opened up now by John Marshall, *John Locke, Toleration and Early Enlightenment Culture* (Cambridge, 2006).

philosopher who came to think that religious diversity was, after all, an aid to the preservation of peace, not least because fragmentation undermined the disruptive capacity of sectarianism. Together they bring us back to John Morrill: as witnesses to the English Revolution, they were forced to think about the interpenetration of religion and politics. The English Revolution was, for all of them in different ways, an act of violent reformation, a war of religion. Those living through it were compelled to ask how civil society could survive among a diversity of religious beliefs, whether such diversity was tolerable at all and how the capacity of religious zeal to turn the world upside down might be contained; they were not compelled to agree on the answers. Their responses might be understood – sometimes – to involve secularizing moves, but they need not be seen as a secularizing process. Even the zealous might participate in such moves, for they had good reasons, whether sincerely felt or not, to wish to combat the impression that they were hell-bent (or heaven-bent) on reducing the world to chaos.

Our examples – the four lead actors and those in minor roles – share a number of things (although in the case of Marshall, our starting point, this is least clear). First, they agreed, faced with the risk of religiously inspired violence and turmoil, that *peace* was a paramount concern. Second, they agreed that in the interest of peace it had to follow that the civil sovereign had some capacity to police the boundaries of acceptable dissent – and this was as true of Locke as it was of Parker, as true of Ireton as of Mayne. The zealous might disagree, finding in a war of religion opportunity rather than hazard; that, however, was the problem. Third, though, they disagreed about the latitude of religious freedom that was compatible with the maintenance of civil peace. Precisely what religious belief or practices posed a threat to peace? That is a rather narrower ground of disagreement between Parliamentarian and Royalist, or (in the terms current from the 1680s) between Whig and Tory, than we might have expected. Its narrowness reflects the overwhelming weight of the legacy of the English Revolution, which served as a warning to many of the need to focus minds on what was necessary to maintain civil peace in a world of zealous enthusiasms.

Perhaps the most important legacy of the English Revolution was that when after 1685 people again faced a monarch of unacceptable religious beliefs, they took steps to ensure that this should not happen again, and that religious diversity would hereafter be as peacefully reconciled with the perpetuation of the Anglican establishment as was possible. Crucially, in 1688 many 'Tory Royalists', unlike their predecessors of the 1640s, opted to be Tory defenders of the protestant Church of England rather than Royalist defenders of James II. They sided, often reluctantly, hesitantly and briefly, with the hated Whig defenders of dissent, sooner than side with the royal defender of a hated Catholicism.[52]

Every argument that I have reviewed, from whatever quarter it comes, has contributed something to our understanding of the central problem with which the English Revolution confronted those who lived through and after it: could civil society survive the religious enthusiasms of its subjects (and its rulers)? It is because so many minds – not all, of course – were so focused on peace, that it was possible for Whig and Tory to work together to maintain peace and to try to find a recipe for religious stability in the so-called Glorious Revolution of 1688–9. The gloriousness of that event lay, above all, in its relative peacefulness. This it would not have had without the reflection, experience and fear that together formed the legacy of the English Revolution.

---

[52] Especially illuminating in this context is Mark Goldie, 'The political thought of the Anglican revolution', in Robert Beddard, ed., *The Revolutions of 1688*, The Andrew Browning Lectures (Oxford, 1991), pp. 102–36.

Bibliography of the major writings of John Morrill, 1967–2009

Compiled by David L. Smith

This bibliography lists the books and major articles that John Morrill has published since 1967. It does not include shorter articles, book reviews or works published in translation into languages other than English. The place of publication is London unless otherwise stated.

1967

(with R. N. Dore) 'The allegiance of the Cheshire gentry in the Great Civil War', *Transactions of the Lancashire & Cheshire Antiquarian Society*, 77 (1967), 47–76

1972

'Mutiny and discontent in English provincial armies, 1645–1647', *Past and Present*, 56 (1972), 49–74

1974

Cheshire, 1630–1660: County Government and Society during the 'English Revolution' (Oxford, 1974)

1975

'William Davenport and the "silent majority" of early Stuart England', *Journal of the Chester and North Wales Archaeological Society*, 58 (1975), 115–29

1976

The Revolt of the Provinces: Conservatives and Radicals in the English Civil War, 1630–1650 (1976)
The Cheshire Grand Jury, 1625–1659: A Social and Administrative Study (Leicester, 1976)
'Puritanism and the Church in the Diocese of Chester', *Northern History*, 12 (1976), 145–55

1977

'The Army Revolt of 1647', in A. C. Duke and C. A. Tamse, eds., *Britain and the Netherlands, volume 6: War and Society* (The Hague, 1977), pp. 54–78
'Provincial squires and "middling sorts" in the Great Rebellion', *Historical Journal*, 20 (1977), 229–36
'English local government in the early modern period', *Archives*, 13 (1977), 41–7
'In search of "Popery and Arbitrary Rule"', *Historical Journal*, 20 (1977), 961–70

1978

'French Absolutism as Limited Monarchy', *Historical Journal*, 21 (1978), 961–72

1979

(with G. E. Aylmer) *The Civil War and Interregnum: Sources for Local Historians* (1979)
'Parliamentary representation, 1543–1974', in B. E. Harris, ed., *Victoria History of the County of Chester, Volume II* (Oxford, 1979), pp. 98–166
'The northern gentry and the Great Rebellion', *Northern History*, 15 (1979), 66–87

1980

Seventeenth-Century Britain, 1603–1714 (Folkestone, 1980)
The Revolt of the Provinces: Conservatives and Radicals in the English Civil War, 1630–1650 (Harlow, 1980)

1981

'The diversity of local history', *Historical Journal*, 24 (1981), 717–29
'King Oliver?', *Cromwelliana* (1981), 20–5

1982

(edited) *Reactions to the English Civil War, 1642–1649* (1982), to which also contributed 'Introduction' (pp. 1–27) and 'The Church in England 1642–9' (pp. 89–114, 230–4)
'Seventeenth-century Scotland', *Journal of Ecclesiastical History*, 33 (1982), 266–71
'Reading History: the English Civil Wars, 1642–1649', *History Today*, 32 (1982), 51–2

1983

(edited with G. E. Aylmer) J. P. Cooper, *Land, Men and Beliefs: Studies in Early Modern History* (1983), to which also contributed 'J. P. Cooper as a teacher' (pp. xiv–xviii)

'Introduction', in J. Wilson, ed., *Buckinghamshire Contributions for Ireland, 1642*, Buckinghamshire Record Society, 21 (1983), pp. vii–xiii

'John Lilburne' and 'Robert Lilburne', in Richard L. Greaves and Robert Zaller, eds., *Biographical Dictionary of British Radicals in the Seventeenth Century, volume 2: G–O* (Brighton, 1983), pp. 186–9, 189–90

1984

'The Stuarts (1603–1688)', in Kenneth O. Morgan, ed., *The Oxford Illustrated History of Britain* (Oxford, 1984), pp. 286–351

'The religious context of the English Civil War', *Transactions of the Royal Historical Society*, 5th series, 34 (1984), 155–78

'What was the English Revolution?', *History Today*, 34 (1984), 11–16

'Recent works (1977–1982) on early modern British history: a review essay', *Tijdschrift voor Geschiedenis*, 97 (1984), 548–54

1985

'Government and politics: England and Wales, 1625–1701', in Christopher Haigh, ed., *The Cambridge Historical Encyclopedia of Great Britain and Ireland* (Cambridge, 1985), pp. 199–205

(with John Walter) 'Order and disorder in the English Revolution', in Anthony Fletcher and John Stevenson, ed., *Order and Disorder in Early Modern England* (Cambridge, 1985), pp. 137–65

'The attack on the Church of England in the Long Parliament, 1640–1642', in Derek Beales and Geoffrey Best, eds., *History, Society and the Churches: Essays in Honour of Owen Chadwick* (Cambridge, 1985), pp. 105–24

'Sir William Brereton and England's Wars of Religion', *Journal of British Studies*, 24 (1985), 311–32

1986

'Between Conventions: the members of Restoration parliaments', *Parliamentary History*, 5 (1986), 125–32

1987

'The ecology of allegiance in the English Revolution', *Journal of British Studies*, 26 (1987), 451–67

'Microform and the Historian', *Microform Review*, 16 (1987), 204–12

1988

(with Christopher W. Daniels) *Charles I* (Cambridge, 1988)

'The later Stuarts: a glorious Restoration?', *History Today*, 38 (1988), 8–16

1989

'Tempered steel: the making of Oliver Cromwell', *Cromwelliana* (1989), 2–9
'Christopher Hill's revolution', *History*, 74 (1989), 243–52

1990

(edited) *Oliver Cromwell and the English Revolution* (Harlow, 1990), to which also contributed 'Introduction' (pp. 1–18), 'The making of Oliver Cromwell' (pp. 19–48), and 'Cromwell and his contemporaries' (pp. 259–81)
(edited) *The Scottish National Covenant in its British Context, 1638–51* (Edinburgh, 1990), to which also contributed 'The National Covenant in its British context' (pp. 1–30)
'John Morrill', in Juliet Gardiner, ed., *The History Debate* (1990), pp. 90–5
'Rhetoric and action: Charles I, tyranny, and the English revolution', in Gordon J. Schochet, Patricia E. Tatspaugh and Carol Brobeck, eds., *Religion, Resistance, and Civil War: Papers Presented at the Folger Institute Seminar 'Political thought in Early Modern England, 1600–1660'* (Washington, DC, 1990), pp. 91–113
'Textualizing and contextualizing Cromwell', *Historical Journal*, 33 (1990), 629–39

1991

(edited) *The Impact of the English Civil War* (1991), to which also contributed 'Introduction' (pp. 8–16) and 'The impact of Puritanism' (pp. 50–66)
'The sensible revolution', in Jonathan I. Israel, ed., *The Anglo-Dutch Moment: Essays on the Glorious Revolution and its World Impact* (Cambridge, 1991), pp. 73–104
'Charles I, Cromwell and Cicero', *Connotations*, 1 (1991), 96–102

1992

(edited) *Revolution and Restoration: England in the 1650s* (1992), to which also contributed 'Introduction' (pp. 8–14) and 'The impact on society' (pp. 91–111)
'The causes of the British Civil Wars', *Journal of Ecclesiastical History*, 43 (1992), 624–33

1993

The Nature of the English Revolution (Harlow, 1993)
(edited with Paul Slack and Daniel Woolf) *Public Duty and Private Conscience in Seventeenth-Century England: Essays presented to G. E. Aylmer* (Oxford, 1993), to which also contributed 'William Dowsing, the bureaucratic Puritan' (pp. 173–203)
'The Britishness of the English Revolution', in Ronald G. Asch, ed., *Three Nations – a Common History? England, Scotland, Ireland and British History, c. 1600–1920* (Bochum, 1993), pp. 83–115

'The historian and the "historical filter"', in Andrew Hegarty, ed., *The Past and the Present: Problems of Understanding* (Oxford, 1993), pp. 93–100

1994

'A British patriarchy? Ecclesiastical imperialism under the early Stuarts', in Anthony Fletcher and Peter Roberts, eds., *Religion, Culture and Society in Early Modern Britain: Essays in Honour of Patrick Collinson* (Cambridge, 1994), pp. 209–37

'The English, the Scots and the British', in Patrick S. Hodge, ed., *Scotland and the Union* (Edinburgh, 1994), pp. 76–86

'Reconstructing the history of early Stuart parliaments', *Archives*, 21 (1994), 67–72

'Conflict probable or inevitable?', *New Left Review*, I/207 (1994), 113–23

1995

'Three kingdoms and one commonwealth? The enigma of mid-seventeenth-century Britain and Ireland', in Alexander Grant and Keith J. Stringer, eds., *Uniting the Kingdom? The Making of British history* (1995), pp. 170–90

'The fashioning of Britain', in Steven G. Ellis and Sarah Barber, eds., *Conquest and Union: Fashioning a British state, 1485–1725* (1995), pp. 8–39

'The unweariableness of Mr Pym: influence and eloquence in the Long Parliament', in Susan D. Amussen and Mark A. Kishlansky, eds., *Political Culture and Cultural Politics in Early Modern England: Essays Presented to David Underdown* (Manchester, 1995), pp. 19–54

'Paying One's D'Ewes', *Parliamentary History*, 14 (1995), 179–86

1996

(edited) *The Oxford Illustrated History of Tudor and Stuart Britain* (Oxford, 1996), to which also contributed 'Three Stuart kingdoms, 1603–1689' (pp. 74–89) and 'Politics in an age of revolution, 1630–1690' (pp. 361–96)

(edited with Brendan Bradshaw) *The British Problem, c. 1534–1707: State Formation in the Atlantic Archipelago* (1996), to which also contributed 'The British problem, c. 1534–1707' (pp. 1–38)

'Getting over D'Ewes', *Parliamentary History*, 15 (1996), 221–30

'Taking liberties with the seventeenth century', *Parliamentary History*, 15 (1996), 379–91

1997

(edited with Stratford Caldecott) *Eternity in Time: Christopher Dawson and the Catholic Idea of History* (Edinburgh, 1997), to which also contributed 'Introduction' (pp. 1–10)

'Historical introduction and overview: the un-English civil war', in John R. Young, ed., *Celtic Dimensions of the British Civil Wars* (Edinburgh, 1997), pp. 1–17

1998

(edited with Ian Gentles and Blair Worden) *Soldiers, Writers and Statesmen of the English Revolution* (Cambridge, 1998), to which also contributed 'Preface' (pp. ix–xi)

(general editor) *The Royal Historical Society Bibliography on CD-ROM: the History of Britain, Ireland, and the British Overseas* (Oxford, 1998)

(consultant editor) John Kenyon and Jane Ohlmeyer, eds., *The Civil Wars: A Military History of England, Scotland, and Ireland, 1638–1660* (Oxford, 1998), to which also contributed 'Introduction' (pp. xix–xxiv) and 'Postlude: between war and peace, 1651–1662' (pp. 306–28)

'King killing no murder', *Cromwelliana* (1998), 12–22

'The English church in the seventeenth century', *History Review*, 30 (1998), 18–23

'Through a Venetian glass, darkly', *Parliamentary History*, 17 (1998), 244–7

1999

Revolt in the Provinces: The People of England and the Tragedies of War, 1630–1648, 2nd edn (Harlow, 1999)

'The war(s) of the three kingdoms', in Glenn Burgess, ed., *The New British History: Founding a Modern State, 1603–1715* (1999), pp. 65–91

'John Philipps Kenyon, 1927–1996', *Proceedings of the British Academy*, 101 (1999), 441–61

'"A great and deserved name": commemorating Cromwell', *History Review*, 34 (1999), 22–25

2000

Stuart Britain: A Very Short Introduction (Oxford, 2000)

2001

(consultant editor) *The Penguin Atlas of British and Irish History from Earliest Times to the Present Day* (2001), to which also contributed 'Part Three: Early modern Britain and Ireland: introduction' (pp. 112–13)

'The causes and course of the British Civil Wars', in N. H. Keeble, ed., *The Cambridge Companion to Writing of the English Revolution* (Cambridge, 2001), pp. 13–31

'William Dowsing and the administration of iconoclasm', in Trevor Cooper, ed., *The Journal of William Dowsing: Iconoclasm in East Anglia during the English Civil War* (Woodbridge, 2001), pp. 1–28

'The house of Stuart (1603–1714)', in W. M. Ormrod, ed., *The Kings and Queens of England* (Stroud, 2001), pp. 225–61

(with Philip Baker) 'Oliver Cromwell, the regicide and the Sons of Zeruiah', in Jason Peacey, ed., *The Regicides and the Execution of Charles I* (Basingstoke, 2001), pp. 14–35

(with Philip Baker) 'The case of the armie truly re-stated', in Michael Mendle, ed., *The Putney Debates of 1647: The Army, the Levellers and the English State* (Cambridge, 2001), pp. 103–24

2002

(with David Loewenstein) 'Literature and religion', in David Loewenstein and Janel Mueller, eds., *The Cambridge History of Early Modern English Literature* (Cambridge, 2002), pp. 664–713

'Introduction' to reprint of G. M. Trevelyan, *England under the Stuarts* (2002), pp. ix–xiv

2003

'A liberation theology? Aspects of Puritanism in the English Revolution', in Laura Lunger Knoppers, ed., *Puritanism and its Discontents* (Newark, 2003), pp. 27–48

'Rethinking revolution in seventeenth-century Britain', in Kazuhiko Kondo, ed., *State and Empire in British History* (Kyoto, 2003), pp. 39–57

'Rewriting Cromwell: a case of deafening silences', *Canadian Journal of History*, 38 (2003), 553–78

'Christopher Hill', *History Today*, 53 (2003), 28–29

2004

(consultant editor) *The Oxford Dictionary of National Biography* (Oxford, 2004), to which also contributed articles on Robert Bennett; Sir William Brereton; (with Mark A. Kishlansky) Charles I; Robert Cholmondeley, earl of Leinster; Oliver Cromwell; William Davenport; Robert Devereux, third earl of Essex; William Dowsing; Aaron Guerden; Denzil Holles, first Baron Holles; John Southworth; Robert Venables

(edited) *The Promotion of Knowledge: Lectures to Mark the Centenary of the British Academy, 1902–2002, Proceedings of the British Academy*, 122 (Oxford, 2004), to which also contributed 'Introduction: The British Academy Centenary Lectures' (pp. 1–7)

'Conclusion: king-killing in perspective', in Robert von Friedeburg, ed., *Murder and Monarchy: Regicide in European History, 1300–1800* (Basingstoke, 2004), pp. 293–9

2005

"Uneasy Lies the Head that Wears a Crown": Dynastic Crises in Tudor and Stewart Britain, 1504–1746, The Stenton Lecture for 2003 (Reading, 2005)

'Concluding reflection: confronting the violence of the Irish reformations', in Alan Ford and John McCafferty, eds., *The Origins of Sectarianism in Early Modern Ireland* (Cambridge, 2005), pp. 229–39

'The English, the Scots, and the dilemmas of union, 1638–1654', *Proceedings of the British Academy*, 127 (2005), 57–74

'The Morrill majority: Daniel Snowman meets John Morrill', *History Today*, 55 (2005), 18–20

2006

'Thinking about the new British history', in David Armitage, ed., *British Political Thought in History, Literature and Theory, 1500–1800* (Cambridge, 2006), pp. 23–46

'Afterword: the word became flawed', in Ariel Hessayon and Nicholas Keene, eds., *Scripture and Scholarship in Early Modern England* (Aldershot, 2006), pp. 248–52

2007

Oliver Cromwell (Oxford, 2007)

'The Drogheda Massacre in Cromwellian context', in David Edwards, Pádraig Lenihan and Clodagh Tait, eds., *Age of Atrocity: Violence and Political Conflict in Early Modern Ireland* (Dublin, 2007), pp. 242–65

2008

'Conrad Sebastian Robert Russell, fifth Earl Russell', *Oxford Dictionary of National Biography* (online edition, Oxford, 2008)

'How Oliver Cromwell thought', in John Morrow and Jonathan Scott, eds., *Liberty, Authority, Formality: Political Ideas and Culture, 1600–1900* (Exeter, 2008), pp. 89–111

'The rule of saints and soldiers: the wars of religion in Britain and Ireland, 1638–1660', in Jenny Wormald, ed., *The Short Oxford History of the British Isles: The Seventeenth Century* (Oxford, 2008), pp. 83–115

'The Puritan Revolution', in John Coffey and Paul C. H. Lim, eds., *The Cambridge Companion to Puritanism* (Cambridge, 2008), pp. 67–88

'Foreword: on naming and shaming elephants in the room', in Micheál Ó Siochrú, *Confederate Ireland, 1642–1649: A Constitutional and Political Analysis*, 2nd edn (Dublin, 2008), pp. i–viii

'Austin Herbert Woolrych, 1918–2004', *Proceedings of the British Academy*, 153 (2008), 391–413

2009

'Oliver Cromwell and the Civil Wars', in Susan Doran and Thomas S. Freeman, eds., *Tudors and Stuarts on Film: Historical Perspectives* (Basingstoke, 2009), pp. 204–19

'1662: Charles II pays a heavy price for his Restoration', in Michael Wood, ed., *The Great Turning Points in British History: The 20 Events that Made the Nation* (2009), pp. 129–38

Index